ECONOMIC ANALYSIS AND POLITICAL IDEOLOGY

ECONOMISTS OF THE TWENTIETH CENTURY

General Editors: Mark Perlman, *University Professor of Economics, Emeritus, University of Pittsburgh* and Mark Blaug, *Professor Emeritus, University of London, Professor Emeritus, University of Buckingham and Visiting Professor, University of Exeter*

This innovative series comprises specially invited collections of articles and papers by economists whose work has made an important contribution to economics in the late twentieth century.

The proliferation of new journals and the ever-increasing number of new articles make it difficult for even the most assiduous economist to keep track of all the important recent advances. By focusing on those economists whose work is generally recognized to be at the forefront of the discipline, the series will be an essential reference point for the different specialisms included.

A list of published and future titles in this series is printed at the end of this volume.

Economic Analysis and Political Ideology

The Selected Essays of Karl Brunner
Volume One

edited by

Thomas Lys

John L. and Helen Kellogg Distinguished Associate Professor of Accounting and Information Systems,
J.L. Kellogg Graduate School of Management,
Northwestern University, US

ECONOMISTS OF THE TWENTIETH CENTURY

Edward Elgar
Cheltenham, UK • Brookfield, US

Published by
Edward Elgar Publishing Limited
8 Lansdown Place
Cheltenham
Glos GL50 2HU
UK

Edward Elgar Publishing Company
Old Post Road
Brookfield
Vermont 05036
US

British Library Cataloguing in Publication Data
Brunner, Karl, 1916–1989
    The selected essays of Karl Brunner. – (Economists of the
    twentieth century)
    1.Economics   2.Ideology   3.Political science
    I.Title   II.Series   III.Lys, Thomas
    330.1

Library of Congress Cataloguing in Publication Data
Brunner, Karl, 1916–
    Economic analysis and political ideology : the selected essays of
    Karl Brunner / edited by Thomas Lys.
        (Economists of the twentieth century)
    Includes bibliographical references and index.
    1. Economics.   2. Economic policy.   I. Lys, Thomas, 1950–   .
    II. Title.   III. Series.
    HC118.B68A25   1996
    330.1—dc20   95–42417
                                                                       CIP

ISBN 1 85898 025 9

Printed and bound in Great Britain by
Hartnolls Limited, Bodmin, Cornwall

Contents

Acknowledgements

The editor and publisher wish to thank the following who have kindly given permission for the use of copyright material.

Banco Nazionale del Lavoro Quarterly Review for article: 'A fascination with economics', no. 135, December 1980, 403–26.

Basil Blackwell Publishers for article: 'Economic development, Cancun and the western democracies', *The World Economy*, 5(1), Winter 1982, 61–84.

Cambridge University Press for article: 'My quest for economic knowledge' in *Eminent Economists: Their Life Philosophies*, ed. Michael Szenberg, 1991, 84–97.

Center for Research in Government Policy and Business, University of Rochester, for article: 'The First World, the Third World and the survival of free societies' in *The First World and the Third World: Essays on the New International Economic Order*, 1978, 1–36.

Harper & Row Publishers for article: 'The sociopolitical vision of Keynes' in *The Legacy of Keynes*, ed. David A. Reese, 1987, 23–56.

Helbing & Lichtenhahn Verlag for article: 'Knowledge, values and the choice of economic organization', *Kyklos*, xxiii(3), 1970, 558–79.

Institute of World Studies for article: 'The New International Economic Order: a chapter in protracted confrontation', *Journal of World Affairs*, 20(1), Spring 1976, 103–21.

Kluwer Academic Publishing for article: '"Assumptions" and the cognitive quality of theories', *Synthese*, 20, 1969, 510–25.

National Association of Business Economics for article: 'The poverty of nations', *Business Economics*, January 1985, 5–11.

Ohio State University Press for article: 'The perception of man and the conception of government', *Journal of Money, Credit and Banking*, 9(1), February 1977, 70–85.

Schweizerische Zeitschrift für Volkswirtschaft und Statistik for articles: 'Reflections on the political economy of government: the persistent growth of government', Heft 3, 1978, 649–79; 'The limits of economic policy', Heft 3, 1985, 213–35.

Western Economic Association for article: 'The perception of man and the conception of society: two approaches to understanding society', *Economic Inquiry*, xxv, July 1987, 367–88.

Every effort has been made to trace all the copyright holders but if any have been inadvertently overlooked the publishers will be pleased to make the necessary arrangements at the first opportunity.

The editor gratefully acknowledges the invaluable assistance of Armen Alchian, Thomas Bösch, Ronald Hansen, Franziska Lys, Jean Morris, Bill Meckling, Margaret Neale, Gail Pratt and Anna Schwartz in the preparation of these two volumes.

Preface: Karl Brunner, 1916–1989

Thomas Lys

In the last years of his life, Karl Brunner was severely handicapped by a non-malignant tumour in his spine that eventually proved fatal. Despite this setback he continued to work as he always has: when he lost control of his right hand, he learned to write with his left. When walking became difficult, he learned to rely even more heavily on the telephone to replace the important face-to-face interactions and held classes at his home. When his wife Rosemarie, a devoted companion of 50 years, passed away, he learned to live alone. I visited him for the last time roughly four weeks before his death. He was feverishly working on a series of articles he wanted to publish that he hoped would unify his contributions to the economics and social sciences literatures. Some of those articles had been previously published, others had not. He was concerned that he might not have enough time to finish that task. He asked me to help him in this last undertaking, for the pain was becoming too great when he sat at his desk and he was losing control of his left hand: he could work no more but he had not accomplished what he had hoped. The article 'Religion and the Social Order' was not complete at the time of his death. This article remains unfinished. In compiling and publishing the content of these two volumes, I have attempted to honour his last request.

Karl Brunner died on 9 May 1989. At the time of his death, he was well known not only for his writing in monetary economics but also for the contributions he had made to econometrics, the theory of man, logics, and to the analysis of socio-political problems. Indeed, between 1953 and 1989, he published over 200 articles and books, founded two leading academic journals (*Journal of Money, Credit, and Banking*, and the *Journal of Monetary Economics*), and organized numerous conferences.

Karl was fascinated with economics. At first, he focused primarily on macro-economics. As he matured his understanding of the field broadened and, particularly in the last stage of his career, economics came to include all aspects of human interaction. The evolution of Karl's understanding of economics is best characterized by a quote from an autobiographical essay, in which he said: 'The problem of creating a "good society" was not at the forefront of my search in life: a search for understanding and insights. But in the last stretch of my path it has become a natural consequence of the work and ideas I have pursued over many years. It will occupy my mind as long as it continues to function and my body supports it. My fascinating search, initiated more than fifty years ago, was greatly influenced by many people from whom I learned many things. Life offered me a singular chance.'[1] Karl took advantage of that singular chance, as evidenced by the breadth and depth of his contributions to the social sciences. A unifying theme of his approach, and what distinguishes his work from that of other leading economists, is his focus on institutions and the incentives they create. Whether studying the money supply process, advising central banks on monetary problems, analysing issues related to the Federal Drug Administration, or investigating the United Nations' attempts to manage the world's resources, Karl's analysis not only focused on the purely technical issues but also on the incentive structures created and their likely impact on the behaviour of individuals, institutions and society. It is that depth and breadth of topics and techniques that characterizes Karl's legacy to social sciences.

Over the course of his 73 years, Karl Brunner was known and admired by many. Of his students who became his colleagues and friends, there was the luxury of knowing him both as a mentor and as a collaborator. Karl was born in Zurich, Switzerland on 16 February 1916, the youngest child of three. His father, William Brunner, was descended from a family of textile merchants from the Toggenburg, a mountainous region in eastern Switzerland. His mother, Ida Maulaz, came from a family of farmers in French-speaking St Croix in the Jura Mountains of western Switzerland. Faced with dire economic conditions at home, Karl's parents, while still in their teens, emigrated to Russia. There, they found employment, probably as a fabric merchant and accountant and as a governess. According to family folklore, Karl's parents were introduced in a carriage in the obligatory presence of a chaperone, some time before the turn of the century. Following political turmoil in Russia, both returned to Switzerland, where they were finally married after a seven-year engagement.

Fascinated with astronomy since his youth, Karl's father passed the admission examination of the Swiss Institute of Technology in Zurich and enrolled to study mathematics and physics. Upon his graduation in 1904, he became assistant at the Federal Observatory. This rather low-paying job, however, did not allow him to support his growing family. He accepted a better-paid position teaching mathematics at a high school in Chur, a provincial capital of the Canton of Grison, isolated in the mountains of eastern Switzerland. He remained there for four years, until he found a position as a mathematics instructor at the preparatory school for young ladies in Zurich. Karl's father was delighted about the move as it brought him closer to the academic activities and intellectual challenges at the University of Zurich. He knew that academic positions were scarce in Switzerland, and one had to wait one's turn. Teaching in Zurich, however, rather than in remote Chur, at least kept him visible – just in case there was an opening. Finally, his perseverance paid off. He was appointed professor of astronomy at the Swiss Institute of Technology in Zurich and director of the Federal Observatory in 1926.

It was there at the Observatory that Karl spent some of the happiest times of his childhood. With keen interest he explored the exciting secrets of the Observatory's garden. Encouraged by his father, he also began to read. He became fascinated with books and read with an intensity seldom observed in a young person of his age. When there were not enough interesting books in the library to be borrowed, he ordered examination copies under his father's name from the local bookstore, read them overnight, and returned them the next day explaining that these books did not satisfy his father's expectations.

In 1934, after what Karl referred to as a rather 'indifferent' performance in high school, he enrolled at the University of Zurich as a history major. This was as much a time of intellectual awakening as of growing concern about what to do with his life. Interested in 'the human animal and human society', Karl ultimately decided to study economics. He wrote: 'It was my desire to understand the human riddle, considered in the context of human society, that made me eventually settle upon economics as my lifetime pursuit.'[2]

Studying in Switzerland proved to be a frustrating experience for Karl. Professors had life-long appointments and, tragically, no incentives to stay current. To supplement the rather limited intellectual challenges that this system created, Karl started a discussion circle with three other students. They met weekly at the Café *Grüner Heinrich* (Green Henry) to review economic readings. Professor Jürg Niehans, one of the four, recalls that around 1942 they debated a monograph by Walter Zollinger, an insurance executive and friend of their economics professor Eugen Grossman. Zollinger argued that the quantity theory of money was a dead end, and the four, with Karl the most outspoken, proceeded to defend that theory. It is fair to say, therefore, that Karl's ideas of monetarism were born in the *Grüner Heinrich*, some 26 years before he coined the term in 1968. Despite the brief brush with monetarism, however, Karl's education was founded solidly in Keynsianism.

After spending one year at the London School of Economics, Karl graduated from the University of Zurich in economics in 1939. He then served as a lieutenant in the infantry, but his failing eyesight (a problem that was to handicap him for the rest of his life) led to his discharge. Karl began work on his dissertation during his military service and was granted a doctorate in economics from the University of Zurich in 1943. He was hired as an economist first with the Research Division of the Swiss National Bank (1943–4) and then with the Delegation of Swiss Trade (1944–5). In 1946, he became a lecturer at the Hochschule für Wirtschaftsforschung in St Gallen, a business school in eastern Switzerland. He was dismissed from St Gallen in 1948 for, according to Karl, showing a lack of respect for the established professors.

(Some 35 years later, he was awarded a doctorate *honoris causa* by that same institution.) Subsequently, he became economic adviser to the Swiss Watch Chamber of Commerce (1948–9) and served concurrently as consultant to the Economic Commission for Europe in Geneva (1948–9).

Karl came to the United States in 1949 on a Rockefeller Foundation Grant to visit the Cowles Commission for Research in Economics at the University of Chicago. In reference to the period prior to 1949, Karl often stated that after finishing his studies in Europe, 'the only thing I knew for sure was that I knew nothing about economics'. From his perspective, his inquiry into economics, and thus his academic career, began in 1949 when he was 33. Karl used the remaining 40 years of his life to produce a body of knowledge with a drive and efficiency that was unique. He spent two years at the University of Chicago, and then was hired as an assistant professor at the Department of Economics at UCLA in 1951. Thus, as had his father before him, Karl obtained his first real academic appointment relatively late in life. He was promoted to associate professor in 1953 and to full professor in 1961. After brief visits at the University of Wisconsin and Michigan State University, Karl was appointed as the Everett D. Reese Professor at the Department of Economics at Ohio State in 1966. In 1971, Bill Meckling brought him to the Graduate School of Management at the University of Rochester (now the William E. Simon School of Business). There, he became the Director of the Center for Research in Government Policy and Business (now the Bradley Research Center). In 1979 he was named the Fred H. Gowen Professor of Economics.

The time in Rochester, and also in Bern, Switzerland – where he spent his summers teaching econometrics – were very satisfying for Karl. He devoted considerable time to 'raising' his third and last batch of PhD students (the first had been at UCLA and the second at Ohio State). He not only supervised their dissertations but also created a friendly and nurturing atmosphere for their development. Starting in 1983, he arranged financing to allow two European students per year to study in Rochester for one semester.

Over the years, his interests centred around two topics: monetary economics and public policy, society and religion. The major outlet for these interests were two conferences that Karl organized every summer in Europe. In Konstanz, on the peninsula of Mainau in southern Germany, he organized an annual seminar on Monetary Theory and Monetary Policy. Issues of public policy, society and religion were debated in Interlaken, a resort town in the Bernese Alps. Common to both conferences was the invitation to scholars from all over the world: monetary economists (academics and central bank employees) in Konstanz, and economists, Marxists and philosophers in Interlaken. As many conference participants can attest, the conference discussions were intense, sometimes explosive, but always constructive.

Karl had a singlemindedness of purpose that many found intimidating. His directness and attacks could be brusque and, if you were the focus of such a barrage, the result would often serve at least one purpose: making sure you were better prepared for the next discussion. Yet, the more I came to know him, especially in the last years of his life, the more I discovered a different side of him. Karl mellowed considerably. He rediscovered a love for the mountains of his native Switzerland and we spent many hours hiking in the Bernese Alps. With his wife Rosemarie, who shared Karl's interest in and devotion to his students, he organized barbecue trips along the Aare river. These excursions started in the late afternoon, continued to become intense discussions of economics, politics and any other field where economic analysis could be applied, and ended well into the night with the singing of old Swiss songs accompanied by the soft crackling of a campfire. It was here, reflected in the combination of intellectual discussions and camaraderie that Karl, as a man and a scholar, seemed most complete.

These two volumes provide a glimpse of the man to whom work was life. Volume 1, with a foreword by Nobel Laureate James Buchanan, reproduces articles dealing with Karl's socio-economic analyses. The second, with a foreword written by Karl's student and long-time associate Allen Meltzer, deals with macro economic issues. Jointly, these two volumes represent Karl's last request. For a man, a scholar, to whom his life was, in the end, his work – but not just the articles and books he wrote but the students he trained, the colleagues he influenced, and the policy-makers he informed – this may be the most fitting tribute.

THOMAS LYS
Student, Friend and Executor
J.L. Kellogg Graduate School of Management
Northwestern University
Evanston, Illinois
USA

Notes

1. M. Szenberg (ed.), *Eminent Economists, their Life Philosophies*, Cambridge: Cambridge University Press, 1991, p. 97.
2. Ibid., p. 85.

Introduction: Karl Brunner and economic science

James M. Buchanan

Karl Brunner was an academic entrepreneur over and beyond his activity as an economist, professor and scholar. Among his most successful ventures was the annual Interlaken Conference on 'Analysis and Ideology', which was initially convened in 1974. The stated purpose of this series of conferences was that of introducing (exposing) European, and especially German, economists to their American counterparts, who allegedly brought along analytical baggage that was more 'scientific' (hard-nosed) than that which included much of the Marxist-inspired rhetoric then encountered in Europe's academies.

In this entrepreneurial enterprise, Karl Brunner was motivated by the conviction that economics does, indeed, have scientific content, analogous to, even if quite different from, that of the natural sciences. And this conviction was accompanied by the belief that genuinely scientific argument, along with the empirical evidence that could be marshalled in support, was both necessary and sufficient to overcome the temptation of scholars to engage in ideological romance.

What did Karl Brunner have in mind when he predicted that the exposure of German scholars to 'scientific economics' would exert an impact on academic practice and, ultimately, on the direction of change in political regimes? To get at an answer to this question, it is useful to examine the nature of the scientific content of whatever it is that economists, as professionals, bring to problems of social organization. How does the economist differ in this respect from the philosopher (Posner, 1993)? Is economics more than either a part of contractarian political philosophy or a branch of mathematics (Rosenberg, 1992)? In this Introduction, I shall try to answer the question, and, in so doing, pay tribute to Karl Brunner's intellectual adventure.

I suggest that we think first of the economist in comparison to the ordinary natural scientist. By 'ordinary' here, I refer to the scientist not as a discoverer of new laws of nature, not as someone who is continually pushing outward the boundaries of our knowledge, but, instead, as a human repository of that which is known.

What does such an ordinary scientist do? As a rough answer, consider the definition of the natural or physical feasibility space. The scientist distinguishes between what is and what is not feasible, given the known constraints of the physical universe. Ragnar Frisch (1959) referred to these constraints as *obligative*, which he contrasted with constraints that are *facultative*.

If economics is compared with natural science, economists should be able to define what can and cannot be done with the *human* materials that exist. Economics should allow us to locate a feasibility space, analogous to that generated for the physical universe by natural science. Economics, if it claims scientific status, must invoke laws or uniformities in human nature.

We know that the great moral philosophers of the eighteenth century were excited about the prospects for developing the sciences of man. For Adam Smith, each person's drive to better his or her own position provided a uniform motivational element from which our understanding of economic interaction emerges. And it is important to note that 'betterment' was implicitly assumed to be objectively measurable. Each person's effort to better his or her own position is observed as a striving to secure personal command and use of a larger share of goods that are commonly valued.

The economist's first step toward restricting the domain of attainable positions is to attach signs to 'goods' (or 'bads'). Note that this step is classificatory only; it does not require any postulate to the effect that the trade-offs among goods be identical over separate persons. The classification requires only that the set of goods that are commonly valued to be positive be identical over all potential traders in an exchange nexus.

A categorical difference between the enterprise of the natural scientist and that of the economist emerges as the latter tries to move toward delineation of the boundaries of behavioural feasibility, a difference that makes the economist's task enormously more difficult in some relative sense. The natural scientist is able to, and indeed must, take the universe as it is found, and without the overlay of a complex institutional structure that has evolved, in part constructively, and that operates to channel and to facilitate patterns of behaviour that cannot be classified to be 'natural' in any primitivist sense. Furthermore, the institutional structure is not unique; distinctly different sets of rules may describe separate historical and locational settings. How can the economist, as scientist, even so much as commence to establish boundary marks between the attainable and the unattainable?

One means of reducing the task to manageable proportions is to drop any claim to generality and to introduce historical-institutional specificity. With a postulated set of structural parameters, that is, within a defined set of legal rules (or facultative constraints), the economist can proceed with the basic classificatory exercise without advancing any claim to generalizability to other institutional settings.

Consider, then, the basic institutional framework for the regime that facilitates the emergence and the operation of a market economy. Persons, individually or as members of organizations, are assigned enforcible rights and claims to both human and non-human endowments, rights that allow these endowments to be used as the assigned owners desire, within certain legal limits. Persons, again individually or as members of organizations, possess rights to enter into and complete exchanges one with another, and to transfer rights on reciprocally agreed terms. As persons exercise their assigned rights by choosing and acting along the dimensions within their authority, a network of production, exchange and distributional relationships emerges, and from this network there will be generated an outcome, or patterns of outcomes, that may be described by vectors of prices, allocations of resource inputs, and distributions of final outputs.

This summary is, of course, familiar territory to the economist. But let me make the connection to the classificatory exercise mentioned above. Recall Adam Smith's most famous passage where he states that the butcher offers the supper's meat for sale, not from benevolence, but from self-interest. Economics is widely, and correctly, interpreted as providing understanding/ explanation of Smith's statement which has genuine scientific content in the following way. The imagined 'social state' in which there are no persons offering meat for sale is non-feasible, given the institutional parameters that define the rights or liberties of potential sellers and buyers, and given the motivational postulate of the science. An even more romanticized alternative would be a setting in which sellers offer meat to those who desire this good, but without demanding payment in return. This result, too, may be imagined as a social state that would be most highly preferred by meat consumers, but few would fail to incorporate the elementary elements of economics in thinking that this result could never be realized.

The principle to be emphasized is the necessity of making the distinction between those states of the world, those 'social states', that can be imagined to exist and those states that can be realized, given the inclusive rules within which economic interaction must take place. The set of imagined positions is, of course, much larger than the set of potentially realizable positions, even within the limits imposed by the acknowledged natural or physical constraints. Within any given institutional structure, the difference between the set of imagined positions and the set of attainable positions stems exclusively from the operation of the motivational postulate that is central to the science of economics itself.

Individual preferences are not simply taken as data. Instead, preferences are restricted by the two-part postulate to the effect that (a) persons seek their own betterment, and (b) betterment is objectively measurable in goods that are defined to be commonly valued, whether positively or negatively.

Consider an individual's ordering of two social states, both of which are technologically feasible, but one of which imputes to that individual a larger quantity of a positively valued good, with the same quantities of other goods.

The individual's preferences must be such as to produce a ranking of such a state relatively higher than that accorded to the alternative. Given such an ordering, the individual cannot select the less-preferred to the more-preferred alternative if he or she is assigned rights of choices along the relevant dimension of behaviour.

In application to the last variant of the Smithian example discussed above, where sellers are imagined to offer goods without payment, such a state is to be classified as non-feasible, so long as sellers retain rights of entry into and exit from the exchange relationship. One-sided, or non-reciprocal, 'exchanges' in goods, valued by both parties, are not permissible way-stations toward emergent market outcomes classifiable as feasible.

This conclusion may be accepted, but the critic may immediately resort to the institutional specificity imposed initially on the whole discussion. The offer of goods without return payment, that is, trade without reciprocation, may be acknowledged to be beyond the limits of feasible economic interaction, under the standard rules of the market in which sellers and buyers retain rights of entry and exit from potential exchanges. But, as noted earlier, these rules are not themselves natural, at least in the ordinary sense. Instead, rules of the market may be considered to be artefactual, having themselves evolved historically or been constructively put in place. Is it possible, therefore, both to imagine a social state where goods are offered without a requirement of payment and to classify such a state as potentially realizable under some alternative non-market assignment of rights?

Consider again the supply/demand of meat, classified as a commonly valued good. Suppose that the rules of the market are abrogated, and that these rules are superseded by politicization/bureaucratization of this sector of the economy. Some persons are directed to produce and supply meat to those who are authorized to receive the product, and there is no reciprocal exchange. Relatively little reflection is required to suggest that the situation attained under this regime is *not* likely to be that which might have been imagined to be possible as an alternative to the market counterpart. The producer/supplier will not be observed to respond to the preferences of consumers/demanders; the product itself will not be descriptively equivalent to that traded in markets. By replacing the set of market rules, there will be, of course, a change in the set of attainable or feasible positions. But these positions will differ from those reached under in-market behaviour along many more dimensions of adjustment than economically illiterate imagination could suggest.

Non-romanticized analysis suggests that the economist's classificatory exercise is more general in scope and applicability than might initially seem to be the case. Those social states or positions that can be imagined but never realized by behaviour within the rules of the market cannot necessarily be realized under any alternative set of rules or assignments of rights. Care must be taken to avoid the comparison of false alternatives. That which might be imagined but not realized under one regime cannot necessarily be brought into being by a shift in regime. Given a regime change, the set of imagined social states may once again be subjected to the economist's classificatory scrutiny, with the distinction between the feasible and non-feasible subsets being defined.

The point to be emphasized is that many, indeed the overwhelming majority, of the technologically feasible positions cannot be behaviourally realized *under any regime*. Most of those positions or social states that are romantically imagined to be possible are inconsistent with the motivational postulate of economics, with human nature as it exhibits its uniformities. Economics need not be the dismal science; but it can scarcely avoid being labelled as the non-romantic science. The setting in which producers/sellers offer high-quality goods for nothing while showing interests in the desires of consumers is non-feasible in a generalized sense. There is no regime, no set of rules, no assignments of rights to choose and to act, that will generate such a social state and remain consistent with the central proposition of economic science.

I am fully aware of the fact that I have restated long-familiar arguments that few practising economists, especially those of the Chicago tradition, will criticize. In a real sense, I have done little more than repackage the economists' positive and scientific proposition to the effect that demand curves are down-sloping. I would suggest, none the less, that packaging can on occasion matter, and that perhaps the somewhat different rhetoric of my argument will prove more convincing than the familiar postures.

Economists are frequently accused of committing the naturalist fallacy, the derivation of an 'ought' from an 'is'. The approach taken in this Introduction should help us avoid such a charge. If the economists can observe politically motivated action aimed quite explicitly at the achievement of results that are clearly beyond the boundaries of feasibility, given the existing regime, no norms are violated when and if they call attention to this as scientific fact.

When the economists suggest that 'the market works', no normatively positive charge need be attached to such a claim. Reference is properly limited to the proposition that, if persons are assigned rights of disposition over their own activities (and uses of their endowments), an outcome will emerge from the interaction that falls within the feasibility space. It may well be the case that alternative outcomes or social states may be imagined and ranked ordinally to be more desirable than those outcomes predicted to emerge from markets. But such alternatives may or may not be feasible, and it falls to the economist, as scientist, to carry out the classification that is required. It is in this role as scientist that the economist should be able to prevent ill-fated efforts to organize political action aimed at achieving results that are beyond the boundaries of behavioural feasibility.[1]

I share Karl Brunner's belief that many of the errors in political economy stem from the failure of political decision-makers to separate feasible from non-feasible states of the economy. Karl Brunner personally made a difference in the European economic scene, both through the organization of the annual Interlaken Conference on Analysis and Ideology, and through his active participation in many discussions of policy alternatives with both observers and practitioners from many countries. Karl Brunner was an economic scientist *par excellence* who was firm in his faith that the emplacement of truth has social purpose.

Scientific ignorance, when combined with informed self-seeking on the part of sectional interests, prevents the attainment of results that might often prove beneficial to everyone in the economic nexus. For example, the intense 1993 opposition to NAFTA in the United States was fuelled only in part by the informed self-interests of protected groups fearing damage from any opening-up of markets. The opposition was also grounded on ignorance of ordinary economic science that generated a fear of imagined consequences which could never be brought into reality.

As Karl Brunner recognized, economists as scientists have an important role to play. There is a repository of knowledge that remains within their unique responsibility. They default on their role when they too become romantic dreamers and try to assist misguided politicians in the search for non-attainable and imaginary worlds. We can only hope that Francis Fukuyama (1991) is correct when he suggests that the demise of socialism will mark the final triumph of ordinary economic science.

Note

1. The role of the economist as scientist presented in this Introduction is different from, but not necessarily inconsistent with, the role of the political economist sketched out in my early 1959 paper. In that effort, I was concerned with how the economist, armed with the propositions of positive economics, might participate in the social discussion of policy alternatives. I suggested that the political economist's role should be that of presenting proposals as *hypotheses*, with the ultimate test being the achievement of unanimous agreement on change. In the context of the analysis here, my earlier concern was with the potential role of the political economist in the discussion of social choices among alternatives, all of which are within the set of attainable or feasible positions (see Buchanan, 1959).

References

Buchanan, James M. (1959) 'Positive economics, welfare economics, and political economy', *Journal of Law and Economics*, **2** (October), 124–38.
Frisch, Ragnar (1959) 'On welfare theory and Pareto regimes', *International Economic Papers*, no. 9, London: Macmillan, 1959, pp. 39–92.
Fukuyama, Francis (1991) *The End of History and the Last Man*, New York: Basic Books.
Posner, Richard A. (1993) 'Richard Rorty's politics', *Critical Review*, **7**(1), 33–49.
Rosenberg, Alexander (1992) *Economics – Mathematical Politics or Science of Diminishing Returns*, Chicago: University of Chicago Press.

1 Knowledge, values and the choice of economic organization*

The disintegration of old orientations and the search for new values

Man is the metaphysical animal. He demands an interpretation of the universe which assigns meaning to his existence. Vast resources were invested over the centuries to satisfy this demand. They yielded comprehensive views projecting values and meaning into his environment. Man acquired an orientation which soothed his mind and reconciled his insistence for securely ordered values with the apparent irrationality of universe, nature and society. Disturbing confrontations with nature and society appeared as necessary phases of individual life in a process leading to a spiritual or transcendental world or as unavoidable stages in a history of societies terminating with a secular paradise. The historical survival of the old orientations was thus essentially determined by the satisfying character of the interpretations about the universe or society as a meaningful or potentially meaningful order.

Ancient conceptions of human orientation persisted for thousand years and shaped traditional philosophy and theology. They have effectively placated man's existential anxiety, made suffering more acceptable and dignified human life. The conviction and force of these orientations never rested on their cognitive foundations. It must be attributed to a core of values and valuations governing man's view of his universe. Assertions of values and descriptions of norms, statements indicating approval or disapproval for types of behaviour, institutions, attitudes, thoughts, and events typically occurred with central emphasis. But man's *Weltanschauung* also contained cognitive aspects interwoven with his valuations. The peculiar mixture of cognitive and value aspects probably strengthened the credibility of these orientations. The erosion of the traditional orientations observed over the recent centuries was essentially fostered however, by the same interlocking combination of valuation and cognition. The combination could not persist in the same mixture over the centuries. It was bound to raise questions which induced a gradual separation between cognition and valuation. There emerged a cognition, expressed by the scientific adventure to comprehend

* Originally published in *Kyklos*, xxiii(3), 1970, 558–79. This article is based on lectures given at Antioch College, University of Rochester, Michigan State University and Denison College. Many discussions with Armen Alchian and Allan H. Meltzer are gratefully acknowledged. They are not necessarily absolved from errors committed. They are absolved however from errors of omission.

1

systematically our world, which gradually freed itself from valuational entanglement.[1]

This development endangered the survival of traditional orientations which approached the acquisition of systematic empirical knowledge bearing on our environment in a rich context of value feelings and value judgements. The erosion of the old conceptions about universe, life and society affected particularly the professional articulators in modern society, i.e., the intellectuals. Under the old frameworks events and circumstances were sanctioned by a meaning which appeared inherent with objects and situations. This meaning actually emerged however from the protection of man's own conception. The meaning of universe and society were not given to men, they were and still are created by men. With the erosion of old orientations the meanings vanished, objects, events, and human situations appeared pointless. The world continued, love, hate, indifference and passion, greed and compassion, conflict and reconciliation prevailed in the same old manner. But articulate men lost their frame of reference and this changed radically our sense about the world and ourselves. Men felt lost, naked and cold. A vast literature expresses this sense. There appeared an almost feverish search for new values to replace the old conceptions. A singular consciousness of the need for values and meaningful orientations pervades the circle of professional articulators.

The concern and search of contemporary articulators is not necessarily deplorable. Neither is the concern and search of many housewives for a better window cleaner. Both activities reveal a human desire. No doubt, the demand for a satisfying orientation is much more pervasive than the demand for window cleaners. One can also argue that the supply of satisfying orientations has substantially more far-reaching and powerful effects on social behaviour and the allocation of resources than the production of a better window cleaner. The confused search for new values and orientations is probably quite justified in terms of the perennial human demand for the kind of product potentially emerging. I do not wish to question the rationality of the investment. Its value to man is fully granted at this stage. It is contended however that the contemporary search creates by-products which seriously endanger the central core of man's potentiality.

We observe with rising frequency and impact an implicit denial of cognition, or a serious confusion between articulated valuations and substantive knowledge. The circle of relevant articulators ranges over a vast array of cultural activities, subsuming minimal art, the happenings, the merger of Catholic conceptions of Christianity with Marxist philosophy, the New Left, the technocrats of the Triple Revolution, the preachers (in churches and universities) of 'social involvement' and a host of contemporary Pietro Aretinos. More serious is the frequent and easy sacrifice of cognition at some altar erected to the glory of some valuations in contexts apparently committed to intelligent cognition. The contemporary concern for values and meanings may have permeated our social fabric sufficiently to assume, almost, the form of a counter-revolution to the cognitive revolution initiated centuries ago. This old revolution introduced an important methodological advance by separating cognition from valuation and contributed in this manner decisively to the rapid growth in our substantive knowledge.

The very same separation also disrupted man's inherited thought patterns. The dissociation of cognition from valuation exposed him without protection to a universe undefined and undefinable in terms of cherished values. The destruction of ancient non-cognitive or semi-cognitive belief systems in the confrontation with systematic cognitive efforts created a vacuum which men cannot suffer. And the search for new orientations and new values exhibits dangerous undercurrents obstructing and beclouding the only source of systematic and reliable knowledge we can reasonably acquire in human affairs. This is perhaps nowhere so clearly expressed as in our conflicts bearing on the choice of economic organization. It also forms a dominant theme in the flood of literature describing or bewailing the human lot in modern societies.

The floods of the counterrevolution will also engulf our universities. One can already discern a growing clamor insisting that universities should be concerned with 'teaching values'. It is frequently contended that one branch of the university attends to the 'narrow technologies' of the natural sciences whereas the humanities and the social sciences will teach proper human attitudes and values. This view is often encountered among historians, the literati, our contemporary Gracculi and even among physicists. But this view totally misconstrues the nature of the cognitive adventure expressed in our scientific enterprise, confuses this adventure with technology and is unable to understand the distinct logical function of cognition and valuation. Some aspects of this potentially dangerous trend in contemporary 'intellectualism' are considered in the subsequent sections.

The uneasy role of cognition in 'social criticism'
Every society must solve its economic and political problems by an appropriate choice of organization. Arrangements exist which determine who governs, under what constraints, and how the governing bodies are selected, maintained or replaced. Moreover, every society possesses an array of resources used in a matrix of technological conditions and knowledge. An economic organization determines for what purposes the resources are used and to which extent, how they are to be combined in production activities, and how the output is divided among the members of the society. Two types of organizational devices are available for the continuous solution of a society's basic economic problem, a system of markets associated with the institution of private property and an administrative system coupled with dominantly

collective property. The choice between the market mechanism and an administrative-political procedure also exists for many detailed issues in any society.

The organization structure formed by markets supplemented with the institution of private property has been frequently and even competently examined. We have acquired substantial knowledge pertaining to its mode of operation with respect to the role of government policies and the cultural patterns fostered or permitted under its institutions. The case on behalf of a market system has also been persuasively argued. It is based on careful investigations of the working of a market system and the social attitudes fostered, or obstructed, by private property. The case is by no means closed. Open issues always remain. The very nature of an open society creates new circumstances which pose new questions, and new problems. New circumstances frequently require an intelligent adjustment of inherited institutions in order to assure an effective operation of our social framework.[2] The positive analysis of a market system and of behaviour or attitudes fostered under its institutions exerted little influence on the professional articulations. A separate inquiry will consider at another occasion why intellectuals prefer with a pronounced frequency a posture of 'social criticism' barely justified by systematic analysis.

A vast array of critical objections have been addressed to the market system. The critique was frequently 'based' on some observations, or on empirical conjectures bearing on selected aspects of social behaviour. The factual assertions were combined with valuational attitude and yielded a repetitive condemnation of capitalism. The interplay of cognitive and valuational aspects assured the critique a persuasive force. A closer examination of these arguments exhibits however a peculiar attrition in the role of knowledge. The occurrence of cognitive ingredients cannot be denied, but they are stunted and remain usually undeveloped. Moreover, as a rule the cognitive elements are not sufficient to justify the criticisms advanced. Valuational impatience overpowers cognition too frequently and the morality which denies moral obligations to carefully executed cognition has victoriously influenced many of our professional articulators.

Valuational impatience and the elementary sacrifice of cognition

The sacrifice of cognition is particularly easy to detect in objections to the market system induced by discrepancies between one's desires (usually glorified as social values) and the result of market processes. One dislikes the *results* of the market process. One also is convinced that one knows what the world needs and finds the allocations emerging on the market not satisfactorily tending to these favoured needs. Ergo, the market has failed and should be replaced by an administrative arrangement. One is always convinced that this arrangement operates in the manner desired by one's wishes. The obvious naivete of this critique does not preclude its frequency and appeal to many articulators.[3]

The prevalence of valuational conceptions has also been demonstrated in discussions of nuclear armaments, demographic problems and of the structure of political processes or the response to a textbook in economics recently published. An important book on thermonuclear war by Herman Kahn was attacked on moral grounds and declared beyond the range of admissible intellectual consideration. These moral strictures on cognitive pursuits were propagated in the *Scientific American*, a medium pretending a cognitive commitment. Economic theories of demographic or political processes were rejected and criticized without consideration of their cognitive status, without concern for their adequacy to provide explanation of our observable environment. Critiques were offended by the theories' implicit disregard of moral preconceptions or valuational attitudes surrounding human behavior. Lastly, when Wadsworth Co. published the new textbook by Alchian and Allan (*University Economics: Elements of Inquiry*, Wadsworth Publishing Co. Inc. Belmont, California), a flood of comments vehemently objected on purely valuational grounds. Actually, the authors painfully separated any value statements from cognitive statements and developed one of the best introductions into *empirical* price theory. But this very success of their cognitive effort collided with the prevalent attitude of valuational concerns. In all these cases valuations operated as social taboos to circumscribe 'socially acceptable cognition'. The systematic investigation of important problems was considered immoral *per se* and therefore reprehensible. On other occasions one objected to the results of the analysis on moral grounds without any relevant cognitive argument. Or one objects to the analysis because the categories used are entirely amoral without value implication to fill men's *horror vacui*.[4]

Valuational impatience and the sophisticated sacrifice of cognition
The dominant role of valuations relative to cognition is less apparent in other arguments. Cognitive aspects actually intrude and are combined in some manner with valuational dispositions. Such arguments require more detailed examination in order to assess whether the factual statements combined with specified value statements are sufficient grounds to condemn capitalism and to opt for an alternative organization. Among these arguments the accusation that systematic exploitation is a consequence of private property and markets has an almost venerable history. It has become the dogma of an institutionalized church. This moral posture has been particularly effective due to its association with an apparently cognitive framework. This very fact explains the vast influence exerted by this view on the conception of professional articulators beyond the comparatively

narrow group of the faithful. Another valuation, seemingly based on examinations of behavior patterns associated with the market deplores that the markets 'transform everything into commodities'. Men thus emerge as depersonalized and alienated entities lost in a meaningless universe. On a substantially lower level of 'intellectual achievement' but in a significantly more developed cognitive context one also hears complaints that the market system cannot generate sufficient purchasing power to absorb all resources into employment. The breakdown of the early 1930s or the growing unemployment in the later 1950s is cited with particular frequency in support of such arguments. The apparently ineradicable unemployment among Negroes and the increasing unemployment rate of teenagers over the postwar period are additional observations which seemingly strengthen the claim that the market system has failed. And in a most general sense it is argued that motivations, values and manifest behaviour fostered under the environment of a market system are of a low order not worthy of our human aspirations. Markets and private property suffocate the development of our full potentialities and obstruct the realizations of higher values and motivations.

It is my contention that in all these cases the critique never developed relevant cognitive grounds to justify the substitution of an administrative organization for the market system. Ills and injustice doubtless exist and our values are deeply offended by many events. But moral offence and the deepest indignation about events observed are no grounds for abandoning the market as an organizational device. My moral indignation only reveals that I prefer another state of the world to the state actually observed. Unquestionably, we can always picture more preferable states without taxing our imagination. But our ability to visualize 'better' states more closely reflecting our sensitivity and personal preferences yields no evidence that this state can be realized. Neither does it provide evidence to assure us that the values satisfied have a larger weight than the values unavoidably sacrificed by our endeavor at 'social improvement'. Decisions bearing on alternative economic organizations must be responsibly made on the basis of a detailed empirical examination of these organizations. Such examination traces the *modus operandi* of various systems and describes cultural-attitudinal patterns encouraged by different institutions. We will rationally choose the arrangement that yields results pertaining to economic welfare and human attitudes that rank higher in our value-system. We must acknowledge that there is no assurance of paradise in our choice, no assurance that injustice will be vanquished, or that coercion of man by man is eliminated and that everybody behaves in the enlightened way I like them to behave. The decisive case for the choice made is that the alternative is substantially worse. Moreover, in the open society based on markets and private property we always have an opportunity to deal with injustice and other ills, at a cost however. But this cost becomes prohibitive under an administrative arrangement, and injustice or social ills remain more ineradicably entrenched.

'Social involvement' has usually been concerned with moral aspects and cultural attitudes. This preconception naturally induced violent criticisms of the system relying on markets and private property. Such criticism was usually based on the contention that private property exerts an evil influence on human character, attitudes and values. These attacks do not emerge from any careful analysis and evidence pertaining to adequately specified *alternative* institutional arrangements. They form typically the response of a romantic attitude or of a moral impatience to a highly imperfect world. It is argued on the other side that the relevant choice confronting mature minds lies between imperfect states. The real question appears which state is less systematically pernicious, more open-ended, more conducive to continuous reconsideration of established patterns and entrenched positions.

The prevalence of private property assures the diffusion of 'economic power', the existence of alternatives to potential exchanges. But alternatives are not accessible at zero cost. Still, such costs are frequently quite small. This circumstance characterizes competitive situations. Costs of access are on occasion, however, substantial. It is precisely under administrative arrangements where the cost of access to alternatives rises sharply, and frequently becomes prohibitive. Moreover, the existence of alternatives at non-prohibitive costs (of access) is the best protection of human integrity. A competitive arrangement emerging from the diffusion of private property is however not a sufficient condition of human dignity. Still, it appears to be a necessary condition. In the absence of genuine alternatives a behaviour reflecting fear, subservience and cautious servility dominates human patterns. Pressures and uncertainties suffocate independence and the creative search for new forms and ideas. Successful survival in non-competitive organizational careers depends crucially on a man's ability to anticipate his superiors' whims and to please him with personal non-performance traits. Successful search for an array of ways to work pleasingly on superiors' idiosyncracies is at a premium. These character traits are not prohibited under a voluntaristic regime based on private property. But the market system is effectively designed to *attenuate* these traits. The administrative system provides on the other hand *systematic incentives* to develop such characteristics and rewards acquisition of such traits comparatively more abundantly than under a market system.

The prevalent disregard of the effect exerted by various institutions on human behavior and attitudes also erodes the cognitive significance of contentions about 'exploitation' and 'oppression'. The Marxist literature never formulated a theory of social processes under capitalism satisfying the logical criteria of an empirical theory. And the discussion of social processes under socialism never moved beyond hippies' dreams. It should not be denied that the Marxist could be explicated by a meaningful empirical analysis of social processes. Neither do I wish to deny that 'exploitation' in some meaningful sense can occur and probably does occur under specified circumstances. But useful explication of these terms in contexts of relevant empirical theories will probably divulge that 'exploitation' and 'oppression' is more pervasive in administrative than in market systems. One would probably also find that the existence of 'exploitation' and 'oppression' is more effectively hidden and beclouded with a barrage of emotive language supplied by Intellectuals under an administrative-political mechanism.

The type of objections surveyed above exhibits a remarkably uniform pattern: certain observations pertaining to economic situations or men's behaviour are noted. These observations are measured on a moral scale and a judgement, 'based on observation', is passed on the type of economic organization which permitted or generated the circumstances observed. And in the last stage of the critique's argumentation comes usually a proposal of a better or New Society. This pattern contains at best suggestive hints for a prolegomenon introducing a never developed analysis of capitalist processes. As a matter (almost) of principle the critiques would never use economic analysis. Moreover, analysis of alternative organizations is totally missing as a rule. A semi-religious attitude expressed in extensive verbalizations replaces the detailed examination of institutional arrangements. This situation occurs with particular clarity in contexts asserting that a market system necessarily generates a state of permanent underemployment of human resources. Such assertions are most frequently associated with frameworks (in the Marxist tradition) never adequately explicated as cognitively acceptable constructions, or associated with frameworks (simple Keynesian formulations) possessing a very low degree of empirical confirmation. The observations initiating the indignant criticisms are thereby not contested. But the dominantly romantic or impressionistic reaction to these observations fails to consider seriously their relevant explanation provided by economic analysis. It thereby also fails to consider relevant remedies to the social ills deplored.

The fundamental confusion of contemporary articulators: knowledge of values and knowledge of the world
The effectiveness of the criticism advanced is probably attributable to the peculiar interplay of valuation and cognition. One particular pattern emerged with a pervasive force in recent publications of leading professional articulators, viz. the development of valuations and value statements in the form of cognitive statements. The discursive evolutions exploring an 'Affluent Society' persistently suggest a cognitive use of statements, the use of sentences to

convey factual information about our environment. Actually, the grammatical form of our language is misused in order to insert a valuational content into an apparently cognitive form. One's value judgements are imparted to the public as if they were cognitive statements pertaining to the structure of our environment.[5]

The confused entanglement of valuation and cognition is a pervasive characteristic of old orientations. They may be dead for our articulators, but an important residual feature remains and strongly affects the contemporary search for 'values and meanings'. This residual feature also affected attitudes towards alternative economic organizations. This aspect can be recognized in the meshing of valuational and normative attitudes with elements of substantive knowledge. Naive thought patterns do not recognize any relevant difference between these two aspects. The traditional orientations yielded an immediate answer to the most pressing needs. They provided values to be followed; they contained norms of conduct, designs of procedures and attitudes, mixed in with some descriptive outline of man's natural and social environment. Knowledge of the environment and knowledge of values appeared to be of the same kind and to be validated by the same reason. The view of the world conveyed by the ancient orientations transmitted to us through philosophy and theology is essentially a view of values and a rationalization of the world in terms of these values.

The identification of knowledge concerning the structure of the environment with knowledge about values has shaped the forms of ordinary language. Ordinary language does not differentiate between factual statements and value statements. Both have the same grammatical form, a predicate term is combined with a subject term to form a sentence. A clear recognition of the fundamental difference between the two types of statements is, however, of crucial importance. This recognition emerged only very slowly in our cognitive efforts and was effectively clarified in recent developments of the logical analysis of the language used in this effort. Early traces of the distinction between valuation and cognition can be found with Malebranche and Spinoza. Hume was already quite explicit on their logical separation. It became clear that valuating assertions possess no theoretical-cognitive content. They convey no factual information about the structure of the world. They convey no interpersonally assessable knowledge about objects and events, about their patterns of regularity and interconnection. It also follows that valuations cannot be inferred from observations or factual assertions, or logically justified on the basis of empirical evidence.[6]

The full recognition of the separate domains of human endeavour represented by cognition and valuation has still another facet. The most perfect cognition, the most complete knowledge about the structure of the universe and social processes provides no answer to the existential problems of human life. The recognition of the logical difference of knowledge and values (or valuation) should not be misused to castigate our search for existential meaning. Man responds to this challenge and expresses whatever answer he may find in his own life. Some of the most basic ideas of contemporary existentialism are thus most acceptable and thoroughly relevant in our perennial 'quest for being'. We reject, however, the adolescent weepiness, the peculiar 'existentialist sickness', exhibited by the circumstance that problems are not so much systematically *thought* about as suffered and *agonized* over.[7]

We accept that valuational attitudes are indispensable for our response to the existential problem. This acceptance remains coupled, however, to a watchful recognition of the logical separation and radical distinction between the two types of statements. The joint function of both statement types in any choice between alternative organization must also be fully acknowledged. A careful and explicit perception of the nature of their interaction in rational decision-making determines actually our choice. The logical structure of this interaction has been clarified both by logicians, statisticians and economists. It is unfortunate that the inherited pattern of value-drenched objections and moral criticisms to the market system persists in almost total disregard of the necessary logical instrumentation for a meaningful dialogue and persuasion.

The inadequate cognition induced by valuational impatience: inadequate analysis of capitalism
It is apparently necessary to emphasize that valuations (or motivations) are not sufficient to determine the preferred economic organization. Neither are they sufficient in general to determine rationally a desired course of policy. Even their supplementation with specific observations is not sufficient. Two cognitive strands essential in a rational decision are missing in the general type of objections and criticisms summarized above. These two requirements are discussed in the present and the subsequent section.

It should be noted first that isolated observations have no meaning without incorporation into an explicitly constructed theory which outlines the structure of the pertinent processes. On the other hand, vaguely suggestive ideas are not theories, they provide at best a guidepost in the search for a theory. Some examples are appropriate in this context. The large-scale deflation of the economy from August 1929 until March 1933 is frequently represented as an inherently unavoidable result of the market system. It cannot be sufficiently emphasized that this idea has never been translated into an explicitly and completely constructed theory. It remains a suggestive idea of considerable power. We possess, on the other hand, empirical theories explaining the general dynamics of a market economy and particularly the extreme severity of the Great Depression. A large amount of evidence has been accumulated by researchers over the last ten years establishing the catastrophic effects of a misconceived monetary-fiscal policy. The monetary authorities persisted with a non-policy of drift and indecision and aggravated the deflationary impulses. On several occasions the deflationary chain reaction decayed clearly, but was reactivated by some inappropriate policy-actions.

Or consider the persistent fluctuations in economic activity. They are frequently attributed to an inherent instability of the market mechanism. Larger-scale deviations from the trend were, however, not due to the inherent instability of markets, but to the instabilities and uncertainties surrounding government policies. The market system operates as a shock-absorber with built-in stabilizers which would not operate within an administrative system. The experience of 1929–33 and also the events in 1937–8 do not support the contentions of failures attributed to the market system. They yield more relevantly evidence bearing on the vagaries of administrative operations and the absence of incentives in the political mechanism designed to induce policies rationally determined on the basis of systematically assessed empirical hypotheses. There is very little evidence in support of the contention implicit in much of the criticism that the operators of administrative designs will exhibit a superior and detached skill in exploiting information and use relevant knowledge for rational decision-making. It appears that survival in the context of politico-administrative mechanisms is not fostered by intelligent use of knowledge for *general* welfare.

It is also asserted on occasion as a general proposition that the market system cannot possibly generate sufficient purchasing power to absorb available resources into productive employment. Simplistic Keynesian-type hypotheses were the only explicit theories formulated thus far as a logical basis for this proposition. The results of empirical investigations decisively disavowed these theories, and empirical researchers slowly acknowledge the comparatively small effect of government expenditures. Moreover, it is recognized that the market system generates search patterns formalized and explained by adaptive stochastic processes which reveal the nature of built-in shock-absorbers and stabilizers.

But what about persistent unemployment of Negroes and increasing unemployment among teenagers? The observations are not disputed, but the interpretation advanced by the critiques is rejected. This interpretation emerges again through an impressionistic short-cut. The contention of 'inherent market failures' is not subsumed under a testable theory of market processes. It occurs in a cognitive limbo as a valuational judgment attached to the observations cited. On the other hand, we do possess a highly confirmed hypothesis explaining the response of distinct labour types to increases in minimum wages. This successfully explains the patterns of persistent unemployment pockets. The hypothesis in question implies nothing with respect to our values. It says nothing about whether we should help the poor or the rich. It only says that if we help the poor by raising minimum wages, then the frequency of unemployment among the poor will rise. Given our determination to help the poor, the theory *supplemented by our* valuation, implies that other procedures are more effective than raising minimum wages. It is strange and puzzling that most well-meaning articulators with socially acceptable values strenuously object to this empirical theory and insist on using minimum wages as a supposedly efficacious means to aid 'the underprivileged'. Their rejection has never been based on relevant empirical investigation. This would require that they formulate an alternative hypothesis which denies the employment effect of minimum wages. It also requires discriminating evidence supporting the alternative hypothesis. In the absence of an explicit alternative the protesting articulators have no basis to interpret observations as evidence. Furthermore, the critiques usually feel that the theory endangers their values. They frequently object to it on these very grounds. It is noteworthy, however, that these values are logically quite consistent with the empirical theory. There is no collision on this level. The theory only endangers the obsessive fixation with respect to the choice of particular means to achieve some of the goal-values. Relevant cognition endangers only the conditional association between values and impressionistically determined means. This case yields a clear example of the precarious position of cognition in our policy discussions. Intelligent policy and the poor both suffer as a consequence.

The pattern of inadequate analysis of an organization based on private property intrudes even on highly sophisticated arguments. Neighbourhood effects of individual actions, the so-called externalities, have become a major concern of a sizeable group. Individual actions are often accompanied by effects not impounded into the cost and yield considerations which determine the conditions of exchange. The occurrence of such external effects is usually characterized as a 'market failure' justifying the imposition of administrative procedures. There is no doubt that important side effects exist. They challenge our ingenuity to find institutional arrangements which minimize their relevance. A broad comparison of different property systems would probably establish that private property lowers substantially the prevailing level of externalities. A system of communal property generates typically higher levels of externalities. This does not imply that a restructuring of rights within a system of private property cannot lower further some of the prevailing external effects. It is important however to avoid the standard fallacy which presents the occurrence of 'external' effects as a sufficient condition for the imposition of an administrative design. The absence of any market on which external effects are traded may be due to the circumstance that the social cost of the creation of a market exceeds the marginal benefit to potential transactors on the market. Furthermore, the imposition of an administrative design does not proceed without cost. Resources with alternative uses must be allocated to the construction of the new arrangement. Moreover, the discussion of externalities usually assumes without supporting evidence that administrative machineries never create externalities and have no side effects. Lastly, the optimal response to neighbourhood effects is not necessarily an administrative design. Such designs make it actually very difficult to assess reliably the welfare effects of government policy. The signals revealing voluntary decisions and summarizing the social evaluations of resources have been removed. Meaningful cost-benefit evaluations are prohibited and replaced by imaginative estimates advanced. The imposition of administrative arrangements cannot be ruled out *a priori* for all neighbourhood effects. But a strong case should be made for their application based on cost-benefit estimates not produced by an interested bureaucracy. Furthermore, other designs relying essentially on the market and voluntary exchanges are frequently possible. Imaginative search for effective devices which yield a more reliable increase in welfare has too frequently been sacrificed to an easy extension of existing administrative arrangements. Alternative devices may involve restructuring of property rights more likely to generate appropriate (but voluntary) behaviour. They may also exploit possible discrepancies in the social and private marginal cost of information production. Information costs are frequently a decisive obstacle in the 'production' of a market and the supply of information at lower social (and private) costs extends the range of voluntary coordination and is bound to raise economic welfare.

Other examples should be drawn from the literature of moral indignation. The moral principle of mutual responsibility is adduced in justification of vast social security arrangements constructed along non-voluntaristic, compulsory designs. The same principle combined with the assertion that many members of our society lack adequate information and exhibit poor judgement is used to support administrative systems supplying medical and health services. In all these cases one notes a conspicuous absence of any cognitive basis. The organizational conclusion is immediately attached to the moral presuppositions. One searches in vain for the necessary analysis of social or institutional behaviour which effectively relates in a logically acceptable manner the stipulated valuations with the organizational proposals.[8]

The inadequate cognition induced by valuational impatience: complete absence of analysis of alternatives, and a reason for this state of affairs
The connection between moral presupposition and empirical conclusion is not the only cognitive component usually missing in the rejection of markets and private property. The replacement of capitalism is proposed not only without substantive analysis of the actual working of the market system and the potentialities of *intelligent* government action within this framework.

Administrative systems are also proposed without any endeavour at assessment of their detailed working, of the behaviour patterns generated in their context and the cultural attitudes fostered by their implicit incentive mechanisms. Administrative designs yield a peculiar impression of thorough controllability of results. With sufficient power at one's disposal one can achieve all desired good results. Knowledge of 'true values' and the will to construct administrative systems of sufficient thoroughness necessarily guarantees the achievement of our goal. This posture reflects actually a remarkable conception of the world radically at variance with our cognitive presuppositions. The latter asserts that our environment behaves according to an underlying structure. The processes governed by this structure determine the outcome of our actions. It implies in particular that there is no assured correlation between motivations of actions and the moral status of the outcome. In the absence of knowledge about the structure of the process the choice of actions shaped by our values usually yields results barely consistent with our motivating values. The conception implicit in the posture of moral indignation views the world as a structureless, amorphous mass to be shaped in the light of our values. The environment appears like clay in the hands of a potter. And our 'knowledge of values' is deemed sufficient to impose the true form on our matter. Analysis of institutional behavior in the context of administrative designs becomes naturally redundant under this conception. The obvious absence of such analysis from the Marxist literature, or the literary outpowerings of the New Left or similar writing by value-conscious articulators becomes thus quite understandable.

We contend that the weight of evidence is against such positions. Organizational designs generate processes with an inherent structure which modifies the outcome of our wishful actions. Administrative designs attenuate the wealth incentives, a motive with bad name and low value among the critiques of capitalism. But they fail to recognize that it replaces the wealth incentive by the power incentive. And the working of this incentive system is indeed corrosive for human values. The behaviour of individuals under a communist system, intent on maximizing their survival probabilities under an arrangement which enlarges their exposure to an encompassing control, has been described on several occasions. There is ample evidence revealing the systematic cultivations of cautious servility, or the pervasive betrayal of trusts and affection. There is also evidence from non-communist countries. Wherever government controls cover extensive sectors, behaviour is systematically shaped by incentives quite inconsistent with the high motives and values so generally aspired. The experience of Winston Churchill during the interwar period demonstrates the danger posed to freedom of expression and controversy by a government-owned communications system. He was prevented from lecturing on the BBC about foreign policy. Government policies prohibited the existence of alternative avenues for expression on radio. The cost of access to alternatives was high indeed under these circumstances. It is precisely the wealth incentives operating in the context of private property which raise the probability of access to communication systems for highly controversial positions and views. This probability is substantially lowered under an administrative-political mechanism. The open flow of controversial views endangers the survival probabilities, or advancement probabilities' of bureaucrats and thus induces a systematic behaviour discriminating against controversial views. Where large sectors of industry depend completely on the government for the supply of funds, one observes that the managerial class carefully avoids opposition or disagreement with government policies. Selection of managers will also depend to a much larger extent on personal traits and personal relations with powerful members of the administration and substantially less on technical competence or performance characteristics. There exists a correlation between wealth incentives and general economic welfare under a competitive organization. This organization also provides adequate alternatives which weakens an individual's dependence on any particular employment. This weakened dependence is a better protection of one's personality and dignity than legally sanctioned administrative designs. The case of blacklisted communists or fellow travellers, or of the security risks dismissed by the US government, is an excellent illustration. They all found employment in private business. The competitive pressure of private business forces a comparative disregard of personality traits in favour of performance characteristics. The monopolistic pattern of administrative arrangements fosters on the contrary attitudes assigning substantial weights to personality traits in advancement and survival criteria. The blacklisted communists would have lost their jobs in a government-owned movie industry, and with a dominant government sector the security risks discussed would have suffered substantially more. Employment would have been difficult to find.

It is thus contended that an administrative system does not shape an amorphous and malleable environment in the light of our 'knowledge of values'. The administrative design unleashes social processes with characteristics systematically associated with the control apparatus. And the most fashionable designs generate patterns which endanger the very values so often adduced for their justification. The continuous appeal to higher motivations of subordinates is, of course, an integral part of the pressure mechanism characteristic of administrative systems. It is a behaviour of superiors which contributes to their political survival and advancement. But naiveté should not be stretched too far. We cannot accept the veil of words cast up by the very control mechanism under investigation as the meaning and substance of this mechanism. The motivational and behaviouristic response of the administered is not correlated with the context of the official appeals. These motivations and responses are shaped in the context of survival strategies applied to environmental pressures peculiar to the system. And the pressures of pervasive anxiety and uncertainty are even greater under an administrative design than under the alternative arrangement. The crucial point, however, remains that this is neither a matter of metaphysical speculation nor of valuational dispositions. It remains fundamentally an empirical issue, to be investigated intelligently through suitable theory construction and evidential assessment. Little work has been done in this field and least of all by the professional articulators preaching the virtues of alternative organizations. The state of permanent moral indignation appears not very conducive to the disintegration of ideological confrontations. Meaningful progress will only be achieved by uncovering relevant issues with respect to the working patterns of distinct institutional arrangement under the tortured veil of ideologically committed valuations.

And lastly, some final remarks
The importance of values cannot be denied. The contemporary concern for values is understandable and deserves our sympathetic support. This concern is an integral part of our life and we express this concern in the *form* of our life. We do respond to questions concerning the sense of our existence forced on us apart from any cognition, questions we can never avoid, simply because we are alive. But this concern should not be misused to disregard the contribution of properly executed cognition in the determination of intelligent action. Neither should it justify the dangerous confusion that knowledge of our environment is subsumable under 'knowledge of values'. The intelligent choice between economic organization requires a detailed assessment of empirical theories bearing on the working of organizational patterns. Values and valuations alone yield no rational decision and cannot guide intelligent actions by themselves.

This problem extends also to government policy within the range of action circumscribed by a libertarian position based on markets and the price system. Public agencies remain confronted with important problems. The history of our monetary policy yields disturbing examples that the intelligent exploitation of relevant knowledge for rational decisions affecting our welfare still has to be learned. How to achieve this remains an open issue. But so long as the issue exists there is little reason to expect systematically good effects from any extension of our administrative mechanisms, and the range of political mechanisms in our society does become a serious issue. Some economists, less enlightened by metaphysical insights than most professional articulators, would persist in searching for institutional arrangements which minimize the dependence of our fates on the chance occurrence of superior wisdom, love, consideration and rational intelligence among the operators of the administrative apparatus.

Notes

1. The uneasy position of cognition in man's historical endeavours to understand himself and his environment has been explored particularly by Ernst Topitsch. The reader will find the following two books by this author very useful. The first book, entitled *Vom Ursprung und Ende der Metaphysik* (Vienna: Springer Verlag, 1958) analyses the patterns characterizing non-cognitive belief systems beginning with ancient mythologies and proceeding to conceptions expressed by traditional philosophy and theology. The second book is a collection of essays: *Sozialphilosophie zwischen Ideologie und Wissenschaft* (Neuwied, Germany: Herman Luchterhand Verlag, 1961).
2. The definition of new property rights in response to technological developments forms an interesting example.
3. The author visited for one month in the summer 1964 the Center for the Study of Democratic Institutions in Santa Barbara (Calif.). Arguments of the general type described in the text were the standard fare of the discussion. The discussions clearly revealed that valuational concern was considered a sufficient reason to disregard relevant analysis.
4. Valuational impatience is also revealed on occasion in discussions of specific empirical issues. It is usually manifested by an explicit rejection of any pertinent evidence bearing on the issue. A classic example occurred at a seminar sponsored by General Electric in January 1967 when the evidence pertaining to a particular issue was rejected by some economists with the comments: 'We feel in our bones that this cannot be so.' This metaphysical attitude successfully adjusts cognition to one's valuational taboos.
5. The reference to J.K. Galbraith's *Affluent Society* is most deliberate. It is an outstanding example of a dominant pattern among professional articulators. The unwary reader feels that the product offered him by the articulators contains a description of the world when actually it is but a tract advertising the superiority of the author's moral preconception or value judgement. Value judgements are thus sold to the public as if they were cognitive statements informing about the structure of our environment. The same articulators who protest vehemently and with fine indignation the false advertisements of private business carelessly mislead the public with respect to the precise nature of their own product.
6. It is still contended on occasion that value statements and cognitive statements are 'really the same'. The confusion arises from inadequate analysis of distinct types of 'value statements'. I rest my case with Topitsch's work previously cited and also with Rudolf Carnap's analysis of 'purely putative sentences' in the volume *The Philosophy of Rudolf Carnap*, ed: Paul Arthur Schilpp (La Salle, Ill., 1963).
7. It is intriguing to note that articulators of 'minimal art' consider this art form an apt revelation of man's 'lack of answers and solutions to problems'. The problems discussed involve essentially values and moral attitudes. And the 'answers and solutions' missing are answers and solutions assuring an effective acceptance by everybody of proper values and moral attitudes. There is an immediate connection between this position and the attitude of a physicist who complained to me that 'social sciences are useless and have failed, because they have not resulted in the moral attitudes' preventing all the observed deplorable social ills. The absence of such solutions and answers ultimately provides a wonderful opportunity to justify a continuous verbal agonizing over and wallowing in problems. Actually, the 'lack of answers' only exists because the wrong questions have been asked.
8. A protean source of professional articulatism supplied the examples in the text. They were from various publications issued by the Center for the Study of Democratic Institutions in Santa Barbara.

2   My quest for economic knowledge*

The topic I have been asked to write about may invite an elaboration of a 'philosophy' in the sense of an explicit and encompassing orientation. But another sense expressed by the road I have travelled in life seems more relevant for my purpose. The ideas and decisions that shape the meandering of one's path reveal, beyond the circumstances encountered, the basic attitudes and orientations of one's life.

The origins set at least the initial segment of one's life and affect some of one's attitudes and ideas. My parents descended from the 'lower orders' of society. My mother was born into the family of a peasant and factory worker in the western Jura Mountains along the Swiss–French border. My father grew up in the Toggenburg, a mountain valley in eastern Switzerland, as the tenth child of a very small textile merchant who travelled around the villages and little towns in the hill country. Both parents emigrated as teenagers to Russia in order to escape their local poverty and confinement. My father eventually managed to study mathematics and astronomy at the Swiss Institute of Technology in Zürich. Astronomy had already attracted his interest as a teenager and dominated his dreams and hopes. Confrontation with reality destroyed those dreams. Still, late in life, he was appointed professor of astronomy at the Swiss Institute of Technology. My love of books and ideas I derived from my father, who encouraged my reading at an early age. Resilience, persistence and determination I inherited from my mother.

After an indifferent performance in high school, I entered the university in 1934 with a sense of liberation and joy. Thus began a very new phase in my life. It was a time of intellectual awakening and growing intellectual excitement. It was also a time of wondering and questioning what to do with my life. I searched for an avenue that would always remain a challenge. Concern about a safe career was overshadowed by my dream of being involved in the pursuit of ideas. It was entirely unclear to me how this could be achieved in the severely confined circumstances of Swiss society. My immediate problem was a choice of fields. Essentially by chance, I encountered economics. That settled my course. This choice was not motivated by any concern for solving so-called social problems by appeal to God, History or the State. The major social and political influences in my family reflected a tradition committed to individual liberty with opportunities to shape one's own life. My move to

*   Originally published in *Eminent Economists: Their Life Philosophies*, ed. Michael Szenberg, Cambridge: Cambridge University Press, 1991, 84–97.

18

economics expressed an entirely different and deep urge. The 'human animal' and human society attracted me with an overpowering fascination. The events evolving north of the Rhine River stirred me and many other young Swiss, and I pondered and worried about it. It was my desire to understand the human riddle, considered in the context of human society, that made me eventually settle upon economics as my lifetime pursuit. I do not really know why I felt that economics could satisfy my dominant urge. At the time there were no good grounds for my belief or my decision. But in retrospect, I do know that my belief turned out to be correct and my decision right. The same urge also shaped a good part of my professional interests to the last segment of my life. At the same time, I made the second of the two fundamental decisions. I met my future wife and from that moment on evolved a close companionship for 51 years. The loving but not uncritical support that I received from my wife decisively shaped my life.

In the winter of 1936–7 I registered for one year at the London School of Economics for wider exposure. A new world opened up as I encountered books and names I had never heard about at the University of Zürich. I spent most of my time in the library reading widely. This was my first experience of modern economic analysis and I enjoyed it. It made me feel that I might be on the right track. But it also posed a problem. After resuming my studies at the University of Zurich in October 1938, with a delay resulting from military service, it gradually occurred to me that I could not expect to acquire an understanding of economics from the professors at the university. This recognition convinced me that I had to lay out my own course of learning. For this purpose I had to rely on library books. My ignorance and the absence of any guidance, however, created some difficulties. Much of my time was wasted with irrelevant or poor selections of literature. Early in 1939 I approached one of the professors to discuss a topic for my doctoral dissertation. In order to impose on myself the task of digging deeply into mainstream English and American literature, I proposed 'Investigations in Anglo-Saxon Theory of International Trade'. Progress on my thesis was much delayed by the war. But I managed to finish it by the end of 1942.

At this stage a new phase opened in my life. A job had to be found. My ultimate dream confronted its first hard test. There were long arguments with my father. I tried, and failed, to explain to him why I did not care for just any safe job. There were at the time no avenues for young people to pursue academic or intellectual interests. The faculty consisted only of full professors (*ordinarius*) or associate professors (*extraordinarius*). Those with a teaching appointment of any sort had to be independently wealthy or employed full time in the government or private sector. They had, quite generally, no time or opportunity to engage in serious intellectual pursuits.

The issue was ultimately resolved when I took a job in the Economics Department of the Swiss National Bank. Within a few months I understood that this department was a blind alley where one grew old peacefully by not ever writing or saying anything substantial, particularly not about monetary problems. The job gave me an opportunity, however, to acquaint myself with some interesting policy problems. Special assignments from the president's office allowed me to study in detail the minutes of the policy-making group and other internal documents. This information contributed to the evolution of my thinking on matters of economic policy. An examination of the detailed policy record with the supporting arguments convinced me that self-declared practical men of affairs frequently are, without seeming to realize it, ardent theorists. The minutes showed that evaluations and actions resulted from a dominant conception about monetary affairs. In order to understand the responses of policy to specific events and problems, we need first to understand the 'theory' guiding that policy, i.e., the policy-makers' ruling conception or vision of their segment of the world. I applied this recognition 20 years later in a study of Federal Reserve policy-making developed jointly with Allan H. Meltzer. During the 1930s and 1940s, the Swiss National Bank managed to combine a real bills doctrine, enlarged to admit Treasury bills, with an emphatic commitment to a gold standard with a large gold reserve and a quantity theory based on note circulation.

There was more to learn, however. This experience initiated a slow erosion of my implicit faith in the public interest theory, or goodwill theory, of public agencies. The final result of the process, interrupted for many years by other work, surfaced to extensive and explicit attention 30 years later. The question arose in my mind why Central Bankers held to their particular beliefs and why they generally avoided pondering and assessing the problems associated with their conceptions. A study of the crises and problems confronting these policy-makers over time revealed that no serious attempt had ever been made to understand the issues in some relevant mode beyond the clichés of the public market.

Late in 1944 it was time to move on. A short interlude followed. In April 1945 I joined a research institute at the University of St Gall. I was also appointed lecturer. This appointment could have been the basis of a permanent career at this university leading from the habilitation thesis to '*Privat-Dozent*' and finally professor, provided that I would play the game right. But I did not. The problem centred around the quality of our work. It seemed to me, and in retrospect I still maintain this position, that our endeavours at empirical research remained, at the very best, very amateurish and journalistic, with a very meagre and dubious economic content. I recognized the problem, but because of my inadequate experience I failed to offer a solution. My suggestion to invite an experienced scholar from the United States was coldly received. It was unavoidable that I disrupted the prevailing sense of satisfaction and posed a problem. My discharge came in March 1948. Thirty-five years later I received an honorary degree from the same university.

The prospects of following my dreams seemed at this stage very sombre indeed. There simply appeared no avenue for my hopes. But I rather quickly found a position at the Watch Chamber of Commerce in La Chaux de Fonds, the centre of the Swiss watch industry. Some interesting and real problems required my attention: the two-tier exchange rate system prevailing at the time in Switzerland and the Trade Charter, a forerunner of GATT, under discussion at an international conference in Havana.

Amid the uncertain pressures and murky future, some friends banded together for systematic learning and discussion. We met every Saturday afternoon in a quiet coffee house in Zürich. We discussed chapter by chapter, section by section, Keynes's *General Theory*. These discussions prepared me for a critical re-examination of Keynesian theory some years later. The important point, however, was that this study group helped me to maintain my hope of finding some way out, somewhere. By the end of the war I was wondering whether I should emigrate to the United States. The thought grew while I was in St Gall and became definite with my dismissal. I applied to the Rockefeller Foundation, which offered a special programme for European scholars. A fellowship was granted, and in September by wife and I moved to the United States. We sensed the beginning of a new life, and so it was. After one semester in Harvard, we stayed for one and a half years at the University of Chicago, interrupted by a long summer's visit to the University of California at Berkeley. The two years under the fellowship were a turning point. They were also years of confusion and search bearing on the nature of my work in economics.

I joined the (then) Cowles Commission for Research in Economics as a guest. My purpose was to acquaint myself with econometrics and the application of mathematics to economic analysis. I enjoyed a good working relation with Carl Christ and Harry Markowitz. Carl Christ and I worked together through Samuelson's *Foundations of Economic Analysis*, and subsequently Harry Markowitz and I studied von Neumann-Morgenstern's *Theory of Games*. These sessions, occurring over many months, were very useful. There were also regular seminars at the commission with an increasingly mathematical flavor. Beyond the commission, of course, was the Department of Economics – a somewhat different world. I became exposed to a group around Aaron Director, Frank Knight and Milton Friedman. The group met with some regularity for discussions ranging over a wide array of problems. The thrust of these differed radically from that of the seminars at the Cowles Commission. They emphatically advanced the relevance of economic analysis as an important means of understanding the world, in a manner that I had never encountered before. I received a clear sense of economics as an empirical science beyond the formal exercises and statistical apparatus of econometrics, which in my experience often obscured the basic cognitive problem. I found this both confusing and strangely appealing. In contrast, many papers presented at the Cowles Commission seminars and their discussion puzzled me deeply. What the criteria of a good paper and an interesting problem really were remained quite obscure.

The issues raised in my mind during this period were not resolved by the time I left Chicago and joined the faculty of UCLA in September 1951. One question, however, became clearer: What is the nature of the intellectual game we actually play or might pursue in economics? So my search for an understanding of how to understand the world continued. Two things ultimately contributed clarity. The first was my many discussions with Armen A. Alchian, who, engaged in a similar search, was strongly conditioned by his prior basic training in statistics. The second was my encounter with Reichenbach's *Prediction and Experience*, which I read avidly. There followed a period of substantial investment in logic and the philosophy of science. I began to feel more at ease with a growing understanding of the only meaningful purpose of my intellectual activities in economics. The nature of the cognitive process gradually emerged in clear lines. This included an understanding of the structure of hypotheses and theories, the search for a useful and adequate formulation, the role of a formal apparatus, the evaluation of the intellectual product and the relevant criteria, and finally the relation between econometric practice and the relevant cognitive procedure and criteria.

The immediate victim of this phase of understanding the cognitive process was my Keynesian conviction, which I had developed by the mid-1940s. There seemed to me very little ground for accepting this theory. It failed miserably, most particularly its basic version expressed by the Keynesian cross, to explain the postwar transition and the longer-term postwar experience. My 'liberation' from Keynesian conceptions revived my earlier interests in monetary analysis. In the past 30 years, I have allocated a substantial portion of my time and effort to work in this field. This phase opened with a project investigating the money supply process. This period also marked the beginning of a long and fruitful association with Allan Meltzer that continues to be an important part of my life. Our innumerable discussions on wide-ranging subjects have shaped my thinking over the almost 30 years we have worked together and sharpened my sense of the issues. It should come as no surprise that, to a large extent, our views have merged into a similar pattern. Our collaboration began with my suggestion that Allan examine the French money supply process. It appeared to me that this topic offered a good choice for a doctoral dissertation. My interest in money supply actually awoke in

1953–4. Reviewing the literature and a large number of textbooks, it struck me that there was no coherent hypothesis of the money supply process. The usual story of bank credit expansion was, of course, standard material. But it failed to satisfy the requirements of a useful hypothesis. It offered no propositions about the determination of the money stock or the interaction between money, credit, and interest rates with a full account of the nature of the process.

This failure was somewhat remarkable in view of the many assertions concerning the money supply process advanced by the profession and in the public market. My attention was increasingly directed toward developing some empirical hypotheses about the money supply process. It seemed particularly desirable to construct an analysis yielding empirical propositions about the relative importance of the monetary authorities, as well as the public's and the banks' behaviour in the short- and long-run evolution of money stock and bank credit. A completely specified framework would also clarify the nature of 'reverse causation', i.e., the conditions under which the observed correlation between money and income expresses a causal direction from income to money. It seemed rarely understood that this is not inherent but results from specific institutional choices. Once the conditions of reverse causation were elaborated, its relevance could be systematically assessed. More generally, a useful money supply theory would facilitate our understanding of different institutional arrangements. We would wish to know whether a shrinking membership of commercial banks in the Federal Reserve system actually impaired the efficacy of monetary policy, as was asserted by the Federal Reserve authorities over many years. Similarly, we would expect that an adequate money supply theory would offer useful answers to questions bearing on financial regulation and deregulation. Finally, we would wish to determine the degree of controllability of money stock and monetary growth. These problems motivated my work in money supply theory pursued jointly with Allan Meltzer. The framework we developed over the years offered answers to all these questions.

In the summer of 1963 Allan and I were approached to prepare a study on Federal Reserve policy-making for Congressman Patman's Committee on Banking and Currency. We gladly accepted an obligation that seemed closely associated with our projects. This work very much influenced my subsequent views and thinking about the behaviour of the Central Bank. The examination of monetary policy-making revived an idea I had developed during my short association with the Swiss National Bank. In order to understand the behaviour of the Federal Reserve authorities, we need to know their dominant conception, i.e., their theory about the process they wish to influence. This knowledge, even though not sufficient, is certainly necessary to understand the Fed's policy-making behaviour. It needs to be supplemented, however, by some knowledge of the Fed's objectives. This second dimension was not included in our study and captured our attention much later. We still were influenced at the time, as were most economists in my experience, by a goodwill, or public interest, theory of government. We were inclined to believe that the Fed would act in the correct way once it properly understood the nature of the process confronting it. Our work made us realize that the Fed's views exhibited little resemblance to economic analysis and were actually in conflict with it. There was no trace in the professional literature, particularly in the textbooks, that prepared us for the encounter with the Fed's view. This view centred at the time on free reserves, i.e., the difference between excess reserves and bank borrowing from the Fed. Free reserves formed the centrepiece of the causal nexus linking monetary policy with bank credit. An increase in free reserves meant, in this view, an expansionary event raising the rate of expansion of bank credit. A reduction in free reserves was interpreted as a contractive move.

This conception determined the choice of free reserves as an indicator guiding the interpretation of monetary affairs. Its frequent use as a target guiding the authorities' actions also followed from this basic conception. We showed that this conception had emerged in the 1920s and had prevailed with some evolution into the 1960s. It explains the puzzlingly large increase in reserve requirements in 1936–7. We also demonstrated that the Fed's policy pronouncements, according to the Record of Policy, were significantly positively correlated with the movement of free reserves. In contrast, these policy pronouncements were significantly negatively correlated with actual behaviour. Viewing free reserves as a crucial link between monetary policy and bank credit caused a systematic misinterpretation of monetary affairs and monetary policy. Restrictive policies were frequently sold to the public as expansionary moves, as in the early 1930s, in 1949 and in 1960, and expansionary policies metamorphosed into restrictive policies. To a large extent, the failure of the Federal Reserve can be attributed to such misinterpretations. By the late 1960s, the ruling conception was modified. Elements of a possible transition became visible in the early 1960s among the policy-makers. But important fragments of the older ideas have reemerged in the past eleven years, particularly the contractive interpretation of 'borrowed reserves' in contrast to non-borrowed reserves.

The Federal Reserve study alerted me to an important policy problem rather neglected in the professional literature, i.e., the indicator and the target problem. The indicator problem involves the optimal choice of a one-dimensional scale guiding the interpretation of policy actions in terms of their consequences on the pace of output. In contrast, the target involves the optimal choice of an observable magnitude guiding the regular adjustment of policy actions. Neither problem is contrived. Any careful observer of the

Fed's tactical procedures necessarily encounters these problems. We also encounter them as an inherent component of all discussions, which typically characterize policies in classificatory terms (easy, tight) or in comparative terms (easier, tighter). In the first case we need to determine a unidimensional binary classification and in the second case a unidimensional ordinal scale (Brunner and Meltzer, 1967). The problem was generally neglected. Many economists argued that we need to look at 'many things' or 'everything'. Both classificatory and comparative statements presuppose, however, a unidimensional scale. In the absence of a scale there is no justification for the statements typically made.

The nature of monetary transmissions caught my attention by the late 1950s. My concern about the nature of the transmission mechanism made me recognize the limitations of the IS/LM model. This paradigm telescopes the array of assets into two groups, money and 'bonds'. Three interpretations of this paradigmatic approach are possible. The first asserts that money substitutes only with 'bonds'. Real capital remains beyond the substitution nexus surrounding money. This means that the interest rate on financial assets forms the crucial link between monetary impulses, on the one hand, and economic activity and price level, on the other. The second interpretation accepts that money substitutes over the whole range of assets. This array is reduced to two assets in order to fit an analysis with a single portfolio equation. The reduction is achieved with the assumption that financial and real assets are perfect substitutes. The third interpretation also accepts the general substitution nexus of all assets but denies the perfect substitutability assumption. This assumption is replaced by a restriction on the range of admissible applications of the analysis. It needs to be confined to events and episodes with small variations in relative market conditions between financial and real assets compared with the movements of the major phenomenon under investigation. The first two interpretations involve hypotheses that I always judged to be quite untenable on empirical grounds. The third interpretation involves no potentially falsifiable hypothesis. It offers a rule guiding the domain of useful application of the paradigm. The problem encountered here bears on the limited range of use, which excludes all but extraordinary events. Moreover, the monetary system occurs in a severely emasculated form. Issues bearing on the interaction between money and credit market, or problems of deregulation and regulation of the financial industry, cannot be subsumed under the paradigm and cannot be effectively clarified within this framework. Any policy analysis executed with the aid of this framework could hardly expect to cope usefully with the relevant problems encountered. The Federal Reserve cannot control interest rates. It faces a whole structure of interest rates exhibiting different responses to shifting mixtures of perceived transitory and permanent shocks. In my judgement we clearly required an alternative view of the transmission mechanism.

The theme was initiated around 1960 and was subsequently elaborated in a long series of papers mostly written with Allan H. Meltzer. My review of the report prepared by the Commission on Money and Credit (Brunner, 1961) offered an outline of the alternative analysis. The broader view of the transmission mechanism emphasizing an imperfect substitutability between all assets, between assets and their services, and between assets and output substantially modifies major propositions of the IS/LM model augmented with the Phillips relation. In particular, this analysis changed the nature of monetary shocks influencing output or price level. Money stock and accustomed monetary growth exert little effect on output. Both are mostly absorbed by the price level. However, perceived deviations from accustomed growth affect current output. Unavoidably, such deviations remain more or less transitory events. Persistent deviations induce revisions of the accustomed growth rate.

Among other issues in monetary theory that attracted our attention were the impulse or shock problem, the interpretation of normal output, and the use (or existence) of money in transactions. Twenty years ago we accepted the thesis of a dominant shock pattern in the form of monetary shocks. In contrast, today we accept a thesis emphasizing unpredictably shifting combinations of shocks.

Until recently the use of money was taken for granted. Monetary analysis offered no explanation for the existence of money. Long discussions with Armen Alchian in the early 1960s contributed to our thinking. We understood that information and transaction costs are necessary conditions for the phenomenon to occur. The basic idea was subsequently developed in a paper (Brunner and Meltzer, 1971). This work initiated a more general interest bearing on the emergence and role of social institutions.

Several issues attracted my attention over the years as a result of my continued interest in the philosophy of science and logic. Milton Friedman's (1953) article questioning the emphasis on the 'realism' of assumptions generated some heated objections. Friedman's logical instincts led him on the right track. But his arguments concentrated on metaphors and illustrations and neglected the core of the essentially logical issue. The objections also missed the logical issue. This situation motivated my attention (Brunner, 1969). The term 'assumption' was used by economists in very different ways. The precise logical characterization of these different uses of the term showed, moreover, that in no case was it possible to infer the confirmation of a hypothesis (or theory) from the confirmation of 'its assumption'.

The cognitive process represented by econometric practice presented another important issue. I felt increasing concern about questionable logical aspects of much of our practice. The language used to convey the results of an empirical investigation was frequently quite misleading. Categorical conclusions or objections were offered that required highly corroborated hypotheses for justification. Such hypotheses were sometimes not even formulated and many times not evaluated against serious alternative contenders. The large-scale econometric models presented some special problems. The degree of freedom problem typically confronting such models was usually resolved by resorting to a set of instrumental variables. But each choice of such a set imposed an implicit class of unspecified hypotheses. Such an intellectual game was, in my judgement, more nearly numerology than science (Brunner, 1973).

Finally, most of our disputes involve systematic alternative hypotheses, but much of our work seems satisfied to show significant inconsistency with the null (i.e., chance) hypothesis. There is, of course, a deeper layer of questions bearing on possibly inherent difficulties in developing real tests. I leave this aside and consider some methodological issues posed by the emergence of the new classical macroeconomics. Rational expectations analysis generalized Marshak's rationale for structural formulation and estimation. The sensitivity of the structure to changes in policy regime suggested the need for a deeper level of invariance. 'Technology' represented by a production function and tastes seemed to offer the required anchor. Thus emerged the methodological theme that all analysis should be derived from such 'first principles'. This position, however, involves two major fallacies. First, we should recognize that there are no 'first principles'. This is a Cartesian illusion. There is no rock bottom, neither of certainty nor of invariance. The general point has been effectively made by Sir Karl Popper. Jensen and Meckling (1979) demonstrated in our particular case that the production function is not invariant with respect to institutional changes. Moreover, the production function involves more than technology. Optimizing behaviour is already at work shaping its form. Second, the methodological thesis seemed also to have convinced new classical macroeconomists that all work need start from 'first principles', anything else being unacceptable. Such methodological legislation is a travesty of science. We possess much useful knowledge, particularly in medicine and even in economics, about empirical regularities without an adequate underlying theory. The advice of new classical macroeconomists to throw this knowledge away makes no sense. The methodological thesis supplemented with the requirement of full 'rigorization' may cause them to box themselves into a corner that omits the most relevant problems.

Some unattended issues inherited from the Federal Reserve study kept surfacing off and on. They centred around the questions: Why do Central Banks behave the way they do, why do they accept the strategies and tactical procedures actually observed, why do they generally oppose any pre-commitment, and why do they generally exhibit a high level of determined ignorance about the processes addressed by their activity? These questions generally destroyed the more or less unconsciously held goodwill theory of political institutions. In the early 1970s, these questions led to some deeper questions. It occurred to me that we could explain the major differences in our approach to political institutions in terms of two alternative hypotheses about man supplemented by two alternative conceptions of justice. Two traditions compete in the social sciences for our attention (Brunner and Meckling, 1977; Brunner, 1987). Both traditions originated in the eighteenth century, one in Scotland with Mandeville, Ferguson and Smith, the other in France with the Enlightenment. The first evolved into the core of economic analysis with the hypothesis of a resourceful, evaluating, and maximizing man. A crucial element of this hypothesis is the proper interpretation of self-interested (not identical with egotistic) behaviour and the biological basis of this behaviour. This approach implies in particular that the 'human animal's' basic disposition, his self-interest, operates independently of specific institutions. They operate in commercial contexts and in contexts of political institutions without private property and profits. Differences in institutional arrangements imply very different specific expressions of self-interested behaviour. The French tradition became in the hands of Marx and Durkheim the sociological model of this century, which probably influences most of the intelligentsia and also a number of economists' thinking about social problems.

The sociological model sees man as a passive agent of society. Basic human nature is quite malleable and can be shaped by social engineering. The two hypotheses yield very different implications about the working of political institutions. The 'Scottish hypothesis' generally determines a constitutionalist approach to government imposing clear and severe constraints on the government's agenda. The sociological model encourages and justifies an open-ended agenda for the state and its agencies, including the judiciary. It appears that much of the detail of our disputes bearing on questions of political economy can thus be explained in terms of the two competing hypotheses. They are, however, not quite sufficient. They are reinforced by suitable notions of justice, the outcome patterns, and the process view. The criteria of justice in the first case pertains to a particular pattern of outcome of the social process (e.g., some preferred income distribution). The criteria refer in the second case to characteristics of the social process. There is an important relation between the perception of man and the conception of justice. The Scottish hypothesis cannot be reconciled with the outcome pattern view, whereas the sociological model offers a rational underpinning justifying the choice of an outcome pattern as criterion of justice.

These issues also bear on two fundamentally different approaches to economic policy. The conflict between the two approaches covers a wide range including monetary and regulatory policy. One approach emphasizes the choice of institutional arrangements and general rules of procedures. The other, in contrast, addresses detailed and contingent actions specific to time and place. The dispute is clearly visible in the field of monetary policy. Discretionary policy and pre-commitment directed to longer-term consideration and predictability continue to be argued. The central issue in this debate often seems somewhat obscured. It involves the hypothesis about man and the information he may command. Human nature and the reliable information at hand crucially condition the working and consequences ᴼᶠ different political institutions. Advocacy of activist and discretionary policy is a rational consequence of the sociological model of man supplemented with full and reliable information about the structure of the relevant processes. For many years I have argued that these conditions do not hold. I had concluded that the sociological model; particularly in its form as the public interest, or goodwill, theory of government, is empirically untenable. Moreover, the information requirement imposed by an activist policy can never be satisfied. The social process continuously generates and disseminates new information. The resulting modification of perceived opportunities induces revisions of optimal behaviour patterns, and thus variations in the economic structure over time. The best we can achieve is the choice of institutional arrangements that minimize uncertainty and offer as many women and men as possible a chance to shape their own lives.

The human spirit is a remarkable phenomenon. The soaring spires and vaults of a Gothic cathedral may be seen as a pure and beautiful expression of this spirit. They seem also to symbolize the human search for knowledge. But we should remember that these beautiful expressions of an aspiring spirit were frequently motivated by less than noble motives. The Bible tells us that grubby life persisted even around the holiest place of ancient Israel. We are thus reminded that our intellectual pursuits are not separated from 'society' in the purity of a monastery or in Hermann Hesse's world of the 'Glassbead Game'. Intellectual life remains embedded in a social and political context. Temptations and incentives reaching beyond purely cognitive criteria thus shape the behaviour of all participants in the intellectual game. It also follows that intellectual pursuits are tied to institutional arrangements that condition its character. It occurred to me in the early 1960s that it would be interesting to examine the effect of different arrangements on the patterns of intellectual life, and I observed the role of institutions in our profession. This observation motivated me to develop a regular series of conferences. The idea was initiated in 1964 at UCLA. This endeavour evolved by 1973 into a joint venture with Allan Meltzer: the Carnegie–Rochester Conference on Public Policy. The Konstanz Conference on Monetary Theory and Monetary Policy began in 1970, and in 1974 the annual Interlaken Seminar on Analysis and Ideology.

The latter was deliberately planned as a forum for the 'imperial' application of 'economic analysis' over the whole range of the social sciences. The development of two professional journals, the *Journal of Money, Credit and Banking* and, subsequently, the *Journal of Monetary Economics*, was similarly motivated. One consideration, among others, was the desire to offer alternative opportunities to younger, not quite established professionals and to prevent a closed shop. The Shadow Open Market Committee, jointly founded in 1973 with Allan Meltzer, was deliberately set in another mode. It is a small, homogeneous group designed to articulate publicly our concerns about the drift in monetary, fiscal and international economic policy. Though it had no direct effect on policy-making, we were gratified to see the interest it stimulated.

The problem of creating a 'good society' was not at the forefront of my search in life: a search for understanding and insights. But in the last stretch of my path it has become a natural consequence of the work and ideas I have pursued over many years. It will occupy my mind as long as it continues to function and my body supports it. My fascinating search, initiated more than 50 years ago, was greatly influenced by many people from whom I learned many things. Life offered me thus a singular chance.

References

Brunner, Karl (1961) 'The Report of the Commission on Money and Credit', *Journal of Political Economy*, **69**, 605–20.

—— (1969) '"Assumptions" and the cognitive quality of theories', *Synthese*, **20**(4), 501–25.

—— (1973) 'Review: Economic models of cyclical behavior (Bert G. Hickman)', *Journal of Economic Literature*, **11**(3), 927–33.

—— (1987) 'The perception of man and the conception of "society": two approaches to understanding society', *Economic Inquiry*, **25**, 367–88.

—— and William H. Meckling (1977) 'The perception of man and the conception of government', *Journal of Money, Credit, and Banking*, **9**(1), Part 1, 70–85.

—— and Allan H. Meltzer, (1967) 'The meaning of monetary indicators', in *Monetary Process and Policy: A Symposium*, ed. George Howrich, Homewood, Ill.: Irwin.

—— and —— (1971) 'The uses of money: money in the theory of an exchange economy', *American Economic Review*, **61**(5), 784–805.

Friedman, Milton (1953) 'Methodology of positive economics', in *Essays in Positive Economics*, Chicago: University of Chicago Press.

Jensen, Michael C. and William H. Meckling (1979) 'Rights and production functions: an application to labor-managed firms and codetermination', *Journal of Business*, **52**(4), 469–506.

3   The poverty of nations*

The condition of poverty and the creation of wealth

Poverty remains an endemic state of man. The curse imposed by an angry god on Adam and his descendants describes the human fate. Man experienced over history, with rare exceptions, toil, hardship and oppression. The uncertain and stringent conditions of life challenged man's awareness. He sought for answers explaining this fate and these were couched in the form of myths and legends. An imaginative human mind invoked a fall from grace or a curse imposed by gods. Such orientations naturally affected man's expectations of 'liberation' from the grinding burden of toil and hardship. The 'restoration of grace' appeared to be the crucial condition for such liberation.

This elementary message emerged over the centuries in very different forms and in widely varying detail. The basic story of man's fate conveyed by ancient myths still persists with a subtle and pervasive influence. The dominant ideologies of our time promise the restoration of (at least secular) grace with the liberation from human bondage to poverty. This promise of liberation should be realized by a 'collective action' imposing a set of explicitly designed *political* institutions as the dominant mechanism for the coordination of society.

The ancient themes still reverberate under new labels in various branches of sociology or social psychology. But their influential repercussions on the intelligentsia market have been challenged for two hundred years by the evolution of economic analysis. This analysis, initiated by the Scottish philosophers of the eighteenth century, offered a revolutionary insight into the social context of man's life. This insight has hardly been absorbed or understood by the educated middle classes of western societies and even less by the professional articulators.

This tradition of economic analysis explains the emergence of social groups and the 'great societies' moving social interaction with a scope far beyond the face-to-face associations. It explains thus the emergence of political structures without metaphor or invocation of metaphysical entities. This tradition shows in particular how social structure emerges from the interaction between coping, groping, resourceful human agents intent to improve their lot according to their judgement and understanding. Social structure appears in

* Originally published in *Business Economics*, January 1985, 5–11. This was the third annual Adam Smith Address: delivered at the 26th Annual Meeting of the National Association of Business Economists, 23–26 September 1984, Atlanta, Georgia.

31

this manner as an important, but quite unintentional byproduct of this interaction.

The same analysis also addresses the condition of poverty and the creation of wealth. The 'wealth of nations', expressed by the standard of living of their people, depends foremost on effort, ingenuity and an imaginative coping applied by men to their environment. The natural environment with the resources provided by nature can make a substantial difference for a nation's opportunities. These opportunities offered by nature condition the pattern of activities and the use of available human and other resources. But the possessions of natural resources do not determine a nation's wealth and do not, *per se*, suspend Adam's curse. Nature's heritage forms, contrary to widely held beliefs well represented by the Brandt Report on the North–South dialogue, neither a necessary nor a sufficient condition for high or rising levels of wealth. More than 50 years ago Argentina was expected to evolve on the basis of its natural resources into one of the world's wealthiest nations. It approached in contrast a pattern of permanent stagnation. We still encounter 'experts' informing us that Argentina with its vast resources should really be expected to overcome, in due course, its current difficulties. Brazil should also be on this count among the wealthiest nations today. Switzerland, less favoured with natural resources than Zaire, Nigeria, Mexico and other nations, should appear among the poorer nations appealing for aid from Argentina, Brazil, Mexico and others. We may also compare Hongkong, South Korea, Taiwan, Singapore with more-favoured nations. Or consider the permanent stagnation in poverty characterizing Tanzania and Zimbabwe in Africa or of Bolivia and Peru in South America.

Political power has frequently been singled out as a crucial factor of a more widely conceived 'natural environment' which decisively affects the wealth of nations. The Brandt Report exemplifies once again this view. But history and economic analysis fail to support this claim. Nations with little power experienced over the past hundred years or more a remarkable increase in wealth. This accrual of wealth occurred moreover not at the cost of other (more powerful?) nations but contributed actually to benefit others through an expanded economic interaction.

Poverty expresses a small production of goods and services. The creation of wealth involves an expansion of this production. Western nations experienced this process over the last 200 years on a scale never before recorded in history. Power can simply not explain this phenomenon. 'Power' does not *produce* goods. It *absorbs* and *uses* goods to maintain the power apparatus, a 'nomenclatura'. But power may be applied to *extract* wealth from those who *produced* it. But this exercise does not *create* wealth, it actually destroys wealth in the final analysis to be discussed subsequently. The emphasis on 'power' thus confuses the *creation* and the *redistribution* of wealth. It also fails to understand the longer-run consequences of redistributive power. The argument based on power frequently occurs in a context linking the accumulation of wealth in western nations with colonialism. But Adam Smith already elaborated the crucial implications of colonialism. He recognized that colonialism meant a loss in wealth for the colonizing nation combined with a domestic redistribution favouring specific groups involved in the process. This redistribution, and not any general accrual of wealth, was the historical driving force of colonization. The exercise of power applied to colonial efforts thus imposed an economic burden on the 'mother country'.

Our attention clearly must be directed beyond natural resources and power to human effort and resourceful ingenuity. The 'founding fathers' of modern economic analysis recognized the central importance of 'human capital' and investment in human capital as a condition of the 'wealth of nations'. The development of the German economy after World War II dramatically confirms this contention. But effort and resourceful ingenuity are not 'sociological data' determined by the mysteries of a 'mental attitude', a 'religious commitment' or an inherited 'work ethic'. Customs, traditions and cultural values may play a role for a while. They will not survive, however, and behaviour will adjust once the supporting conditions have eroded. Economic analysis informs us that effort and resourceful probing emerges with substantially greater frequency and intensity whenever human agents encounter opportunities offering reasonable expectations of benefits resulting from applications of searching efforts and coping ingenuity. Without the incentives of potential opportunities agents will find it hardly worthwhile to expend much effort and ingenuity. The magnitude and quality of effort and the intensity of search for imaginative innovations in types and use of resources is generally closely linked with the expectation of capturing the returns from these endeavours. The incentives of potential opportunities thus condition the current level of human endeavours. They also shape the accumulations of human capital expressed by the level and quality of skills and the development of non-human resources with the productive modification of the environment.

The power argument outlined above completely fails to comprehend the central role of opportunities and of the link between investment of efforts and capture of expected returns. It proceeds as if there operated no incentive feedback from the distribution of the product to its supply. The argument suggests on the contrary that all goods are available as 'pies from the skies' to be grabbed by participants in a social game. The powerful acquire the lions' share of the pies and the losers get the crumbs. Naturally, one concludes from this romantic vision that the balance of power needs to be changed.

The message conveyed by economic analysis thus directs our attention to the conditions which encourage the application of human effort and ingenuity to the inheritance determined by history and environment. These conditions do not depend on nature. They are determined by the social organization characterizing a society. The prevailing socio-political institutions condition the potential opportunities facing human agents. They ultimately shape the incentives guiding effort and ingenuity which evolve over time into customs, habits and traditions. But such customs and traditions can be destroyed by changes in institutions which lower the expectation of a link between effort and real benefit. We recognize this in the pattern of existing socio-political institutions the crucial condition for both wealth creation and the persistence of widespread poverty. A stagnation in permanent poverty expresses thus not a curse of vengeful gods (in heavens or in history) to be atoned by a purifying collective action. Such stagnation results essentially from the inheritance of social institutions affecting the behaviour of people in society.

The ambivalence of political structure: the state as umpire of a positive-sum game and operator of a negative-sum game
The nature of institutions maintaining poverty or fostering wealth creation requires some further attention. The role of political structure, and specifically of the state, needs to be clarified in this context.

The social productivity of political structure is best understood in comparison with a state of anarchy. An agent arranging his affairs under anarchy has the following options for the use of his resources: he can invest in production, in trade, in attempts of robbery and in defence against others. The exposure to potential loss of resources due to piracy by others lowers the incentive to invest in production. It also constrains the opportunity to trade. Productive activity addressed to wealth creation remains under the circumstances at a low level. All agents seem to be caught in the trap of a prisoner's dilemma. The repetitive occurrence of the basic social problem posed by anarchy induces however the interacting responses so well described by the founders of economic analysis and more recently further elaborated in great detail by Hayek. The evolution of political institutions offers in this respect a solution to the prisoner's dilemma inherent in a state of anarchy.

So consider now the options available to an agent arranging his activities in the context of political structure. He can use his resources again in four different ways: invest in production; trade; invest in the political process in order to redistribute wealth on his behalf; and lastly, invest in the political process as a defence against wealth redistribution schemes advanced by others. Anarchy and political structure are thus not distinguished by presence or absence of a zero- (or possibly even negative-) sum game of social interaction. We recognize at this stage the peculiar ambivalence of political structure. This structure establishes rules of the social game. Such rules substantially confine (but never eliminate totally, as exemplified by Mafia, Camorra, etc.) the wealth-impeding activities of anarchy to a comparatively low level. They provide thus a 'monopoly of violence' anchored by the political structure. This monopoly forms a necessary condition for the specification of property rights and their enforcement. Investment in production and in activities raising the level and quality of human and non-human resources is encouraged as a result of the greater expectation of capturing the returns under the rules of the social game. Specification and enforcement of property rights also encourages a wider range of possible transactions and opens new opportunities for mutually beneficial trade. The resulting increase in the creation of wealth expresses the remarkable productivity of political structure.

But magnitude and extent of the benefits accruing from political structure still depend on the institutional arrangements guiding the co-ordination of socio-economic activities. Private property exhibits in this context a crucial advantage poorly understood by most professional articulators in the public arena. The assignment of property rights resolves a physical impossibility associated with potential social conflicts. Scarce resources cannot be controlled simultaneously by several persons. The structure of rights determines who can do what with respect to which scarce object. This structure fully reflects the inherited patterns of resources. It mirrors in this sense the constraints imposed by nature. All resources need be owned by some person and beyond this no rights should be assigned. This condition rules out the wide array of market closing and entry restricting arrangements under any name. Lastly, private property rights guarantee the important link between efforts and returns emphasized above. This link is actually generalized under such a system to transactors beyond the range of owners of non-human resources.

But no rules of the social game can preclude a new form of wealth impeding activities replacing the ancient patterns of anarchic wealth impediments. The problem actually adheres to any set of rules. All political structures determine potential opportunities for manipulation *within* the rules accepted for their operations. They unavoidably offer incentives to be used for purposes of wealth redistribution among the participants of the social game. There is hardly a political institution which does not yield consequences with respect to the distribution of wealth. Agents respond to this state by investing resources in the political process in order to generate wealth transfers from others or to ward off attempted transfers by others. This aspect of political structure involves basically a negative-sum game within the context of the socially productive positive-sum game provided by a stable set of rules. The incentives to invest in the political process for purposes of acquiring wealth from others or for protective political action lowers the allocation of resources to socially productive activities. The taxes imposed by implicit or explicit wealth transfers occurring in one form or another lower moreover the incentive to invest in production, trade and the accumulation of resources.

These consequences determine the inherent ambiguity of the state expressed by the joint operation of a positive and negative sum game proceeding in the context of political institutions organizing the social interaction.

All political structure thus involves simultaneously a wealth-creating and a wealth-impeding dimension. The wealth-obstructing activities proceed, however, in contrast to the state of anarchy, in accordance to a recognized and generally accepted set of rules. Political structure thus lowers, but does not remove, the uncertainty confronting agents' socially productive activities. The magnitude of the lowered uncertainty or, in other words, the extent of the wealth-impeding range of activities associated with political structure depends crucially on the detail of the socio-political institution. Every set of political institutions produces its specific mix of positive- and negative-sum social games. The weight of wealth-impeding activities depends thus on the socio-political arrangements of nations.

The nature of wealth-fostering and wealth-impeding political institutions may be usefully described in rough outline. The distinction between the two dimensions of the state may be usefully introduced for this purpose. These dimensions refer to the 'protective state' and the 'redistributive state'. This classification is essentially justified in terms of the purpose addressed with political institutions and holds only approximately in terms of their consequences. Robert Nozick and James Buchanan amply demonstrated the redistributive dimension unavoidably embedded in the protective state. The protective state encompasses a set of political institutions which define general rules offering a stable framework for agents' productive activities. Such rules involve most particularly the definition of private property, the protective arrangements of police and courts associated with this definition, enforceability of privately negotiated contracts, and stable and predictable fiscal procedures including monetary policy. The rules bearing on the government's financial affairs need explicit recognition in this context. Unpredictable explicit changes in taxation or implicit changes via erratic inflation in a world of tax rates addressed to nominal values can substantially lower the incentives of the positive-sum social game. A rich variety of observations informs us that the detail of the political framework shaping the social institutions listed above substantially influences the productivity of the social game. Well-designed political structures foster the evolution of markets. They improve their functioning and encourage, with the associated higher level of predictability, the accumulation of resources. These consequences are essential strands of a wealth-creating social process. This follows from the fundamental fact that the social institutions protected by the type of political structure under consideration assure, on the average, a systematic link between effort and ingenuity applied on the one side and the resulting returns on the other. We may formulate this more generally as a set of institutions which raise the probability of a link between the consequences of actions and the agents committing these actions. They also lower the likelihood of market-closing and entry-restricting activities.

An alternative set of rules or institutions embodied in political structures represented by the redistributive state typically produce wealth-impeding consequences. The class of these political institutions exhibits a rich detail testifying to man's inventiveness. We may summarize this vast detail into two broad groups for our purposes. One group involves constraints on choices bearing on contractual arrangements and the tenure of property. The other group contains structures with direct distributional consequences and associated distortions of incentives. This division is neither neat nor clean, but a better organization of the material may emerge from further discussion. But it will serve our purpose for the moment.

The argument outlined above suggests that the creation of wealth or entrenched poverty is substantially conditioned by both levels of the political apparatus, the 'protective state' and the 'redistributional state'. Too little of the first and too much of the second obstruct wealth creation and maintain pockets of poverty or even mass poverty. An uncertain or more or less deliberate failure to execute the basic protective function erodes the link between *productive* effort and capture of expected returns. This experience can be observed over history and continues to our time. I already mentioned Argentina. We may also notice the permanent political instability and longer-run uncertainty bearing on important socio-political institutions in Bolivia, Peru, possibly Chile in South America, Zimbabwe and other nations in Africa. The social context of these nations provides few, or hesitant, incentives to create wealth through productive investment. The context spurs incentives directed toward conquest of political control with the acquisition of the associated spoils. The resulting pattern of entrenched poverty cannot be alleviated by doses of foreign aid. Such aid essentially contributes to raise the resources available to the local nomenclatura. It cannot replace or offset the absence of an adequate protective state.

The realization of the basic protective function may be offset to some extent by the state's 'redistributional activities'. Constraints on contractual arrangements and the effect of socio-political conditions on property tenure exemplify this aspect. The usual textbook treatment of production obscures this important point. We read that output is linked with an array of inputs via a production function. This function purportedly represents the underlying technology. This interpretation is thoroughly misleading, however. The nature of the production function is sensitively conditioned by socio-political circumstances. The 'production function' actually forms the outcome of agents' optimizing responses to these conditions. It follows that variations in the admissible range of contractual arrangements or associated organizational forms modify the 'production function'. Constraints on admissible contractual arrangements tend to lower output for any given input. Consequently they impoverish a society and obstruct the imaginative search for new modes of wealth creation. The imposition of self-management or co-determination illustrates the issue. The organization forms may survive successfully in competition with the corporation and other forms. They may exhibit a comparative advantage for specific activities. Our experience clearly indicates however that this comparative advantage occurs in a very limited range. A coercive imposition of these forms forces, therefore, the organization of production into a mould less adapted to the co-ordination of resources in production. A comparative decline in output thus emerges. Detailed investigations of the incentives prevailing under self-management and co-determination confirm the results of economic analysis. These investigations also show that self-management in particular creates new social tensions and conflicts between younger and older workers, or between established workers and potential new workers entering the market.

Corporate governance is another fashionable issue which should be mentioned here. Modifications of governance are proposed in order to achieve purportedly desirable social goals. The sense of these proposals usually conveys that they impose *no* social costs and *will* achieve the desired effects. Economic analysis dismally disillusions us on both counts. The social costs in particular will rise with the severity of constraints controlling corporate organizations.

The change in the law governing insolvency in Germany and the 'comparable worth' movement in the USA offer further examples of contractual constraints. The assignment of priority rights to several months' salary beyond the date of filing for bankruptcy raises the cost of capital, impedes investments and affects employment. A systematic application of 'comparable worth' procedures would seriously impede the organization of production and impose social costs in terms of lessened output of goods and services.

Pharmaceutical regulations and the admissible range for the forms of property tenure are the last examples of constraints on the production function potentially lowering welfare. The prevailing regulation of pharmaceutical products confines both contractual procedures and the choice of production processes. It raised the cost of operation and via the reduction in the relevant economic duration of the patent it also lowered the expected return. The constraints lowered new pharmaceutical innovation and lowered consequently the achievable state of health.

The modification of the patent's relevant duration actually abrogates established property rights. Constraints on the form of property tenure can significantly impair the nature of the social production function. In many countries around the world land is frequently tended by peasants under a usufruct system. Irrespective of the political motives behind this tenure system an examination of its operation reveals that it obstructs productivity of agricultural labour, obstructs quality-raising investment in land and encourages population growth in the countryside. The collectivization of agriculture offers a particularly emphatic example of obstructive institutionalization. It eroded incentives to produce and raised incentives for a wasteful use of resources. Agricultural output naturally suffers. Socialist nations from Tanzania to Russia exemplify our case with remarkable clearness. The land tenure system imposed assured a permanent agricultural crisis.

The second strand of the 'redistributional state' encompasses examples from the welfare system of western societies, the oligarchic power structure of nations in the Third World, the 'nomenclatura' of socialist countries, or some patterns of non-socialist dictatorships. The welfare system of western nations imposed a massively accelerated redistribution which lowered incentives to work, invest and save. It raised, on the other hand, incentives to invest resources in the negative-sum game of political processes.

The oligarchies of many nations in the Third World depend on their survival on a persistent redistribution of wealth from the countryside to the cities. Their political base is usually anchored with the populace in the cities. In order to maintain their power the ruling oligarchies find it advisable to impose low prices on agricultural products. This pattern destroys incentives to produce food, erodes incentives to invest resources in agricultural operations, and creates incentives to abandon fertile land and join the masses in the cities.

Most socialist countries operate a vast system redistributing wealth from the potentially productive sector to the 'nomenclatura', for all practical purposes a socially unproductive sector. This nomenclatura is composed of a huge military complex, an internal security and economic control apparatus. And again this redistribution system lowers incentives for the productive use of resources. Non-socialist military dictatorships also require for their survival a redistribution favouring the military apparatus with similar consequences for the wealth-creating dimension of the social process.

The evolution of labour markets over the past sixteen years reveals that western nations participated in their own way to obstruct, usually with the best intentions, the wealth-creating process. Unemployment in European countries stayed very low until about the end of the sixties. The pattern changed dramatically during the seventies. Unemployment rates rose into the double-digit range. Belgium and the Netherlands measured recently unemployment rates above 15 per cent. With the exception of Switzerland, almost all European nations experienced massive increases in measured unemployment. Politicians and the media frequently attribute this development to new technologies. One also encounters in the public arena comparisons with the Great

Depression. This comparison fails, however. The rising trend in European unemployment occurred, in contrast to the thirties, during a period of expansionary financial policies. Technology, moreover, as we learn from economic analysis, cannot explain this unemployment either. Technological innovations change opportunities. Old jobs disappear and new jobs emerge. The American experience of the last 30 years demonstrates that reasonably functioning market processes continuously create new jobs and offer new employment. The crucial conditions pertain to the socio-political institutions under which markets operate. Most European countries experienced, in this context, major changes. A variety of arrangements affecting the operation of labour markets were introduced by European governments. These arrangements include measures of 'employment protection', liberalizations of unemployment support, increasing payroll and social security taxes imposed on employers and similar measures. 'Employment protection', represented among other procedures by increased compensation payments upon dismissal, raised the expected real cost of employment relative to the real return expected from employment. The same result holds for increased payroll taxes and other obligations associated with employment. It follows that either net real wages fall or employment declines relatively. These adjustments are unavoidable. As it happened, the resulting adjustments occurred in most nations dominantly in the dimensions of employment–unemployment. No single step or single measure introduced in this evolution involved any dramatic or crucial changes. But their cumulative effect over time did change the operation of the economy. Whatever the motivation and intention of the political decisions shaping this evolution they produced a stagnant labour market. Vast human resources are poorly used and the nations are significantly poorer than they otherwise could be. The petrification of labour markets caused by a long sequence of political decisions also endangers the future course of western societies. Technological innovations, a necessary condition of rising wealth in our history, will increasingly evolve, in the context of petrified markets, as a social threat. The resulting political decisions tend under the circumstances to obstruct the wealth-creating process even further. Proposals to lower the working time per week to 35 or 25 hours illustrate this point.

The evolution of labour markets, however important, offers just one strand to our theme about wealth and poverty of nations. The government's fiscal operations deserve some attention in this respect. In an investigation of the consequences of taxes and government expenditures on the pattern of resource, it was estimated that general welfare in the United Kingdom was lowered by about 8 per cent as a result. Taxes, and most particularly expenditure patterns, severely distorted the allocation of resources. Lastly, the lecture can hardly be terminated without a reference to the rising tide of protectionism. The range of protectionist schemes expanded and they evolved in imaginatively subtle complexity. Their rationale barely changed over the centuries, neither did their welfare implications. They redistribute wealth, benefiting special groups at the expense of the rest of society. The highly visible benefit of the favoured group in conjunction with the widely dispersed and thus less-visible social costs, or welfare losses, misleads politicians and publicists into believing that protectionist institutions raise general wealth. The redistribution produced is, however, associated with a comparative social impoverishment. But the ideology and illusion of protectionism as a condition fostering wealth creation permeates France, South America and influential groups in many other nations.

And so ...

History demonstrates, analogously to biological experimentation via mutation, an endless experimentation with social organizations and associated cultural terms, attitudes and values. These organizations yield very different survival characteristics in competition with other social groups. They also determine the long-run chances of rising wealth or entrenched poverty and disease. The intentional, and frequently unintentional, evolution of the socio-political institutions decisively determines, ultimately, the conditions of poverty or wealth-creation irrespective of the evolution's motivating conceptions. The role of political structure, represented by the state and its apparatus, thus deserves careful and intense attention in this context. The illusion is widely held that the state *produces* wealth, and, more particularly, that little wealth will be created without the *detailed* and *controlling intervention* of the state. Another illusion dominating our time and well represented among the Christian churches holds that government intervention addressed to massive redistribution cannot affect the incentives guiding the social process of wealth creation. The translation of moral fervour 'to help the poor' into institutional arrangements which lower opportunities and entrench poverty forms one of the saddest ironies of our age. It is a small step from such beliefs to the view, implicit in the legal thesis of 'tax-expenditures', that all wealth belongs 'really' to the state and is conditionally and revocably leased to individual agents. Our discussion reveals the nature of the misconception asserting a *direct* productivity of the state. The state is not a producer of wealth. It shapes *conditions* which encourage the creation of wealth. But it also frequently represents political institutions which impede expanding welfare. The state can, and frequently does, obstruct the wealth-creating process and contributes to sustained poverty. Its wealth-impeding activities yield an economic rent to a small group with access to the socio-political institutions. The emerging social organization of western societies will thus determine whether a nation *accumulates* wealth or *persists* in poverty.

4 'Assumptions' and the cognitive quality of theories*

Language games and empirical science

Many aspects of our social activities may be usefully interpreted as language games. Such a frame of reference could subsume cocktail parties, our teaching, or Don Juan's approach to a beautiful woman. Our intellectual activities naturally fit the frame of a language game. Such games are played for radically different purposes and the rules of the game tend to reflect the dominant goals guiding the participants in a particular language game.

Major portions of our intellectual language games originated in man's attempt to provide a satisfying orientation about the universe and himself. The traditional games expressed by theology and metaphysics are gradually modified, however. New types of games describe important features of contemporary theological or metaphysical discourse. These modifications do not affect the crucial properties which distinguish these games from the language games constituting empirical science. The latter also provide an orientation about man's environment. Metaphysics and empirical science share this general purpose. But the games differ radically in a subset of their characteristic rules. Every intellectual game has a more or less explicit subset of rules controlling the assessment of competing orientations constructed according to another subset of rules. The construction rules of metaphysical or empirical science games need not be different; they actually seem to coincide on many occasions. But the rules governing the survival of competing orientations decisively separate the two groups of games. The assessment rules of metaphysical games select orientations with greater viability relative to prevailing psychological, sociological and political conditions. Such rules were not totally absent from the actual game historically played in empirical science. But they remained an alien and obstructive intrusion. The relevant assessment rules sort and rank theories and hypotheses providing the desired orientation by suitable exposure to pertinent observation. Such exposure may occur quite indirectly with lengthy chains linking theories or hypotheses with the statements directly confronted with appropriate observation. The crucial feature of empirical science language games should nevertheless be recognized in a strict dependence of cognitive quality on competitive survival in repeated exposures to relevant observations.

* Originally published in *Synthese*, **20**, 1969, 501–25.

Participants in a language game characterized by empirical science would generally grant the importance of observations in assessments of competing theories and hypotheses. This much seems quite definite. But admission of such importance does not determine a unique or even relevant choice of assessment rules governing the exploitation of observations for an evaluation of rival theories. The rules of an empirical science game should effectively discriminate between contending beliefs according to their cognitive quality. The history of our language games shows, however, that the nature of such effective discrimination and the nature of the relation between observations and the intellectual products has frequently been unclear, disputed and confused. Appropriate rules were usually developed in the context of a continuous game situation. The essential purpose of the game, viz. the acquisition of orientations which are intersubjectively and repeatedly assessable in terms of relevant observations, gradually strengthened an awareness concerning the general nature of the assessment rules required for the desired cognitive purposes. This awareness has not penetrated the games played by economists. Our discussions, including the discussions associated with our econometric practice, reveal a pervasive uncertainty and confusion concerning the more detailed nature of the assessment rules guiding the use of observations.[1]

The dispute about the role of 'assumptions' and their 'realism' exemplifies the uncertainty and confusion associated with the consensus that observations govern the cognitive quality of theories. The dispute erupted in response to a critique of some prevalent procedures originally formulated by Milton Friedman.[2] Friedman addressed his critique to the following argument pattern frequently encountered among the language games played by economists:

1.   a class of assumptions A is associated with a theory T;
2.   (a)   the realism of the class A is questioned and found to be of low degree;
    (b)   the class A is accepted as plausible and realistic;
3.   (a)   in case 2(a) it is then argued that the unrealism of the assumptions A of T impels us to reject T;
    (b)   in case 2(b) the realism of A is purported to strengthen the case for T.

Friedman objected emphatically to an assessment of theories based on the realism or unrealism of their assumptions. He argued vigorously that the cognitive quality of a theory cannot be judged by the realism of 'assumptions' but must be judged by the confrontation of its implications with suitable observations.

Friedman's critique of a particular but widely used form of economists' language games proceeded essentially in the context of the ordinary idiom and used extensively analogies and even examples from pictorial language usages.

This essentially intuitive procedure with heavy emphasis on vague analogies compounded the confusions. The subsequent discussion was more directed by the illustrations used in Friedman's paper than by the requirements of logical explications. A number of papers were published which critically examined Friedman's thesis.[3] A session of the annual meetings of the American Economic Association was also devoted to the issue raised by Friedman.[4] Samuelson objected with particular vigour at this session to his interpretation of Friedman's thesis, viz. that only the realism of a theory's consequences, *independent of the realism of the theory itself or of its assumption*, mattered for our judgement of its cognitive quality. He argued in general terms and by means of examples that we cannot ignore the unrealism of a theory or of its assumptions, whatever the realism of some of its consequences may be. It appears that Samuelson still expresses a majority opinion concerning important aspects of our language games. His objection accepts the entrenched practice which assesses theories in terms of the realism of its assumptions. It is of minor interest whether Samuelson characterizes Friedman's position properly. Samuelson expresses himself at least some nominal doubt on this score. The intuitive, analogistic and pictorial nature of Friedman's discourse does not permit an unambiguous decision in this respect. The crucial issue raised implicitly by Friedman and explicitly reaffirmed by Samuelson remains focussed on the 'direct' confirmability of theories and assumptions. Samuelson argues that the realism or unrealism of theories and their assumptions can be judged independently of the realism or unrealism of their non-trivial consequences. The traditional position seems thus vindicated. Once we accept an assessment of theories which apparently requires no evaluation of observable consequences, one becomes naturally suspicious about the rationale of Friedman's thesis. His thesis seems either irrelevant or at worst an obstacle to cognitive progress and obviously appears to be an instrument of ideological warfare.

The remainder of this paper reconsiders the adequacy of the traditional language game played by economists and reaffirmed by Samuelson. Such reconsideration proceeds relative to the generally acknowledged goal of language games associated with empirical science. We require for this purpose an explication of the terms 'assumption of a theory' and 'realism of statements'. A critical survey of the discussion originated by Friedman establishes that both terms are highly ambiguous. We will disregard the array of logical problems associated with the ambiguous use of the term 'realism of a statement' and concentrate on the role and logical structure of 'assumptions'. We select for our purposes one particular meaning of realism, expressed by truth of confirmation of a statement.[5] We consider thus the question whether language games governed by rules which determine the truth or confirmation of a theory by means of truth or confirmation of 'assumptions' are well-designed cognitive games. Our answer is radically negative. Our analysis

examines an array of uses of the term 'assumptions of a theory' in economists' language games. It will be demonstrated that some assumption types
have no truth values or cannot be confirmed. They are not statements but only
open formulae. Other assumption types can be assigned truth values or can be
confirmed. But in no case is the truth value or confirmation of a theory
determined by truth or confirmation of its assumptions. There exists no
systematic association between truth or confirmation of 'assumptions' and
truth or confirmation of theories. The subsequent analysis establishes that
truth or confirmation of assumptions yields no information about the cognitive quality of a theory – except in a question begging sense, in case the
'assumptions' constitute the theory itself. There still remains in this case the
question, how do we establish truth or confirmation of such assumptions.[6]

The examination of the cognitive role of assumptions is prepared in the
next section by a sketchy survey of some important properties of language
structures which constrain admissible procedures in our language games. The
survey is essentially addressed to economists and emphasizes some properties of relevant language games which are usually disregarded in reflections
bearing on our intellectual enterprise.

On the division of our cognitive language into a theoretical and observational sub-language

Most of the time we manage to communicate very successfully with the aid
of ordinary language. Similarly, we communicate effectively our intellectual
endeavours in the context of a somewhat improved version of ordinary language. This improvement may frequently include mathematics. But even in
these contexts our usage of the (improved) ordinary language is typically
unreflectedly 'rough and ready', semi-intuitive and loaded with psychologistic
intrusions. These inadequacies of our ordinary communications are neither
deadly nor necessarily bad. As a matter of fact, they emerge from an unavoidable dilemma imposed on effective communication. A glance at the math-
ematicians' standard procedure elucidates the point. If mathematical
arguments were constrained to proceed with total explicitness in the context of
a completely formalized language system even simple proofs would extend
over a terrifying length. The proof of complex theorems might require whole
books and communications would near a dangerous breakdown. Effective
communication depends to a substantial extent on short-cuts, on context, and
a willingness to compress many detailed steps into single big jumps. All this
is perfectly appropriate and even very useful. Not infrequently, however, the
formal inadequacies, so useful for effective communication, create trouble.
They generate misconceptions, logical confusions and render the arguments
murky. In such cases we are forced to replace our familiar procedure, whether
in the context of ordinary or improved idioms, by an explicit logical analysis

of the particular trouble spots. The discussion on the role of assumptions demonstrates the dangers of clarifying inadequacies and confusions generated by our ordinary communications instrument by means of the very same instrument. I do not argue that a carefully constructed and explicit language system be generally substituted for our ordinary instrumentation. I argue, however, that such a language system, supplied by modern logic, be substituted for the ordinary instrument in all attempts at clarification of problems arising in the context of our ordinary language.

Logicians found it useful to divide the language of science into two sub-languages, the observation language and the theoretical language.[7] The observation language contains an elementary logic (up to and including the first-level predicate calculus), whereas the theoretical language contains also the non-elementary parts of logic, particularly class theory, and includes mathematics. All the predicates and individual constants of the observation language are observable terms. A social group using these terms has developed a standard response to their usage which relates them to specific observable entities. A semantic rule is thus assigned to all the descriptive terms of the observation language.[8] The terms of this sub-language thus possess a direct empirical meaning for the members of the group. The terms of the theoretical language, on the other hand, have no direct observational meaning. No semantic rules are assigned to these terms and they have no direct connection with observable entities. Numerous examples of such theoretical terms are usually drawn from physics. But economic theory also abounds with such terms.[9] The division between the two sub-languages should not be visualized as an unambiguous and fixed linguistic pattern to be characterized by purely semantical means. It is an essentially pragmatic phenomenon. Our overt behaviour, the manner in which we communicate and respond to affirmations or denials of statements, reveals the existence of the partition. The division is shaped over the long run by our communications process and the changing knowledge situation of the group. Nevertheless, it remains reasonably clear at any particular stage.

Our intellectual adventure has been engrossed with the construction of theories explaining our observable environment. It is therefore remarkable that the codifications of our systematic knowledge in form of theories and hypotheses were not restricted to the observation language. The explanatory power of theories and hypotheses was substantially raised by using formulations reaching beyond the somewhat narrow confines of the observation language. This situation also applies to economic theories. There may be hypotheses which are, or could be, formulated completely in the observation language. Our most useful theories, however, contain ingredients from the theoretical language. It follows therefore, that an empirically relevant theory need not satisfy the operationist ideal which demands that all terms be assigned a semantic rule specifying a direct observable counterpart. This request would suffocate our cognitive endeavours. The occurrence of theoretical terms does not detract from the empirical character of a theory. What matters is our ability to establish a logical connection between the theories and test-sentences (i.e. the so-called basic sentences) formulated in the observation language. Such connections should enable us in particular to interpret verifications of test statements as confirmations, and falsifications of basic sentences as disconfirmations of theories investigated.[10]

Theories exhibit, in addition to the occurrence of theoretical terms, another logical feature affecting their evaluation. This second feature also occurs among hypotheses formulated in the observation language. They contain statements of an essentially general character. Formally, they appear as quantified formulae with the variables ranging over an infinite or open-ended domain.[11] Such statements are not logically equivalent to any finite combination of sentences which summarize our observational results.

Universality and occurrence of theoretical terms impose important logical constraints on the nature of our evaluations. They also prohibit a variety of arguments typically advanced in the context of our problem. The following list summarizes some of these consequences attributable to the structure of the language used in the construction of economic theory.

1. Universality alone is sufficient to render a theory (or even a hypothesis in the observation language) in principle unverifiable. Whatever the amount of true test statements supporting a theory (or hypothesis) the *truth* of the theory cannot be logically inferred. It follows that a theory is never *directly* assessed by observation. Only appropriate test statements derived from the theory can be directly assessed by confrontation with observation. Verifications of these test statements yield confirming instances for the theory and falsifications disconfirming instances.
2. Unverifiability does not preclude confirmation by suitably discriminating test statements.
3. In the absence of any existential operator woven into the theory it will also be refutable. It is, however, important to emphasize that actual refutation by a falsifying test statement is a necessary but far from sufficient reason to reject a theory. Our choice is frequently between quite imperfect theories, i.e. theories which had been exposed to *some* falsifying test statements. The comparative extent of falsification shapes the decision and not falsification as such.
4. In case an unrestricted existential operator ranges over an infinite or open-ended domain of objects the theory is also irrefutable. Confirmability still remains and so does a competitive evaluation of alternative theories. The same characterization applies also to stochastic hypotheses or theories.

5. No finite combination of statements summarizing our observational re-
    sults implies (logically) any theory (or hypotheses) completely formu-
    lated in the observation language.
6. The occurrence of theoretical terms in a theory precludes any application
    of the traditional notion of induction by enumeration to the relation
    between observations and theory.

The relation between assumptions and theories

The methodological discussions did not recognize the ambiguous use of the
term 'assumptions' in our language games.[12] It seemed to apply naturally to
the antecedent of a material or logical implication. But the language games
actually executed by economists exhibit a greater variety. The term appears in
different contexts and with distinct meanings. These meanings are explicated
to some extent in subsequent sections. This explication permits a critical
examination of the role of 'assumptions' and most particularly of the thesis
so vigorously reaffirmed by Samuelson and other economists.

'Assumptions' as constituent sentences of theories or hypotheses

*Theory as a deductive system and assumptions as the non-logical postulates
of the system*   On occasion the term 'theory' is applied not to a body of
general laws but to a deductive system as a whole.[13] It has been shown that a
complete deductive system can be constituted by a logical and a nonlogical
branch.[14] The logical branch introduces the primitive sentences of logic (i.e.
axioms of logic) and definitions involving only logical signs. All statements
of the logical branch are derivable from logical primitive sentences by means
of the transformation rules governing deductive procedures. The nonlogical
branch introduces primitive sentences pertaining to a subject-matter beyond
logic (or mathematics). These primitive sentences are on occasion described
as nonlogical or subject-matter postulates. Whenever 'theory' refers to a
deductive system as a whole containing nonlogical postulates the term 'assumption' is frequently used to cover these very postulates. Thus 'assumptions' denote what is more typically referred to as a theory.

A hurried reader of recent discussions may easily be misled into believing
that the choice of (nonlogical) postulates in the context of a given deductive
system is arbitrary. The interchangeability of theorems and postulates has been
strongly emphasized and these substitution possibilities no doubt exist. The
(finite) interchangeability is seriously restricted however. In particular, the
nonlogical postulates typically contain theoretical terms and usually exhibit a
quantification structure. Relative to the domain of discourse occurring in science they imply a vast array of sentences of which no (finite) sub-class could be
substituted for any of the postulates without altering the deductive system.

The standard argument under investigation suggests in the present context that the empirical adequacy of the deductive system is determined by the truth or confirmation of the nonlogical postulates. This argument appears to suggest that confirmation or truth applies initially to the nonlogical postulates and is then transferred by logical implication to the other sentences of the deductive system. This view is totally misconceived. The logical structure of the nonlogical postulates described in the previous section renders a direct confirmation or truth attribution independent of observation statements in simplest form (i.e. of basic sentences) impossible. Both confirmation and assignment of meaning move actually in the direction opposite to the lines of logical deduction. Direct observations permit assignments of truth values to observation statements of a particularly simple form, our test statements or basic sentences. The truth of the simple observation statements confirm the first-level generalizations occurring in the deductive system. And the confirmation is transmitted step by step following exactly the lines of deduction upwards until it reaches in the *last* stage the nonlogical postulates.[15]

Theory in the usual sense as a class of universal sentences describing the body of general laws and assumptions as constituent sentences of a theory
Not infrequently, particularly in papers on mathematical economics, we find the term 'assumption' used to single out a sub-set of specific statements constituting the theory. The term 'theory' is used in this paragraph in the *narrower* sense, viz. as the class (or conjunction) of general sentences describing the basic laws of the subject matter considered. It does not refer to a deductive system as a whole but only to its nonlogical postulates. The separation of the specific subclass A is selected in such a manner that together with the remaining statements T^1 sentences I of particular interest can be derived which could not be derived from T^1 alone. What happens in this context may be described as follows: The analyst has already formulated T^1 and is very much interested to demonstrate a particular class of sentences I. He then searches for an additional class of statements A, such that the conjunction $A \cdot T^1$ logically implies I, whereas T^1 does not logically imply I.[16]

In general, the class A is not unique relative to any particular T^1 and I. This means that another class A^1 may be found which in conjunction with T^1 logically implies I. The separation of the total theory T into A and T^1 might thus reflect an implicit ordering of the statements in T by the analyst. He may be more strongly inclined to maintain the T^1 component of T and more willing to replace the other component in case T runs into difficulties.[17] Or he may be interested to establish a comparatively simple set of relative sufficiency condition for the class I which is intended to play a crucial role in the evaluation of a given deductive system. Because of the logical equivalence between

$$A \cdot T^1 \supset I \text{ and } T^1 \supset (A \supset I)$$

one is permitted to describe A as a sufficient condition for I relative to T^1. The mode of speech or writing followed by many analysts typically suggests that A is a sufficient condition for I. This is due to the fact that, once stated on the first page, T^1 never occurs any more explicitly. Moreover, theorems or statements actually derivable only from the conjunction A and T^1 refer explicitly only to A, and the explicit formulation of the theorem is in the form of the conditional statement $A \supset I$. The mode of articulation thus generates a psychological response which tends to overlook that this conditional statement, $A \supset I$, is logically implied by T^1, and in particular, that I is not a logical consequence of A. The same psychological response is strengthened by the habit induced by the apparent independent standing of the conditional ($A \supset I$), to present A as (the ?) assumptions of I.

These misconceptions effectively beclouded important logical features of this assumption type. A rigorous reformulation of the sentences constituting A reveals their *general* character, i.e. they involve quantification (or generalization) over an infinite or open-ended domain in an essential manner. They also contain usually theoretical terms. It is therefore logically impossible to verify them on the basis of a finite number of observations summarized by molecular, nongeneral sentences. Given the nature of our universe of discourse a general sentence is not derivable from a molecular observation sentence. The truth of the latter, established by suitable observations can thus not be transferred to the general sentence. The general sentence may still be false. The trouble with synthetic sentences generalized over infinite or open-ended domains is that we never *know* their truth, even if they are true. But we can always *confirm* them, and their confirmation, jointly with T^1, depends on the truth value assigned to a selected class of relevant basic statements. The confirmation is transmitted from the 'bottom' of the deductive system built around $A \cdot T^1$ to its top formed by $A \cdot T^1$ in the manner described by the previous paragraph.

The possibility of indirect confirmation also offered an opportunity to misinterpret the logical relation between sentences and evidence. Some test statements may bear directly on some implications of the theory $A \cdot T^1$ other than I and yield no information concerning I. The test statements thus provide a confirmation of $A \cdot T^1$, and supply via the deductive relation from $A \cdot T^1$ to I an indirect confirmation of I. An attention geared to a truncated segment of the indirect confirmation procedure together with the habit of concentrating on the conditional $A \supset I$, often creates a pervasive impression that truth (or confirmation) is immediately assigned to assumptions A, which all by themselves transfer this truth to the class I. By exhibiting A as 'assumptions' for the class I of particular concern to us, the analyst suggests that all we need to establish is the truth of A and he appears also to say that this truth is immediately decidable by direct confrontation with pertinent observations. The sentences occurring in A are thus misconstrued as basic sentences of the observation language while they actually belong to the theoretical language.

The misconceptions in this position should be clear: (a) the relation between A and I does not permit us to transfer truth from A to I independent of T^1. The conditional does not formulate a logical implication; and (b) the logical structure of A, characterized by occurrence of theoretical terms and general sentences, does not permit an immediate assignment of truth or an immediate, direct confirmation independent of testable implications.

Assumptions as sentences not constituting the theory or hypothesis under consideration

Assumptions of a theory or hypothesis constituting a higher level theory   We shall speak of a theory or hypothesis in the usual and narrower sense of the term. The terms do not refer to a deductive system as a whole, but only to a finite class of general sentences describing the basic laws of behaviour bearing on a specified subject matter. We find numerous contexts where a theory T has been formulated and reference is made to a finite class of general sentences A, not identical to T, but which logically implies T. The class A is then frequently described as containing (the ?) assumptions of T. The procedure is usually couched in words which suggest that the formulation of A supplies a justification of T. Sometimes T is felt to be implausible and in need of some justification. So A is formulated and T is exhibited as a logical consequence of A. Finally, a plausible case is advanced on behalf of A which is then transferred to T by means of the deductive chain leading from A to T.[18]

Unfortunately, this procedure, so obviously convincing, is thoroughly fallacious. It thrives on a confusion between our psychologistic responses conditioned by well-entrenched linguistic habits with a logical analysis of statements and evidence. The logical relation between A and T requires that A possesses at least the same degree of generality as T and contains at least the same theoretical terms as T. It follows that it is impossible to evaluate A directly. As T itself, A is unverifiable but confirmable. And the confirmation of A also begins with the assignment of truth values to specific observation statements of simplest form. This assignment is then transmitted backwards along the line of deduction to A. The logical relation between A and T implies that all the confirmation transmitted to T from suitable observation statements is transferred onwards via T to A. Confirmation of A thus depends on T.

However, confirmation of A may not depend on T only. This fact is closely associated with the peculiar function of the construction of higher-level hypotheses. Given *T*, the formulation of *A* would contribute very little if *A* only permits derivation of *T* and nothing else. The significance of the construction lies in the circumstances that *A* also implies a class of statements *S* with a different range than *T*. This other class may occur as theories or hypotheses bearing on aspects of phenomena not subsumed under *T*. In this case the formulation of *A* enables us to marshal observations for an appraisal of *T* which previously could not be used for this purpose. The construction of *A* is thus designed to raise the value of the information extractable from a given set of observations. Observations bearing on basic statements associated with *S* may be used to confirm *T* indirectly, or to raise the degree of confirmation already assigned to *T*. The confirmation of *S* is transferred in the manner already indicated previously to *A* and is transmitted from *A* with the deductive chain to *T*. The existence of indirect confirmation via higher-level theories and an impressionistic view of the partial segment from *A* to *T* of the total confirmation process may have contributed to the misconception that the realism of assumptions determines the relative adequacy of a theory. The decision about *T* would still be made on the basis of the total evidence, and it is logically possible to be faced with an evidential situation which induces us to reject *T* but accept *A*, due to very bad evidence from basic statements associated with *T* but not with *S*.

Assumptions as selected types of observation statements   Theories and hypotheses are typically used in explanations and predictions of specific observable events. The logical patterns of both explanation and prediction are identical. The two activities differ according to their pragmatic contexts. Suppose *T* designates a theory, O^1 indicates a molecular combination of basic observation sentences, and O^2 is also a molecular combination, but of a different set of basic sentences. Moreover, let O^1 and O^2 be such that the conjunction of O^1 and *T* logically implies the conjunction O^2, i.e. we have as a logically valid statement

$$O^1 \cdot T \supset O^2.$$

In case we have performed suitable observations and verified O^1 we move in the pragmatic context of a prediction. The conjunction of the verified O^1 with *T* enables us to derive the observation sentence O^2. Suitable observations indicate the assignment of an appropriate truth value to O^2. If O^2 is true, another confirming instance has been added to raise the corroboration of *T*. If on the other hand O^2 is falsified, then the conjunction $O^1 \cdot T$ is also falsified. Falsehood of the conjunction together with the truth of O^1 implies the falsehood of *T*. A false prediction thus implies a refutation for the theory. Still, we should not reject the theory simply because a disconfirming, refuting instance occurred. Theories should be rejected according to their *comparative* confirmatory (or disconfirmatory) status. Even imperfect theories are better than no theories.

In the case of an explanation we made an observation summarized by O^2 and wish to explain the event expressed in this sentence. We use for this purpose a theory T and show that an event expressed by O^1 would lead to the event to be explained. Such explanation would be of a purely interpretative nature if O^1 has not been verified and T never been confirmed. A stronger level of explanation exists in the case that the theory T has been substantially confirmed by previous observations and is used to advance the event expressed by O^1 as the causal factor generating the event summarized by O^2. Because the first event has not been observed the imputation of O^2 to O^1 depends completely on the cognitive status of the theory T. The strongest case of explanation is achieved when T is highly validated and the sentence O^1 had been subsequently verified, or at least partially confirmed.

In the context of these explanation and prediction patterns the term 'assumptions' is frequently used to refer to the molecular observation sentence O^1. An 'assumption' O^1 conjoined to a theory T, becomes an 'assumption of T' and this permits an explanation or prediction of O^2. However, the truth of O^1 does not determine a truth-value of T. O^1 may be true and still T quite false, or O^1 may be quite false and T wonderfully true. Moreover, there is no connection between the truth value of O^1 and the degree of confirmation of T. The realism of an assumption in this sense has simply no bearing on the relative adequacy of a theory. The 'realism' of O^1 only determines whether the event expressed by O^1 belongs to the realm of T or not – an entirely different matter indeed.

There is another usage of the term assumption closely associated with the usage just indicated. On occasion the term appears to refer to the antecedent of a material implication, i.e. of a conditional statement which is not logically valid. But in the context of a material implication, i.e. a simple if–then statement involving no logical relation between antecedent and consequent, there exists no logical connection between the truth values of the antecedent and consequent permitting an inference from the truth of the antecedent to the truth of the consequent. This would presuppose the truth of the conditional, but this truth must be inferred from the truth of the consequent. So the whole argumentation breaks down in this case.

The material implication whose antecedent is singled out seems however in most discussions implicitly related to a general implication. The discussion may explicitly deal with a conditional statement $O^1 \supset O^2$. The context may however contain a theory T, such that T logically implies $(O^1 \supset O^2)$. Due to the logical equivalence of $T \supset (O^1 \supset O^2)$ and $O^1 \cdot T \supset O^2$ this case would then exactly correspond to the previously discussed situation. The event designated by O^1 would be an assumption for the occurrence of the event O^2 *only relative to the theory T*. And given *T*, the 'realism' of O^1 can be used to infer the 'realism' of O^2. However, the realism inferred is not the realism of a theory, but of an observational prediction, which may turn out to be utterly unrealistic.[19]

Assumption as the antecedent of a general implication, or as a selected component of such antecedent
The ordinary idiom uses a bewildering array of devices to express generality. For most of our everyday purposes this array does not impair our communication. We seem to manage quite well over a large range of typically occurring circumstances. We also observe, however, that many confusions are due to the ambiguities of ordinary idiom. Such confusions arise most frequently when we reflect on the reasons for affirming or denying specific sentences or classes of sentences. On such occasions a clarification of the issues requires suitable translation of the statements formulated in ordinary idiom into sentences of an explicit and carefully regimented language system. The latter sentences will exhibit the relevant logical structure which affects our procedure in affirming or denying the sentences and thus remove some of the semantical shadows obstructing the evaluation process.

We select for our purposes in this paragraph a simple-minded example to illustrate the point. More immediately relevant examples of empirical laws drawn from economic theory require unfortunately too much preparation concerning the necessary logical vocabulary. Fortunately, simple examples are sufficient to state our point in this paragraph. Consider the three statements:

(a)   The lion lives in Africa.
(b)   Lions live in Africa.
(c)   All lions live in Africa.

All three are uniformly translated into the sentence

1. $(x) [Lx \supset Ax]$,

where *L* designates the property of being a lion and *A* the property of living in Africa. The expression (x) is the quantifier and expresses the generalization applied to the open sentence $Ax \supset Bx$, which may render

2.   If it is a lion, then it lives in Africa.

Quite evidently, this is not a sentence. The 'it' hangs completely in the air and thus expresses the essential dummy character of the variable *x* which is taken to range over the class of all objects. Prefixing the quantifier may be viewed as attaching the term 'Whatever you may consider' in front of the last expression. The quantified expression is a sentence, whereas the bracketed expression is not a sentence. We refer to it as an open sentence. We remind the reader that such formulae possess no truth-value.

Sentences of type 1 play an important role in science. Most of our empirical laws or statements constituting a theory can be usefully cast into this mould. Of course, quantification usually extends over a battery of variables and the simple atomic formula Lx and Ax are typically replaced by complex formulae involving essential occurrences of free variables. The important role played by patterns exhibited in 1 justified a special name. Such sentences are called *general implications*. They are constituted by two major building blocks, viz. a universal quantifier (x) expressing generality applied to an operand expression $S_1(x) \supset S_2(x)$ in conditional form, where $S_1(x)$ designates a complex open formula with x as a free variable and $S_2(x)$ denotes another complex open formula with x as a free variable. The term 'assumption' happens now to be used on occasion to refer to the antecedent of the open conditional occurring as a component expression of the general implication. The open formula $S_1(x)$, or in our specific example above, Lx, would be called on occasion an assumption.

This usage of the term 'assumption' occurs also with a certain refinement. The open formula $S_1(x)$ may frequently occur as a conjunction in the form $S_{11}(x) \cdot S_{12}(x)$, where both expressions again denote open formulae involving free occurrences of the variable x. One of these components can then usually be shown to play a special role. It operates as a sort of screening device to filter the applicability of the law. It is included to delimit the realm of application or the 'social space' of a given hypothesis. An appropriate specification of the expected range of application is an essential part of a completely formulated theory or hypothesis. And such specifications can usually be introduced through selected components of the antecedent in the operand expression of the general implication. In the context of our simple-minded examples we might rewrite the general implication as

$$(x) \, [Lx \cdot - Cx \supset Ax],$$

where C designates the attribute of being in captivity and the dash designates the sentential operator 'not'. The component '$-Cx$' of the antecedent thus functions to filter the range of phenomena and select only the lions not in captivity as the relevant space which could potentially falsify the general implication. The addition of components to the antecedent, which are neither logically incompatible with, nor logically implications of, the previous components, necessarily narrows the realm of application. There is no doubt that the quality of 'assumptions' in the sense covered by this paragraph plays an important role in the competitive evaluation of alternative theories. With other performance characteristics the same, we prefer a theory with larger realm of application to a theory with a smaller realm. The term 'assumption' refers, according to the present interpretation, to a logically significant entity with a specific role in the appraisal of theories. However, this role cannot be reasonably translated into the argument pattern under discussion. Assumptions in the sense of the present paragraph are open formulae and possess no truth value. It is logically impossible to assign truth values to these assumptions or to confirm them absolutely or comparatively. Thus it is logically impossible to decide about the adequacy of a theory on the basis of the realism of such assumptions. However, if 'realism' should be understood as the range of a sentence or the range associated with an open formula (i.e. the intersection of the ranges of all sentences generated from the open formula by suitable substitution), then we would certainly attach significance to this 'realism' in our evaluation. But this significance of a particular meaning of 'realism' should not be twisted around into the idea that truth or confirmation of the theory is transmitted from the assumptions.[20]

Assumptions as semantic rules
The existence of semantic rules is a necessary but not a sufficient condition to assure us that a given theory or hypothesis has a positive empirical content.[21] These rules effectively shape the meaning of theories and hypotheses formulated in a given language system L^1. Variations in the rules must be recognized as changes of the language system within which theories are constructed. These changes are unavoidably transmitted to the interpretation of theories. Even in the context of an unchanged formal structure the meaning of theories has been modified. A shift in semantic rules changes in general the empirical content. The separation of the realm of potential observations between those consistent with the theory and those inconsistent with the theory is usually affected by the modification of semantic rules. This is clearly reflected in our shifting responses to affirmations or denials of sentences of otherwise invariant formal composition.

Semantic rules are not formulated as sentences of the language used to constitute the theory, i.e. they do not belong to the object-language. These rules speak *about* linguistic entities in the object-language. They associate observable phenomena in the domain (or universe) of discourse with linguistic entities in the object-language. These rules, like all the other rules constituting a language system used to formulate 'subject-matter theories', are themselves formulated in the meta-language. The semantic rules of designation may be introduced as a function D on the signs in the object language into the power set of the domain U. A given (object) language system is thus described by a triplet (U, D, O) where O refers to the other rules describing a (semantic) language system (e.g. list of signs, rules of truth, of range and of values).[22] The sentences composing the designation rules D have no meaningful truth-condition. They express conventions like the rules of a game and we either accept them or replace them with other conventions. But we cannot meaningfully discuss their truth. It follows that their 'realism' cannot determine the realism of the theory. Theories formulated in the object-language are neither logically consistent with nor implied by 'assumptions' in the sense of semantic rules. These and other logical relations apply to sentences in the same language, whereas the 'assumptions', i.e. the semantic rules, constitute the language itself.

The standard argument has thus no applicability to this case. Nevertheless, the short sketch of the logical status of semantic rules should reveal their important functions. Moreover, an admission that the categories of truth or falsity do not apply to these rules does not preclude an appraisal of their comparative adequacy. In particular, we can evaluate and confirm competing theories which differ in the choice of semantic rules. Substantial improvements may occur on occasion in a particular line of inquiry only as a result of more appropriate specifications of semantic rules. The comparative adequacy of distinct semantic rules is thus reduced to the relative confirmation of competing theories formulated in languages characterized by these different rules. The relevant situation pertaining to these 'assumptions' can, however, never be meaningfully expressed in terms of the prevailing linguistic practice. Once more this practice only obstructs the recognition of the proper role of a logically significant category in the construction and evaluation of empirical theories.

Psychologism and logical analysis

Discussions of 'theories and their assumptions' frequently suffer from a pervasive intrusion of psychologistic considerations. They usually occur as conditioned reflexes in the form of specific linguistic dispositions which replace a logical analysis of sentences and of the relation between sentences. The usage of the term 'logical' offers some interesting clues. Most occurrences of this term have little relation with logic or logical analysis. The term is used to express approval governed by one's pattern of thought-association or word-association to which one has become conditioned. Unaccustomed associations are illogical, even if a truly logical analysis of the relevant sentences finds the material thoroughly acceptable. Such approvals and disapprovals have little value for cognitive purposes.

In the context of discussions evolving around theories and their assumption three different types of psychologisms may be frequently observed. One may encounter, for instance, a reference to 'assumptions of a theory' as 'intelligible first principles explaining the theory'. Marginal productivity theory may thus be introduced with an impressive list of 'assumptions' laying down a host of esoteric conditions bearing on 'rationality', 'certainty', etc. In general, it is logically impossible to derive the theory under investigation from these 'assumptions'. Moreover, these 'assumptions' do not occur as sentences constituting the theory, neither as sentences which may be conjoined with the theory to derive observation statements. They seem to operate in the traditional Aristotelian sense of 'intelligible first principles', designed to render the theory psychologically palatable and convey a meaning independent and beyond its empirical content. But such procedures yield actually little help in understanding the relevant content of a theory. In particular, our conditioned responses are mistakenly assigned a cognitive significance which they simply do not have. At the very best one may on occasion interpret the attention applied to 'intelligible first principles' as preliminary and intuitive steps in a search for 'higher level theories'.

Another potent psychologism is the idea of a unique set of 'assumptions'. This idea rarely occurs in stark explicitness. It is, however, implicit in frequently occurring linguistic patterns. Among these may be noted phrases which indicate that such and such class of statements requires these and these assumptions. There are equivalent formulations, as for instance that given statements 'imply' or presuppose specific assumptions. In all such cases a unique set of assumptions is selected. The context of these discussions suggests that the assumptions selected are to be understood to imply (in a logical sense) the statements under consideration, i.e. the assumptions are hopefully introduced as sufficient conditions for the given statements. Such sufficiency conditions are, however, never unique. We are again misled by our conditioned responses into falsely equating our constrained ingenuity with non-existing logical uniqueness. There is no logical (i.e. *logical*) justification to assert that a statement S presupposes, requires, etc., assumptions A. These linguistic patterns reveal only so many inherited bad habits which clog our cognitive mechanisms.

The last psychologism is closely related to the second. After having selected the 'assumptions presupposed' by a statement S according to a psychological process governed by acquired reflexes one proceeds to discuss these assumptions. In case we find them untenable and decide on their falsehood, we feel furthermore justified to transmit this falsehood to the statement S under investigation. The logical fallacy of assigning uniqueness to a set of assumptions is thus compounded by another logical fallacy which has been deemed sufficiently important by logicians to rate a specific name, viz. the fallacy of denying the antecedent. The truth of the matter is that logical implication transfers truth; it does not transfer falsehood. Thus if A logically implies S, i.e. the conditional $A \supset S$ is true simply by virtue of the meaning of the logical signs occurring in the statement, then S must be true whenever A is true. In case A should be false we have, from this alone, no information about the truth-value of S. Thus we conclude that 'assumptions' are neither unique nor does their falsehood affect the truth-value of the statement investigated.

Concluding remarks

The actual usage of the term 'assumptions of a theory' suggested a number of distinct logical categories to which this term is interchangeably applied. There is no case in which a previously or independently determined 'realism' of 'assumptions' can be used to determine the 'realism' of a theory. Such notions simply result from various strands of logical misconceptions and most particularly a confusion between one's psychology and logical analysis. Such radical rejection of prevailing habits should not be misconstrued into an assertion that 'assumptions' have no cognitive function. They most certainly do perform important functions as semantic rules, as open sentences specifying the social space of a hypothesis, as initial conditions to be conjoined with a theory for purposes of prediction or explanation, as higher level theories or as selected sub-classes of the statement constituting a given theory. However, none of the functions performed by 'assumptions' in construction and evaluation of our cognitive products can be meaningfully explicated by the prevailing verbalization. The language games characterized by the inherited argument pattern centred on the notion of 'realism of assumptions' exhibit at the very best a dubious and uncertain relation to the acknowledged cognitive purpose. They contribute to the entrenched confusion between logic and conditioned reflexes to the use of words and sentences. Intonation of 'observations' and 'realism' is thus not an adequate guide for the development of language games satisfying the cognitive purposes of empirical science. Our endeavors still require a more explicit recognition of the nature of cognitive language games. Such recognition does not assure success in our intellectual struggles to comprehend our environment. It will only preclude the morass of irresoluble contentions resulting from a misuse of our language games.

Notes and references

Useful comments were made on earlier drafts by Armen Alchian and Lee Hausen. Critical comments by Carl Hempel also guided the revision of earlier versions. Many discussions with Allan H. Meltzer shaped the final outcome. These comments and discussions are gratefully acknowledged.

1. The reader may wish to consult three papers bearing on this and related issues by the present author: 'A case study on the importance of appropriate rules for the competitive market in ideas and beliefs', *Schweizerische Zeitschrift für Volkswirtschaft und Statistik*, **103** (1967), no. 2; 'Some reflections on current econometric practice', in *Essays in Honor of Richard Buchner*, Zürich, 1969; and 'A critique of current econometric practice', in *The*

Ohio State University Symposium on Econometrics, forthcoming in 1969. When I prepared my last version of the paper I found by chance the stimulating paper by Hans
Albert, 'Theorie und Prognose in den Sozialwissenschaften', in *Logik der Sozialforschung*,
ed. Ernst Topitsch, Lengerich, 1967.

2. The reader should consult the first essay in the *Essays in Positive Economics*, Chicago:
    University of Chicago Press, 1953.

3. J. Melitz, 'Friedman and Machlup on the significance of testing economics assumptions',
    Journal of Political Economy, **78** (1965), 37–60; Eugene Rotwein, 'The methodology of
    positive economics', *Quarterly Journal of Economics*, **73** (1959), 554–75.

4. *Papers and Proceedings of the American Economic Association*, May 1963. These *Pro-
    ceedings* covered the session of December 1962. The session included papers by Andreas
    G. Papandreou, Ernst Nagel and Sherman Krupp; discussants were G.C. Archibald, Herbert
    A. Simon, and Paul A. Samuelson.

5. Other meanings occurred in the discussion. They are clearly visible already in Friedman's
    original paper. Their term refers on occasion to the range of a theory or statement, i.e. the
    set of state descriptions in which a statement holds. It seems also to express on other
    occasions a monotone function over the power set of the set of predicate and functor signs
    occurring in a language system. These and other meanings relate to relevant aspects of a
    semantic analysis of theories and their proper assessment. These aspects will be examined
    at another occasion. It should be noted that these aspects appear in the stronger version of
    Samuelson's interpretation of Friedman's thesis and should be clearly separated from the
    question whether or not truth or confirmation of theories is based on truth or confirmation
    of logical implications or proceeds by assessment of truth or confirmation of a 'theory's
    assumption'.

6. Ernst Nagel clarified some issues of the problem in his contribution to the session of the
    American Economics Association in December 1962 (see note 4). The central portion of
    the subsequent explications was originally presented at the Annual meetings of the Econo-
    metric Society in December 1960.

7. The reader may usefully consult the contribution of Rudolf Carnap to the *Minnesota
    Studies in the Philosophy of Science*, vol. I, ed. Herbert Feigl and Michael Scriven,
    Minneapolis: University of Minnesota Press, 1956. The title of the contribution is 'The
    methodological character of theoretical concepts'. The reader may also consult the contri-
    bution by Carl G. Hempel to the same studies, 'Deductive-nomological versus statistical
    explanation', vol. III, ed. Herbert Feigl and Grover Maxwell, Minneapolis: University of
    Minnesota Press, 1962. The paper contributed by Paul Bernays to the *Essays in Honor of
    Rudolf Carnap, Logic and Language*, ed. B.H. Kazemier and D. Vuysje, Dordrecht,
    Holland: D. Reidel, 1962, is also illuminating.

8. A semantic rule formulates an association between descriptive terms of a given language
    L and observable phenomena outside this language. The rule is formulated in a meta-
    language of *L*, not in *L* itself. The rule does not *use* signs of *L* to speak *about* the subject-
    matter but speaks *about* some signs of *L*. It is consequently not advisable to formulate the
    rule as a sentence of *L*. Professor Papandreou's attempt to develop a canonical form for
    sentences constituting economic theories foundered on this particular problem.

9. Some economists apparently fail to recognize the importance of this aspect. Jack Melitz
    writes, for instance: 'However, the difficulty of testing the physical postulates in any
    relatively straight forward manner is easy to diagnose; it arises from the fact that these
    postulates contain various highly abstract terms, such as atom and molecule, whose
    counterparts in nature are not subject to immediate sensory observation. It does not follow
    that there are significant barriers to direct testing of postulates in other disciplines, par-
    ticularly in a field as distantly related to physics as economics' (op. cit., *Journal of
    Political Economy*, **78** (1965), 55).

10. The occurrence of theoretical terms in empirical theories raises a difficult issue pertaining
    to the demarcation between language games associated with empirical science and the
    'noncognitive' language games. The separation between cognitively meaningful, the
    cognitively nonmeaningful or the noncognitively meaningful has traditionally posed a
    hard issue. Logicians have struggled for rigorous syntactical or semantical solutions. A

rigorous explication is still missing. This does not remove the phenomenon and our behaviour reveals that we do acknowledge the existence of boundaries. And even fuzzy and blurred boundaries are useful if the realms separated are large enough, with a substantial and well-separated core. This certainly applies to the demarcation between empirical science and 'meta-physics', or more appropriately, between the associated language games. One should add that failure to formulate sufficiency conditions does not eliminate the existence of some useful necessary conditions characterizing empirical science language games.

11.   Universality is conveyed in ordinary idiom by means of a variety of devices. All, every, any, the indefinite article or nouns formulated in plural may all be used interchangeably. This shifting usage may create serious problems on occasion, particularly in the context of complex sentences. Logic introduces therefore a regimented language system to avoid the confusions which unavoidably accompany our ordinary idiom.

12.   Ernst Nagel clearly recognized the ambiguity of the term in his paper contributed to the session of the American Economic Association, in *Papers and Proceedings of the American Economic Association*, May 1963.

13.   Tjalling Koopmans, *Three Essays on the State of Economic Science*, New York, Toronto, London: McGraw-Hill, 1957.

14.   Rudolf Carnap, *The Foundations of Logic and Mathematics, International Encyclopedia of Unified Science*, vols I and II, *Foundations of the Unity of Science*, vol. I, no. 3, Chicago: University of Chicago Press, 1963.

15.   The material mentioned in note 14 discusses in detail this relation of meaning-assignment. Economists arguing on behalf of the view critically examined in the text usually impose a molecular form on the nonlogical postulates. Koopman's discussion reveals quite clearly that he attributed a nongeneral form to these postulates. The logical structure of empirical theories is thus completely misconceived. Ernst Nagel properly emphasized this aspect in Koopman's discussion. Koopman's mistake precludes an adequate analysis of the relation between 'assumptions' and the 'cognitive quality of a theory'. Samuelson's contribution to the session organized by the American Economic Association imposes another constraint which prohibits with similar effectiveness any relevant clarification: assumptions A of a theory T are introduced as classes of statements which contain the statements constituting T as a sub-class. This mould is not very useful for our purposes. Most important however, it leads Samuelson to an identity statement involving the theory B and the class C of all of its logical consequences; i.e. $B \equiv C$. Both terms of the formula denote sets (or classes). The formula satisfies thus standard rules of language, but happens to be false for most theories. The complete class of logical consequences (i.e. the logical content) of a theory expressed by the set of statements constituting it is not identical with the theory. The class C contains elements which do not occur in class B. B appears as a proper subset of C. Consider for example a theory consisting of the single statement $(x)\ [Ax \supset Hx]$ where the predicates A and H refer to some attributes. Class B is $\{(x)\ [Ax \supset Hx]\}$ and class C consists of all singular sentences $Aa \supset Ha$, $Ab \supset Hb$, etc., where a and b denote objects in the domain. Even for the case of finite domains the classes are not identical. In case Samuelson meant to interpret the sign '$\equiv$' not as identity (equality) but as equivalence (i.e. as a binary sentential connective and not as a binary functor) the formula $B \equiv C$ is false for languages with infinite domains and without transfinite transformation rules.

16.   Let for instance T^1 denote a generic formulation of a market system and let I designate sentences about the stability of the system or asserting the existence of an equilibrium solution. A consists then of statements further constraining the relations describing the market system.

17.   This was precisely the intention of our own procedure in 'Predicting velocity: implications for theory and policy', *Journal of Finance*, May 1963. We introduced a general demand function for money in the following manner: T^1 covers the specifications $M = \gamma(i, r, h, W)$ where i is a vector of financial rates, r is a vector of yields on real and h on human capital. The signs of the derivatives of γ are also laid down. A consists then of two parts: (a) aggregations of the vectors into single magnitudes and (b) auxiliary hypothesis relating the aggregate index of r to the aggregate index of h.

18. The reader may find James Tobin's description of his purpose introducing a higher level hypothesis for the slope hypothesis of money demand instructive. See 'Liquidity preference as behavior towards risk', in *Risk Aversion and Portfolio Choice*, ed. Donald D. Hester and James Tobin, New York: John Wiley 1967. It has also been argued (Robert Dorfmann, Paul Samuelson and Robert Solow, *Linear Programming and Economic Analysis*, New York, 1958) that the expected utility hypothesis, with its peculiar linearity property is rather implausible. It requires obviously 'justification'. Such 'justification' is advanced by subsuming the hypothesis under 'more plausible assumptions'. The standard postulates of Neumann-Morgenstern (NM) utility are usually introduced for this purpose. I do not wish to belabor the point that I find it very puzzling why these 'axioms' should be 'more plausible' than the expected utility hypothesis. But let us disregard this point. We also disregard the logical fallacy that subsuming a hypothesis under a set of assumptions contributes *per se* to raise the cognitive status of a hypothesis. It should be emphasized, however, that the NM axioms cannot justify the expected utility hypothesis even in the sense desired or claimed. The NM axioms do not imply the expected utility hypothesis. They imply an *existential* assertion ranging over a set of utility-functions, viz. that among infinitely many utility functions consistent with the NM axioms there exists a utility function linear in the probabilities. However, as there are infinitely many utility functions nonlinear in the probabilities which are equally consistent with the NM axioms, it is difficult to see how these axioms yield any justification for the 'implausible' linearity property of the expected utility hypotheses.

19. Jack Melitz addressed his discussion mostly to the antecedent of a material implication. The role of 'assumptions' in our cognitive games can barely be explicated by such a constraint. The discussion suffered moreover from serious logical errors. On p. 54 the author asserts: 'The statement "if *x*, then *y*" does not imply anything about the world at any particular spatio-temporal location unless it is brought together with an affirmation that *x* is true. The combined assertion of "if *x*, then *y*" and "*x* is true" implies y... . In a literal sense the author is of course correct. The quoted sentence 'if *x*, then *y*' contains sentential variables or schematic letters (it is not clear which) and thus says nothing about the world. Footnote 43 on the same page, however, reveals that the author applies his assertion to the case where *x* and *y* are to be understood as abbreviations for definite sentences of molecular composition. In this case the author is easily repudiated by elementary logic. The conditional statement 'if *x*, then *y* , contrary to the author, does yield information about the conditions of the world. It asserts that observable conditions which make the sentence '*x*' true and the sentence '*y*' false do not occur. Actual occurrence of such conditions would thus falsify the conditional statement. The conditional has empirical content. It should be furthermore noted that the quoted passage also confuses two distinct language levels, sentences of the object language (if *x*, then *y*) and the metalanguage ('*x*' is true) are combined in a manner violating the relevant rules of language necessary to avoid logical inconsistencies.

20. The assumption type considered in this section occurs in the context of Friedman's original discussion. It occurs particularly at the occasion of his discussion of Galileo's Law. Samuelson's objection to this discussion completely misses the peculiar role of this assumption type in theory constructions.

21. This content may be determined as the class of all basic sentences which are logically inconsistent with the theory. The empirical content can actually be specified in terms of a smaller class involving only state-descriptions. The latter are the 'largest' possible basic sentences formulatable in a given language.

22. These general properties of semantic systems are lucidly developed in Rudolf Carnap's *Introduction to Semantics*. The reader may also usefully consult Wolfgang Stegmüller's *Das Wahrheitsproblem und die Idee der Semantik*, Vienna, 1957.

5   The perception of man and the conception of government*

Introduction

The long-run tendency toward expansion of government that has dominated social developments in the western democracies for many years is attracting increasing attention from an array of social science scholars in search of a systematic explanation. This paper is an attempt to contribute a small fragment to that discussion. It addresses the rationale underlying conflicting views about the role, range and function of government. Alternative intellectual approaches to the 'limits of government' appear to us to be critically influenced by the models of man employed by the various discussants.[1] The set of characteristics with which man is endowed in the development of social science theory inevitably controls the body of theory that is forthcoming. What is less-frequently recognized is the impact that views about the nature of man have on the evaluation of political and market institutions.[2]

Alternative conceptions of man in the social sciences

While the various social sciences address many of the same or at least widely overlapping phenomena, the division of labour among the various disciplines – political science, sociology, economics, anthropology, psychology – is difficult to rationalize. To some extent it is an accident of history. Economics deals primarily with the economic organization and man's behaviour in that context. Political science, on the other hand, examines man's political organization. 'Sociologists concern themselves mostly with the social effects of cultural heritage, mores, customs, ethnic background, taboos, value systems, and social classes in modern societies. ... Psychology embraces an almost endless array of more or less disjointed topics ...' (Meckling, 1976). Organizational or social psychology offers a more focused connection with the central concern of social sciences, since it looks at man's behaviour in specified organizational contexts (e.g. the business firm).

*   This paper (written with William H. Meckling) was presented by Karl Brunner at Ohio State University on 30 April 1976, in recognition of Everett D. Reese's contributions to the university. It was originally published in *Journal of Money, Credit and Banking*, **9** (1), Part 1, February 1977, 70–85. The paper has been influenced by many discussions with Allan H. Meltzer and Michael Jensen. The authors also gratefully acknowledge valuable comments offered by William Dewald on a first draft.

The various disciplines have also tended to establish claims to specified subject areas. Crime 'belongs' to sociology, markets and exchange to economics, government and political institutions to political science and primitive tribes to anthropology. Recent developments have somewhat blurred and eroded these classifications. Many economists, for example, have begun to write and research subjects traditionally assigned to political science, sociology, psychology, and even anthropology. For our discussion here, it will be useful to distinguish intellectual endeavours directed toward understanding social institutions and processes on the basis of the perceptions of man employed in those efforts. Four different models of man can be distinguished: (a) REMM – Resourceful, Evaluating, Maximizing Man – the model of man developed in economics; (b) the 'sociological' model of man; (c) the 'political' model of man; and (d) the 'psychological' model of man.

These labels express the relative dominance of the ideas in the various fields, but the use of the models by various social scientists is not confined to the fields from which the labels are taken. For example, the political or sociological models of man are often encountered in the literature produced or arguments developed by economists, while at the same time, sociologists and political scientists sometimes use REMM as the basis of their research and analysis. The following summary of the characteristics of each of these models of man is largely based on Meckling (1976).

REMM – Resourceful, Evaluating, Maximizing Man

The codification of the characteristics of man as a unit of analysis in economics is the product of at least 200 years of research. While intensive attention to the formal codification can and has occasionally sidetracked attention from the underlying substance, this substance can be summarized in terms of three crucial strands:

1. Man is an evaluator. He is not indifferent. He cares about the world around him. He differentiates, sorts, and orders[3] states of the world, and in this ordering he reduces all entities encountered to a commensurable dimension. Things valued positively are preferred in larger magnitudes. Moreover, the evaluation depends on the context. Any given increment of a positively valued object suffers a lower evaluation as the total available to the individual rises. Man is willing to trade off in all dimensions. He is always willing to forfeit some quantity of any given valued item for a quantity of some alternative item that he values more highly. His evaluations tend to be transitive, expressing a consistency in his value system.

2. Maximizing man recognizes that all resources are limited, including his own time. Whatever his resources, man attempts to achieve the best position he can under the constraints facing him. This optimization

occurs on the basis of less than perfect information, and it recognizes that decision making itself involves costs.

3. The resourceful aspect of man is analytically the most troublesome to handle. Resourcefulness emerges whenever man is confronted with new and unfamiliar opportunities, or when man searches for ways to modify the constraints and opportunities. Coping, groping, and learning all express man's resourcefulness and form an essential aspect of his systematic behavior.

The REMM model does not describe man as a brainy but heartless calculating machine. Charitable behaviour, love of family, compassions, can be consistently subsumed. Man appears as a search organism, responding systematically to incentives and stimuli. These are systematically associated with institutional arrangements surrounding man. Market and nonmarket institutions can be analysed in terms of the incentives structures they generate. In contrast with the other models, the REMM model explains man's behavior as a consequence of interaction between the *individual's* value system and constraints or opportunities. This formulation is usually supplemented with the assumption that the variability of the constraining conditions dominates the variability of the preference system.[4] Changes in behaviour are thus dominantly attributed to variations in opportunities and not to variations in values.[5]

The basic ideas of the REMM model were introduced more than 200 years ago by Mandeville, Ferguson, and Adam Smith. The idea of REMM was an essential building block in the analysis that led them to conclude that a social equilibrium results as an unintended by-product of the interaction of self-seeking men.

The sociological model of man

> Sociological man is conformist and conventional. His behavior is a product of his cultural environment; the taboos, customs, mores, traditions, etc., of the society in which he is born and raised. ... If behavior is determined by acculturation, then choice, or purpose, or conscious adaptation are meaningless. ... Sociological man is not an *evaluator*, any more than ants, bees and termites are evaluators. (Meckling, 1976)

Cultural conditions and historical forces certainly affect human behaviour, but the sociological and the REMM model differ in their treatment of this effect. In the REMM model acculturation conditions the constraints and the preferences of the individual in his coping, groping and interested behaviour. In contrast, the sociological model asserts that individual behaviour is directly determined by social factors and cultural conditions. Man is neither resourceful nor an evaluator, he is a conformist enslaved by conventions.

Structuralist interpretations of sociology reveal some basic properties of the model. Members of a society are essentially viewed as role players. Society determines an array of social positions that determine roles assumed by members of society with specific role obligations. Social anticipations concerning the performance of specific role obligations are supplemented with appropriate sanctions to assure adequate performance. The interaction between social positions, role anticipations and sanctions determines individual behaviour. There is no room for adaptive creativity, or for evaluating responses to incentives. The sociological model attributes a crucial significance to the exogenous existence of social values and social norms. These values and norms establish the social order independently of individuals.

The sociological view of man is particularly prominent in Marxian writings. Lukasz stresses the role of 'social totality' as an entity above and beyond all individuals and their interaction. This view is repeated by Adorno, who maintains that all social phenomena, including the individual, depend on the social totality. Others argue that a reduction of social phenomena to the behaviour of men, i.e. the explanation of social phenomena in terms of individual behaviour, is basically false and inadmissible. These scholars insist that individual behaviour be traced to a social whole. Society determines individual behaviour, not the other way around.[6]

The impact that the use of alternative models of man has upon the analysis of social phenomena and attitudes toward such phenomena is nowhere more apparent than in matters concerning crime. Those who start with a sociological view of man regard criminal activity as a reflection of the social environment. The sociological model fosters the view that society creates crime; that crime is the unavoidable consequence of particular types of social order exogenously imposed on individuals. This view denies that the range and frequency of criminal activities depends on opportunities. Actions designed to modify relative opportunities (i.e. changes in expected costs and gains of criminal activities) are useless given the sociological interpretation of crime. Punishment itself is also useless. Crime can be brought under control only by changes in the social environment. Conviction of criminals can only be justified as a means of social rehabilitation. If conviction and deprivation of liberty palpably fail to rehabilitate, the rationale for conviction disappears. In one of the more extreme modern variants, the sociological model transforms criminals into more or less conscious political activists responding to a brutalizing social environment.

While the REMM model does not deny the role of social institutions, it directs attention to other factors. In particular, it directs attention to the individual's resourceful adjustment to relative opportunities – to the conditions shaping expected gains and costs associated with criminal and alternative activities. It suggests examination of the legal system, and how its operation lowers or raises the probabilities of conviction and of various degrees of punishment. It also leads to the study of the incentives shaping the behaviour of policemen, judges and prosecutors functioning in the legal system.[7] It is hardly surprising that the policy conclusions drawn from the two alternative conceptions differ so radically.

Political man

Political man is an evaluator and maximizer, but he evaluates and maximizes on behalf of the public interest, rather than his own. Political man predominates in public policy discussions, where goodwill or public interest guides the behaviour of politicians, legislators and functionaries in the bureaucracy. An increasing number of economists and political scientists have turned their attention in the past ten years to developing a better body of theory explaining the results produced by the political sector. Many of these attempts abandon the public interest theory and admit a measure of self-seeking behaviour. Legislators are assumed to maximize their changes of re-election, or incumbent parties to maximize the proportion of votes cast in their favour. While these formulations approximate the REMM model, they are not identical to individual welfare maximization. Moreover, the public interest theory of political behaviour continues to be widely employed by social scientists though in a subtle implicit manner. Thus, one of the favourite pastimes of economists is searching for circumstances (externalities, public goods, moral hazards) in which markets are nonoptimal. Once such circumstances are found, it is customary to jump immediately to the conclusion that government should intervene.[8] Government is the *deus ex machina* that can be relied upon to remove negative external effects and produce positive external effects. Moreover, normative statements involving optimization of social aggregates (optimal rate of inflation, optimal budgeting, optimal consumption and capital accumulation, etc.) are converted into positive statements about the world by suitable conjunction with a public interest theory. Much of the so-called theory of economic policy only makes sense in the context of a public interest theory.[9]

Psychological man

Psychological man differs both from sociological man and REMM because his evaluations are incommensurable. His valuations are structured in a hierarchy. His needs are absolute. He will not trade off some of one source of value, e.g. physical hunger for another, e.g. security, until the former is completely satisfied. The psychological model of man produces an array of *ad hoc* motivational explanations with little systematic analytic coherence. Moreover, these motivational explanations are usually incompatible with evaluating trade-offs and with the notion of resourceful search to adjust relative opportunities. This sketch of psychological man is included for the sake of completeness, but will not be used in the subsequent discussion.

The role of the perception of man for the conception of society and government

In the following three sections we attempt to clarify the role played by the conception of man in social and political discussions. Socialist doctrine and the liberal doctrine respectively offer excellent vehicles for this purpose. In the last section the problem of corruption provides a specific example showing how the sociological and REMM models yield fundamentally different evaluations of governmental institutions.

Socialist doctrine

The ideal socialist state   The vision of the ideal socialist state has an important influence in contemporary society. It conditions the views of the intellectual establishment in western societies in many and often very subtle ways. The socialist argument opens with a moral condemnation of the capitalist system. Market economies are inherently evil. They destroy man and prevent the development of his human faculties. Capitalist societies are suffused with commercial values that dominate human relations. These values obstruct the evolution of finer values. Men become the tools of corporate interests; and corporations are compelled by their place in the social totality to pursue dehumanizing behaviour.

This perception of economies organized on the basis of markets, private property and voluntary exchanges is juxtaposed to the socialist vision of a New Society. This New Society is egalitarian and assembles men in a communal fraternity. It opens avenues for man's perfectability and the realization of his full human faculties. The prehistory of man in capitalism will be ended with the advent of the socialist state, and the true history of true man will emerge. The vision emphasizes the change in man's attitudes and nature that unavoidably occurs in the new society replacing the old capitalist system. The socialist argument looks to a society with men 'acting according to finer motives than accumulation, to better values than manipulation, and evolving an ethic beyond the appetite of self' (attributed to Irwin Howe in Miller, 1976). An authentic socialism introduces a cooperative fraternity and equality without the individual competition so pernicious to finer human values.

Sociological man in the socialist vision   Although this general theme has many variations, the essence of the argument is clear. The sociological model of man plays a crucial role in this socialist argument. The evil and injustice of capitalism are built into the social order. Men ensnared and enmeshed in the system are shaped by the social pressures of this totality. They cannot avoid behaving according to a pattern imposed by society. They are compelled to pursue roles determined by the social positions they have been allotted. The uselessness of efforts to patch up the market system is a natural consequence of this view.

In a curious way, the sociological model attributes self-seeking behaviour to men in commercialized societies. Self-seeking, of course, really means economic man in the narrowest and meanest sense. But more than that, such behaviour is not a matter of conscious choice on the part of individuals, nor a part of man's nature given the fact of scarcity. Self-seeking behaviour is imposed by the social totality. Man is self-seeking in the same sense that ants and termites are self-seeking, but his self-seeking behaviour is not genetic nor purposeful. It is culturally determined, in particular, by the existence of markets, private property and exchange.

In centring attention on the *Produktiansverhaltsuisse*, the pattern of owner-ship in nonhuman resources, self-seeking behaviour is equated with the profit motive and the predominance of commercial values. The theologian Niebuhr exemplifies this position with his admonition that self-interest is the cause of injustice and conflict. He argues that 'the power residing in economic owner-ship cannot be made responsible' and, therefore, 'must be destroyed'. Self-seeking behaviour ad irresponsible control over resources will only disappear with a change in the social order, and the sociological model of man assures us that a new society will generate a new life-style, liberating man from the bonds of self-seeking behaviour. Neither vision nor argument expresses any doubt that the restructuring of society with the abolition of private property will create a man with a new moral vision.

The apparent perfectability and malleability of man's basic nature, which is inherent in all socialist arguments, follows directly from the sociological model. In the Marxian versions, this result is linked with the materialist interpretation of history. Marx's interpretation of history depends crucially on the class struggle, which is nothing more than the reduction of indi-vidual behaviour to the social totality. The social totality as an entity *sui generis* exhibits an *Eigengesetzlichkeit*, i.e. it is subject to its own laws, independent of interacting individual behaviour. This *Eigengesetzlichkeit* is expressed by the laws of motion of history, which move the social process to its eschatological fulfilment. Sociological man is a crucial ingredient. He is a necessary condition to the social *Eigengesetzlichkeit*. With the indi-vidualist approach properly exorcised, an explanation of the social totality can only occur in terms of an *Eigengesetzlichker* process, subject to its own and independent laws of historical motion. Moreover, these laws imply that all specifically social laws are relativized to a phase in history characterized by the prevailing social order. This relativization of social laws assures an opportunity for alterations in the behaviour of an essentially malleable man.[10]

Socialist doctrine and the emergence of social order   Beginning with the work of the Scottish philosophers, economic analysis has demonstrated that social order (equilibrium) emerges from interaction among REMMs in the market place. Market conditions confront each individual as an objective reality, but the same market conditions are also the net result of individuals' actions. The usefulness of the notion that equilibrium emerges from the interaction among individuals is, of course, not limited to the market place, but extends to a wide variety of organizational structures, e.g. the political organization.

It is important to recognize the unintended character of this social equilibrium. The social order does not emerge from intentional individual behaviour directed to *that* purpose. This unintentional consequence, so clearly formulated by Adam Smith, was either uncomprehended, overlooked or rejected in the sociological literature of the nineteenth century. Since in every individual's personal experience consequences seemed to be associated with directed, intentional behaviour, the idea that social order would emerge from the interaction of REMMs without direction was ignored or rejected. It follows that society, social order and institutions are the 'total alien, objective reality outside and beyond all individuals'. Every individual encounters society as an external force imposed on his activity and life experience. This psychological impression was the basis of the social determinism more or less explicit in the sociological model. These impressions, combined with an implicit argument that consequences and intentions must be correlated suggested the thesis that social phenomena and the social totality are ontological entities beyond individual volition, and 'cannot be reduced to individual behavior'.[11]

The socialist doctrine and ideology   The socialist vision and the socialist critique of capitalism are never accompanied by a description of the institutional arrangements that will prevail, much less a searching examination of the impact those institutional arrangements would have. The REMM model has led to the construction of a coherent body of theory relating individual behaviour to specific institutional contexts. It has (testable) implications for behaviour not only in the context of markets, but in the context of nonmarket organizations as well. It implies, for example (in contrast to the suggestion emanating from the sociological model as it is applied in the socialist argument), that there exists no society and no social order without individual competition. Such competition occurs in very different forms determined by the incentives fostered by the prevailing institutions. In the presence of scarcity, human wants conflict. An understanding of this fundamental fact directs our attention to the crucial question: how is this conflict resolved? Markets and private ownership represent one set of institutions that resolve this conflict; nonmarket institutions represent another. What is the nature of the competition generated by alternative institutional settings? The REMM model explicitly directs our attention to a range of questions that cannot be addressed in the context of the socialist argument because of the fundamental nature of the sociological model of man. The fact that every individual's goals conflict with the goals of others is swept aside with vague allusions to fraternity and community.

The pervasive neglect of institutional arrangements and incentive structures implicitly fostered by the sociological model separates the socialist vision from all sense of reality. This autonomy of the vision should alert us to its significance as a marketing technique in the sale of socialism as a way of life. Brunner has emphasized on another occasion (Brunner, 1970) that man is the metaphysical animal. For millenia, man has manifested a pervasive and persistent demand for sweeping, all-embracing orientations. The viability of these orientations depends on a felicitous mixture of factual references, emotively satisfying valuations, and vast inherently unassessable speculations. The orientations offered to western societies by Christian vision and theology have been gradually decaying over the past few centuries, and in this century have faded to a pale shadow. But man demands a vision, and socialism has thus found a receptive market.

The socialist argument as developed and cultivated by the new clerics (i.e. the intelligentsia) provides the necessary theology by combining factual references and valuational speculation in a viable new mixture. But this implies that it is useless to expect adherence to relevant cognitive standards in the socialist argument, or to insist that the vision be disciplined by systematic reflection on persistent patterns of human nature operating under specifiable alternative institutions. Such cognitive requests miss the politico-religious purpose of the socialist argument.[12]

The liberal argument
Though the socialist argument is more prominent in Europe than in the United States, it is also very influential in intellectual and political circles here. It is, however, what we might call the *liberal vision* that dominates the intellectual establishment in the United States. The very diffusion of the liberal position makes it difficult to summarize its content. We have therefore chosen a specific example, Okun (1975), as a basis for our discussion. Okun's standing as a professional economist assures us that we should find the liberal argument presented with as much skill and balance as can reasonably be expected.

The liberal view   The liberal argument is cautiously reserved and somewhat suspicious of markets, or, more generally, of the role of voluntary exchange as a means of social co-ordination and organization. It recognizes that markets and exchange contribute to the efficient use of resources. It even concedes that efficiency results from REMMs interacting in the right (perfectly competitive) environment. But there is also substantial distrust of market institutions. They create inequalities, foster the appreciation of dollar values, and endanger the viability of noncommercial values: 'The imperialism of the market's valuation accounts for its contribution, and for its threat to other institutions. It can destroy every other value in sight.' The tyranny of the dollar 'would sweep away all other values' (Okun, 1975).

The 'admissible' range available for market operations must be limited, moreover, by deliberate political action: 'The basic transgression of the market place on equal rights must be curbed by specific detailed rules on what money should not buy' (ibid., 31). Political processes and institutions are necessary to balance the social effect of market mechanisms and market institutions. The apprehension concerning the 'one-dimensional human values' resulting from market processes are not matched by similar apprehension concerning the political process. 'The good sense of public officials and professional codes of ethics' (ibid., 26) can be expected to protect the working of political institutions. There are allusions to some problems associated with political institutions and political control, but these concerns are vague and muted. The relative size of the government sector or the range of government activities does not threaten individual liberty or the range of individual choices. Private ownership of resources does not involve 'the same kind of basic liberty as freedom of speech or universal suffrage' [ibid., 38]. Moreover, 'the issue of government versus private ownership of industry has little to do with freedom, but much to do with efficiency' (ibid., 61).

This view of government is in large measure a result of the central role of egalitarian objectives in the liberal vision. The liberal economist recognizes constraints encountered in the realization of the vision. Efficiency is lowered and material welfare sacrificed. Government's central function is to make the liberal vision a reality at as small a sacrifice in material welfare as possible.

Liberal doctrine and sociological man   Okun's book shows clearly the intrusion of both the sociological and political models of man in the liberal argument. These models of man appear in the discussion simultaneously with REMM. Such eclectic combination of contradictory cognitive building blocks is characteristic of the liberal argument. The obvious contradictions are removed by suitably partitioning the argument. REMM is confined to market processes; political man operates in the nonprofit environment, i.e. in government; and sociological man emerges in the discussion of broad social issues.

This partitioning reflects the influence of the central theme in the sociological model – that the social environment determines man's life-style and individual values. Individuals enmeshed in market processes are socially compelled to pursue dollar values at the cost of other values. Individuals embedded in the political process, i.e. politicians and bureaucrats, behave as political man. They act in the public interest, meaning in accord with whatever the particular expositor would like.

Okun's contraposition of commercial values and other values provides a classic illustration of the application of the sociological model. The normative appeal of the argument is enhanced by identifying REMM with dollar signs, i.e. with the pursuit of commercial values, even though REMM behaviour is perfectly consistent with the list of ultimate values (family, marriage, friendship, love, etc.) that Okun himself extols.

The influence of the sociological model can also be found in the discussion of political rights. Business and wealth endanger these rights and produce counterfeit votes, whereas the political manipulation exercised by labour unions and other special interest groups are no cause for concern. The dangers to noncommercial values (such as family, companionship, friendship and love) arise from self-interested behaviour in markets, but there is no danger that REMM behaviour in the political arena might stifle the cultivation of higher values.

Okun's vision of the good society parallels the socialist vision in its failure to specify what institutional structures will be invoked, or provide any analysis of their impact. We are told that 'equality of income would give added recognition to the moral worth of every citizen, to the mutual respect of citizens for one another and the equivalent value of membership in the society for all' (Okun, 1975, 47). Hardly anyone would use this language to describe the effect of *any* of the income transfer programmes we now have in the United States. Surely the opposite would be more accurate. Welfare must be one of the major sources of alienation – alienation of the recipients from the welfare bureaucracy, alienation of the welfare bureaucracy from the taxpayer, and alienation of the taxpayer from the recipients. The REMM model suggests that egalitarian patterns will have to be coercively imposed, and it is hard to see how such coercion can be used with the felicitous results so lyrically proclaimed by Okun. He finesses this problem with sociological man. When the vision is realized we will all happily accede to equality *of outcome*. Acculturation will make it so.

The sociological model is also reflected in the tendency to lend organizations, particularly society, human qualities, i.e. to treat them as if they were individuals choosing and acting on the basis of their own objective function. Thus, we read, 'society does not try to ration the exercise of rights' (ibid., 7). 'Society refuses to turn itself into a giant vending machine that delivers anything and everything in return for the proper number of counts' (p. 13). 'Society decides it will not let old people starve' (p. 19). 'It explains why the political process rather than the market place must judge the legitimacy of some preferences' (p. 78). References to 'the need for collective action or choices' whenever the 'market fails in one respect or another' (p. 99) provide another example. The terminology 'collective action or choice' obscures the fact that only individuals can act or choose. What is different about different choice situations is not that some are collective and some individual. What is different is the institutional framework through which the choices are exercised. The 'collective choice' terminology injects a Rousseauesque flavour with the correct overtones of goodwill and public interest. In a similar vein, we note that the 'Consumer Protection Agency ... is one worthwhile step to strengthen the public's power' (p. 29). We are left to determine who that public is.

One of the most interesting facets of Okun's analysis is that he apparently understands the agency problem – the problem a principal has in getting an agent to maximize the principal's welfare – but he never realizes that this problem exists in government. Thus, he points out that 'managers ... have interests and objectives of their own, quite distinct from the profitability of their firm' (p. 42). On the other hand, we are asked to believe that bureaucrats, legislators, the judiciary, etc., do not *'have interests and objectives of their own'*, or at least will not have such interests and objectives when the vision is realized. (This is discussed in Jensen and Meckling, 1976.)

Liberal doctrine and political man   Okun's book skilfully demonstrates the usefulness of the sociological model as a sales technique in the political market. 'Society', treated as an entity with human characteristics, appears as a guardian of the ethical principle. The discussion is sprinkled with normative admonitions – 'rights granted by society ought not to be traded' (Okun, 1975, 25), or men 'ought not to spend money for the purpose of influencing votes' (p. 78), or 'the legitimacy of individual preferences ought to be judged by society' (p. 31), or lastly, that society should judge the admissible range of voluntary exchange.

Government's role as ethical guardian means that the political model of man takes on crucial significance. Because of political man we can safely expect the results emanating from the political process to coincide with society's (Okun's?) goals. The political model eliminates the danger that the actual performance of politicians and bureaucrats responding as REMMs to specific institutional incentives will violate the ethical principles expressed by society. Okun's faith in political man is unswerving. We are assured that 'closing a bad escape valve (via the market) may be an efficient way of promoting the development of better ones through the political process' (p. 21).

We are also told that 'absurdly low paid or risky jobs should be kept out of the market place'. No concern is exhibited that the institutions replacing or controlling the market might introduce incentives that convert the initial intention into radically different results.

The public-interest theory of government service appears with remarkable explicitness in the view advanced that 'the safeguards against special pleading' or the pressures and temptations resulting from lobbying activities 'must lie in the good sense (and informed skepticism) of the public official and in stronger professional codes of ethics' (p. 26). Because they are political men, officials will adhere to moral codes in spite of the incentives created by the new institutions.

The liberal vision and freedom Perhaps the most important issue raised by the liberal argument bears on the relation between individual freedom and the role of government. The liberal argument generally denies any threat to individual freedom from an expanding government sector and the persistent replacement of market mechanisms with political institutions or processes. Okun asserts that the relation between collective and private ownership 'has little to do with freedom, but much to do with efficiency' (Okun, 1975, 61). The institution of private ownership can therefore only be justified in terms of efficiency (pp. 37–8). It is furthermore suggested that the 'misuse of powers by the government sector' occurs independently of the relative size of the government sector and its budget (p. 39). The sociological model of man encourages this posture. Social dangers can only lurk in activities suffused with 'dollar values'. Whatever dangers exist in institutions that control nonowned resources or regulate private activities are easily exorcised with professional codes of ethics. The public interest theory of government behaviour, of course, re-enforces this view. With freedom dismissed as an issue, the private sector can be justified only on efficiency grounds, and the case for an expanding government sector follows more easily. Again, the issue is of crucial significance in marketing the liberal vision.

Okun's discussion of property rights and freedom comes down to a denial that private ownership has any relationship to freedom. He concludes that discussion with the statement: 'Yet some people argue the case for private ownership of such items as though it were the same kind of basic liberty as freedom of speech or universal suffrage.' That statement makes the error so commonly made by those who employ sociological and political man, namely, confusing normative and positive propositions. As a positive matter, the right to property, the right to free speech, and suffrage, are on all fours. In each case, the law simply provides that the police powers of the state will be used to ensure with high probability that an individual will be permitted to engage in certain behaviour – voting, speaking, selling, or what have you. What

Okun is really trying to persuade his readers to accept is the proposition that these various rights do not occupy the same moral grounds – that property rights, the right to own a house or car, for example, should not be valued as highly as the right to vote or the right to speak out. If he had put his proposition in those terms, he would have encountered a much less sympathetic audience. The implicit normative nature of his argument is less damaging to his views than his outright denial that rights in property are freedoms. Carried to its logical conclusion, his argument implies that we would all be equally free if there were *no* private rights in *any* property, e.g. if *all* property were held in the name of the state. He is led to this conclusion by an argument perfectly analogous to the following. If a law is passed denying Okun the right to reply to these comments, we cannot tell whether that increases or decreases the range of human freedom. His freedom (right) to speak out has been decreased, but our freedom (right) not to have his comments appear has been increased – ergo, freedom of speech, *per se*, is not a value that we must be concerned about.

The case of corruption
The problem of so-called corporate corruption has attracted much attention in recent months. This problem offers a useful vehicle for contrasting the results of an analysis of a social problem using REMM, and an analysis of that same problem using the sociological and political models of man. We are not here concerned with the question of whether or not the corrupt behaviour is immoral. What we are concerned with is explanations for the phenomenon. Unless we understand the institutional factors that foster the corruption, policy measures are likely to do more harm than good. Moral indignation, unaided by substantive analysis, usually produces measures extending the conditions favouring corruption or curtailing individual freedom of action without solving the underlying problem.[13]

Ranking members of the intellectual establishment have recently presented their views in two articles published in the *Wall Street Journal* (Schlesinger, 1976; Nader and Green, 1976). Arthur Schlesinger Jr contrasts a 'self-policing' public (i.e. government) sector with a private sector apparently suffering under pervasive habits of corrupt behaviour. Corruption in Schlesinger's judgement shows a clear case of delinquency on the part of business. The basic responsibility lies with the business sector. The low moral level of businessmen affects the government sector. Corrupt behaviour by officials results from the influence of bad guys, i.e. the businessmen. All this means, of course, a 'crisis in legitimacy of business'. Schlesinger states moreover that 'if business cannot clean its own house, the government will clean the house of business'. He concludes with a warning that business must show a greater 'capacity for collective self-discipline'.

Ralph Nader and Mark Green (1976) argue that corrupt activities are criminal and should be subject to serious punishment. They also suggest that corrupt business behaviour is the crux of the problem. Government corruption is a consequence of business corruption. A solution of the problem can be found, according to Nader and Green, with severe penalties imposed on businessmen and more extensive regulation of business by government.

Once again we see the influence of the sociological model of man combined with the public-interest view of government service. Profit-seeking is at the heart of the corruption. The involvement of government officials in these corrupt transactions is a 'fall from grace', but is not inherent in the role government is being asked to play. To protect itself and the public, the government sector must extend its role and powers even further.[14]

A radically different interpretation of the phenomenon and very different policy conclusions emerge from an application of the REMM model. The REMM model directs attention to the large array of government agencies with arbitrary powers to interpret mandates and regulations. Shifting interpretations, procedures and criteria can and do involve for 'the clientele of the agencies' large capital gains and losses. Thus, controls and regulations offer an opportunity to the controllers and regulators to accept (or extract) payments of money or favours in exchange for favourable treatment.

Transactions involving purchase or acquisition of resources (including appointments of staff) or sales and disposal of resources (sale of land, supply of various licenses, etc.) also offer opportunities for government officials to engage in corrupt exchanges. The expectation of corruption associated with sales and disposal (e.g. licenses) are enhanced to the extent that the item supplied is officially priced below its market value.

A recent review of nationalized banking in India provides an excellent example of the kind of analysis of the corruption phenomenon the REMM model produces:

Because profit criteria are, as a matter of policy, no longer being stringently applied to many of the banks' operations, opportunities for corruption also have increased and the chances of detection diminished. Once loans are made on the basis of social and political rather than commercial criteria these can easily be juggled to the mutual profit of the recipient and the bank official. ... It is perhaps not surprising that the most popular Marathi play currently being performed in Bombay (*Kashi Kai Wat Chuklan*? or *How come you lost your way in this poor neighbourhood?*) deals with the problem of bank corruption in India!

Even before nationalization there was, admittedly, a problem of fraud and senior bank officials were sometimes known to use bank funds to buttress their own private businesses. However, there were strong independent checks on them provided by the auditors, the government inspectors and the law courts. Since nationalization these groups are not radically separate bodies acting as a constraint on the banks from outside; rather they are all part of a shapeless inter-related government bureaucracy. Furthermore, there is no clear owner who loses by these depredations and who might be expected to combat them vigorously since his self-interest demanded it. Since nationalization, fraud has become democratic in the sense that far more people have an opportunity to participate in it and the new fraud-enfranchised groups have not been slow to exploit these opportunities.   (Meckling, 1976, 1205–6)

The existence of potential gains from corruption does not by itself imply that the potential will be exploited. The extent to which corruption occurs will also depend upon the costs confronted by government officials, and those costs will be a function of the probability of detection as well as of the size of the penalties assessed if detected. As the article on corruption in the Indian banking system suggests, there are some analytical reasons for suspecting that the costs a government servant can *expect* to suffer as a result of corruption are lower than what his business counterpart can expect, probably because detection costs are higher in government. This is not inconsistent with the fact that most of the corruption that has been brought to light has taken the form of payments to government officials rather than payments to executives in other private firms.

Neither the inadequate analysis nor the sketchy evidence we present here on the corruption problem is intended to be definitive. We are simply trying to emphasize that the REMM model generates one framework within which to consider such questions, while the sociological and/or political models may yield an entirely different framework within which to consider those questions.

Concluding remarks

The conflict between those who believe that human welfare can be improved only by enlarging the role of government and those who believe the opposite has occupied centre stage in the social sciences for many years. Differences of view in that debate are often attributed to different ideological commitments. What appears to be ideological, however, often turns out to be substantive. One of the most important substantive issues that lies at the bottom of differences about the role of government is the perception of man used in analysis of social questions. In the social sciences two radically different models of man have come to be used: REMM and sociological man. Political man has been introduced as a special case derivable from the sociological model. REMM and sociological man yield substantially different analyses of the operation of political and market organizations, and have very different policy implications. Much of the conflict about government can thus be reduced to the conflict between alternative models of man.

These models contain propositions about man and his behaviour that are in principle assessable. This assessability pushes questions of value, ideology and social norms another step backward in resolving the disputes over the role of government. The dispute contains a cognitive core that we propose to emphasize in the market place for ideas.

Notes

1. Normative views about the role of government are also conditioned by the conception of justice employed. An enquiry into the impact of alternative views of justice on political and social ideas is postponed to another occasion.
2. Professional articulators usually explain the dispute between advocates of severely limited government and the proponents of large and not clearly limited government in terms of different ideological commitments. This is a rather shallow and unrevealing answer. It is easily understandable, however, in terms of the characteristics of the 'market for words' conditioning the intelligentsia's behaviour. Of course, ideological dimensions enter all our intellectual endeavours. The occurrence of these ideological components does not justify *per se* the rejection of any hypothesis or theory. Whatever the ideological influences at work, the informative value of a hypothesis can only be judged by appropriate cognitive procedures.
3. It is often argued by the intelligentsia that 'men are not concerned and do not care'. What they really mean is that many men do not care as much, comparatively, for the things the intelligentsia is concerned about. Men differentiate and sort; and different men sort differently.
4. This assumption has been useful for explanation of many phenomena. It does not preclude an examination of conditions shaping preferences. The historical or cultural conditioning of preferences does not change the crucial propositions of the REMM model. Even changes in preferences are subject to REMM behavior.
5. The emphasis on variations in values is frequently quite confused; two senses of the changes in values are, in much of the social science literature, not adequately distinguished. One sense means changes in the preference system and the other means changes in location of the state point within a fixed preference field. The latter occurs, of course, as a result of changing opportunities.
6. A detailed analysis of the sociological conception can be found in Vanberg (1975). Vanberg's excellent study also covers the individualistic approach developed by Georg C. Homans. A survey prepared by Hans Georg Monissen for the Third Interlaken Seminar on Analysis and Ideology indicates, however, that variations on the sociological model dominate the thinking and work of German academic sociologists. Vanberg also notes the tension between the sweeping and essentially programmatic meta-discussions elaborating in general terms the sociological model and the *ad hoc* individualism emerging in allusions to concrete problems of situations. A similar point was made by Meckling (1976). But these allusions are not subsumed under a coherent framework. They occur as loose, disconnected fragments violating the essential thrust of the programmatic orientation. The reader may also find useful information bearing on the thesis developed in the text in Tenbruck (1961).
7. The reader may find an interesting description of the issue in Tullock and McKenzie (1975). Economists, using a REMM model, increasingly contributed to the analysis of criminal or illegitimate activities. The work of Gary Becker should of course be mentioned foremost in this respect.
8. One of the unhappy results of this practice is the enormous talent and effort regularly devoted to unearthing some new set of circumstances under which markets are nonoptimal. If a fraction of that energy were devoted to understanding political processes, the social sciences would be in a far better position than they are to say some useful things in the policy arena.
9. The reader should consider as an example the discussion of the relation between number of targets and number of instruments and the applications made over the range of policy problems, or the more recent analysis on controllability.

10. It is noteworthy that an endless literature invoking the laws of motion and producing mountains of discussions, meta-discussion and (meta)^n-discussions never formulated such laws. We obtain vague classificatory sequential allusions in a descriptive *ex post facto* mood.

11. The continuing prevalence of these views is nowhere more evident than in discussions of national economic planning. Thus, a recent advertisement, endorsed by Nobel Prize winner Wassily Leontieff, which advocated national planning, said: 'No reliable mechanism in the modern economy relates needs to available manpower, plant and materials ... the most striking fact about the way we organize our economic life is that we leave so much to chance. We give little thought to the direction in which we would like to go.'

12. The development of Protestant theology within the last hundred years offers interesting examples bearing on the general argument in the text. Bartley (1962) said, 'The Protestant liberals considered revolution in human motivation to be the chief political need of their time.' Liberal theology argued that motives of helpfulness and goodwill must replace the motive for private gain, selfless behaviour should replace self-seeking behaviour. Bartley continues: 'The vague liberal assumption about man's dignity; and their Kantian belief that the obligation to do one's duty was a universal human experience, led many of them to feel that such a change of attitude was possible on a large scale. Few of them were definite about just what kind of social institutions would accompany that change. But they agreed that in principle social and economic institutions existed which would be compatible with the ethic of the Sermon [on the Mount]. Human motivation and social justice could, in principle, be reconciled' (1: 34–5). Bartley effectively describes the substitution of religious commitment for an assessable empirical analysis of behaviour under alternative institutional arrangements. The socialist theology continues thus a well-established tradition.

13. A peculiar immorality of professional moralizing can be observed at this point: they refuse a moral commitment to recognize the proper conditions for effective action.

14. It is noteworthy and typical for arguments influenced by the sociological-political model that corporate criminality is viewed somewhat differently than street criminality. Both criminals are the product of their social environment, but corporate criminality results from the evil greed of corporate profit motives, whereas street criminality results from socially deprived, disadvantaged and brutalizing conditions. The street criminal deserves compassion and understanding, whereas the corporate criminal deserves harsh injunctions and penalties. This attitude is clearly reflected in Nader and Green's piece. It is also remarkable that some legal procedures affecting Swedes accused of tax law violations are much harsher than Swedes accused of street criminality.

References

Bartley, William Warren III (1962) *The Retreat to Commitment*, New York: Knopf.

Brunner, Karl (1970) 'Knowledge, values and the choice of economic organizations', *Kyklos* **23**, 558–68.

Davies, Christie (1974) 'The shady side of nationalization in India', *The Banker*, **124**.

Jensen, Michael C. and William H. Meckling (1976) 'Theory of the firm: managerial behavior, agency costs and ownership structure', *Journal of Financial Economics*, **3**, 305–59.

Meckling, William H. (1976) 'Values and the choice of the model of the individual in the social sciences', paper presented at the Second Interlaken Seminar on Analysis and Ideology, 1975, *Schweizerische Zeitschrift für Volkswirtschaft und Statistik*, Fall.

Miller, Stephen (1976) 'The poverty of socialist thought', *Commentary*, August.

Nader, Ralph and Mark Green (1976) 'What to do about corporate corruption', *Wall Street Journal*, 12 March.

Okun, Arthur M. (1975) *Equality and Efficiency: The Big Trade-off*, Washington, D.C.: Brookings Institution.

Schlesinger, Arthur Jr. (1976) 'Government, business and morality', *Wall Street Journal*, 12 March.

Tenbruck, Friedrich H. (1961) 'Zur Deutschen Rezeption der Rollentheorie', *Kölner Zeitschrift fur Soziologie und Sozialpsychologie*, **13**, 1–40.
Tullock, Gordon and Richard B. McKenzie (1975) *The New World of Economics: Explorations into the Human Experience*, Homewood, Ill.: Irwin.
Vanberg, Viktor (1975) *Die Zwei Soziologien*, Tubingen: Mohr.

6 The perception of man and the conception of society: two approaches to understanding society*

Approaches to 'society'

The 'social and institutional embeddedness' of man has attracted the attention of social philosophers since Aristotle. Man's social integration motivated Adam Smith's revolutionary analysis of a 'spontaneous order'. This problem of social and institutional embeddedness has attracted in particular the interests of sociologists; social values and the corresponding embeddedness became the central themes of a useful social science. Such values appear in the form of opinions, attitudes, orientations, norms of behaviour or rules of conduct. Although these patterns clearly shape individuals' behaviour, values as social phenomena appeared to sociologists to be beyond the initiative and decision of individuals. Since Durkheim (1961) this perception has controlled most of sociology. Seeing values as an independent force justified an analysis in terms of social conditions and forces constituting a social process somewhat independent of individual behaviour and interaction.

This conception contrasts fundamentally with the paradigm developed in economics and initiated by Adam Smith, where the individual is the focus of values. Social values are generally recognized and commonly held individual values. Social processes and social values are determined by the nature of the interaction between individual members of the social group.

But economists' interest in sociological issues has waned since Adam Smith's time. There developed a concentration on a narrow range of social phenomena represented by market transactions. While impressive analytic progress has been achieved in this manner, the procedure has excluded a wide range of social and institutional reality which shapes social processes and the nature of market transactions. Whenever economists ventured beyond the range of market transactions, they easily adopted the sociologists' mode of argument. They seem to be unaware of or unconcerned about the intellectual inconsistency of their behaviour. In playing the dominant intellectual game, some economists choose to disregard reality, apparently because it does not offer sufficient opportunity for a rigorous approach or because it appears to

* Originally published in *Economic Inquiry*, xxv, July 1987, 367–88. This paper was the basis for a lecture presented on 2 July 1986 at the annual meetings of the Western Economic Association in San Francisco. Discussions with Thomas Lys, William Meckling and Allan H. Meltzer are gratefully acknowledged.

be ideologically contaminated. But the history of science reveals the basic flaw of such objections. Serious problems beyond the range of interests considered over the past hundred years deserve, and actually require, the economists' attention, if human society is to be adequately understood. A less than fully rigorous account may still provide useful knowledge or at least important steps in the development of further knowledge. Broader social issues are not inherently ideological, and even the ideological contamination introduced by social issues does not exclude competent social analysis.

Economics has experienced a major new thrust over the past quarter-century. Gary Becker and others, joined by some sociologists, extended economic analysis to a wide range of traditionally sociological problems. Political scientists adapted the general framework developed in economics to their range of interests, reinforced by the re-emergence of political economy under Buchanan's (1975) influence. Alchian (1950) developed the property rights analysis which merged with other trends emphasizing the role of transaction and information costs. Thus appeared the 'new institutional economics'; it explores the rationale and consequences of institutional arrangements associated with either market transactions or nonmarket pursuits.

This intellectual evolution offers a new vision and a new understanding of social institutions. It appears that the basic hypothesis about (or model of) man developed in economics to explain behaviour in the context of market activities can be effectively generalized to subsume social phenomena beyond the accustomed range. The sociological model thus appears, contrary to Talcott Parsons' (1951) claim, as a special case of the economic model. An opportunity for a unified approach to social science has thus emerged. It should be noted, however, that much of the descriptive work supplied by anthropologists and sociologists can be productively exploited. Among the issues most particularly benefiting from the nonsociological approach to sociological problems may be listed the emergence and role of social values. This analysis expresses the nature of the fallacy that justifies moral relativism in terms of the observed wide diversity of moral systems. In this examination we obtain also a better insight into the nature of social coherence mechanisms, or the relation between social values and social order.

The last theme bears on an old issue and combines a variety of ideas. Some suggest an influence from the social order to social values. Others emphasize influence in the opposite direction. A third argument combines the first and the second in a dialectical process. And of course, all these groups of ideas occur with more or less subtle differentiations, exemplified by Schumpeter's (1942) and Horkeimer's (1947) accounts of capitalism's demise. The relationship between social (and human) values and social order has in recent years been forcefully thrust into the public's attention by 'professional moralizers' constituting the bureaucracy of the established churches.

The two models of man

A common strand unites most of the discussions bearing on values and the social order. This strand appears in attempts at both explanatory accounts and normative re-evaluations, which typically address self-interested behaviour as a crucial characteristic of any social order based on markets and private property. Many of the apparently nonnormative accounts suggest that the spread of self-interest in Western societies is a modern phenomenon. In the eighteenth and nineteenth centuries, conservative commentators deplored the erosion of traditional values (expressed by 'rank and ancestry') under the influence of an expanding market orientation. This attitude is still reflected, albeit in some modified and moderated form, among contemporary neoconservatives – for example, in Irving Kristol's (1978) muted cheers ('two cheers for capitalism') for a market-oriented society. Neoconservative thinking is in such cases closely associated with a normative position that assigns to the state the role of a moral guardian; this guardianship should control the admissible range of the public's preferences.

To a large extent theologians move on a parallel path but frequently express a more extreme point of view. In their eyes, self-interested individualism engrossed with commercial values obstructs the creation of a humane society. They claim, however, that earthly salvation can be achieved through the manipulation of political structures. Such manipulation, guided by the counsel of theologians, can impose a moral society on immoral man, who is swayed by his own self-interest.

The socialist tradition shares some elements with the neoconservative attitude and many more with contemporary theologians. According to socialist thinking, self-interested behaviour is imposed by the characteristic arrangements of the social order. This notion is much more developed in the socialist than in the theological literature, and emphasizes that a radical change in the social order will produce a 'new man' with a new set of motivations.

This summary of the intellectual scene immediately reveals the crucial role of a substantive hypothesis. The vision of the nature of man conditions most thinking about values and the social order. We naturally expect social science to offer us guidance on this issue, and indeed we find various alternative models of man (see Brunner and Meckling, 1977) expressing very different visions. There is not necessarily contradiction between these visions. They were usually associated with different realms of our reality, in accordance with the 'shoe box' theory of the social sciences. Each box represented an underlying model of man. 'Economic man' controlled the box labelled 'Economics' and 'sociological man' the box entitled 'Sociology'; 'political man' and 'anthropological man' were special cases of 'sociological man'. 'Psychological man' still occurs in textbooks and papers characterized by the Maslanian scheme. This heritage is disregarded here, as leading scholars in psychology (particularly in the field of learning theory) now pursue a converging course with developments in economics.

Economic man was generally understood to condense the most relevant aspects of human behaviour in the 'everyday pursuits of market affairs'. According to a widely expressed view, it provided a picture of man completely governed by economic motives. He was quite egotistical in the sense that his motives addressed only his personal well-being. Thus emerged to many students and professionals a picture of a dried-up, shrivelled homunculus, a dubious representation of reality. This picture may have helped to clarify certain basic allocation problems confronting man, and may have conveyed an important sense of the allocative behaviour that reflects the underlying subjective substitution potentials inherent in man's choice processes. But these important points were dwarfed by the narrow focus somehow created by the notion of economic man. It contributed to a pervasive sense that economic analysis was ontologically confined to aspects of economic motives. This ontologically based methodological rule impoverished economic analysis and seemed to justify the role and importance of sociological man to address the dominant range of social reality. Noneconomic motives seemed clearly suggested by observable behaviour. And man's obvious concern, interest and attention directed to others undermined the more or less tacit understanding of an 'egoist'.

This procedure and interpretation dominating the social sciences encounters two major objections, one methodological and the other substantive. It is unsatisfactory on methodological grounds to accept *a priori* an ontological representation of human reality with different and actually inconsistent behaviour hypotheses, and to avoid contradictions by imposing suitable restrictions on their realms of application. Cases of apparently segmented human behaviour patterns may just reflect information and learning problems that can be integrated into a unified approach.

Substantively, the sociological model is seriously flawed. The separation or segmentation of social phenomena and processes from individual behaviour and interaction ultimately fails to explain social phenomena. To invoke society as creator or producer of social entities seems to beg the question. Society is not an actor; it results from individual action and interaction. The existence of social entities is revealed by specific regular patterns in individual behaviour. Parsons' (1951) belief that no bridge could possibly connect individual behaviour with social categories confined sociology to a description or narrative without analytic explanation, and implied a retreat to mystification.

REMM, the economic model

The difficulties encountered by the sociological model can be avoided. A properly reformulated model of man beyond the caricature of a homunculus yields great promise for a unified approach in the social sciences. This model draws together strands introduced into the literature since Adam Smith. The label REMM – Resourceful, Evaluative, Maximizing Man – appears in Meckling (1976) and in Brunner and Meckling (1977). Discussions over the years have suggested that several issues bearing especially on economic motives (i.e. self-interest and egotism) and on the nature of constraints and 'bounded rationality' still require detailed attention.

The central building blocks of the model are the preference field with its specific structure and the constraints that determine the opportunity set. It will be shown that these building blocks fundamentally differentiate REMM from the sociological model, with far-reaching implications for our understanding of social phenomena. The discussion proceeds in the sequence of the acronym (REMM).

Resourcefulness, evaluating and maximizing behaviour possess a common basis. Recent contributions from evolutionary analysis and sociobiology or bioeconomics need to be recognized at this stage. We understand that the individual is not born as an empty slate (Barrash, 1979) to be subsequently covered by social experiences, but rather is born with a biological and genetic heritage. Two aspects of this heritage must be emphasized. One pertains to a common aspect shared by all people. This includes the broad potential and general disposition of behaviour. Both disposition and potentiality are independent of the social environment. In fact they influence the behaviour patterns emerging in response to the social environment, including dominant institutional arrangements. The slate cannot be rewritten arbitrarily by radical social engineering. The biological-genetic heritage exhibits great variation in specific form and intensity of the common core. We observe a rich diversity in individual endowment. Such differences impose further limitations on social engineering.

Resourcefulness and its variations among individuals forms an important strand of the biological heritage. The cultural and social evolution of humankind over 100,000 years offers an array of observations revealing remarkable resourcefulness. Man searches, probes, copes and experiments and is not a passive entity. Such experimentation reaches from the trivial to the majestic. But the cumulative effect of comparatively trivial events affects over time humanity's opportunities and survival conditions. The selection of plants or animals for food and the development of tools and instruments over prehistory exemplify my point. So does the behaviour of modern bankers experimenting with an array of financial innovations in order to cope with new conditions. Resourceful experimentation appears as a driving force of cultural and social evolution and interacts, as discussed by Popper (1957), with biological evolution. Resourcefulness thus prepares the ground for the evolutionary analysis emphasized in recent years by Hayek.

Resourcefulness also bears on the interpretation of the opportunity set which the individual confronts at any moment. But resourceful behaviour modifies this set over time. Agents invest resources to probe and explore in order to expand their opportunity sets. Probing and exploring may change the environmental conditions or the information about these conditions which specify the relevant opportunity set. An adequate formalization of resourcefulness has not so far been achieved. Brunner and Meltzer (1971) made an attempt in a special context, where agents operating with incomplete information jointly optimize their choices of opportunity set and position within the set. The opportunity set is not immediately and fully determined by prevailing natural, social or technological conditions. It reflects instead the individual's perception of these conditions. Incomplete information characterizes our reality and controls this perception, and thus influences the relevant opportunity set.

Resourceful man also evaluates. Three topics are important here: the form of the preference field, the separation between economic and noneconomic motives, and the meaning of self-interest and egotism. A quote from Brunner and Meckling (1977, 71–2) helps to clarify some aspects of evaluating behaviour:

> Man is an evaluator. He is not indifferent. He cares about the world around him. He differentiates, sorts, and orders states of the world, and in this ordering he reduces all entities encountered to a commensurable dimension. Things valued positively are preferred in larger magnitudes. Moreover, the evaluation depends on the context. Any given increment of a positively valued object suffers a lower evaluation as the total available to the individual rises. Man is willing to trade off in all dimensions. He is always willing to forfeit some quantity of any given valued item for a quantity of some alternative item that he values more highly. His evaluations tend to be transitive, expressing a consistency in his value system.

The crucial properties of the individual's preference structure are clearly suggested by the quote: the relative evaluation for a positively valued object diminishes with its increasing quantity, and trade-off or substitutability occurs in all directions.

The assumption of a generalized trade-off between positively valued objects, events or states implicitly denies the relevance of the traditional separation between economic and noneconomic motives. This separation has been used to justify the shoe-box view of the social sciences, where economic analysis is essentially confined to behaviour springing from economic motives. Further reflection demonstrates the questionable character of this interpretation. The range of all allocations extends much beyond wealth maximization and potentially includes enjoyment of books, theatre, concerts, ice-cream, beer, wine, football, and so on. Can we meaningfully describe decisions about these as involving only economic motives? The same question extends to the enjoyment of status influence and friendship. Any *a priori* delineation of economic versus noneconomic motives offers no useful basis for analysis. This holds in particular as the generalized trade-off (i.e. substitutability) subsumes the potential range of all positively valued states, events, objects or aspects. The recognition of such open-ended trade-off behaviour is a crucial condition for any useful analysis of broad social conditions. This applies most particularly to the evolution of social arrangements. On the other hand we do encounter problems that do not always require explicit acknowledgement of the 'full intellectual baggage'. We frequently assume the constancy of some variables with full awareness that the assumption is not literally true. We may postulate, rightly or wrongly, that the relative variability is modest and poses only a second-order problem. Or we may restrict our attention to a subset of the full range of motives (i.e. events) occurring in individuals' utility functions. This procedure is quite appropriate where the trade-off between the recognized subset and the disregarded subset creates at most a second-order problem in the question under consideration. Such approximations neither imply nor suggest the irrelevancy of the generalized trade-off.

There remains a fundamental question concerning the ultimate location of evaluation. REMM refers unambiguously to the individual. This raises the egotism issue. Egotistical behaviour may be characterized as single-minded attention to one's own welfare without reference to the welfare of any other person. (On the other hand, altruistic behaviour means that a person's utility function includes attention to other persons' welfare.) This specification of an egotist is consistent with REMM but fails to account for important social institutions such as family and friendship. The egotism postulate may safely be applied, however, to many problems as a useful approximation. Our basic assumption is one of self-interest. This means that in general individuals refuse to delegate permanently and unconditionally decision powers pertaining to their personal affairs, given such a choice. In other words, individuals prefer to maintain power over a range of personal decisions. It follows that evaluations proceed in accordance with the individual's own assessments, understanding and interpretation. The individual is the ultimate locus of values.

At this point, we encounter a second question raised by Marx and other sociologists; namely, that private interests are socially determined interests, determined by society in a process of socialization and internalization. The operation of such processes is hardly disputable. But these processes do not establish the Marxian thesis of a 'social Lysenkoism'. REMM emphasizes a biological-genetic heritage which controls (up to a point) the nature of 'the slate' and modifies the writing by socialization and internalization on the slate. The processes of socialization and internalization are thus filtered by the biological-genetic endowment. Self-interest is a central component of this endowment. The role of this endowment becomes obvious in the remarkable variations in the detailed aspects of life (quality and extent of resourcefulness, nature of trade-offs), even among individuals with similar cultural and social conditioning.

Lastly, we turn to maximizing man with another quote from Brunner and Meckling (1977, 72).

> Maximizing man recognizes that all resources are limited, including his own time. Whatever his resources, man attempts to achieve the best position he can under the constraints facing him. This optimization occurs on the basis of less than perfect information, and it recognizes that decision making itself involves costs.

The representation of formal maximization under constraints may offer a useful approximation to behaviour under many circumstances and for a wide range of problems. Its general applicability is not material here. What is material is that resourceful exploration and action within constraints are not purposeless ramblings but are instead driven by efforts to improve one's welfare. Fundamentally, the model emphasizes that individuals are rational. Rationality is perhaps a more basic component of the hypothesis than maximizing behaviour. Rational behaviour is directed toward a goal or purpose, expressed by a utility function. It means in particular that the individual does not willingly or knowingly sacrifice a goal within the relevant opportunity set. Limited computational facilities of computers and human minds, the cost of gathering and interpreting information, and often a diffuse uncertainty prevent the expression of rational behaviour in terms of straightforward maximization. Rational behaviour produces instead a set of more or less conscious rules of procedure.

The sociological model

Objection to an emphasis on individual private interest is a central feature of the sociological model. This section presents the basic structure and central emphasis of this model. The sociologists' model assigns autonomy and primacy to society, i.e. to social institutions, norms and rules of conduct. It suggests that the individual confronts social arrangements which influence his behaviour but are clearly beyond his influence. Durkheim, the 'father of modern sociology', developed this theme in two different ways, according to the Dutch sociologist Lindenberg (1985). The social determination of individual behaviour takes the form of either moral systems or social currents. The processes of socialization and internalization are invoked, with sanctions for deviants, to assure desired moral behaviour. Society is clearly an ontological entity separate from individuals. Durkheim (1961) writes:

> Moral goals, then, are those the object of which is *society*. To act morally is to act in terms of the collective interest.   (p. 59)

> The collective interest, if it is only the sum of self-interests, is itself amoral. If society is to be considered as the normal goal of moral conduct, then it must be possible to see in it something other than a sum of individuals; it must constitute a being *sui generis*, which has its own special character distinct from that of its members ...   (p. 60)

Whereas morality characterizes the comparatively stable and long-term components of society, social currents address temporary influences expressed in passing opinions and emotions. Parsons (1951, 502) repeated this position in the most explicit terms: 'That personalities are above all oriented to the optimization of gratification as the fundamental directional principle, while social systems are oriented toward cultural change, is an inference from and a way of stating, the mutual independence of the two classes of systems.' Marxian sociologists may object to the last clause of the sentence. It does contradict more or less explicit sociological references to socialized man. The crucial point for our purposes, however, is the explicit emphasis on the independence of the social system shared by Marxian and non-Marxian sociology, as emphasized in Brunner and Meckling (1977).

The basic strands of the sociological model are usefully summarized by the acronym SRSM, juxtaposed by Lindenberg (1985) to REMM. The acronym addresses the three essential elements of sociological man, whose blank slate is arbitrarily filled by society: Socialized Man, Role-playing Man and Sanctioned Man. The first element expresses the ontological primacy of society and the resulting social determination of the individual sphere. Man emerges fully programmed by his social context. An analogy with bees and ants may be invoked, but we need to recognize that the programming of ants and bees with respect to the details of their life pattern derives from a biological-genetic basis. The sociological model implicitly assigns no significance to this base and attributes programming completely to society.

Role-playing follows from the socialization process. Society is structured into an array of roles and individuals are fitted into specific roles with socially determined characteristics and obligations. The established role system and role behaviour determine stable expectational patterns. Members of society can to some degree anticipate each other's behaviour. Still, deviations from role-playing due to incomplete socialization need to be controlled. Sanctions supplement and reinforce the processes of socialization.

Lindenberg introduced a second model with the acronym OSAM (Opinionated, Sensitive, Acting Man), associated with empirical sociology. This branch of sociology typically addresses social processes centred on 'opinions, attitudes and orientations', all socially determined. Sociologists are thus prone to approach labour market phenomena in terms of a work ethic or work 'orientation'.

According to this model, man is opinionated and forms opinions about aspects of his environment. Man is also sensitive (i.e. his opinions are easily influenced by his surroundings). Lastly, man acts in response to his opinions. OSAM seems to be simply a special case of SRSM with attention confined to specific processes.

Lindenberg notes that SRSM is not resourceful and is subject only to the restrictions of sanctions and role expectations. Scarcity has only an indirect effect on SRSM, in so far as role expectations have been moulded by the premise that 'ought implies can'. SRSM expects only role behaviour of others and evaluates events only in terms of conformity and deviation. Choice (substitutability) is ruled out and thus nothing is maximized.

OSAM lacks resourcefulness and restrictions. Attitudes and sensitivity to social influences involve expectations and evaluations, but it is important to note the expectations and evaluations do not relate to a process of choice and maximization. Rather, they create 'situationally specific activations of behavioral patterns'.

The nature of social processes
A description of fundamental models hardly produces sufficient clarification of the relevant issues. The nature of the basic conflict between the two models is poorly understood. This situation is substantially influenced by a nonanalytic tone that is common in sociology. A description is often interpreted as a theory (i.e. a hypothesis). However, this does not necessarily distract from the description's usefulness as an observational basis for the development of an adequate analysis. In a similar vein, the telling of a story is sometimes equated with the analysis of a problem. It has been claimed that REMM is empty, and that whatever it says is contained, with more, in sociological accounts. The first claim can be dismissed immediately, since the R and E components are inconsistent with specifiable behaviour patterns. The second claim is best addressed in the context of specific groups of problems. This approach reveals most effectively the fundamental conflict between the two models and the usefulness of the REMM model as a unified hypothesis for the social sciences. The following four sections pursue this course.

The invisible hand: the emergence of social phenomena from interaction between individuals
The sociological approach reflects an old problem addressed by political philosophers. How can we expect society, represented by social institutions, norms of behaviour or rules of conduct, to emerge from the actions of self-

interested individuals? The prevailing fact of self-interest behaviour among individuals seems to prevent an explanation of social arrangements, including social values, in terms of initiatives and actions pursued by individuals. There seems to exist no transition from the individual member to society, a point repeatedly emphasized by Marxian and non-Marxian sociologists. Society cannot possibly be explained as a sum of self-interested individuals or a collection of individuals. Society must be recognized as a distinct ontological entity with structures and behaviour patterns not reducible to individual behaviour.

The structure of general equilibrium in economics reveals in a simple fashion the flaw in the sociological argument. Prices confront individual agents in a competitive market as given uncontrollable social facts. But we learn from basic price theory that prices are not separate social facts unrelated to individual behaviour. On the contrary, prices are reducible to individual behaviour. They emerge from a process of specific interaction between self-interested individuals with little attention to or knowledge about the nature of the process shaped by their joint behaviour. This interaction process thus involves more than just a collection of individuals. Such descriptions are bound to fail in any attempt at linking social phenomena with individual behaviour. The very formulation reveals a remarkable analytic naiveté. This is particularly remarkable when we consider Adam Smith's revolutionary contribution to the problem. More than 200 years ago he developed the basic notion of the nature of the social interaction process generating social patterns unintended and unplanned by self-interested individuals. He coined the famous term 'invisible hand'; i.e. he examined an interaction process producing social patterns as if guided by an invisible hand, without anybody intentionally directing the emerging patterns. The invisible hand has frequently been ridiculed; but the ridicule completely misses the crucial analytic point, viz., the occurrence of an interaction process linking social phenomena with the behaviour of self-interested individuals.

Invisible-hand explanations form the core of any analysis based on the REMM model and addressed to social institutions and aspects of social embeddedness. Hayek has developed this point substantially over the past 20 years, emphasizing in particular the emergence of abstract impersonal rules of conduct as a precondition of a viable greater society beyond the reach of the emotively anchored small band roaming the earth in human prehistory.

This approach also offers an opportunity to stress the forces encouraging coherence in human society. 'Moral communities', in Buchanan's (1975) sense, may still operate in a 'greater society'. Such communities involve an emotively based binding force, a strong individual commitment to a personal relation with other members of the group. Religion forms a principal example of the basis for binding moral communities. But greater societies hardly form a single moral community, particularly in modern times. With a multiplicity of competing moral communities within a single society, the moral order established by general norms of behaviour and abstract rules of conduct is decisively important. Such rules have to guide behaviour between the different moral communities and for the individuals outside such communities. They lower uncertainty among members of society concerning the probable range of each other's behaviour. They contribute in this way to the co-ordination of social life in complex societies. Norms and rules thus act as constraints which are advantageously respected.

No society without a moral order can function and survive in competition with other societies with more moral order. Disorder indicates either a transition to a new moral order or gradual disintegration. Religious rituals, norms and rules evolve in the context of awesome historical or evolutionary experimentation. The invisible-hand analysis explains the emergence of this social embeddedness. An evolutionary approach explains, moreover, that we should expect a wide diversity of moral communities and moral orders. Supergame theory offers in this respect an analytic complement with its emphasis on the nonuniqueness of the institutional equilibrium (Schotter, 1981). This evolutionary experimentation, unplanned and without human intentions, exhibits some analogies with biological evolution. The diversity of moral communities and moral orders and their changes over time produce substantial variations among societies bearing on their economic development and their long-term survival. Moreover, the interaction between members of a society shaping social values is an ongoing process modifying norms and rules over time.

An important aspect deserves special attention. The rich diversity of moral communities and moral order, of which the western intelligentsia has become increasingly aware, has contributed to a noteworthy erosion of the latter's moral order. The diversity has been interpreted to justify a pronounced moral relativism. A spreading relativism has meant a substantial weakening of emotive commitments to inherited norms and rules. This weakening has not proceeded as a result of the general emergence of new social values providing a regulatory framework. This evolution has meant that socialization suffers from an uncertain drift. The inference from the diversity of moral systems to moral relativism and its behavioural consequences fails to understand the evolutionary aspect of moral systems associated with man's more or less resourceful coping. It also fails to recognize and understand the fundamental fact that a society without a moral order lacks sufficient coherence and suffers from an increasing range and intensity of conflicts and uncertainty.

Supergame theory offers additional insights into our problems beyond the nonuniqueness of institutional equilibria. An examination of 'prisoners dilemma' situations demonstrates the possible emergence of co-operative social patterns even with self-interested individuals. In an experimental investigation, Axelrod (1984) has exhibited the longer-run superiority of a tit-for-tat strategy. This strategy ultimately dominates many other strategies and produces eventually a dominant pattern of social co-operativeness. Moreover, the same analysis clarifies the nature of the widespread fallacy which juxtaposes conflict (or competition) and co-operation as mutually exclusive behaviour patterns. The co-operative behaviour occurs even with conflicting interests of self-interested individuals. This analysis explains a remarkable incident observed in World War I. Axelrod describes trench warfare where opposing units occasionally confronted each other for a lengthy time. This provided a natural opportunity to signal possibilities of co-operative behaviour with the aid of an approximate tit-for-tat strategy; thus appeared a 'live and let live' accommodation between hostile troops. Under this arrangement troops would deliberately aim their fire so as to miss the enemy. Violations committed by one side were punished by the other side with similar unco-operative behaviour. This pattern was ultimately destroyed by the High Command with the aid of a simple stratagem: it shifted troops around frequently, so that the time required to develop a co-operative pattern and the incentive to maintain it was not available.

A special set of rules produced by social interaction should be further considered here. It was noted in an earlier section that maximizing behaviour may not occur under all circumstances. The concept of rational behaviour was introduced as a more fundamental notion to be approximated on frequent occasions by maximizing behaviour. Man's physical capacities are also a limited resource to be used in a resourceful manner. This issue has been addressed in the literature under the term 'bounded rationality', a somewhat misleading term which seems to equate rational and maximizing behaviour. The issues addressed under the term are, however, quite relevant for our purposes. The problem may be compared to a situation that occurs in operations research, where there exists on occasion an algorithm for a maximizing solution. But this algorithm may be complex and particularly costly. Alternative algorithms, easier and cheaper to operate, often yield useful approximations to the maximizing solution. The loss due to deviations from a maximizing solution can be offset under the circumstances by a more economical algorithm. This simply means that rational behaviour takes into account the cost and inconvenience of probing for a best solution. Limited physical capacity condemns man to operate permanently under severely incomplete information, so rational behaviour may on many occasions not result in standard maximizing behaviour. It is precisely rational and resourceful behaviour that produces this result. Resourceful coping and groping yields in such cases rules of thumb; social interaction between individuals distributes information about such rules over the social group. The same process also assures a competitive sorting out among alternative rules of rational behaviour. According to Alchian (1950), social groups with better-adjusted rules will survive more effectively in the long run.

Invisible-hand explanations have been successfully applied to the emerging of a minimal state (Nozick, 1974) or the emergence of a natural equilibrium under anarchy as a provisional step to a minimal state (Buchanan, 1975); an interesting case is the formation of a property rights structure in the gold fields of California (Umbeck, 1981). This sort of development substantially undermines the sociological thesis of society's autonomy built into the sociological model. The analysis of the invisible-hand process demonstrates the falsehood of sociologists' claims that there is no possible channel leading from individual behaviour to society. This explanation offers also a useful programme of research into the processes generating and modifying social values, moving much beyond a descriptive treatment supplemented with speculation.

Evolution and the relation between the two models
The evolutionary theme introduced in the previous sections should be somewhat expanded. The process of sociocultural evolution reveals the emergency of norms and rules in response to new circumstances. Major social adjustments reflecting changes in important underlying conditions seem usually to be accompanied by changes in norms and rules. Lindenberg (1985) directed our attention to this by usefully clarifying the relation and substantive difference between REMM and SRSM. He argues cogently that SRSM may offer a programme for a descriptive blueprint of a stationary society but fails to offer any explanation of the consequences induced by underlying changes. A stationary society does not exhibit resourcefulness, choice or substitution; the potential is dormant, possibly confined by inherited restrictive institutions. But this fact does not mean that resourcefulness and choice are absent. They are simply not operative. The following passage from Lindenberg (1985, 102) develops this point:

> It is a defensible proposition, that in very stable societies most, if not all, relevant restrictions will have found their way into role expectations and sanctions. In these situations, SRSM is a handy shorthand expression of institutions, structural constraints and social behavior all in one. This boils down to situations in which the expected behavior always belongs to the set of viable alternatives and in which the expected rewards minus the expected costs are always highest for the behavior alternative that is prescribed by the role expectations. Imagine an organization in which everybody behaves the way he or she is told. Then all we need to do in order to predict the behavior of each individual in a certain position is to recreate the blueprint of the organization (that is, the description of interlocking role expectations). It is not surprising that anthropologists have frequently applied this blueprint approach to small, stable societies, using SRSM as their model of man. Yet it is important to notice that [REMM] behaves under these restrictive

conditions *as if* he were a SRSM. The moment these restrictive conditions do not apply anymore, SRSM gives us no clue as to how behavior might change.

The REMM model emphasizes the resourceful adaptation expressed by rational choice behaviour. The searching, coping, groping and exploring behaviour summarized by resourcefulness is, according to REMM, not a given constant. Its force and intensity vary with the stakes perceived by individuals.

For example, take a primitive society of hunters and gatherers in which males are socialized into the role of the hunter and females into the role of the gatherer. Now let the population of this and surrounding bands increase so that the (biologically determined) stock of resources (edible wild animals, berries, etc.) is slowly depleted. What will happen? Men will continue to hunt and women will continue to gather but the marginal productivity of their (role-conforming) efforts will decline. The number of individuals for whom role-conforming behavior is the most rewarding behavior will also decline, creating a situation in which [REMM] will act less and less as a SRSM. Although [REMM] does not allow us to say what alternatives become more rewarding than the ones prescribed by role expectations, we know that [REMM] is resourceful, i.e., he is able to learn and is inventive. Let one band begin to check its population growth (say by infanticide); let another band create taboos about hunting and gathering on certain days, thus restricting exploitation of the resources; let a third band use a number of their hunters to guard a territory against other bands. Each band is resourceful in a different way, but the third band has created a totally new situation: within its guarded territory, any further resourcefulness of its members will benefit only its members, greatly increasing the marginal value of this kind of behavior to the band. Attempts to keep edible animals within the guarded territory is likely to lead to the domestication of some of them. Attempts to increase yields from plants within the territory is likely to lead to the search for new edible plants and to some knowledge of seeds and cultivation. Slowly a sedentary agricultural society will develop with very different roles than the hunting and gathering type of society. Because the scarce resources in an agricultural society (livestock, arable land) can be accumulated, resourceful and maximizing behavior will lead to much more social inequality than existed in a society in which scarce resources (wild animals, berries, etc.) could not be accumulated. (Ibid., 102)

The SRSM model implicitly assumes that the cost-return pattern encourages established role playing and penalizes deviations, or that individuals are immune to variations in cost-return patterns induced by perceived environmental changes. The second assumption cannot survive an impressive array of observations bearing on human behaviour. The first assumption may hold in a stationary society but fails unavoidably in an evolving environment. The resourceful character of man may be sufficient in societies with less tightly or rigidly structured institutions to change cost-return patterns continuously against conformity with inherited role playing. Lindenberg (1985) refers in this context to an interesting and telling inconsistency in Parsons' (1951) argument:

for Parsons, the stable, integrated process of interaction in terms of established role relationships 'is the fundamental point of reference for all dynamic motivational analysis of social process' (p. 205). Yet, he also observes that 'changes in the fundamental reward system of the society' are continual. 'Organizations are continually restructured, old ones die out or decline while new ones rise, and the role structure within those which continue is altered' (p. 513). The 'fundamental point of reference' is so much built into SRSM that the observation about continual change in the 'reward system of the society' cannot possibly lead to an adjustment in the simplifying assumptions. The individual as a focus of initiative is thereby permanently placed *outside* the framework of analysis. (Ibid., 103)

Other examples may be addressed to elaborate the flaw in the SRSM model. Demsetz (1967) examined the adjustment in the property rights structure of an Indian tribe. Before opportunities of exchange with white traders emerged the land was the communal property of the tribe. When trade opened up, the existence of communal property imposed severe externalities. Maximizing behaviour led to overhunting. The consequence induced, resourcefully, a change in social institutions. Communal property was replaced by family property in sections of land. This institutional change removed the externality and modified the incentives to hunt. The consequences of a family's action were no more imposed on the whole tribe but were born directly by the family.

The evolutionary consequences of resourceful, evaluating and rational behaviour can be explored in many more cases. During the past 20 years major changes in the US financial sector have occurred. Deregulation and financial innovations have produced radically new patterns, a process exemplifying the resourceful coping and exploring of new circumstances by rational agents. A climate of increasing risk and uncertainty coupled with deregulation eroded the cost-returns advantage of conforming behaviour. Shifting cost-returns patterns fostered the search for new services, financial instruments, and technologies. The result is a massive change in the nature and structure of the financial sector over the last few decades. Similarly, the institutional change expressed by deregulation emerged in response to the effect of persistent inflation on interest rates.

We need not confine our vision to the modern world. The historian Lynn White (1962) traced in a fascinating book many medieval technological innovations, including the stirrup, the harness for horses, the heavy plough, a more functional chimney, and the functional button. These innovations resulted from the endeavours of many struggling and rational individual agents. They were not imposed by society. They modified warfare, changed the social structure and raised agricultural productivity. The feudal system resulted, as well as the possibility of the emergence of cities. Such an evolutionary course confounds SRSM. The dormant REMM behind the SRSM emerges, destroying the correlation between the optimal cost-return pattern evaluated in terms of individuals' preferences and the inherited conforming behaviour. The pattern of evolutionary adjustments reveals that the SRSM model offers at best a limited description of reality with a misleading sense of an analytic undertone.

One fundamental issue should be noted here. The resourceful coping and exploring of opportunities produces innovation and the evolutionary process but remains essentially unpredictable; this point has been developed more generally by Sir Karl Popper (1957). The innovations mentioned above were hardly predictable. We know from the history of technology that even innovations based on known inventions were not readily predictable. The jet engine was judged by leading experts to be useless for airplanes at a time when its technology was fully understood, with prototypes already used by the German Luftwaffe. The unpredictability emphasized here does not mean that no useful prediction can be made in socioeconomic affairs. Conditional predictions bearing on limited ranges of our relevant reality are often possible and may have useful information value. We may also frequently note the general nature and direction of substitution processes induced by changes in underlying conditions. An understanding of the general nature of socio-economic evolutionary processes is not prohibited by their essential unpredictability.

Changes in values
The formation of social values in a process of social interaction between self-interested individuals has been elaborated in earlier sections. At any moment of time, the inherited social capital of norms and rules also influences individual behaviour. Social values exert this influence via individuals' more or less conscious or deliberate acceptance of them as part of their relevant constraints or preferences. Changes in values can be expected to modify behaviour. This relation certainly forms an important component of socio-cultural evolution. In order to approach this complex problem some other issues need to be laid aside first. We need to examine critically the sociologist's inclination to explain changes or differences in observed behaviour in terms of changes in values. It is argued here that nonvaluational components of constraints frequently offer a better and more relevant explanation.

Any explanation of social phenomena involves two analytic levels, individual behaviour on the first level and social interaction on the second level. The first level centres on individuals' preferences and constraints. Variations in social phenomena are traced in the context of this social analysis to changes in individual preferences or constraints. The traditional research strategy pursued by economists usually concentrates attention first on changes in the constraints. We should not deny, however, that changes in preferences can and do occur. But the basic sense of the traditional strategy cautions us to invoke difficult to assess and mostly very speculative changes in values. Sociologists, on the other hand, have no reason to be cautious. The sociological model contains no interrelation between preferences and constraints. OSAM suggests that changes in values constitute an explanation of observed social variations. But the social analysis developed by economists reveals a basic ambiguity in this strategy. It never seems clear what 'changes in values' really means. The mode of discussion about values unavoidably produces this result. Values have no structure and their relation to individual behaviour remains obscure and purely impressionistic.

An examination of the interrelation between preferences and constraints reveals that changes in values may actually involve two radically different situations with substantially distinct interpretations. A change in the preference field (i.e. the value system) typically produces a change in behaviour represented by the location of the optimal choice in the preference field, even with unchanged constraints. But a change in the constraints modifies behaviour with an unchanged value system. The change in the optimal choice induced by the change in constraints is associated with a change of the relative evaluation (i.e. marginal rates of substitutions) of the various relevant objects, aspects, etc. A change in values may thus mean a change in the value system or a change in relative evaluations within an unchanged system. The former proceeds independently of any change in constraints, whereas the latter is caused by and reducible to changes in constraints. The importance of this difference may be emphasized with the aid of some illustrative examples.

Hirschman (1982) noted, in a survey of intellectual assessments of social organizations co-ordinated by markets, that western societies were rather suddenly gripped by self-interest early in the last [eighteenth] century. Some observers in the eighteenth century lamented that the sense of 'rank and ancestry' was destroyed by a spreading self-interest. Such arguments suggest a fundamental change not just of the preference field, but in human disposition. They suggest that self-interested behaviour is a historically bounded and conditioned human pattern. However, historical experience and sociobiology tell us a different story. The range of actions expressing self-interested behaviour have substantially varied over humankind's historical experience. The binding institutions of a society committed to rank and ancestry narrowed the opportunity set for the optimal choice. Moreover, the binding social conditions sometimes produced corner solutions. A wide range of behaviour thus appeared unrelated to any self-interest, but revealed the immediate influence of society. This argument fallaciously believes that self-interest does not exist because it is not given sufficient opportunity to express itself. A change in constraints, enlarging the opportunity set, provides then a greater range of admissible actions expressing innate self-interest. The evolution of an institutional structure incorporating expanding capitalism thus created the impression of a change in values. But a closer examination of behaviour under a wide range of confining social conditions reveals patterns of resourceful adjustments. Such patterns frequently involve adjustments modifying the degree, extent and content of the social constraints. We should not infer the reality of life and behaviour, just from a blueprint of a society. The occurrence of self-interested behaviour can be demonstrated with substantially less subtlety in the cases of officials of the church and lay persons who benefited from a system of rank and ancestry. The erosion of this system and rising opportunity for self-interested actions by others were naturally deplored.

Many social patterns usually attributed to variations in attitudes and orientations are at least partly the consequences of different constraints. Major differences in mutual attention between individuals has been observed under a variety of circumstances, usually explained in terms of different human values. Such variations in possibly altruistic behavior may occur. There is, however, an alternative explanation based on variations in constraints and applicable to cases of different population densities. Attention is an activity with a substantial time dimension. Social contexts involving large differences in encounter densities necessarily induce very different allocations of available time to attention expressed in terms of relative frequencies of encounters. In regions with low encounter density much more attention will be invested *per* encounter than in regions with high-encounter densities, even with the same set of values. Attention in low-encounter regions may even be reinforced by the fact that it is a good investment under the circumstances. In regions with low population density, people rely more on each other for mutual help in emergencies.

Anthropologists and sociologists have commented on the behaviour of African farmers in British colonies. Farmers appeared interested in achieving only a very modest target income. Although it seemed obvious that their values differed from those of western farmers, further examination revealed an entirely different situation (Jones, 1960). Some colonial regimes imposed severe constraints on farmers, who were obliged to sell to an export monopoly setting the price at a comparatively low level. The incentive to produce suffered as a result. Without such constraints, African farmers behaved much like western farmers in terms of their responses to incentives.

More examples could be assembled, but the essential nature of the issue should be recognizable. The problem arises because the sociological model includes neither constraints nor structured preferences which yield a generalized substitution potential.

J.R. Ewing and the commissar

This paper argues that norms and rules of conduct guiding the behaviour of members of a social group emerge from the interaction of self-interested individuals, and that prevalent values depend on the range of existing institutional arrangements. These arrangements determine opportunity sets and therefore the resulting specific location of choice in the preference field. The social order thus influences prevailing values, at least in the sense of relative evaluations (at the margins).

There is a more fundamental issue to be addressed. A well-established intellectual tradition deplores the human qualities, or lack of them, fostered under the social order represented by capitalism. Greed and narrow egotism are considered characteristic of capitalism; the competitive patterns permeating this social order encourage conflict and obstruct the development of cooperative attitudes. Capitalism apparently systematically selects lower quality values and rejects higher quality values. Even Frank Knight (1935) joined with the voices in this chorus. This theme dominates the modern intelligentsia, and the media often expresses the views of this group. J.R. Ewing in the television series *Dallas* provides an interesting case. He is representative of the human type conditioned by capitalism. The Marxian literature expressed most forcefully and in the most explicit context the view that overriding self-interest (equated with egotistical profit maximization) is the unavoidable consequence of private property. Individuals cannot escape the conditioning imposed by this social order. It determines the roles its members have to play, and there is no escape from this fate within the given order.

However, the sociological model promises the possibility of salvation. A radical change in the social order totally modifies the nature of role assignments and thus of behaviour. The suspension of private property is actually supposed to achieve more: man becomes liberated from his bondage to a false consciousness. He will be liberated in particular from self-interest, which atrophies under socialism, and noncommercial values of higher quality can flourish. Okun (1975) developed a similar idea inherent in the sociological model. In a market-oriented context with private property men are slaves to commercial values and profits. Within nonmarket contexts and in the absence of private property, behaviour will be guided by noncommercial values expressing higher and socially more constructive values.

Theologians have in recent years attended to this issue with increased intensity. The quest for a new man in a new society already occupied the church fathers. Protestant and Catholic theologians of our day jointly deplore the evils of capitalism and the destructive power of self-interest. Thus they propose to mobilize political forces with the intention to change the social order. In one form or another, their dreams direct our attention to an ultimate socialist society, ideally guided by theologians.

Their position appears somewhat ambivalent at this point. They do wish to create, like the Marxists, a society of liberated men and communal love. But it is not clear whether they generally accept the Marxian argument based on the sociological model and thus expect a natural evolution of a new man. (Gutierrez, the leading liberation theologist in South America, explicitly acknowledges the Marxian version of the sociological model as a foundation of his arguments.) On the other hand, they may find it simply necessary and justifiable to force members of society into the *forms* of a community but without its *substance*. An apparently moral society would thus coercively impose its will on immoral man. But an adequately functioning moral society satisfying theological dreams can only be expected on the basis of the sociological model.

The basic issue in all these laments and dreams is the relevance of a fundamental assumption separating the REMM and the sociological model. The latter describes man as an empty slate to be filled with writing by the social order. According to REMM man is born with a conditioning biological disposition. This disposition includes, among other basic strands, self-interested behaviour. A self-interested behaviour *and* disposition occurs in man's makeup independently of the variation in the social order. It follows that the somewhat naive equating of self-interest with profit-seeking misses an important point. This procedure is bound to conclude that an abolition of private property removes profits and profit-seeking evaporates. But profit-seeking is one particular component in the total expression of self-interested behaviour. The pattern of the manifold expression of self-interested behaviour depends, in contrast to the basic self-interested disposition, on the social order. Profit-seeking (or better, private wealth accumulation) is certainly an important expression of self-interest in a market economy. But self-interest does not vanish under the social arrangements of a socialist state. This is the crucial point. REMM alerts us to the fact that self-interest expresses itself in such a social context in very different and unexpected ways. A detailed observation of the behaviour of peasants, managers, workers and party functionaries would note the resourceful coping of the various social groups in response to their circumstances. The reality is usually hidden in a dense veil of words that extol the human virtues of a socialist society in accordance with the blueprints of the dream. The widespread willingness of the intelligentsia to accept the words as the final reality is a remarkable phenomenon. We may here usefully remember the difficulty that (then) General Eisenhower had in countering Marshall Schukow's argument that communism stands for brotherly love, communality and equality.

The pervasive occurrence of self-interested behaviour implies a similarly pervasive occurrence of competition. Recognition of this basic fact seems hard to accept for many people. Substantial conditioning causes competition to be perceived as a social process confined to market-oriented systems. No competition could possibly arise under socialist institutions. Competition was supposed to characterize capitalism; and co-operation, on the other hand, socialism. The invisible-hand analysis revealed, however, the co-operative aspect built into social processes under capitalism. It is important to emphasize the counterpart of this for socialism, viz., the competition inherent in its social structure. One will not discover this competition by looking for capitalistic patterns of competitive behaviour. The nature of competition depends sensitively on the social order and prevalent institutions. Individuals' resourceful coping and experimentation ultimately determine the nature of competitive mechanisms operating in society. The REMM model suggests that socialist institutions foster a pattern relying substantially on the interplay of personality traits and political relations or on the use of the accessible political apparatus.

A careful evaluation of alternative social orders should examine in particular the human patterns produced under different competitive processes. We need to explore specifically the consequences for human integrity, honesty, mutual attention and concerns, friendships, etc. One specific aspect deserves particular attention. Socialist and market-oriented systems differ substantially in the range of choice available to members of society expressed by the acceptable range of voluntary transactions. Under socialism, the representative individual remains to a large extent permanently exposed to the 'commissar'. Under capitalism, exposure to the J.R. Ewings is a matter of choice. We can avoid them, but we cannot choose to avoid the commissar. The sociobiological component of the REMM model would suggest, moreover, that the Ewings are hardly monopolized by capitalism. Such character types will randomly emerge both under socialism and capitalism. But they will nonrandomly drift to and be selected for commissar positions. They probably exhibit superior survival characteristics under socialist institutions. In fact, a socialist society offers to the potential Ewings of the world substantially more promising opportunities. It is noteworthy that Lenin deliberately manned his enforcement apparatus with the worst human dregs. He could be sure that a merciless extermination of undesired classes would be faithfully executed without conscience or scruples, possibly even reinforced by some enjoyment.

The supergame analysis of a prisoners' dilemma situation (summarized earlier) demonstrates the emergence of co-operative behaviour among self-interested people. Such co-operative features foster some measure of mutual attention and regard. The institutional arrangements of a socialist society offer in contrast little incentive to be attentive to its 'customers'. Moreover, the tension felt between the reality of life under socialist institutions and the official ideology is hardly conducive to the spread of higher values. We should of course also recognize the permanent human ambivalence of capitalism. Greed, meanness and ruthless egotism can indeed be found; but we observe also expressions of important noncommercial values and humane considerations. The institution of an open society allows a wide range of experimentation in the search for values and meaning. It also allows any individual to protest injustices observed and to convince others to pursue a course in life attending to (in his view) better values. This human ambivalence seems ultimately the best one can expect from fallible individuals. On the other hand, the attempt to create a moral society imposes rigid institutional arrangements with incentives which are not conducive to the cultivation of humane values.

Final remarks

This essay continues the basic line of argument developed in a previous article by Brunner and Meckling (1977). The arguments emphasize that different visions of society encountered in the intellectual world and the public arena are ultimately determined by conflicting hypotheses about the nature of man. This thesis was elaborated in that article in terms of differing views about the working of political institutions and the conditions fostering corruption.

This essay has described the crucial properties of the conflicting views of man in more detail, with special emphasis on neglected or frequently misunderstood aspects. It argues that the political and intellectual battle bearing on the future of Western societies rests finally on the empirical relevance of the conflicting visions of man. More immediately important at this stage, however, is a fundamental cognitive issue confronting social science. This essay argues that the sociological model offers no useful hypothesis about social reality. It rejects the shoe-box theory of knowledge implicit in much of the social science literature. It argues that REMM offers a unified approach for social science, so that social science can emerge as a single discipline with branches differentiated (similar to the situation within economics) by a variety of problems, aspects and issues. This development will depend to some extent on further developments in the analytic formulation of basic ideas. This includes in particular the emergence of social values, the evolution and the influence of values, and quite generally the nature of the relation between social values, individual behaviour and the social interaction of individuals. Work is already underway to incorporate social norms and rules into the basic choice model. The conditions inducing modification of this social capital with public good characteristics need to be explored in detail. Of particular importance for our times is a deeper understanding of the attrition in this social capital. One suspects that the range of conflicts will grow and that pervasive uncertainty will increase, with further consequences for economic affairs and social coherence. The course has been laid out, and it presents us with a challenging research agenda.

References

Alchian, Armen A. (1950) 'Uncertainty, evolution and economic theory', *Journal of Political Economy*, June, 211–21.

Axelrod, Robert A. (1984) *The Evolution of Cooperation*, New York: Basic Books.

Barrash, David (1979) *The Whisperings Within*, New York: Harper & Row.

Brunner, Karl and William H. Meckling (1977) 'The perception of man and the conception of government', *Journal of Money, Credit, and Banking*, February, 60–85.

Brunner, Karl and Allan H. Meltzer (1971) 'The uses of money: money in the theory of an exchange', *American Economic Review*, December, 784–805.

Buchanan, James (1975) *The Limits of Liberty*, Chicago: University of Chicago Press.

Demsetz, Harold (1975) 'Toward a theory of property rights', *American Economic Review*, May, 347–59.

Durkheim, E. (1961) *Moral Education: A Study in the Theory and Application of the Sociology of Education*, New York: Free Press.

Hirschman, Albert O. (1982) 'Rival interpretations of market societies: civilizing, destructive, or feeble', *Journal of Economic Literature*, December, 1463–84.

Horkeimer, Max (1947) *Eclipse of Reason*, New York: Oxford University Press.

Jones, William O. (1960) 'Economic man in Africa', reprinted from *Food Research Institute Studies*, I(2), 107–34.

Knight, Frank H. (1935) 'The ethics of competition', in *The Ethics of Competition and Other Essays*, Freeport, NY: The Book for Libraries Press, 41–75.

Kristol, Irving (1978) *Two Cheers for Capitalism*, New York: Basic Books.

Lindenberg, Siegwart (1985) 'An assessment of the new political economy: its potential for the social sciences and for sociology in particular', *Sociological Theory*, Spring, 99–113.

Meckling, William H. (1976) 'Values and the choice of the model of the individual in the social sciences (REMM)', *Schweizerische Zeitschrift für Volkswirtschaft und Statistik*, **4**, 545–60.

Nozick, Robert (1974) *Anarchy, State, Utopia*, New York: Basic Books.

Okun, Arthur M. (1975) *Equality and Efficiency: The Big Trade-off*, Washington, D.C.: Brookings Institution.

Parsons, T. (1951) *The Social System*, Glencoe, Ill.: Free Press.

Popper, Karl (1957) *The Poverty of Historicism*, London: Routledge & Kegan Paul.

Schotter, Andrew (1981) *The Economic Theory of Social Institutions*, Cambridge: Cambridge University Press.

Schumpeter, J.A. (1942) *Capitalism, Socialism and Democracy*, New York: Harper.

Umbeck, John (1951) 'Might makes rights: a theory of the formation and initial distribution of property rights', *Economic Inquiry*, January, 38–59.

White, Lynn (1962) *Medieval Technology and Social Change*, Oxford: Clarendon Press.

7 Reflections on 'theology and the social order'*

The battle about the future of our society

A pervasive battle embroils western democracies. This battle determines the future of our societies. It shapes the reality of government veiled by the traditional forms and influences the nature of economic organization. The outcome decides whether men will live under governments with limited powers and relying for the solution of society's economic problems on private property and markets, or whether men will cope with an unlimited government exercising a vast system of detailed controls over all affairs. The fate of human dignity and freedom is at the very centre of this issue. One side argues that an economic organization based on markets and private property functioning under a limited government offers the best chance for the emergence of freedom and human opportunities. The other side on the political and intellectual battlefield claims that human dignity can only flourish under a socialist organization of society.

For some years now, the Christian churches entered the ongoing battle. Theologians addressed with rising frequency basic socio-political issues of our time. Theology claims with increasing vigour that it offers a message for a social order answering man's basic humanity (*menschengerechte Ordnung*). The concern for social justice as a manifestation of central theological themes dominates general content and detail of theologians' approach to the '*menschengerecht*' social order. It is moreover understood that the realization of social justice requires political action. Such action unavoidably engages the powers of the state in a manner guided by the socialist dream. Socialism in one form or another appears thus as the natural consequence of the Christian churches' social message. This consequence conditioned by a particular view of justice and the nature of political institutions cannot be explained in terms of the biblical message purportedly at the heart of theology. One wonders, therefore, whether the current theological theme involves an historical adaptation induced by confrontation with an environment offering competing and appealing orientations beyond the traditional churches. This question poses a serious problem for a social scientist but need not be further considered for my present purpose. My reflections address some crucial intellectual strands in what I would label the 'theology of socialism'. The thoughts

---

*   Working paper, University of Rochester, 1986.

developed remain therefore somewhat provisional at this stage. More or less subtle variations in theologians' thinking need some further attention in the future. My present note addressed to our fundamental problem concentrates on issues of particular importance in this context.

Some strands constituting the 'theology of socialism'

The central theme is justice. Justice is the motivating force and the criterion in all attempts to reshape the social order. An array of pronunciations and writings make the sense of 'justice' quite clear. Justice is equality, i.e. equality in the distribution of goods and services. A rigid outcome pattern or 'end state' conception thus prevails. We read in the context that this is the only admissible notion. It is the proper concept determined by 'reason of linguistic logic' (*sprachlogische Grunde*). We are also told that we all share equally in Jesus' love for man and share equally in the promise of salvation. So it seems to follow that justice must mean equality in distribution. Some further theological elaborations explain that equality corresponds to the theological sense of justice as an 'adequate and necessary' response dictated by love. Justice as equality also expresses the theological concept of 'communality of love' (*Verbunden-Sein in Liebe*). There occur, however, some 'dialectic qualifications' of the theme. Justice is also attributed to a social process *approaching* equality. We hear thus that justice means a 'decline of human suffering'.

A central strand associated with the theological interpretation of justice is the requirement that society form a 'moral community'. All social relations should be guided by deep personal involvement and affection. The standards of a (good) husband–wife relation should characterize *all* human interaction. The personal meaningfulness of face-to-face encounters, of *Du und ich*' relations, should permeate the whole society. Thus emerges a sense of encompassing solidarity which unites all persons in love and mutual compassion. It follows that 'to be a Christian is to build a community in the world and to oppose capitalism'. Capitalism is the great enemy of a 'moral community'. It destroys such communities, destroys 'human values' and human dignity. The theologian Moltman recognizes in capitalism only 'power and the will to power'. He concludes, therefore, that economic reality must be subjected to moral theology.

The theological argument is occasionally supplemented by some (rather casual) empirical considerations. One theologian cautions us that theological arguments need not only be concerned with a human and just social order, but also with the realizability of their proposals. The question was thus addressed whether the political imposition of equality would not destroy the wealth of societies and actually produce general poverty. But we are told that there is no empirical evidence linking inequality with wealth-creating institutional conditions. Equality could thus be expected *not* to lower production and the available future resources. Myrdal is approvingly quoted to assert that equality produces a socio-psychological environment actually raising productivity and production. Hollis Chenery's work at the World Bank is used to demonstrate that greater inequality does not raise real income of a nation. Such short references typically exhaust the attention invested into the feasibility requirement.

Some critical reflections on the basic strands
My comments are organized in three sections. The first section examines the basic fallacy associated with the requirement that the whole society be shaped into a moral community. The empirical issue concerning the relation between wealth-creating institutions and equality is considered in the second section. The last section discusses some general aspects of theological discussions bearing on the social order and the role of political institutions.

Moral community and its political solution
The idea of a 'moral community' confronts us in our times with an appealing force. But the belief that we should transform whole societies into a moral community is a dangerous dream. Hayek analysed this dream in a series of lectures and Buchanan examined the social role of 'moral communities' in a somewhat different context.

Hayek explores the evolutionary heritage of our sense of solidarity. Men lived for the dominant part of their history from the earliest beginnings millions of years ago in small bands. Men could not survive alone and neither could large groups at the time. The survival of the small band depended crucially on the close mutual interaction between members of the band. The survival process was most particularly conditioned by close personal relations among the members. Small bands evolving a sense of solidarity within the group experienced larger survival probabilities in a hostile environment. This sense of solidarity emerged as a biological product of the evolutionary process. But within the last ten thousand years social and cultural evolution went beyond the small band. Larger groups began to form for a variety of reasons. This process extending the social group posed difficult adjustment problems still observable at this time. The mechanism of social coherence appropriate and adequate for the small band could not operate in the greater societies. The sense of solidarity built into man's biological heritage requires, apart from exceptional and comparatively short-run experiences for its useful operation, 'face-to-face' groups with essentially personal relations among all their members. Once men moved into the broader range of larger societies, the personal face-to-face contacts remained confined to a small sub-group within the greater society. Most of the encounters involve somewhat impersonal contacts and relations. This replacement of personal relations with dominantly impersonal relations in the greater societies is quite unavoidable. Personal relations in an extensive face-to-face context involve much investment of time and effort. It is physically impossible in the context of the natural constraints on our life to extend a pattern of personal relations to all members of the greater society. Social coherence requires, under the circumstances, alternative mechanisms. The 'moral order' of the greater society, to use Buchanan's terminology, cannot rely on the processes operating within the small band. Buchanan emphasizes the role of organized religions which can and historically have provided important mechanisms of social coherence. The Greek city states of antiquity and the formation of the Jewish nation out of clans and tribes over many centuries offer interesting examples. But organized religion was not sufficient for the detailed functioning of greater societies. Such functioning depended on the emergence of abstract, impersonal rules of conduct guiding all members of society. Hayek examined over the past decades in great depth the socio-cultural evolution of these rules and the spontaneous order (i.e. the 'invisible-hand order') created by the interaction between individuals. These rules of conduct, frequently uncodified and somewhat implicit, constitute a crucial building block in the moral order contributing to the survival of greater societies. The erosion of such rules would endanger the survival of any society over time.

The theological perspective of social justice may be explored somewhat further. This perspective anchors the social experience of justice on the Christian concept of love. The 'communality of love' finds ultimately an 'adequate or necessary' expression in a society exhibiting the patterns of social justice. The argument thus presents the Christian 'communality of love' as a sufficient condition for the social justice envisaged by the theological perspective. This proposition, once we accept the notion of Christian love used in this context, is hardly controversial. The problem arises, however, on confrontation with reality, in the attempt to extend the moral community (i.e. the desired communality of love) to the whole of the greater society.

The social evolution into the greater society occurred within a time span quite short when compared to the processes of biological evolution. The conditioning by these processes working over hundreds of thousands of years of living in small bands still affects our thinking and emotions in modern times. The biological heritage is not fully attuned to life in the greater society with its specific coherence mechanism adapted to the new social environment. Thus emerges a perennial tension for men living in greater societies. The moral order based on abstract, impersonal rules of conduct clashes with man's biologically inherited desire for a 'moral community'. This tension explains why the dreams of transforming greater societies into a 'moral community' are so appealing to many persons. An understanding of the social coherence mechanism operating in smaller groups and larger societies reveals, however, the impossibility of such transformation. Whatever knowledge we possess informs us that the greater society cannot function without a pervasive reliance on abstract, impersonal rules of conduct guiding impersonal relations. Attempts to *impose* a moral community, implicit in any appeal to a political solution, create a reality far removed from the motivating dream. The politically imposed attempt requires an extensive political apparatus with a massive concentration of power in the state. This institutional apparatus shapes incentives and opportunities which coping and groping man will exploit to his advantage. This advantage will be most particularly available to the small group of persons controlling the apparatus. The transformed society continues to rely, moreover, to a *large extent* on abstract and impersonal rules. The operation of these rules proceeds, however, in the context of rigid institutional arrangements lowering the chances for human dignity and creative freedom.

The fundamental fallacy of the theological argument can now be recognized as follows. The uninhibited recourse to a 'political solution' for the realization of a Christian perspective reveals a peculiar and unfounded intellectual somersault. The sufficiency condition mentioned is essentially inverted. The pattern of social justice appears as a sufficient condition of the communality of love. Theological insistence on the link between social justice and the communality of love combined with the proposed recourse to political action unavoidably requires the above inversion. We find, however, no reason in this theological argument why this inversion should be accepted. It remains totally obscure why the institutional implementation of social justice should be expected to produce a pervasive pattern of Christian love.

Some theologians may concede the fallacy of the inversion. They may also recognize that a communality of love coinciding with an extended society remains an eschatological dream. But the achievement of 'social justice', understood in the prevalent meaning, still remains in their view a feasible option. The more or less explicit goal is a 'moral society for immoral men'. The appearance of moral behaviour is imposed coercively by suitable institutional implementation. The institutional imposition thus coerces essentially immoral people into a pattern satisfying the standards of a 'moral society'. A crucial problem burdens, however, the creation of a 'moral society' based on the police powers of the state. Economic analysis informs us since Adam Smith that institutional implementations typically produce unanticipated results poorly correlated with the motivating intentions. The institutional imposition of 'social justice' is thus quite likely to generate behaviour patterns difficult to reconcile with any meaningful sense of a 'moral society'. This problem is closely related with issues surrounding the concept of 'social justice' so singlemindedly advanced by theologians with very little thought and justification. These issues are addressed in the next section.

The theological decision to invoke the police powers of the state as the instrument for the creation of a moral society poses in my judgement a fundamental dilemma for any serious Christian. The biblical message emphasizes that man is created in God's image. Man is provided with conscienceness, a conscience and an innate freedom. He is free, in particular, to choose his course in life. But the Christian message also emphasizes that man bears a responsibility toward other persons. Ultimately man is, moreover, accountable about what he did with his freedom. The 'theology of socialism' essentially rejects a crucial dimension of the Christian message. The recourse to the state's police powers means that man's freedom to choose a course of responsibility should be revoked. If man fails to pursue the course of a life in responsibility (*'ein Sein in Verantwortung'*) then he need be coerced into a pattern copying this behaviour. Dostoyevsky's Grand Inquisitor would approve and so do theologians who deplore the 'condemnation to freedom' in an open society. It is crucial in the Christian vision that God did not create a pre-programmed man automatically following the way pointed by Jesus. Man's freedom is decisive for the *moral* dimension of his course in life. There is neither morality nor immorality without this freedom. There is, in particular, no moral virtue in behaviour resulting from coerced copying of the desired patterns. The 'moral society' discussed above possesses thus no moral quality whatsoever. This society is difficult to reconcile with the basic Christian message. The 'moral order' of an open society, relying on private property and markets as society's organizational devices, offers the Christian message better opportunities.

Two short comments need be added bearing on the 'communality of love' or a 'moral community'. Koestler understood the depths of this problem. He had Rubaschow meditate in jail on the 'love for mankind' proclaimed by one of our major ('the' major?) 'secular religions' competing with the Christian churches for man's mind. He reflects in particular on the irony that this abstract love for mankind never gets translated into love or compassion for particular persons. The latter experience on the contrary the impersonal cruelty of an all-embracing apparatus. Koestler–Rubaschow recognized that the institutional enforcement of 'love thy neighbour' as a sweeping social pattern only destroys love and compassion with freedom.

My critique of theologians desiring to transform a greater society into a 'moral community' guided by deep personal relations neither implies nor suggests the historical irrelevance of moral communities or of wider-reaching organized religions as a strand in our moral order. Men's behaviour demonstrates that there is a demand for 'moral communities' and organized religions. It is precisely the greater society based on abstract impersonal rules which permits the satisfaction of this demand. Greater societies with open institutions allow the competitive supply of moral communities and organized religions.

Men are not 'condemned to freedom in a faceless world'. They can satisfy their elemental desire for the protective womb of a moral community and *choose* among the alternatives available. But all moral communities and organized religions must also abide by the moral order of the greater society constituted by the prevailing abstract rules of conduct. The rejection of this moral order leads to the anarchy not of individuals, but of conflicting moral communities.

Equality and the conditions of wealth-creation
At a recent meeting in Vancouver of the World Council of Churches, one of its officials was reported to have asserted that the scarcity problem had been solved and our attention need be shifted therefore to the problem of distribution. It appears that the theological concerns for distribution, and most particularly for equality in distribution, assume that conditions of wealth-creation exist independently of the conditions regulating distribution. A Swiss theologian actually asserted in his discussion of social justice that no empirical evidence connects the two sets of conditions. The issue is sometimes approached with the question whether more inequality in distribution raises productivity. The answer is usually negative as many cross-country data would suggest. One concludes therefore that removal of inequality will not lower the (God-given) productivity of society. But the question is ill-designed for our purposes and misses the core of the problem.

The conditions fostering the 'wealth of nations' have been described for many years in the economic literature. But the pieces of theological literature so far examined thoroughly neglect the contribution made by economic analysis since Adam Smith. The wealth of nations does not depend on their respective power or their possession of natural resources contrary to some intelligentsia clichés, also encountered among theologians, well integrated into the Brandt Report on the North–South Dialogue. In order to express this fact somewhat more precisely, power and natural resources are not a necessary condition for wealth. Power, in particular, contributes nothing to the *creation* of social wealth. A comparison of nations over time and at any particular point in time supports this proposition. The power of Soviet Russia is incontestable but the wealth of its population, i.e. its living standard, is and will remain comparatively low. On the other hand, a number of powerless small nations belong to the wealthiest groups in the world. Similarly, Argentina's natural resources seemed to promise more than 50 years ago a golden future, but it wallows for decades in economic stagnation.

The crucial conditions fostering or discouraging the creation of wealth are located beyond natural resources and powers in the institutional arrangements of a nation. Institutions which connect an imaginative effort with its expected benefits are both a necessary and sufficient condition for the creation of wealth. Our historical experiences indicate that a wide array of social organizations loosen the connection between investment of effort and capture of its benefits. Nations will languish and stagnate whenever such arrangements increasingly dominate their affairs. Many nations in South America, Africa and even in Europe demonstrate this basic fact. The adoption of the Russian model of agricultural organization in Tansania systematically obstructs agricultural development and assures that the domestic supply of food will linger at a comparatively low level. More generally, the pattern of price controls imposed on agricultural products in many Third World nations is the major cause of inadequate food production and the large fraction of potentially usable but untended land.

The institutional conditions fostering the creation of wealth operate thus by linking the conditions of distribution with the conditions of production. Men respond in general to the expropriation of their product and produce, save and invest less. Centuries of economic analysis and research establish this fundamental fact, a fact singularly neglected in theologians' attempt to praise the Christian virtue of an egalitarian or socialist organization of society. Theologians thus sell the 'socialist package' on the public market with the promise that the 'moral society' can be realized at no expense in terms of economic welfare.

An attention to power and national resources as sufficient and necessary conditions of wealth naturally follows from any failure to understand the relevant processes and institutional arrangements. This failure fosters the misconception that wealth is somehow 'given' independently of man's social arrangements. And a theological perspective naturally emphasizes national wealth as a gift of God. Unavoidably, as production is presented to be invariant with respect to all possible distributional patterns 'moral theologians' can propose with inpunity an egalitarian solution. Natural resources may occur with an abundant richness and still be useless. They must be exploited first before they contribute to the wealth of a nation. And this exploitation will depend on prevailing institutions. Social arrangements and political patterns frequently obstruct the wealth-creating exploitation of natural resources. These resources are indeed given, but their *discovery*, *use* and their resulting *contribution* to national wealth is not 'given'. They depend on man's imaginative activities conditioned by the expected private benefits shaped by the prevailing institutions. Similarly, the emphasis on power is hardly astonishing when the institutional context of wealth-creation is not understood. Indeed, once we feel that 'everything is given' then distribution appears to operate without a social function. It serves simply the product of power. So power can also be used to achieve the 'moral society' at no social costs. One additional comment may be necessary. 'Power' exercised by various monopolies and political institutions does affect the actual distribution. But power does not create social wealth, it redistributes it among the members of society. And this redistribution shapes incentives which tend to lower the nation's wealth.

Wealth-creating institutional arrangements do not assure equality in distribution of goods and services. And so it follows that these institutions cannot be accepted in a 'moral society' shaped in accordance with the canons of moral theology with its views of social justice. The egalitarian message is of course easiest to sell if the public can be assured that implementation of the message produces neither economic stagnation nor a loss of freedom. We suspend attention to the latter issue and attend here to the relation between 'inequality and productivity'.

The inequality observed under wealth-creating arrangements reflects partly chance and partly variations in the natural or social endowments of persons. Variations in natural endowment exist and affect the prospects of the persons involved. Variations in social endowment (inherited social position and wealth) also exist with similar effects on prospects. But we need to caution against some exaggerated views associated with the existence of the social endowment. The open institutions encouraging the creation of wealth also foster a 'circulation of the elites'. We find in general a pervasive 'regression phenomenon'. The average income of children whose parents had more than average income is usually *below* their parents' income and children of parents with below-average income experience in the average a higher income than their parents. We observe a 'circulation of the elites' even under the more rigid structures of medieval society. Barbara Tuchman noted in her story about fourteenth century France that the average span of a family in the aristocracy lasted only three generations. There is little evidence for the inherent operation of a 'poverty trap' condemning the poorer groups to a permanent fate in poverty. The occurrence of a 'poverty trap' is a typically associated with social conditions and arrangements obstructing the process of general wealth creation.

A similar condition affects the relation between inequality and productivity. There prevail in many nations, and most particularly in nations of the Third World, institutions and political arrangements which simultaneously raise inequality and lower productivity. Many changes occurring in the past decades impaired social productivity and probably sharpened inequality in several respects. Inequality is thus far from being a sufficient condition of social productivity. Economic analysis offers no claim for a positive correlation between inequality and levels of social productivity. Economic analysis tells us, however, that chance and variations of the endowment naturally associate some measure of inequality with the operation of wealth-creating institutions. Inequality appears thus as a *necessary* condition of wealth-creating processes. But we cannot say that larger or more rapid wealth creation will in general raise the degree of inequality. Neither can we say that larger inequality will raise social productivity. The crucial aspect for wealth creation and economic progress is not inequality but a set of institutions which provide incentives for the application of personal (and socially) productive efforts. And with the demonstrable fact of man's basic nature this requires institutions which produce reasonable expectations that the benefits resulting from efforts applied can be captured by those investing the efforts.

The notion of justice, miracle explanations and the institutional vacuum

The notion of justice   The observable fact of inequality in the distribution of goods and services seems to dominate all other concerns in theological thinking about the social order. We may also perceive this concern as an expression of the belief that an egalitarian state will solve major human or social problems. The egalitarian state is hopefully expected to raise the level of human dignity and freedom or to offer better opportunities for the realization of higher human values. Equality in distribution becomes thus the manifestation of justice. The degree of inequality measures under the circumstances the extent of injustice prevailing in society. As at least one theologian makes clear, there is no other theory of justice. This assertion is a remarkable expression of ignorance or wilful intellectual blindness. We owe to Hayek and Nozick a serious and important alternative view of justice. This alternative view seems somewhat neglected in the theological literature bearing on social problems.

The egalitarian position is an especially straightforward version of the 'end-state' or outcome-pattern notion of justice. According to this view, justice is defined in terms of specific patterns to be imposed on the outcome of the social process. The alternative notion characterizes justice in terms of selected properties of the social process largely independent of the *specific* outcomes emerging from the process. The evaluation of the criteria is however not independent of the *general* outcome produced by social processes satisfying the selected criteria. The process view may also be somewhat modified by suitable general constraints on the outcome. The negative income tax offers a useful example in this respect.

The independence of 'processual justice' from specific and detailed outcome patterns makes it essentially unacceptable to ambitious political or 'socially committed' intellectuals. It should be obvious that this notion of justice violently clashes with any view requiring specific distributional results in one form or another. It certainly clashes with most of the prevailing justifications for a welfare state and *all* justifications for a socialist society. It appears that the two opposite notions of justice could be usefully evaluated by some detailed examination of their respective consequences.

The two notions of justice determine very different attitudes about the state and the role of political institutions. A process conception is compatible with a minimal state. It is in particular consistent with the basic justification of a constitutional government, i.e. a government with a range of political institutions explicitly and deliberately limited to broad functions of protection and the provision of the most obvious 'public goods'. A process conception hardly justifies detailed interventions or extensive replacement of market mechanisms by political institutions based on budget or police powers. On the other hand, the patterning of outcomes produced by the social process required under an end-state conception invokes extensive structuring with the aid of political agencies. In the absence of political institutions arranging or controlling the use of resources, the required patterning of outcomes will necessarily fail. Voluntary private transactions produce results substantially deviating in general from any particular end-state principle. The enforcement of this principle can thus only proceed in the context of political institutions controlling the use of resources with the application of appropriate police powers. The array of political institutions associated with any end-state principle implies moreover that the range of voluntary transactions and private opportunities is coercively reduced. Nozick concludes on this point that 'end-state and most patterned principles of distributive justice institute (partial) ownership by others of people and their actions. These principles involve a shift from the classical liberals' notion of self-ownership to a notion of (partial) property rights in other people.' The partial loss in self-ownership follows unavoidably from the operation of the political institutions according to the intentions of the end-state principle selected.

The tradition of economic analysis reveals the fundamental flaw built into the end-state conception of justice. It makes us understand that political institutions are not governed by their original intentions and justifications. Every institution characteristically evolves specific incentives and disincentives embedded in the arrangement. The persons exercising the policy powers associated with the institution and other persons confronting the institutions respond to these incentives and disincentives. There emerges, under the circumstances, unintended and unanticipated behaviour patterns which threaten the realization of the end-state principle. Further institutionalization of police power will be necessary to correct these unintended outcomes in order to modify the results according to the requirements of the end-state principle.

The problem addressed in the last paragraph deserves some further discussion. An examination of Rawls's theory of justice may clarify some relevant aspects. It should also be noted, incidentally, that I found no trace of recognition of Rawls's theory in the theological products investigated thus far. It appears that Rawls could not survive the unreflected and arbitrary egalitarian precommitment exhibited by many theologians. Nozick convincingly argued that Rawls's criterion of justice (the difference principle) operates in the nature of an end-state principle. The difference principle imposes a constraint on the admissible distributions of resources or entitlements. Social arrangements are ranked according to this principle by the comparative position of the least-endowed or least-'entitled' social group. The discussion of Rawlsian theory proceeds in this context according to a long philosophical tradition which essentially *disregards* the institutional context associated with constraints on distributional patterns. These contexts form the crucial material for the proper examination of the social consequences associated with any attempt at institutionalization of end-state principles. Such principles do not operate automatically and by themselves in a vacuum. New opportunities for political manipulation are unavoidably created with any political agency designed to enforce the patterning required. These opportunities result from a fundamental ambivalence of all political structures. I have described this problem on another occasion with the following words: 'The starting point is the fundamental ambivalence of government. This ambivalence is expressed by the mixture of benefits and risks associated with a political structure.' Hobbes and others have eloquently described the state of anarchy. We also note that anarchy or unstructured social processes appear, at most, as transition phases. Nozick and Buchanan offer a lucid and detailed analysis of the transition from anarchy to elementary forms of political structure. Both authors demonstrate that anarchy is not a viable state and spontaneously evolves forms of political structure. This spontaneous evolution requires no mysterious 'social' forces beyond man's interests and resourceful endeavours. The social interaction between self-interested men produces the transition into patterns of political structure.

The benefits to individual members of these associations are very substantial indeed. Their security is enhanced and the political structure encourages an economic organization raising the productivity of labour and thus improving the standards of living. This story is clear enough. But the emergence of political structure shifts opportunities and incentives in a peculiar way. Nozick addresses this aspect when he notes that already the constitution of a 'minimal state' unavoidably involves some measure of coercive redistribution of wealth.

In a state of anarchy, each individual has essentially three options: to engage in productive activity or voluntary exchange; to allocate efforts to protect his produce and possessions; or to engage in piracy and acquire wealth through violent extraction from others. It should be obvious that only the first option increases social wealth. The occurrence of the other two options determines the brutal uncertainty of anarchy and the vanishing incentive to invest any resources or efforts for returns beyond the immediate horizon. The appearance of political structure replaces this vast uncertainty confronting the individual with some 'rules of the social game' represented by specific political institutions. The crucial fact requiring some emphasis in this context bears on the range of options available to individual members of the political association. These options include, of course, the application of resources controlled by individuals to produce wealth. The evolution of political structure enhances and safeguards this option. But the very nature of political institutions cannot prevent alternative options. Their existence offers opportunities to invest resources in political activity, guided by implicit (or explicit) rules of the institutions, in order to extract wealth from other members of the political association. The occurrence of this option implies the existence of a last option, i.e. investment in political activities designed to fend off extraction of wealth threatened by the political activities of other groups. Under both anarchy and a state of political structure, individual agents can thus acquire wealth by productive effort and voluntary exchange or via extractions from others. The ambivalence of political structure is defined by the persistence of socially nonproductive private wealth extraction. This kind of wealth acquisition does not distinguish anarchy from systems exhibiting political structure. The crucial difference appears in the range of uncertainty and the existence of rules confining the processes of wealth extraction in the context of political structure. Such rules lower the uncertainty confronting individual agents. This difference implies that opportunities for socially productive wealth acquisition via productive efforts and voluntary exchange are enhanced. Such enhancement assures the viability of the political structure. Viability is endangered whenever political institutions develop complex and pervasive incentives for potential wealth extraction. There emerge, under the circumstances, ever-widening organizational efforts to exploit the political process for persistent acquisition of wealth at the expense of others. The change from anarchy to political structure may also be formulated as a shifting mixture of a positive-sum game. The negative-sum game looms so large under anarchy that most political structures offer a better mixture of positive- and negative-sum games. But the crucial fact is that every political structure necessarily contains characteristic incentives yielding its own peculiar range of negative sum games.

Fundamental ambivalence of political structure thus induces forces which make it quite unlikely that any institutionalization of an end-state principle offers a stable solution settling around the desired pattern. The existence of political institutions tears the 'veil of ignorance' and encourages their extensive manipulation for the self-interested purposes of all those with better information and access to these agencies and their respective police powers. The consensus established behind the 'veil of ignorance' and expressed by a class of distributions thus eventually dissolves when members of the social group actually confront the institutional reality of the end-state principle.

This dissolution of the consensus implies, furthermore, that the end-state principle remains a ritualistic invocation with an essentially different reality. This reality will remain untractable relative to the demands of the end-state principle, even with systematic attempts to enlarge the police powers and rectify the 'aberrations'.

The ambivalence of political structure, discussed in the passage quoted above, bears with particular force in the 'end-state' notion of justice. The detailed and extensive implementation required by this notion confronts us with a serious obligation. Feasibility and realizability requirements emphasized by Karl Popper and acknowledged by at least one theologian, essentially address a crucial question. This question ultimately involves an intelligent evaluation of social and human consequences produced by the institutional implementations. The hopeful expectation that an approximation to social justice lowers human suffering would seem to impose a cognitive obligation on the theologians. This obligation would require a careful examination of the nature of possible implementations. This examination needs to be extended to the actual working of the institutional arrangements and also needs to consider their effect on human values and dignity. This cognitive obligation is remarkably neglected by theologians' intrusions in social affairs. One is sorely tempted to speak about a peculiar immorality exhibited by many theologians expressed by the violations of a moral commitment to the required cognition.

The conversion problem and the institutional vacuum   Theological thinking on social matters shares with the Marxian literature the general sense of condemnation of social organizations based on private property and markets. Such organizations are condemned for their alleged basic human failure. The theological literature also shares with the variety of Marxian versions the general idea that a conversion of society in accordance with socialist principles assures the human liberation, i.e. 'the solidarity in freedom and the freedom of solidarity', expressing the canons of Christian love. But the common rejection of capitalism and the common dream of paradise on earth still leaves a crucial difference between the theological and Marxian positions. The difference reveals and also explains the intellectual vulnerability to Marxian intrusions of theological thinking in these matters. Socialist analysis offers a specific argument justifying the feasibility of the conversion into a socialist society. The argument relies on a sociological model of man. This model asserts the encompassing cultural and institutional conditioning of man's behaviour. Man is in all respects the product of his social environment. Specifically, attention to 'commercial values' and profit-seeking behaviour is imposed on man by a society based on private property and markets. Such attention and behaviour will vanish once a 'commercial society' has been

replaced by a social structure without private property and markets. A socialist organization fosters different attention and behaviour. Self-interest and
self-realization will disappear under the new social condition which will
produce a 'new man'.

The social analysis developed by economists over the past 200 years
denies the relevance of the sociological model underlying the socialist argument. This alternative model of man emphasizes that 'self-interested' behaviour is a basic biologically conditioned pattern invariant over history or
cultural-institutional conditions. The *specific* content of such self-interested
behaviour will, on the other hand, be affected by environmental conditions. It
follows thus that self-interested behaviour cannot be equated with profit-
seeking. Such behaviour will continue in the context of non-profit institutions
including the Vatican and the World Council of Churches. The search for
power and influence replaces in these contexts the pursuit of profits. Men
quite generally pursue actions which promise to help or improve their position. The nature of these specific patterns depends on the institutional context. The wide array of institutional contexts within a nation or between
nations at any one time, and also observed over history, offers much evidence
bearing on the comparative relevance of the sociological model supporting
the socialist argument and also the end-state conception of justice. The
hypothesis introduced by the Scottish moral philosophers in the eighteenth
century revealed, moreover, the fallacy of a central socialist view accepted by
theologians. They chastise the destructive influence of competition permeating capitalism. They fail to understand in this context that competition reigns
in all societies. The nature and forms of competition change with the socio-
political organization and so do the human characteristics associated with
these organizations.

The socialist argument is sufficiently explicit to reveal its empirical inadequacy. There is, in contrast, simply no theological argument bearing on the
conversion to the desired egalitarian state. We obtain no clue why the egalitarian state will actually function according to expectations. A major strand of the
Marxian argument seems, moreover, explicitly rejected by the theological argument. Socialist analysis usually emphasizes the '*Eigengesetzlichheit*' of the
social process, i.e. loosely expressed as the internal self-determinism of the
social process. This self-determinism removes any independent feedback
from individual self-realizations to the total behaviour of society. It assures,
thus, the conversion into a socialist state and the latter's workability. Theologians leave us at best with an unexplained miracle. Somehow politics can
be invoked to produce the transition and all will work according to the good
intentions.

The intellectual vacuum of theological thinking on this point reveals a
fundamental flaw. The discussion of the alternative notions of justice empha-

sized that desired outcome patterns reflecting an end-state principle need be addressed with some institutional implementation. The discussion also emphasized the basic problem associated with such implementation. Theological arguments apparently avoid this problem. We do not learn what kind of detailed institutional implementation is required to produce an egalitarian state. And we do not observe any attempt to cope with the consequences of the incentives built into the required institutions. We learn very little beyond the invocation that an egalitarian system expresses the canons of Christian love and satisfies the moral community to be achieved. This involves a remarkable intellectual quantum jump. The Christian love permeating a moral community produces equality in distribution. So a somehow imposed egalitarian system can be expected to reflect or produce this moral community. The egalitarian state does not emerge from voluntary individual decisions and transactions. Such emergence would correspond to an egalitarian state based on Christian love practised by all members. But this dream world cannot reasonably be expected to ever exist. The theological dream of an earthly paradise motivates, therefore, ultimately a political activism. This activism expresses a programme of coercive actions by the state imposing the result on all members of society. The moral community of Christian love must thus be *enforced* by open-ended and extensive police powers of the state regulating the detail of all personal life. As the theologian Moltman puts it: 'Moral theology should control society.' The Ayatollahs seem to agree. Our latter-day theological message conveys thus that people either reluctantly express the Christian love expected of them, or else the state will make them behave according to patterns desired by moral theologians. Some people might feel that this is a travesty of the essential biblical message, and, incidentally, involves just plain bad social analysis.

Our responsibility, and a moral responsibility it is indeed, is to cope with the real world we live in. We have, in particular, a responsibility to examine what kind of institutions raise the chance of human dignity and freedom. This obligation is thoroughly neglected in theological thinking. Economists contributed over the past decades substantially to our understanding of behaviour patterns fostered by institutional arrangements. We learned to appreciate the consequences of different property rights structures. We learned, in particular, that the juxtaposition of 'competition' and 'co-operation' as characteristics of alternative social organizations obscures the relevant issues. Competition and co-operation prevail in all social organizations. What actually characterizes alternative social organizations is the *nature* of prevalent competition conditioned by prevailing institutions. Competition for profits hardly characterizes the behaviour in the Vatican, the World Council of Churches, the public agencies in Washington or the Kremlin. But competition for power, influence and status controls behaviour in many subtle variations. We are ultimately confronted by the question *what kind of competition* offers better chances for human dignity and freedom. This question is never considered in the theological literature. This failure is unavoidable once one interprets 'capitalism' with Moltman as 'power and the will to power'. This characterization abysmally fails to penetrate beyond the shallowest clichés of our time. It fails to understand the crucial operational characteristics of market institutions and of a socialist organization. Socialist organizations concentrate great and detailed power over a wide range of society within the state apparatus. Competition is thus shifted from markets and wealth acquisition to power and political status. But this competition has no social function raising the wealth of societies. The power concentration of socialist societies creates strong incentives to influence agencies and political institutions which control vast resources. The power problem emerges with particular force in all attempts to implement an egalitarian state. It requires severely coercive arrangements with a dominant political apparatus. This apparatus will need a total monopoly over all economic affairs and needs to control all resources in order to proceed in accordance with an egalitarian principle. The same apparatus will enjoy, moreover, a total concentration of political power. It is most unlikely that such an apparatus will be the subject of democratic control by members of society. The democratic *forms* may continue to exist. But they will operate as conduits of control and the exercise of power by the apparatus. The egalitarian state thus confronts an ancient problem. Who guards the guardians? The institutions imposing the political control necessary for a coercive distributional pattern yield little chance for a feedback control from members of society. Such feedback could and probably would violate the canons of moral theology applying to distribution. The striving for an egalitarian state thus produces a social system with extreme concentration of all power in the hands of a small group, the nomenclatura of a theological state.

Final comments
The excursion of theologians into the range of social affairs offers a remarkable phenomenon. The recommendations made and the social goals or standards advanced float in a peculiar intellectual vacuum. No adequate analysis appears and the problem of institutional implementation associated with any social reform remains buried. The occurrence of shoddy or irrelevant arguments replaces an application of useful analysis. I note in this context the casual disregard of alternative notions of justice. The reader may note in particular the argument that 'linguistic logic' determines economic equality as the sense of social justice. This is simply pretentious nonsense. The reader may also consider that 'equality in distribution follows from the fact of all men's even participation in Jesus' love'. The logic of this argument resembles medieval philosophers' claim that there are

seven openings in the human head and thus follows the existence of seven planets circling the earth.

The excursion into social affairs without social analysis may be associated with some distinct intellectual situations in theology. Protestant theology increasingly developed an essentially atheistic position. An atheistic theology does involve of course a strange use of language. But the term is still used to cover actually a denial of the essential Christian message. One wonders therefore whether the attention to social affairs and the achievement of 'paradise on earth' emerged as a substitute for the vanishing content in modern Protestant theology.

Another strand can be encountered in Catholic thought and teaching. My perusal of some representative literature reveals a subtle hostility to economic analysis. This attitude is expressed in various modes. The reservations hardly involve relevant cognitive considerations. They usually involve objections to the use of a positive analysis. Analysis should 'integrate' social valuations and reflect in its execution these valuations. But a positive analysis formulating and assessing empirical hypotheses is our best hope to understand the world we live in. It is also a necessary instrument to understand the probable consequences of major and minor institutional reforms. The imposition of valuational constraints generally endangers the ultimate cognitive purpose. And thus results the confusion of 'ought' and 'is' or 'ought' and 'probably could be'. This state of affairs encourages some historical speculation. The pronounced reservations addressed by the Catholic church towards the natural sciences in the sixteenth century gradually vanished over time. But reservations to the cognitive enterprise did not disappear. They shifted simply their ground and re-emerged with a different address: the social science expressed by economics.

This theme deserves much more extensive attention on a future occasion. It involves ultimately a study of the nature and conditions of the intellectual obstacles built into contemporary Protestant and Catholic theology. These obstacles render it difficult to accept a competent economic analysis. The same obstacles also condition theologians to become easy victims of Marxian rhetoric and thought. This situation does concern all of us. The future of the few free societies with 'open institutions' is at stake. But sincere and well-meant advice from 'moral authorities' may well lead us into a society with little chance at human dignity, more entrenched poverty and less human opportunity and freedom. Ultimately the assertion of 'moral authority' in the absence of any serious cognitive effort hardly offers us any reliable guide.

8 Religion and the social order*

Introduction

Economics emerged in the late eighteenth and early nineteenth centuries with a broad social vision. The vision narrowed during the later phases of the nineteenth and the first half of the twentieth centuries. The profession lost some perspective on many social problems but gained substantially in analytic articulation. This period was, however, an important phase in the development of economics. It also prepared the groundwork for the revival of a broad perspective involving the systematic application of the articulated analysis to an open-ended range of social and institutional problems. Public-choice theory, property rights analysis and Gary Becker's excursions into 'sociology' may be mentioned among the pioneering efforts. This intellectual revival of an old theme, implicit in Adam Smith's work, has expanded into a broader stream over the past 20 years.

A major human experience in society has so far hardly been touched by this intellectual development. The 'human animal' has been characterized in many different ways. But one particular characteristic deserves more attention on our part. Beginning in the grey zones of prehistory, 'religion', understood in a wide sense, shaped human experience. It was expressed by specific attitudes and practices. Religion has persisted throughout history as a pervasive social phenomenon to this day. It may be tempting to argue that 'religion' and its associated institutions and activities should remain, or should stay, outside the intellectual pursuits of economists. But the remarkable persistence of 'religion' over the history of human experiences suggests that man, whatever else he may be, is essentially also a 'metaphysical animal'. Such persistent aspects of human experience should not be excluded from our vision and their existence needs to be acknowledged by our intellectual endeavours. Some of the intellectual developments of recent years, most particularly Hayek's evolutionary approach, may offer clues to an understanding of this essentially human phenomenon. The religious experience is moreover associated with social institutions and behaviour bearing on the socio-economic conditions of society. Two major groups of problems may be addressed under the general heading of 'religion and the social order'. One group addresses the social role of religion. This includes also the role of its

* Editor's note: The article 'Religion and Social Order' was not complete at the time of Karl Brunner's death. I chose to include this article in its unfinished form as a symbol of Karl Brunner's commitment to his work.

institutional establishment with the codification of a specific vision. The other group examines the socio-political views cultivated by the institutional apparatus of a religion. The paper explores most tentatively the first issue and moves more firmly on a specific strand of the second issue that is of particular importance at this time.

The social role of religion

The origins of the phenomena collected under the term 'religion' seem closely associated with the evolution of human consciousness. Karl Popper emphasized in his evolutionary analysis the non-explainable major evolutionary quantum jumps: the emergence of complex life forms after billions of years of only the simplest life forms, or the emergence of consciousness and ultimately of human consciousness. This last step offered an opportunity for human self-awareness and languages as a rich instrument of communication. This cultural evolution interacted with the biological evolution affecting the brain and specific organs. The human animal thus developed an apparatus to cope more effectively with the environment, a biological and cultural apparatus which offered the conditions for a more flexible adaptation to changing circumstances.

The apparatus that improved the survival conditions of man also made him aware of his existential problems. Birth, hunger, disease and death intruded on his expanding consciousness. And so did many intricate regularities of nature observed over time. The basic existential problems and both the nondramatic regularities and the dramatic events of nature challenged the human animal's growing consciousness. Interpretations and stories emerged weaving the array of experiences together. These stories addressed in particular experiences beyond human control. They expressed, moreover, an incipient human urge to probe 'behind' the immediate experience. Thus emerged over the ages encompassing orientations about man's position in life, his relation with his environment and the universe. This evolution shaped not only the greater societies formed along the rivers in Mesopotamia and the Nile but also the diversity of more or less minor tribal groups all over the world (Topitsch, 1958). These world visions typically combine factual descriptions, expressions of values, valuations and normative prescriptions together with interpretations based on prevalent understanding. This peculiar mixture determined the social and intellectual effectiveness of the encompassing orientation. The three distinct components of the world vision reinforced their effects and receptivity. It characterizes the history of religion to this day.

The crucial aspect for our purposes still needs attention. The evolution of religion, as an encompassing orientation guiding man through life, should probably be understood as an essential component in the formation of human societies. Hayek's argument offers a useful starting point for our purposes. The survival of the small band which originally dominated human existence depended on a close integration of its members. A well-understood pattern of co-operation and a reliable attention to specific functions in the collective hunt for animals, the search for other foods, or the preparation of tools was a necessary condition for successful survival. The pattern is supported by norms of conduct and values which guide and control the behaviour of the members in the group. Such norms and values foster behaviour which ensures the group a better chance in the competition for life. These elements of group cohesion probably did not occur in the form of a simple enumeration, but in the context of stories about the life of the group. They acquired thus binding and steering power. This slow development forms an important part of an early segment of mankind's cultural evolution. This process reflected, similar to biological evolution, a pervasive experimentation by 'nature'. A wide array of stories and orientations emerged providing a valuational anchor to maintain the groups and identify their members. Such arrays persist to this day even in western societies. The survival value of these stories for the various groups probably differs. Some may be better attuned to encourage behaviour beneficial for the group and others may be less successful in this respect. Some orientation with their valuational guidelines may encourage more flexible behaviour, or more probing or easier adaptation to new circumstances.

At some stage, in various parts of the world, a major transition of social organization emerged. Smaller bands coalesced in the 'greater society'. This imposed radical readjustments and adaptations in man's life. The valuational context of the small bands' steering behaviour was quite inadequate to provide coherence and guidance for the members of the greater society. The norms of conduct successfully structuring the highly personal interaction of a 'face-to-face society' could not apply to the pervasively anonymous relations in the greater society. This is Hayek's central theme. The greater society requires new coherence mechanisms. They are in general not imposed by an authority but emerge from the interaction between self-interested individuals as an unplanned and undesigned by-product of the social process. Abstract rules of behaviour, or norms of conduct, replace in the greater society the personal relations of the small band. These rules and norms guide the behaviour in anonymous and impersonal encounters characterizing the greater society.

But the formation of the greater society involves probably more. It is at this stage that 'religion', i.e. the encompassing orientations, enters with an important social function. The transition from the moral order of a face-to-face society to the moral order of a greater society was a difficult and prolonged process stretching probably over many centuries. It was moreover not the purely spontaneous and voluntaristic process implicitly conveyed by Hayek.

Stages of conquest and subjection very probably intervened. But even in this case the rules and norms of the whole moral order constituting a society became more effective, more acceptable and more attentively observed in case they were incorporated within an emotionally binding context. The general orientations provide this function. The abstract rules and norms are in some sense 'sanctified' as an integral component of the embracing orientations. The disadvantage the greater society suffered in comparison to the emotionally anchored moral order of the small groups is overcome in this manner. An emotionally appealing context is provided to strengthen the authority of rules and norms. It should be clearly understood that the role of religion is not exogenously imposed, as it were, but evolves simultaneously and in interaction with the rules and norms. The prevalent religion thus enhances the coherence of an otherwise anonymous society. It also contributes to its self-awareness and self-understanding. This identification forms an important part of the coherence contributed by religion.

Some historical examples may be usefully adduced to exemplify my point. Religion appears as an important element in the formation of ancient Israel. The process leading from family clans to tribes and ultimately to a nation was protracted and frequently fragile. The associated evolution of an identifying orientation substantially supported this process. This orientation probably absorbed elements from diverse sources and from different historical backgrounds and experiences. They were gradually integrated into a stylized and more or less unified story. We note also among the ancient Greek cities an important social and political role of religion. Special days were devoted for religious exercise, reinforcing the self-awareness and self-understanding of the social group formed by the city. The Roman practice of acknowledging the emperor as a god, confronting the fledgling Christian community with a serious spiritual problem, also reflected an aspect of the social and political role of religion. It is not clear to what extent this practice was seriously understood in a literal sense. But even if we doubt this, the integrative function of the practice reflects the ancient role of religious visions and practices.

The socio-political influence of religion as a stabilizing and controlling orientation can be recognized also in the political exploitation of the pervasive demand for such orientation throughout human history. Some of the ancient orientations contained a major socio-morphic component (Topitsch, 1958). The vision of a universal order, most explicitly expressed in stories about stars and gods, appears to result from a projection of the society's social structure, i.e. the universal order is conceived in analogy to the prevailing social order. Once structured in this way the orientations are used to sanctify and justify the existing socio-political order. The link between the ruler and a universal order established in this manner deepens the awe which members of society feel toward political power.

The merging of a 'religious organization' with the political apparatus prevailed throughout most of human history. We can hardly attribute this persistence to mere chance. My argument bearing on the social role of religion suggests on the contrary that it expresses an important social function of religion in a specific mode. The idea of a connection between religious visions and a socio-political order, or of a metaphysical anchor for society, have not faded in our modernity. The Catholic church offers not only liberation theology but its official stance accepts the basic connection as an essential element of its social doctrine. Protestant theologians argue explicitly that political power should be guided and applied in the light of advice provided by theology. And then of course we observe the Ayatollah society and quite generally the Islamic fundamentalist movement. We need to mention in this list also the modern communist state. Keynes (1932) understood very well that communism appeared on the historical horizon as a new religion with all the traditional components which characterize such general world orientations. This holds also for its institutional trappings. We do encounter of course the question whether and to what extent communism as a world vision and metaphysical foundation of a power structure is seriously believed by the members of society. It may be taken more seriously as an orientation by persons and groups outside the communist bloc. Even so, it is noteworthy that this orientation with its institutional trappings and rituals continues to be exploited to justify the power structure and its policies. Ancient Egypt and medieval Spain offer two major examples from the past of the merger of political power with a religious control apparatus. However different the two situations, they coincide in the extensive use of the opportunities offered by religion to unify and control the country. Egypt in particular operated very much in the nature of a theocracy with a priestly class, supplementing the court's bureaucracy, supporting the Pharaoh to control the society with the help of an institutionalized orientation. The temples of Karnak and Abu Simbel reveal the vast resources invested for this purpose. The case of Spain may be understood as an attempt to use the religious feelings to unify the country after the final elimination of the Moors. It thus offered the king a useful instrument to enhance his power by using an existing and well-established religious organization. A similar situation characterizes the alliance between the Pope and the French king in order to destroy the Albigensian heresy among the rich and semi-independent dukedom of southern France.

Author's *note*:
Insert here section on separation between church and state; the role of capitalism in contrast to Tawney and Weber; the role of pluralism in orientations and the erosion of moral order with the withering of inherited orientations.

The general orientations existing and influential over human history did not operate on the human mind in a social vacuum. It was already noted that they were usually combined with a set of social institutions (organizations, customs, rituals, etc.) designed to guard the tradition and transmit it to posterity. We also observe here that cultural evolution introduced a wide range of experimental solutions expressing man's perennial attention, in one form or another, to his existential questions. The differences between Christianity, Judaism, Islam and Buddhism are indeed remarkable. This subject is, however, left aside. The interpretations and codifications of the broad underlying orientations is more immediately relevant for purposes pursued in this paper. We may also notice on this count vast differences between the world's major religious experiences.

My argument concentrates, however, on the Christian tradition, i.e. we consider the role and evolution of theology. The small Christian community of the first century hardly required extensive theological interpretation of the original message. This state could not persist, however. The faithful could not fail to note over time that their eschatological vision increasingly conflicted with reality. The second coming with the end of the world and the final judgment seemed suspended. Theological discourse emerged essentially over the early periods in order to resolve the ensuing crisis. A diversity of reinterpretations appeared over the following centuries until eventually the 'Roman interpretation' prevailed. The losers in this competitive struggle between contending theological interpretations and reinterpretations of the message were declared as heresies. Thus was initiated a process which endures to our days. The Christian message and its theology have been described as expressing over the centuries a constant search for a philosophical interpretation. Its evolution over almost two thousand years shows major changes in theology and fostered adaptation to reality and philosophical trends. Aquinas's *Summa Theologia* attempted to merge the inheritance of Greek philosophy with Christian theology.

Major theological reinterpretations and battles erupted during the reformation. Their relation to the socio-political context would be interesting to explore. A rough survey of European history suggests that such relations did affect the pattern of reformation. The contrast between France and Germany could be quite instructive in this respect. This short recognition of the problem must be sufficient at this stage. The nineteenth century witnessed again major adaptations in theological thinking. And the most recent developments, both in Catholic and Protestant theological thinking, show a further adaptation to the socio-political reality confronting the Christian churches.

A major competing religion has appeared on the horizon over the past century. Socialism, in one form or another, seriously contends for the public's allegiance beyond the membership of the socialist parties. The modern mind may also find it difficult to cope with the traditional rendering of the Christian message. The changes in the socio-political structure in western and Latin American societies over this [twentieth] century has raised the political influence of the social group below the median income. The incentive to adjust theology to this social evolution may have worked its will on contemporary theologians.

The adjustment of theology to a social message

General remarks
The most recent evolution of theology was probably conditioned to some extent by the interaction between basic elements of the Christian message and the emerging social and intellectual environment. The core of the inherited story conveys a promise of salvation and freedom from the burden of existential problems. The translation of the central message into an ethics guiding our behaviour during our finite life remained a perennial problem for the churches. It was comparatively simple for the earliest Christian community waiting for the 'second coming'. The problem appeared when the churches had to address the fact that the Christian community had to settle down for continued existence on this earth. The churches' teaching thus needed to reconcile its message with the human need to extract a living in a process involving a complex interaction between persons. A more or less subtle intellectual and emotional tension endured over the centuries in this task. The ethical question also found a variety of different answers over the long history of the different churches.

The central message and ethical problem made the churches' position in our modern world increasingly vulnerable. The intellectual revolution generated by Marxian ideas beyond the groups of professed or organized faithful challenged both the message and the moral position of the churches. This influence merged with a swelling trend of (non-Marxian) social critique that offered a similar thrust deploring the iniquities of the existing social and economic order. These influences merged into a broad and influential stream of an essentially socialist conception. One may easily be misled about this development by thinking in terms of explicit socialist parties and organizations. We may observe a substantial exposure to such ideas among non-socialist parties in Europe and the USA.

It is interesting to reflect that the appearance of socialism, as a vision and a programme, was importantly influenced by the Christian tradition. Topitsch (1958) demonstrated in detail the influence of various Christian traditions and heresies on Marx's philosophy and social vision. The idea of some sort of salvation and freedom from existential problems motivates much of socialism's appeal. Its vision and ultimate promise of a society without frustration and injustice exploits a verbal tradition and vision long cultivated by the churches in a very different intellectual context. The churches and theology found it necessary to cope with this threatening challenge to its inherited authority. Both were forced to consider more explicitly the question of the social and economic organization of human society. The message of the Bible does not necessarily translate into a programme for a socialist society. Such translations were frequently accomplished by various groups of bishops of the Catholic church, the liberation theologians and the World Council of Churches. We observe, however, beyond such translations a pattern exemplified by the social doctrine of the Catholic church and the pastoral letter of the US bishops. The Christian message is translated into an array of moral injunctions to be imposed on society and its economic life. These injunctions involve occasionally very specific details bearing on social and economic conditions. The implementation of these conditions and the nature and consequences of the institutions required are never explored, however. There simply appears to be a general sense that government and politics could always offer a solution.

There seems to prevail a deep aversion to the use of economic analysis in order to understand the nature of the issues addressed. This analysis poses a serious intellectual problem. It seems to endanger the goals formulated and is difficult to reconcile with the emotional commitment already invested. An interesting discussion of Catholic social doctrine reveals this problem (Koslowski, 1984). Economic analysis is not faulted on cognitive grounds, but for being too 'mechanical'. This objection translates into the explicit critique that it lacks normative postulates expressing desirable social values.

The aversion to economic analysis contributes to the churches' and theologians' vulnerability to socialist ideas and conceptions. The rhetoric of the churches resembles to a large extent the socialist rhetoric juxtaposing the iniquity and evils of our existing orders with the promise of a socialist society. This similarity of rhetoric is very seductive. It seems to have seduced an influential strand of churches and theologians to embrace arguments and ideas of the socialist tradition in the absence of any adequate analysis. The result is an intellectual position which produces some emotional satisfaction but offers a singularly flawed product. This flaw is not confined to details but affects the basic core of the intellectual position represented by liberation theology, the World Council of Churches, the Australian and Canadian Catholic bishops, some officials of Protestant denominations in the USA and in selected issues by the official Catholic social doctrine and the US bishops' pastoral letter.

Motivation and justification

A cluster of social problems is frequently mentioned as the motivating force of theological thinking addressed to questions of social and economic organization. We find listed here alienation, inequality in power and wealth, rampant injustice and poverty. Dependence on central industrial nations is particularly emphasized in Latin America. Alienation from work and between people expresses the increasing frustration experienced by people as a result of the sense of loss of control over their fate. It is a phenomenon unavoidably tied to the prevailing institutional structures associated with the concentration of power and wealth. The result is dehumanization and atrophy of human spirit. Piecemeal reform or repair of the existing structures cannot change the deplorable situation. A radical change needs to be accomplished. The Christian message advises all Christians to share their gifts received from God. In accordance with this message, so we read, power and wealth need to be shared among all members of society. Equality in power, wealth and income appears thus as a central objective. Society needs to be restructured to realize this goal. The arguments do not explicitly develop why inequality in wealth and power is unjust. It seems that all inequality in wealth means deprivation for some. This is tied to the admonition to share. Such sharing apparently must be imposed by political action in case 'the system' does not produce it spontaneously. Such restructuring creates a society, guided by the churches and theologians, which will realize human potential and exorcise alienation and oppression (or repression). The purpose of the whole endeavour is to create ultimately a true community. This community should express a brotherhood, or a fellowship, of man bound together in mutual love and attention.

The motivational force is thus determined by the rejection of the existing society burdened with evil and iniquity and the fervent hope of realizing a dream of a just society. The institutional restructuring centred on the redistribution of power and wealth follows from the two components of that motivation. This pattern closely parallels the socialist movement. All this is presented by the churches and theologians with a sense of 'moral authority' justifying their critique and their hope. One wonders unavoidably what the basis for this moral authority and justification really is. We can find some answer in a statement prepared by a (Protestant) theologian. He argues that 'the authority can rest only on the cogency of the argument that they advance' (Preston, 1987). He supports this position with a reference to the Bible which directs appeals to 'every man's conscience in the sight of God'. We read furthermore that 'theologians have a world view'. Others, for example the liberation theologian Gutierrez, justify their position in terms of the 'exact scientific character' of his argument. The writings appear also to suggest that the moral tone as such, expressed by the condemnation of existing evil and the lofty dream, assures moral authority. These justifications and claims challenge a critical examination of the argument. I do not wish to denigrate the dreams. It seems a part of our human experience. But a sympathy for this dream should guide us to consider carefully the nature of the social and economic organizations which offer the best human chance.

An unresolved issue

The reliance on moral tone and moral fervour offers no justification of the argument. Any argument addressing social reorganization as a means to achieve certain ends (the dream) involves statements beyond normative appeals and moral injunctions. It must invoke, in order to be complete, cognitive statements about the world and the working of political institutions, social and economic processes. The validity of such statements cannot be assessed on moral grounds or in terms of a moral criterion. The cognitive adventure expressed by the evolution of empirical science developed in its practice the relevant criteria to choose among contending alternative ideas in terms of the best correspondence with reality. Preston's argument is sufficiently ambiguous to be consistent with the requirement of an empirical analysis. The nature of the cogency emphasized is left unclear. We are not told what the relevant criterion of this 'cogency of arguments' should be. The appeal to the passage in Paul's Epistle to the Corinthians would even suggest some moral or ethical criterion. I suspect, based on the nature of the prevalent literature, that most church people and theologians would interpret Preston's requirement in moral terms. But this would not satisfy the requirement of the relevant cognitive justification. Consider, therefore, that it is addressed to cognitive cogency. Then we encounter the problem implicit in much theological thinking and most particularly even in official Catholic social doctrine. An earlier paragraph stated that this doctrine objects to economic analysis because of its neglect of 'values and norms'. The objection could of course not be answered by referring to the role of value systems expressed as preferences or the Hayekian analysis explaining the emergence of norms and rules in the social process. The objection addresses the absence of moral postulates. So let us ponder the consequences of adding moral postulates of one sort or another to our economic analysis.

Such postulates could be formulated as additional constraints on the behaviour of the various groups of individuals including policy-makers. This would most probably quite radically modify the logical context of the analysis. The juxtaposition of different implications, obtained with or without moral postulates, or with alternative moral postulates, would confront us with a choice. The resulting logical and empirical content needs to be assessed against relevant observation. The imposition of moral postulates would not suspend the requirement of systematic empirical assessment in terms of a relevant cognitive criterion. But the tenor of much of the writing suggests very different behaviour. In case the observable world fails to conform to the implication of an analysis subject to moral postulates, the churches and theologians seem willing and ready to invoke the police powers of the state to impose the desired pattern with the aid of an array of institutional restrictions. The cognitive commitment seems poorly developed in a theology addressed to matters of our empirical world. The aversion to the cognitive endeavour, represented by empirical science, practised by the Catholic church in order to protect its traditional orientation and interpretation of the world, became forcefully visible in the case of Giordano Bruno and Galileo Galilei. The church, however, made its peace with the natural sciences, at least with physics and astronomy. Some Protestant churches or sects still find it impossible to make their peace with the natural sciences, most particularly with astronomy and biology. But the aversion of the churches toward economics as an empirical science still lingers. They feel uncomfortable or threatened in their basic orientations bearing on man and society. The subsequent sections argue, however, that this aversion actually endangers their very motivation to examine the blueprint of a society offering all men and women a chance to shape their lives.

The 'new man' and 'socialism'

The cognitive ambivalence, hesitation or confusion in theological thinking directed to the world is nowhere more clearly visible than in the conception of a 'new man' and quite generally in its 'anthropology'. The laments about an imperfect human nature engrossed with a greedy accumulation of wealth and power resemble quite closely the condemnations characteristically advanced by the socialist literature. The capitalist system ensnares the human soul and mind and directs man's attention to lower values. Higher values expressed by mutual empathy, attention with a sense of brotherhood or fellowship cannot flower under the institutional condition of capitalism. The pursuit of profit and wealth suffocates the truly human values. A society attuned to Christian teaching must overcome this sorry state. A 'Kingdom of God' on earth seems to form the guiding paradigm. The socialists, most characteristically represented by the Marxian literature, invoke a social process transforming human nature to a pattern of mutual and pervasive attention approved by theologians. The abolition of private property, at least in the means of production, is supposed to emasculate the profit and wealth motive. The 'real human values' thus emerge and have an opportunity to develop. Mutual attention and altruism will eventually dominate the social process after suitable adjustments to the new institutional arrangements. A radical change in human nature and behaviour can thus be expected, according to this story. The theological story is not very clear in this respect. The emergence of a 'new man' is somehow taken for granted in some of the literature.

It also conveys a sense that the restructuring of society contributed to this human transformation. In general we obtain the impression that the 'new man' has a better chance to surface and overcome the 'old Adam' under social organization 'sharing' power and wealth.

This position of the churches and theologians involves a fundamental issue shared by the socialist conception. Their 'anthropology', or view of man, radically conflicts with the perception developed in some strand of the social sciences since the Scottish moral philosophers of the eighteenth century and reinforced in recent years by developments in biology. The total malleability of human nature in response to institutional restructuring, postulated by the socialist literature and implicitly in much of recent theological thinking on social issues, does not represent an adequate understanding of human nature operating in society. We need to recognize that men and women are not born as empty slates to be covered with any writing produced by the social context. People are born with a genetic endowment shaped by a long evolutionary process. The crucial aspect of this endowment is the self-interested nature and corresponding behaviour of men and women.

The nature of self-interest is frequently misunderstood. It should not be equated with egotism (Brunner, 1987). It essentially expresses the fact that human beings prefer, in general, to make their own decisions in accordance with their understanding of things. In particular, people do not willingly cede in general and irrevocably their right to make decisions about minor or major aspects of their lives. The concept is thus not empty but extends beyond the usual understanding of egotism and includes altruistic behaviour, friendship, family life, etc. (Brunner, 1987). This hypothesis about human nature offers a much better foundation for understanding the world than the expectation of actual or hopeful malleability into a 'new man'. In particular we need to recognize that human nature is invariant with respect to variations in institutional arrangements. This does not mean that institutions have no effect on human behaviour. The same basic nature expressed by self-interested coping and groping with the environment produces very different behaviour in response to the shifting incentive associated with variations in institutional arrangements. The resourceful and evaluating self-interest responds with a wide array of specific behaviour patterns conditioned by incentives in different social organizations. It is naive to believe that the abolition of private property and the removal of profit and wealth accumulation suspend any self-interested nature. They will simply redirect self-interested behaviour into other channels and directions. Profit-seeking and self-interested behaviour are not equivalent. The first is only a particular (and partial) expression of the latter operating under particular circumstances. The misinterpretation of specific behavioural adjustments as a change in basic nature occurs unfortunately much too frequently and produces substantial confusion in matters bearing on questions of social organizations. Such confusions surface in some problems in subsequent sections.

A digression may be considered first, however. It is worthwhile to examine the chapter on 'The Human Element' in Schumpeter's book *Capitalism, Socialism and Democracy* (1942). Schumpeter's discussion is remarkably flawed. He shares in some fashion the major problems of theological thinking. He emphasizes in one paragraph the decline of pecuniary motives among managers. The discussion reveals, however, a confusion between the basic and pervasive human feature of self-interest and some particular form of its expression. It fosters the illusion that a suitable change of institutions which removes one particular kind of expression of the basic pattern actually transforms men and women beyond self-interested behaviour. Theologians fail in particular to understand the interaction between self-interest and opportunities and the variation in *specific* behaviour produced by variations in opportunities. Such variations reflect shifting incentive structures channelling self-interested behaviour in different directions which yield very different expressions.

Schumpeter strangely misses the importance of shifting incentives associated with changing institutional patterns. He ponders whether and to what extent the life of peasants and workers would be affected by a change from capitalism to socialism. He concludes that very little, if anything, would change. This is really an astonishing statement made by one of this century's recognized economists. Some aspects of peasants' and workers' life will indeed be unchanged. Peasants continue to confront the changing seasons and the whims of nature. But both peasants and workers operate under very different organizational structures offering different incentives. A collective farm induces different behaviour than a privately owned farm or the private use of government-owned land. Even with privately-owned farms the peasants' behaviour will be quite different under socialism. The acquisition of resources for use in production and the disposal of output is quite differently organized. The opportunities for peasants and workers do differ substantially once we look more carefully. The variation of institutional arrangements within the socialist bloc (say Russia, Poland, Hungary, Yugoslavia) are already sufficient to establish my point. They are sufficient to produce substantially different performances of the economy in at least the most affected point.

The fatal illusion of a 'new man', reinforced by the confusion of the basic human nature invariant with respect to institutional differences with specific behaviour expressions responding or exploiting institutional variations, severely distorts the churches' and theologians' social vision. This illusion and confusion, at the very foundation of much of Christian social thinking, affects all the major strands of their intellectual structure bearing on society.

Poverty and justice

Poverty forms one of the major motivating forces of the churches' social concern. Their approach to poverty remains, however, remarkably undifferentiated. Poverty in the USA, Europe, India, Brazil or Africa seems to pose the same problems. Schumpeter (1942) commented in his examination of capitalism that further economic growth over a number of decades of the kind experienced during the nineteenth and early twentieth centuries would remove poverty as an important social problem. The response of the churches to such suggestions reveals inadequate attention to two distinct problems. One refers to the average level of real income and the other to the distribution of wealth and income.

Theologians seem hardly touched by Adam Smith's *Inquiry into the Wealth of Nations*. Their general economic illiteracy is nowhere more pronounced than on the first problem. The conditions which foster economic growth and rising standards of living over a broad range of the population are quite generally poorly understood by the churches and theologians. They fail in particular to understand the role of institutions and social organizations. They frequently emphasize the occurrence of natural resources and most particularly their ownership within some national boundaries. But the occurrence of national resources and their pattern of ownership neither explains persistent economic growth of a nation nor the average level of real income. Switzerland and northern Italy are among the wealthiest areas in Europe but have very few natural resources. Brazil is better equipped in natural resources than the USA but experiences a much lower living standard. South-western USA and northern Mexico shared a similar economic fate in the first half of the nineteenth century. Their respective general resource basis was not radically different. However, today the two regions seem worlds apart and the difference in average real income sufficiently large to encourage a massive flow of illegal migration from south to north.

These short allusions must suffice here. The crucial facts are well known among economists. The occurrence of rich resources does not necessarily express economic wealth, raising the average level of real income. The creation of wealth depends crucially on the prevailing incentives that encourage members of a society to improve their skills, develop their productive equipment and apply themselves with ingenuity and sufficient intensity to their economic pursuits. The best chance to produce a rising standard of living which gradually overcomes mass poverty emerges under an institutional arrangement which offers individuals a reasonable opportunity to capture the fruits of their endeavours. A system of open markets with free entry based on private property provides an institutional framework challenging imaginative efforts or explorative experiments over a wide range. Such institutions also encourage the exploration of natural resources and their use. The crucial difference in the wealth of many nations must therefore be recognized in the nature of their prevailing social institutions. The theological literature fails to comprehend that wealth is neither a gift of Nature nor of God, but the result of human effort unleashed by a suitable social organization which effectively exploits people's pervasive self-interested drive. It appears under the circumstances that the social dreams pursued by churches and many theologians actually endanger the opportunities to overcome poverty.

The tenor of the articulated dream reveals substantial ambiguity concerning 'poverty'. The evil seems not so much the low level of average real income but the inequality of distribution. The concern about poverty seems mostly addressed to the fact that there are people experiencing income below the average. This is judged to be immoral. Inequality of income is understood to mean deprivation. The comparatively higher incomes are acquired at the expense of the lower income groups. Justice requires under the circumstances that all members of society enjoy equal income and wealth. Theologians justified this social position in various ways (Brunner, 1986). One particular argument may be considered here. The Bible emphasizes the moral obligation of the wealthier members of society to attend to the poor and deprived. This moral obligation was reinterpreted by modern theologians into a right of the poor to be exercised against all persons with income or wealth above the average. This reinterpretation usefully accommodates the socio-political environment perceived by many theologians. It appears to me, however, irreconcilable with a moral argument and the Christian message (Brunner, 1986). The moral character of an action depends on the fact that it is voluntarily pursued. The person involved could have exercised his or her freedom to decide very differently. It is precisely this freedom which determines the moral quality of an action. We may express this issue deliberately in religious terms in order to recognize the theological flaw implicit in the translation of moral obligations of one party into legal claims of another party. If God wanted to ensure that man and woman always decide for Him he could have programmed mankind that way. But he did not. We are neither bees nor ants. We can choose, and this choice assigns moral meaning to our life. Coerced 'goodness' has no moral standing.

We encounter throughout the theologians' argument a red line. It is clearly exemplified by statements made by functionaries of the World Council of Churches to the effect that 'we have solved the production problem and now we need to attend to the problem of distribution'. Theological thinking apparently assumes that production and distribution are independent social processes with no feedback from distribution to production. Production and the accrual of wealth are, according to a prevalent church view, simply a gift of God to mankind, manna fallen from heaven independently of human effort, imagination and experimentation. The very formulation of the problem of production and distribution reveals the fundamental failure of the churches to exercise moral authority with a useful social vision. Its flawed 'anthropology' distorts its vision and obstructs recognition of the interdependence between production and distribution. Arbitrary redistribution of the results forthcoming from production modify incentives and opportunities confronting agents with a negative effect on the use and development of resources. Some may object that the initial (i.e. before redistribution) distribution of income is essentially random and just a matter of good or bad luck. Chance certainly plays an important role in this process. All endeavours suffer under a pervasive uncertainty about the outcome. But the evaluation of this uncertainty, best represented by a subjective probability distribution, does depend on the human input. The expectation rises with the amount and quality of resources invested in a project. Even in an uncertain world redistribution lowers the incentives to create private and social wealth. It lowers expectations about the results of production and raises the risk.

It is argued occasionally that unequal distribution of income and wealth does not assure economic growth. Arbitrary redistribution therefore seems feasible without endangering the potential of growth and rising general real income. Inequality of income distribution is certainly not a sufficient condition for growth and risking average real income. We can list many countries, most particularly in the third world, which pursue policies that simultaneously obstruct development and higher real income in the future for broad social groups and also produce a highly skewed distribution of wealth benefiting the power elite, its apparatus and associates. But inequality in distribution remains a necessary condition of growth, rising real incomes and opportunities over a wide range. As Schumpeter remarked, this process gradually alleviates poverty understood in an absolute sense. Real income also improves at the lower end of the scale.

This is, however, not acceptable and hardly satisfactory to the clerical articulators. A central objective of their endeavour is a 'just' society. But justice in their view means equality of income and wealth. It appears that they expect all kinds of human wonders from involving the state's police powers to impose such justice on society. My examination of the literature has so far yielded no evidence that they have ever produced an alternative view of justice. One finds on the contrary statements asserting that this particular representation of the 'end-state' conception of justice is the only possible view (Brunner, 1986). They disregard in particular the process view of justice. The end-state notion defines justice in terms of a specific outcome pattern to be produced by the socio-political process. The process view in contrast characterizes justice in terms of the general properties of the process. The choice of these general properties may depend on considerations of probable outcomes and the resulting working of the social process. A process view may even be combined with a suitable 'social safety net' to ensure some protection for those members of society who would slip to the lowest levels of the distribution.

At this point we should note that the two views of justice are importantly related to the 'anthropological' view. In order to maintain an end-state view, most particularly the equality of income and wealth, advocates need to use a 'sociological model of man' (Brunner and Meckling, 1977; Brunner, 1987) or fall back on the hope of a 'new man'. The two positions are essentially equivalent in terms of their support provided for justice expressed by a thoroughly egalitarian society. This perception of man offers the definite expectation that the goal of an egalitarian society can be realized at hardly any cost in economic welfare and freedom. It allows moreover the argument that an egalitarian society raises the opportunity for 'true human values' to dominate life. The whole structure of thought crumbles, however, once we question the basic hypothesis about human behaviour. We need not deny the occurrence or importance of altruism, concern for family, friends and even others, or serious religious commitments. But we need to recognize that self-interested behaviour permeates the social process. There are, moreover, no good grounds in history or biology to expect or even reasonably hope for a transformation into a 'new man' once a radical institutional restructuring has been accomplished.

But this poses a serious problem for an egalitarian society. The advocates of such a society invested little effort in probing the institutional requirements of their dreams. A complex and rigid system of political control would be necessary in order to ensure an egalitarian outcome. Such institutions offer, however, as do all institutions, specific incentives to direct self-interested behaviour into very different channels and expressions than were anticipated. Incentives to use and develop resources to raise the standard of living would suffer. A massive bureaucracy would be needed to ensure an egalitarian system and to replace the price mechanism as a solution for society's allocation problem. This system fosters incentives to exploit the control and power apparatus in a self-interested way. The 'nomenclatura' of the system will explore many imaginative forms to use the existing institutional structure for their personal benefits. Corruption would persist as an 'endemic disease' in such an organization. The formal requirement of equal income may remain satisfied. But control over the use of resources must be assigned in all societies to one person or another. In every society there emerges thus an assignment of 'control rights'. These control rights assume very different forms and meanings under alternative socio-economic organizations. But even a socialist society without property rights in our accustomed 'capitalist' sense must assign some 'control rights' in order to prevent chaos in the use of resources. Such control rights offer opportunities to use some resources, directly or indirectly via trading with other members of the nomenclatura, for some personal benefits. Housing, automobiles, access to many facilities may be mentioned in this context. The actual real income of the nomenclatura can be expected to exceed the opportunities determined by the official egalitarian salary. Similar incentives would operate in private transactions. Many persons enjoy a human endowment appreciated by many others willing to pay extra to see or hear their favourites' performances. The enforcement of an egalitarian society poses under the circumstances almost impossible problems, and if truly enforced by the 'guardians', it will stagnate in apathy and poverty.

Power and oppression
Themes to be discussed:

- the relation between power and wealth;
- the egalitarian principle applied to power;
- institutional issues;
- the idea of a general 'Sovietization'; and
- the illusion of 'power-sharing' in a complex political organization.

Radical communality
Themes to be discussed:

- the confusion between a 'moral order' and a 'moral community'; and
- the confusion between the 'greater societies' and small social groups.

Religion and an open society
Theme:

- the case for an open society based on markets and private property in terms of religion and religious beliefs.

References

Brunner, Karl (1986) 'Reflections on "Theology and the Social Order"', working paper, University of Rochester and ch. 8 this volume.

Brunner, Karl (1987) 'The Perception of Man and the Conception of "Society"', *Economic Inquiry*, xxv, 367–88.

Brunner, Karl and William H. Meckling (1977) 'The Perception of Man and the Conception of Government', *Journal of Money, Credit and Banking*, **9**, no. 1, part 1, 70–85.

Keynes, John Maynard (1932) *Essays in Persuasion*, New York: Harcourt, Brace & Co.

Koslowski, Peter (1984) 'Metaphysics, Christian Religion and the Social Order – With Special Consideration of Catholic Thought', paper presented at the 11th Interlaken Seminar on Analysis and Ideology, June 11–15.

Preston, Ronald H. (1987) 'Christian Socialism Becalmed', paper presented at the 14th Interlaken Seminar on Analysis and Ideology, June 8–12.

Schumpeter, Joseph A. (1942) *Capitalism, Socialism and Democracy*, New York: Harper.
Topitsch, Ernst (1958) *Vom Ursprung und Ende der Metaphysik: Eine Studie zur Weltanschauungskritik*, Wien: Springer-Verlag.

9   The First World, the Third World and the survival of free societies*

A New Marxian–Leninist Manifesto

The history of man is largely a story of oppression, poverty and war, with the sombre fabric occasionally relieved by the freedom of open societies. The institutions of a free society offer man a chance to grope for human dignity and human achievement. They open opportunities to improve standards of living and the quality of life in ways rarely experienced by man. The historical record of western societies offers in this respect a remarkable illustration. 'Capitalism' fostered energetic application of human resources and imaginative innovations. The range of freedom expanded, arbitrary government power shrank, opportunities for broad groups rose, and the human lot improved substantially.

The ideological assault

But the freedom of open societies remains forever fragile. Their very existence threatens the institutions and conceptions of the many tyrannies, whose survival requires that the freedom of an open society be denigrated, perverted, and 're-interpreted' as the 'slavery of a lost society'. Although the details of such assaults may vary over a wide range, the most pervasive and effective forms share a common strand. They exploit man's perennial desire for universal orientations and certainties in a world confined to fallible views and chances.

The essentially human attempt to alleviate 'the burden of reality' – recognized and used to advantage by the assailants – comes to endanger man's striving for freedom. In this respect, the 'ideological warfare' suffered by free societies emanates from fundamental religious conceptions embedded for thousands of years in man's mind. It functions to weaken the intellectual attraction and emotive force of the freedom experienced under open societies. It constitutes, moreover, an effective shield supporting and protecting the tyrannies in the very name of freedom and humanity.

*   Originally published in *The First World and the Third World: Essays on the New International Economic Order*', ed. K. Brunner, Center for Research in Government Policy and Business, University of Rochester, Rochester, NY, USA, 1978, 1–36. The author gratefully acknowledges useful comments made on a first draft by Allan H. Meltzer. The manuscript was prepared during a visit at the Hoover Institution, Stanford, Cal., during the 1977–8 period.

A systematic political campaign reinforces the 'ideological warfare'. This campaign diminishes the power and influence of the free societies and subtly affects their domestic institutions. The trend seems poorly understood, little appreciated, or, in contrast, even welcomed by western bureaucracies and the intelligentsia. The rhetorical camouflage of 'Orwellian inversions' may obscure perception. Recognition is probably also veiled by the nature of the political mechanism increasingly used in the onslaught on free societies. The United Nations was constituted at the end of the Second World War with great expectations as an instrument of peace and political stability in the world. It was supported in the United States over many years and with a considerable emotional investment. Under these conditions, it is difficult to perceive that the United Nations has gradually changed conceptions and operations as its membership has changed. Its institutional apparatus has evolved into an instrument systematically exploited by a majority for their political-economic purposes.

In recent years, the political thrust of the United Nations organization has been increasingly focused around the idea of a 'New International Economic Order' (NIEO). Its various strands are not really new, having been proposed and discussed in UN agencies for almost two decades. But they have emerged with a new design anchored in a broad socio-political conception. With their new ideological coherence, these ideas have found an attentive response in the General Assembly. They increasingly influence, moreover, the operation or the agenda of many international agencies. The NIEO proposals would modify the purpose and role of the United Nations. The contrast between the poverty of the Third World and the affluence of the First World is politically offensive and morally unacceptable to advocates of the NIEO. Their determined attempt to interpret these differences in wealth as a serious 'danger to peace' serves to legitimize the attention of the United Nations and to justify the new focus of its expanding institutions.

The programme advanced under the NIEO encompasses a wide and open-ended range of proposals and instruments.[1] The array and diversity of proposals under the programme of the NIEO reflect a broad strategy to exploit all possible avenues and institutional opportunities for the central purpose: a massive transfer of wealth from the western countries to the Third World.

The strategy emerges in the activities and operations of the Food and Agricultural Organization (FAO) in Rome, in the International Labor Organization (ILO) in Geneva, in the Secretariat of the United Nations Conference on Trade and Development (UNCTAD) and the series of conferences sponsored by this agency. But the crucial and unifying strand of the strategy was probably most explicitly revealed in conferences and negotiations concerning exploitation of the rich resources of the ocean beds. The representatives of the Third World opposed access by private corporations, asserting that ocean-bed resources 'belong to mankind'. This declaration supposedly justifies the political proposal of a single monopoly organizing the extraction of ocean-bed resources and 'owned by the people of the world through their respective governments'. Such rhetoric never fails to impress portions of the media and the intelligentsia. But the significant aspect of the proposal is that the monopoly would in fact be controlled by the voting blocs of the Third World. The required resources and technologies are to be supplied, on the other hand, by the First World. The development of ocean-bed resources should thus proceed under institutions that allow the Third World to impose implicit taxes on US and other western citizens, extracting a wealth transfer irrespective of the wishes and rights of those citizens.

The erosion of freedom
Negotiations designed to structure the exploitations of ocean-bed resources in accordance with an international agreement were suspended in 1977. The United States foreclosed for the moment this access to western wealth. But the central idea still guides the NIEO and influences the array of other proposals or the operations of international agencies. The unifying theme is the development of a political mechanism offering partial control over western resources. That mechanism requires a gradual modification of international institutions in two directions. In the first stage, the secretariats, offices, committees, agenda and broad decision-making are to be controlled by representatives of the Third World. The second stage would then achieve a gradual expansion of UN functions, with a corresponding encroachment on the domestic affairs of western countries.

The threatened erosion of institutions in free societies seems difficult to perceive, however. Recognition of the process linking the operation of international agencies with the domestic scene in western countries is obscured by the diffuse nature of the political mechanism. There are no dramatic evolutions, and the process moves with many unobtrusive and almost innocuous little steps. But the cumulative effect of the trend is not beyond understanding. Senator Daniel P. Moynihan has recognized the basic issue, noting that 'what is going on is the systematic effort to create an international society in which government is the one and only legitimate institution'. The NIEO's vision is dominated, according to Moynihan, by 'an encompassing state, a state which has no provisions for the liberties of individuals'.[2]

The erosion of free societies required by the realities of an NIEO has been explicitly acknowledged and presented as a human achievement by some western advocates. Gunnar Myrdal contends that 'rationality' demands the imposition of coercive institutions to forcibly lower the real consumption of western societies and thus to extract the massive transfer of wealth deemed morally appropriate. Parliamentary democracy and the western institutions assuring the chances of freedom and human opportunities would barely survive in Myrdal's world. Charles W. Haynes, former secretary of the Carnegie Endowment for International Peace, appears as an ardent advocate of the NIEO in the United States. He understands that it would require 'a full abandonment or at least a sharp curtailment of the consumer-oriented society'. This phrase must be recognized as a moralizing obfuscation of the proposed systematic dismantling of the institutions assuring men the pursuit of their own ends by their own lights. This consequence of the proposal is more easily discernible once the required institutional rearrangement is pondered in some detail. Haynes essentially admits that the freedom still enjoyed in western societies must be sacrificed, but he is confident that 'free societies will accept the restraints' to be imposed by an NIEO.[3] The former secretary of the Carnegie Endowment for International Peace is apparently little deterred by such a loss of freedom. Patient and nonideological negotiations carried on at high government levels should lead to the 'peace' of a new international order. The demand for a 'nonideological' approach really means that the West must renounce its commitment to the institutions of a free society. Such renouncement implies, moreover, western acceptance of the ideological theme governing the views and policies of the Third World.

This theme finds little explicit recognition in the western nations. The prevailing disposition is to interpret the New International Economic Order as a diffuse programme bearing on international trade and investments, with an array of somewhat 'boring' detailed technicalities. The details, however, are not so irrelevant, for they reflect a basic purpose and emerge from an encompassing ideological position. It is important to penetrate 'beyond the trees' of technicalities affecting exchange of technologies, communications, preferential tariffs, etc., 'to the woods' providing structure and meaning to the amorphous mass of details. A remarkable article by Senator Moynihan, published in 1975 [*The First World and The Third World*, 1978], directed the attention of a broader public in the United States to the essentially ideological theme embedded in the 'institutional revolution' permeating the United Nations. His recognition of the theme was flawed, however, by a serious misconception of its nature. It was presented as a descendant of Fabian socialism and interpreted as a broad heritage of the educational exposure of the Third World elite to English cultural experiences. Although Fabian socialism may have, at best, prepared the way for the contemporary ideological theme, the central notion of that theme is essentially Marxian in character and contains a discernible Leninist flavour. This Marxian–Leninist orientation permeates the political or social conceptions and rhetoric of the Third World, occurring independently of the communist parties. It explains and motivates crucial parts of domestic arrangements and dominates the details and patterns of international policies. The NIEO thus emerges as a

New Marxian–Leninist Manifesto expressing the political thrust of the Third World and gradually institutionalized by the United Nations.

The Marxian theme

The Marxian-Leninist theme presents man as an entity conditioned by the embedding social organization.[4] The crucial characteristics of society are its *Produktions-Verhältnisse*, the occurrence or nonoccurrence of private property 'in the means of production'. Private property assures the emergence of class conflict, determines exploitation, and obscures consciousness about deeper realities. Conflict, exploitation, oppression and injustice thus occur independently of the personal volitions of members of the 'capitalist class'. Owners of private property are compelled by their role in the social process to exhibit specific attitudes, valuations and behaviour patterns. It follows from this fundamental perception of man and society that only a radical change of the system, the abolition of private property, can remove oppression, conflict, exploitation, and assure the transition from 'necessity to liberty'. Such a 'revolutionary expropriation of the exploiters' modifies the 'social condition of production' and transposes man into a new world without conflict and oppression. The Leninist extension of the Marxian vision, with its stress on imperialism and the political 'avant-garde', has found a particular echo in the Third World, as have the Stalinist additions pertaining to the role of organizations and 'control techniques'. The commitment to a Marxian–Leninist doctrine assures that any human progress or improvement of the human condition under capitalism is really an 'accident' and in contrast to the essential trend or inherent conditions of capitalism 'determined by the fundamental laws of society'. In a corresponding view, all failures and 'Gulagian events' in societies that recognize Marxian principles are remedial accidents not essentially inherent in the social process conditioned by socialist institutions.[5]

Implications and advantages

The ideological theme dominating thought and policies in the Third World yields several important implications for the New Manifesto. The first emphasizes the inherent impossibility of reforming or improving the 'system'; attempts along such lines would obstruct the necessary and final revolution. These endeavours are thus particularly evil and repugnant according to advanced insights into the 'laws of society' offered by historical materialism. This explains the virulent hatred reserved by Marxian faithfuls for social-democratic intellectuals, politicians and parties. The second implication is a close corollary of the first. Recognition of the 'basic social laws' implies that the total destruction and overthrow of the system is the foremost priority of political action. All existing institutions should be systematically used for and applied to this radical purpose. Another implication naturally confines 'imperialism' to political and economic relations with capitalist countries. The central imperialist country in this view is necessarily the United States. The political programme requires, therefore, that the United States be weakened and its socio-political institutions be gradually modified. Moreover, all operations of private foreign corporations in countries of the Third World are necessarily 'neocolonial expressions' of western imperialism. The following message is unavoidable under the circumstances:

> In one world, as in one state, as I am rich because you are poor and I am poor because you are rich, transfer of wealth from rich to poor is a matter of right; it is not an appropriate matter for charity. The objective must be the eradication of poverty and the establishment of a minimum standard of living for all people. This will involve its converse, a ceiling on wealth for individuals and nations, as well as deliberate action to transfer resources from the rich to the poor within and across national boundaries.[6]

According to Marxian doctrine, differences in wealth are symptoms of exploitative class relations. Massive redistributions thus weaken the system of private property, reinforce class conflicts, and eventually destroy the class structure. The same theme emerges also in the views attributed to Mr Boumediène from Algeria:

> The raw material producing countries insist on being masters in their own houses. Developing countries must take control over their natural resources. This implies nationalizing the exploitation of these resources and controlling the machinery governing their prices.[7]

The metaphor of 'master in the house', with the emphasis on 'nationalization' of resources, conveys the basic idea that countries of the Third World must abolish private property and establish the socialist institutions required to 'remedy poverty and oppression'. Boumediène, Nyerere and other representatives of the Third World cultivate a ritualistic 'anti-imperialism' that combines a nationalist fever and socialist intentions formulated in a Marxian context.

The prevalence of this ideological theme among the members of the Third World is hardly a matter of chance. Its propagation offers substantial advantages to the 'ruling elites' of the Third World. The doctrine justifies the replacement of markets based on private property with a complex set of political institutions to control the use of resources. This transformation contributes to the survival of oligarchies and protects the tyrannies established in many countries of the Third World. A society based on private property and markets does not guarantee that dictatorship will never emerge. The 'open institutions' of markets and private property seriously constrain, however, the power and manipulative range of a dictatorship and offer greater opportunities for its removal. The socialist institutions that emerge with the abolition of private property concentrate power in a small oligarchic apparatus suffering little exposure to challenge from outside groups. Moreover, the Marxian theme justifies the power monopoly with satisfying humanitarian language. It exploits the intelligentsia's disposition to confuse words and reality in order to obtain the docile group of clerics that centres of power always require.

The events in Tanzania in past years provide, in this respect, a stark illustration. Coercive collectivization of agriculture has uprooted millions of inhabitants and forced a large social group into a Russian mould. This mould, with its characteristic pattern of disincentives, has produced in Russia a permanent agricultural crisis. Agricultural production also fell, of course, in Tanzania, and we can safely expect its agriculture to flounder and stagnate for many years in the future. But it should also be clear that such collectivization offers vastly increased opportunities for political control over the rural sections of the country. It has become substantially more difficult in the Tanzanian countryside to express or organize opposition to Dr Julius Nyerere and his political apparatus. As Jean-François Revel notes:

> democracy provides a legal mechanism whereby in the normal political process, without civil war or coup d'état, one administration can be replaced by another, if the majority ... so decides. Such a system is captivating to few if any of those who hold power. Once they are informed that their socialist conscience forbids them in the interest of the revolution to permit any provision for their own replacement in power, that conscience will also prevent them from allowing any criticism whatever of themselves.[8]

Such criticism, under the circumstances and according to the interpretation of reality guided by the ideological theme, simply has no function. This implication of the basic theme partly explains the Third World's endeavour to exploit UNESCO as an instrument of information and communication policy. The essential purpose is to control the flow of information, in a sense safeguarding and strengthening the prevailing power structure.

The pervasive ideological theme yields another advantage. It offers opportunities to disguise any mismanagement or failure in domestic policies by attributing all problems to capitalist countries. Responsibility for economic stagnation and drift is shifted by the ruling oligarchies to the 'insensitive and selfish' behaviour of the United States and western Europe. The theme also backs up, with a penumbra of intellectual pretensions, the insistent drum-fire of demands that the 'right' for massive transfers of wealth be honoured and actually implemented by the West. Recent conferences, sponsored by various agencies, have thus increasingly revealed cautiously conciliatory and 'concessionary' gestures by western countries.

Flaws in the Marxian scheme

The political and economic usefulness of the ideological conception governing the NIEO does not establish its validity. It seems appropriate at this stage to examine critically some of its major strands. We note first some facts generally accepted by independent observers not yet ensnared by a new *credo quia absurdum est*. All historical realizations of Marxian societies suffer under a typical pattern of economic problems. One may well speak about a 'structural crisis of socialism'. Agricultural production probably reveals the most obvious case. The problems are lessened to the extent that ideological purity is sacrificed and private property survives as it does, tenuously, in the agricultural sectors of some eastern European countries. The peculiar incentive system confronting managers and bureaucracies induces a wasteful use of resources and low-quality production of those goods with little immediate significance for the political apparatus. Queues, shortages and huge, rigid bureaucracies are permanent characteristics of socialist societies. Moreover, oppression and poverty have not been relieved by the 'destruction of the system' and the appearance of 'socialist institutions'. On the contrary, the systematic pattern of intense oppression occurs as an endemic social disease of Marxian societies. The brutalities of Gulag Archipelagos do not appear in capitalist countries, but they do exist in the Marxian societies. Most western Marxian scholars would find it difficult or impossible to teach or publish in such a society.

Recognition of the 'Russian model's' failure induces two very different responses among Marxian intellectuals in the West. One group has apparently decided that the failure results from ideological impurities. The ideological lapse from eschatological commitment produced a 'pragmatic bureaucratization'; ideological pragmatism neglected the emergence of the New Man in a New Society through the purgatory of sustained 'cultural revolution'. This group looks hopefully to Yugoslavia or to China's Cultural Revolution and may turn to Albania or may admire international terrorism. Their hope will always shift with the eventual accumulation of information about historical realities. We are reminded of the Christian sectarians forever proclaiming (sequentially) another day of reckoning just ahead of us. Other groups, with less religious fervour, grope for alternative forms of 'socialist institutions'. They contend that 'Stalinization' is not a necessary feature of a socialist society evolving according to Marxian precepts. Their discussions usually centre around vague ideas of 'universal sovietization' – a pervasive system of participatory self-management applied to all forms of social organization. The remarkable fact about this 'groping for socialist answers' is the implicit admission that Marxian analysis yields little information about the actual operation of socialist societies.

This failure of Marxian analysis reflects a fundamental flaw in the conception of the 'social conditions of production', defined in terms of man's ownership relation to the means of production. The underlying sociological model of man, traditionally used by Marxians, equates self-interest with the profit motive fostered by the ownership of property in a capitalist society.[9] Self-interested behaviour is thus not a pervasive characteristic of man, according to Marxian views, but the result of a specific social condition in a particular historical context. We can recognize at this juncture the fundamental cognitive flaw of the analysis, a flaw subtly influenced by the metaphysical, or religious, traditions incorporated into Marxian thought.[10] An alternative conception of man, advanced by the Scottish philosophers of the eighteenth century, has been systematically developed over the past 200 years and forms the central core of economic analysis.[11] By this analysis, self-interested behaviour, understood in a broad sense, is fundamental to man's nature and is thus *invariant* with respect to historical changes and social conditions, although these conditions affect the *specific* responses and prevailing patterns emerging from the self-interested attention of individuals enmeshed in a specific social context. It follows that abolishing private property yields no *fundamental* change in man's attitude. Any set of 'socialist institutions' creates new, and characteristic, patterns of incentives and disincentives. Responses to them, however, remain unanalysed in the Marxian scheme because of its denial that self-interest is a fundamental human characteristic. We note, in particular, that the abolition of private property does not remove private control over and private use of resources. Available resources are administered somehow, and they are administered by individuals. The arrangements used determine the opportunities for private use of resources. Socialist institutions thus encourage a *private* use of *public* resources at the expense of the general public.

The basic view of man incorporated in modern analysis, when compared with that of the Marxian sociology, is substantially more compatible with historical experience. It explains, in particular, the failures of the historical realizations of Marxian societies, whose socialist institutions suffer, as it were, a permanent 'capitalist crisis'. It explains most particularly their human failure and the systematic inhumanity produced. It explains also why the search for a 'socialist society with a human face' remains essentially a religious illusion, ending ultimately in the misery and brutality of a Stalinist society. The western European hope for a Marxian society based on 'self-management of all resources' will remain a dream without reality. The analysis emerging from the insights of the Scottish philosophers informs us that the institutionalization of Marxian dreams effectively destroys the historical aberration of freedom and restores the universal human condition of oppression, war, and poverty.[12]

Several more specific strands of the ideological theme behind the NIEO deserve some attention. Nyerere expressed the Marxian belief that the wealth of western nations is due to the poverty of the Third World. Exploitation of the Third World produced, in this view, the living standards of the West. The pervasiveness of this belief follows from its 'obvious' simplicity. It corresponds to the simplistic impression that nobody could live on the other side of the earth without falling off. The relevant facts are very different. Its relations with the West contributed in general to the economic development of the Third World. We also hear laments that the West consumes an inordinate share of the world's wealth, although we never hear that the West also produces an 'inordinate share' of this wealth. Peter Bauer has examined these and related issues in a series of papers, and the reader is referred to his articles included in this volume [i.e. *The First World and the Third World*, 1978]. Justification of the NIEO in terms of an established 'right' based on 'past exploitation' should eventually be recognized as a theme without support in reality. It remains, however, a powerful ideological weapon to lure the support of a gullible western intelligentsia for persistent raids on the wealth of western nations.

We note in this context the medieval misconception of trade as a zero-sum game. Nyerere and his cohorts fail to recognize that wealth is produced by human endeavours in response to incentives and opportunities. Since voluntary trade and transactions actually bring mutual benefits to all participants involved, the resourceful groping for and coping with opportunities by participants in the social game yields substantial rewards. This resourcefulness is an essential characteristic of a social organization based on markets. It assures continual increase in wealth and also distributes the gain, under competitive conditions, over widening social groups. It is precisely Nyerere's institutional dream of an NIEO that would transform the social organization into an essentially zero-sum game. The political institutions of such a society intensify conflict and maximize the rewards to be extracted from political power.

Some arguments offered in justification of the NIEO emphasize specific supplementary aspects more or less linked with the basic theme. Called up as evidence of the need for a transfer of wealth are a persistent decline in the terms of trade confronting the Third World and a decline in its share of international trade. Neither is really supported by relevant observations. The findings of a group of experts selected by UNCTAD from 'developed and developing countries' and using the data prepared by UNCTAD yield no support for the notion, well-advertised in UN circles, that the Third World suffers under the 'old economic order' an inherent decline of the terms of trade. The report concludes: 'There was general agreement that the statistics presented to the group did not provide any clear evidence of a long-term deterioration in the terms of trade of developing countries.'[13] It is also noteworthy that neither the terms of trade nor the movements in shares of trade can be systematically linked to the economic welfare of the countries involved. Falling relative prices do not imply under all circumstances a fall in the real incomes of the producers involved. The link is substantially controlled by additional elements affecting technological developments, productivity and relative input prices in the production process. Similar considerations apply to the movement of trade shares. Many factors determine trade shares with very different influences on real income. The movement of trade shares by itself offers no information without further detailed examination. We may indeed infer, with good reason, that real incomes are lowered by a fall in trade shares produced by domestic export taxes, export controls, domestic obstacles in one form or another imposed on imports, or foreign obstacles to domestic exports. But this consequence results jointly, with the declining trade shares, from the underlying specific events. Lower real incomes are not caused by lower trade shares but by the events indicated. But many other events lower trade shares of countries and simultaneously *raise* their real incomes.

Transfer of wealth is also supposed to alleviate poverty and support economic development. The NIEO programme, however, provides for transfers from western nations to the *governments* of Third World countries. Our analysis of the political institutions prevailing in these countries implies that the resources extracted from the advanced nations are predominantly used to benefit the ruling oligarchies. They will be distributed among selected social groups supporting the regime, and they tend to strengthen the existing power apparatus. The ruling oligarchies experience little incentive under the established sociopolitical institutions to distribute the benefits over broader groups, independently of political status. Poverty will be alleviated for a few at the cost of diminished future opportunities for the majorities. A similar pattern characterizes economic development. Political incentives dominate the choice of projects and their mode of execution or operation. The result is usually a wasteful use of resources with comparatively little permanent or broad effect on real incomes and economic opportunities.[14] The vehement opposition of representatives of the Third World or advocates of the NIEO to a programme of broad opportunities for private investment under reliable 'rules of the game' should be noted in this context. A flow of private investment would benefit wider population groups and raise real income with a lessened dependence on the political intentions of a confined power structure. The development of projects and the expansion of job opportunities beyond manipulation of the political apparatus raises opportunities for potential political competition and offers a basis for independent criticism of domestic policies. In contrast, wealth transfers for governmentally controlled 'economic development' minimize the potential competition for political office and maximize the means of political control.

The western response

Even well-informed citizens of western nations fail to recognize a connection between the thrust for a New International Economic Order, the 'institutional revolution' within the United Nations, and the future evolution of their own societies. A 'sophisticated' or disillusioned attitude finds that the United Nations and its array of agencies is a 'do-nothing speech club' with cocktail parties, chauffeured limousines and plush offices. Common opinion also has it that neither the General Assembly nor its many agencies possess compelling decision-powers affecting our lives and welfare. This complacent view of the matter is dangerously misconceived. The attribution of a 'do-nothing' character to the United Nations follows from a belief that the international organization's function is the protection of peace and the resolution of conflict, as expounded in the official rhetoric that launched it and still sustains its propaganda apparatus in the United States. When this naïve belief is confronted with the unending series of regional wars, conflicts and threats of wars, the natural conclusion is that the United Nations really does nothing. This attitude also fosters a perennial hope that it will eventually 'do something', that is, will act in accordance with official rhetoric. And so we hear that the international organization is man's last hope, requiring our prayerful support. This attitude misses the relevant reality rather completely. Rachel McCulloch investigates, in her contribution to [*The First World and the Third World*], the gradual modifications in the UN structure, governing ideas and mode of operation. The problem does not follow from the United Nations' doing nothing, but from what it actually does. And we need to recognize that the problem is embedded in the very structure of the institution.

The role of passive diplomacy

Western representatives, politicians and media do not perceive sufficiently, thus far, the increasingly focused trend in the operation of international agencies. They appear cautiously reluctant to recognize facts, understand their deeper meaning, or acknowledge a systematic underlying pattern. In his article included in [*The First World and the Third World*], Senator Moynihan discusses the bland obliviousness of western representatives steeped in 'traditional diplomatic courtesies'. Speaking of the human-rights issue in a more recent article, he notes the capitulation of the West in the ongoing ideological war:

> The issue of human rights has long been at the center of international policies. In fact, from the time the Soviets commenced to be so hugely armed that their 'peace' campaign lost credibility, and Khrushchev opted for Russian involvement in 'liberation' struggles, this issue has been acquiring greater and greater salience. Which is to say that in human-rights terms the Western democracies have been attacked without letup. ... Western democracies, having allowed themselves to be

placed on the defensive, finally ceased almost wholly to resist. In the language of diplomatic instructions, this lack of resistance was known as 'danger limitation'. In truth, it was something very like capitulation.

Senator Moynihan also notes the basic flaw in the Carter administration's 'human-rights approach'. The secretary of state essentially refuses, in the senator's view, to place the problem in the relevant political context, and insists on dealing with it as a separate and isolated 'humanitarian issue'.[15] Under the circumstances, the issue may easily fade among the files of a bureaucracy with little interest in or appreciation of the fundamental confrontation of our time. Concern with ideology seems a *de facto* monopoly of the tyrannies in the Second and Third Worlds, a monopoly conceded by western governments. The rising cult of the Third World among the western intelligentsia and government agencies reinforces the distorted vision reflected in western policies and actions. A growing awareness of the fundamental sociopolitical issues staged by the Second and Third Worlds would reflect 'a new American will to resist the advance of totalitarianism'. But Senator Moynihan worries, quite properly, that the 'permanent government' can be expected to push in the opposite direction, toward a policy of 'reassurances and accommodation' to our enemies.[16]

The passive disposition of our State Department bureaucracy has been noted by various observers. In August 1976, a UN agency sponsored an international conference on crime in Geneva. The western nations were subjected throughout the conference to a flood of hostile harangues. The Second and the Third Worlds joined in a common ideological onslaught on the free societies, in rhetoric drenched with Orwellian inversions. The experience offered an excellent illustration of the systematic exploitation of any institution, irrespective of its official or announced purpose, to wage a full-scale socio-political war on the western nations. This barrage was endured with silent passivity. Hostile resolutions even found their way through committees chaired by western representatives. Independent observers reported that delegates from western countries 'did not wish to engage in polemics'.[17] They behaved according to a pattern of 'traditional diplomacy' and maintained a posture of 'reassurances and accommodation'. The same pattern suffused the State Department bureaucracy with respect to the International Labor Organization in Geneva. What is remarkable is that continued participation was advocated even after the ILO sessions held late in the summer of 1977. The sessions revealed with brutal clarity that the majority of the ILO has effectively abandoned its original purpose. A voting bloc from the Second and Third Worlds rejected the documents, prepared in line with the original function of the organization, reporting on the administration of treaties and conventions in member countries. This action and the pervasive socio-political confrontation revealed vividly the new political role imposed on the ILO. It has essentially become another 'institutional weapon' to be used against the free societies by combined forces of the Second and Third Worlds.[18]

The consequences of our disposition to reassure and accommodate reach beyond verbalizations and declarations. The rhetorical barrage reflects political pressure bearing on a wide and open-ended list of demands presented to the western nations. A disposition to 'accommodate' necessarily produces a series of concessions. Any particular event or occurrence in the series may have modest or even negligible significance, but their cumulative effects over many years still emerge with a serious weight. Moreover, even minor concessions supplemented with an array of new committees, commissions, or agencies open new avenues for the exploitation of the 'institutional weapon'. The new institutions tend to evolve very differently from the manner expected or officially announced by western bureaucracies. The experiences already assembled under international agreements or with negotiations developed in the spirit of the NIEO are quite informative.

Institutional extensions
Several years ago the European Economic Community negotiated with a group of Third World countries the so-called Lomé agreement, which initiated an arrangement designed to stabilize the revenues from major exports supplied by participating members of the Third World. The new bureaucracy of the Stabex system rapidly adjusted its operations to the incentives built into the institutional arrangement. Independent observers note difficulties encountered in obtaining relevant information; Stabex operation proceeds behind a protective veil.[19] Such nontransparency expresses a natural interest of the bureaucracy to increase its opportunities to control resources and manipulate their use with minimal pressure from outside monitoring. We note also the systematic disposition on the part of the bureaucracy and political commission to interpret the agreement and its execution in increasingly extensive terms. Stabex operations have been extended to compensate *any* losses or reductions in export revenues, including those clearly attributable to the *domestic* policies of the export countries. One country initiated, for instance, a trade monopoly over lumber, and another set minimum prices on sisal. In both, exports and revenues fell, with prompt compensation by the Stabex system. The two cases are very instructive indeed. Both policy measures involved a transfer of wealth to selected groups in the respective countries. The major transfer by the trade monopoly probably accrues to the government sector, its bureaucracy, and associated 'elites'. Moreover, this transfer proceeds at the cost of citizens in the Common Market countries. The complexity and nontransparency of the arrangement assures that few voters in western Europe will know about the taxes systematically imposed on them

by the Third World.[20] The reader may object that the amounts involved are possibly 'small'. But the two events, however small, illustrate the long-run consequences of the bureaucracy's disposition. The extensive interpretation shapes new opportunities for Third World countries to impose policies on their societies that will effect transfers of wealth to the governing class and its associates and supporters, with the expectation that any losses in revenues produced by such measures are shifted to the western European taxpayer. It raises, thus, the incentives to develop 'innovative policies' endangering exports for the benefit of selected domestic groups. It should be clear that such transfers of wealth from the West neither alleviate mass poverty nor contribute to economic development. They essentially reinforce and benefit the existing political structure and raise the consumption of the government sector. They encourage further misallocation of resources and lower whatever economic progress could otherwise be achieved. It is noteworthy that the Federal Republic of Germany opposed the 'extensive interpretation' but eventually yielded under general political pressure from its associates in the Common Market.

The bureaucracy's extensive interpretation of the agreement covers more dimensions. The number of countries with rights to receive transfers has been increased from 46 to 52. The list of products with guaranteed export revenues has naturally been enlarged, and in some cases revenue is guaranteed even for exports to countries beyond the members of the Common Market. The separate events are modest or even trivial *per se*, but they indicate the step-by-step process evolving under the incentives built into the agency.

This experience bears significantly on the so-called North–South dialogue. It is hardly reasonable to expect that any arrangement emerging from this 'dialogue' will not suffer systematic extensions over the years, with increasing opportunities for the Third World to manipulate implicit taxes on citizens of the First World. Another case in point is offered by the protracted negotiations over the constitution of a common fund to finance an 'integrated commodities program'. In these meetings, the Third World has consistently advocated arrangements with extensive or essentially open-ended mandates and with substantial powers vested in the bureaucracy or crucial voting committees. The Third World thus pushed in recent negotiations (summer 1977) for a wide-ranging interpretation of 'buffer stocks' that would permit open-ended interventions by the new control agencies in the market for raw materials. This feature would support the new bureaucracy's disposition to raise 'regulated' prices beyond any level determined by 'narrow' stabilization purposes. The proposals include, moreover, that plans for diversification, technological development, productivity increases, market research, commercial development, etc., etc., be subsumed under the activities financed by the 'common fund'. As in the Stabex system, the taxpayers of western countries will have no vote in these arrangements. Neither will the western governments have any opportunity to control or even to monitor the use of funds extracted from their citizens to further Third World schemes.

Responsible monitoring of the resources obtained from the West will be prevented or obstructed by the 'anti-imperialist' claims to self-determination and 'sovereignty over resources'. Self-determination and sovereignty include, of course, a 'right', represented by suitable institutions, to raid the western taxpayer. It also includes the expectation that western governments will prod and cajole private corporations under their jurisdiction to invest in countries of the Third World, under conditions dictated by those countries requiring that indigenous managers be employed. And, most particularly, the investor should expect no returns and fully accept the risk that the ventures, once successfully operating, will be expropriated with little or no compensation. Proposals of 'joint ventures' mean, in a similar vein, that the western investor may neither control the management nor expect a return on his investment. It is remarkable to note the occasional willingness of western governments to accept the Third World's suggestive rhetoric in this matter and convey 'appropriate' signals to private industry.

Similar willingness is evident in the events surrounding negotiations aimed at a 'consensus document' on the occasion of the Seventh Special Session of the General Assembly in 1975. The session opened with a speech by Secretary of State Kissinger, read at the time by Ambassador Moynihan. A round of discussions had been initiated with the Third World's submission of a broad list of demands. The United States responded with a set of proposals developed in Kissinger's paper. Several weeks of 'hard bargaining' eventually yielded a consensus resolution. 'However, neither Ambassador Moynihan nor Assistant Secretary Enders, nor the Congressional advisory group mentioned that the specific language of the resolution was much more forceful in advocating certain proposals over others. The proposals which were advocated least strongly were those generally advanced by the United States.'[21] Nevertheless, Assistant Secretary Enders reported, in the best diplomatic tradition, that the document resulted from 'a genuine process of negotiation in order to get an agreed result from which we could all go forward'. The consensus was established, however, with 'many United States concessions (e.g., transfers of real resources, international monetary reform, and even a study of indexing for rather tenuous consideration of United States proposals)'.[22] Several things should be noted about the US proposals. They would enlarge the network of international agencies involving the First World in the Third World's economic policies. The comparatively muted response to the proposals probably reflects the smaller opportunities for eventual political control of the organizations envisioned by the United States. But even such institutions, once in operation, would offer incentives for modification and extension according to a now-customary pattern. Second, Enders' emphasis on 'going forward' from the 'agreed result' extends hope and 'reassurance' to the Third World for future accommodation. Finally, by proposing such international agencies, the United States helps the NIEO and its underlying theme. It has basically accepted the Third World's position and opened the initial round in a state of permanent negotiations bearing on 'concessionary transfers'. Although the United States officially disavowed some of the characteristic language expressing the Third World's ideological theme, it did accept the documents, thereby conveying legitimacy to the basic theme.[23]

A previous paragraph noted the breakdown of negotiations over the exploitation of ocean-bed resources, a breakdown essentially due to the extreme position of the Third World. It seems highly unlikely that this suspension will persist, and one may surmise that the State Department is preparing for new rounds of negotiations. It appears useful, under the circumstances, to examine the US position in this matter. The State Department opposed, under Secretary Kissinger, the full monopoly of a joint international government 'enterprise', instead advocating that private corporations should have limited access for a limited period. This proposal concedes too much and again accepts the basic thrust of the NIEO. It offers a major machinery beyond the control or influence of western nations affecting the use of western resources. It is, moreover, blind to the incentives unleashed. The limited realm of private corporations would be continuously threatened. The very existence of this realm, created by an international political body, would open opportunities to raise issues about the geographical range and the duration of the 'corporate privileges' to exploit 'the people's wealth'. Any acceptance of the US proposal would thus unleash a series of intermittent negotiations that would erode private rights via 'a process of genuine bargaining'. Such erosion of property rights would produce another transfer of wealth at the cost of investors, workers and consumers in the United States. Any signs indicating willingness or interest on the part of the State Department bureaucracy to resume international negotiations in this matter should therefore be viewed with some apprehension.

A tentative explanation of western accommodation

The pattern of accommodation and 'concessionary' moves gradually acquires a sharper focus. This development, and our apparent helplessness or indifference to changes in the role of international organizations, still requires some explanation. This section tentatively advances three reasons, which may partly interact or overlap: a fundamental lack of relevant ideological conception on the part of our foreign service bureaucracy; the incentives and rewards operating on this bureaucracy; and lastly, the partial acceptance by some groups among the intelligentsia, the media, Congress, and also the administration of central elements of the ideological theme embraced by the Third World.

The conceptual vacuum

The western countries show little awareness that a political war has been unleashed on the free societies. The systematic exploitation of the 'institutional weapon' for broad socio-political purposes hardly penetrates public consciousness. The western world recognizes no underlying theme that weaves into a unified pattern the mass of technical detail confronting its representatives and negotiators. But there is such a theme, and it guides the persistent search for new issues, the choice of technical or organizational details, and the change in the use and operation of international institutions. It should be explicitly emphasized that this ideological theme bears on fundamental issues, on matters of *substance* and *fact* affecting the survival of free societies.

For the most part, foreign-service bureaucracies in western countries refuse to recognize the signals. 'Traditional diplomacy' conditions the bureaux to an isolated, piecemeal approach centering on technical detail *per se*, with substantial neglect of the socio-political thrust reflected by the detail. In a persistent confrontation with an opponent trained to view all issues and the most negligible detail as a component of a coherent 'ideological theme', the conceptual failure of the West encourages piecemeal 'concessionary bargaining'. It also fosters the 'concessionary reinterpretations' and adjustments of agreements or institutions.

The United States Treasury, in contrast to the State Department, has occasionally approached some comprehension of the basic issue. It appeared to understand during the Kissinger era that the United States should actively advance its socio-political case for the institutions of a free society and also shape its policy-making in accordance with this case. The evidence suggests that Secretary of State Kissinger rather failed, in matters concerning the NIEO, to see 'the wood for the trees'. The 'ideological theme' underlying the NIEO was brushed aside as 'a sterile debate'. The Secretary of State also concluded, apparently after a discussion with his aides, that the issues raised by the NIEO were 'just a big bore'. This evaluation by political and diplomatic leaders hardly encourages a bureaucracy to penetrate beyond the range of 'traditional diplomacy' into a realm of systematic socio-political confrontations. But Kissinger does not stand alone in this respect. Willy Brandt, the former Chancellor of the Federal Republic of Germany, expressed in the late summer of 1977 the hope that the issues surrounding the NIEO might be safely 'de-ideologized'. Appropriately enough, the preparations for a new international committee provided the background for this expression of hope, which was supplemented with a declaration emphasizing the need for 'concessionary transfers'. Brandt's comments reveal the entrenched Western blindness to the fact that the NIEO *is* the instrument of an ideological assault on the West. It is also remarkable that the Third World's ideological thrust, well designed to engender guilt feelings among western intelligentsia, has never really been answered by the West. No major political leader in a western country has raised his voice to present a case for the free societies or to emphatically reject the barrage of accusations. Minor politicians daring a rejoinder suffer verbal abuse in the media for 'their insensitivity'.

A remarkable illustration of the West's failure to understand the issue and to articulate with courage and determination its case on behalf of free societies appears in President Carter's commencement address delivered at the University of Notre Dame in 1977. The President assures us that 'we will co-operate more closely with the newly influential countries in Latin America, Africa and Asia. We need their friendship and co-operation as the structure of world power changes.' With a new confidence in our own future we are now 'free of the inordinate fear of communism which once led us to embrace any dictator who joined us in that fear'. President Carter also lends some support to the 'new international economic order' with the words of a previous president of the United States: 'More than a hundred years ago Abraham Lincoln said that our nation could not exist half-slave and half-free. We know that a peaceful world cannot exist one-third rich and two-thirds hungry.'[24] We observe just in passing the distortion of facts expressed by 'one-third rich and two-thirds hungry'. President Carter follows intellectual fashion and speaks as if the world's incomes were concentrated at two extreme end-points of a distribution. The facts are very different, however; real incomes, including those of countries beyond the First World, are distributed over a wide scale and exhibit a substantial middle ground. Considerably more serious is President Carter's failure to comprehend the current ideological assault upon the United States. There appears a serious misconception about the confrontation with the Second World over its deliberate ideological imperialism. It requires no 'inordinate fear of communism' to understand the pervasive socio-political and intellectual war waged on western positions. The 'confidence' that dismisses 'inordinate fears' easily fails to appreciate the nature of the conflict. The statement quoted also legitimizes the New Marxian Manifesto, with no apparent awareness that it is an instrument in the worldwide battle to transform the free societies according to the prevailing totalitarian pattern.

The attitudes and views of the Second and Third Worlds reveal a common strand affecting our destiny. The 'old problem' of communism and the 'new problem' raised by the NIEO confront the West with the same basic issues. This seems little understood in President Carter's dismissing 'dictators who feared communism' and offering 'friendship and co-operation' to dictators in the Third World. The facts indicate, however, that the old and the new problem both express the socio-political war on free societies. Recognition of their unity would direct President Carter's attention to an important connection between the sentences quoted. Our contemporary tyrannies subject their citizens to a state of slavery described by Revel as approaching a 'prenatal stage controlling things and people in the same manner',[25] but the *contemporary* world of 'half-slave and half-free' apparently lies beyond our president's perception. Also beyond his comprehension is the fact that the socio-political institutions of those tyrannies – from Uganda or Tanzania to Russia and China – obstruct economic development and entrench the poverty of the masses.

This judgement seems contradicted by President Carter's attention to 'human rights'. The administration's interpretation of the human-rights issue offers, however, another illustration of the conceptual failure or vacuum pervading our political institutions. The nonpolitical or purely humanitarian interpretation of the issue artificially separates the problem from its relevant sociopolitical context. The Second World should have shown the nonsense in such attempts at separation. The very idea of isolating a 'humanitarian issue' is a remarkable exercise in prayerful naiveté about the realities of social and political forces. President Carter's approach and reaction to the Russian stance on human rights reveals a serious misconception in this matter. The French government's fear of provoking the Russian leadership expresses, on the other hand, a keen appreciation of the essentially political nature of the issue.

The 'nonpolitical' reinterpretation of human rights is probably conditioned by a subtle and influential misconception of the social problem, a misconception apparently shared to some extent by Senator Moynihan. To regard human rights as the issue of our time with the greatest bearing on the structure of a free society is to misconstrue the nature of the problem. Recent trends in political language have sharply separated human rights from property rights. Moreover, most discussions of human rights reveal a subtle shift in the meaning of the term 'rights' used in these contexts. In the earlier understanding, the rights of individual members of a social organization, including their rights to property – which are, after all, the rights of humans with respect to specified objects – either circumscribe the range of admissible individual action relative to specific objects and persons or confine the range of governmental action in definite ways. But in its modified meaning, 'rights' have come to represent an allocative claim to specific resources: 'the right' to housing, to food, to a job, to medical care, etc. Such 'rights' also imply, however, detailed claims on society's members. Such claims are imposed by coercive political institutions with a role of determining and supervising the details of resource allocations between individuals or between production units and industries. It follows that the extension in the meaning of the word 'rights' actually endangers the institution supporting the freedom experienced in western societies. The fashionable notion suggests policies and arrangements implicitly advocated by the NIEO and its underlying ideological theme. But under the institutions protecting the power monopoly of an oligarchy, the 'new rights' are converted into obligations to the ruling apparatus. The emphasis on 'human rights' as a political component of our foreign policy is therefore neither sufficient nor really appropriate. It also offers excellent opportunities for suitable reinterpretations according to a Marxian theme.[26] Still, Senator Moynihan deserves credit for grappling with a central issue of US policy. He directs our attention to the fact that there is a socio-political confrontation in our time and advises that our policy be formulated in full awareness of the ideological battle. Indeed, the sociopolitical case for a free society should be a cornerstone of US foreign policy. This requires a characterization of free societies, not in terms of the now-ambivalent 'human rights' concept, but in terms of the relevant institutions assuring the freedom and opportunities we have known. These institutional arrangements include severe constitutional constraints on the range of governmental powers and activities, private property, and a dominant reliance on the market mechanism to guide the allocation of resources.

The bureaucracy's incentives

It seems doubtful that the conceptual failure of the West explains the political behaviour previously described. One naturally wonders why the conceptual vacuum persists. The answer, I suspect, lies in the pattern of incentives embedded in the bureaucratic structure of the foreign services.

People do change beliefs and attitudes whenever the stakes are sufficiently large. Changes are quite costly, however, requiring unpleasant efforts and separation from accustomed habits. They also involve substantial investment in learning new procedures and acquiring new information. Such costs are taken on by most people only in case the return expected is sufficiently large. The bureaucratic structure of nonmarket organizations tends to raise the costs and lower the returns associated with its individual members' investments in changing their views or the surrounding beliefs. The pattern of incentives assures the survival of the inherited 'admissible range of procedures and views' to which the higher echelons of the permanent government have become attuned.

Another important aspect concerns the manner of determining achievement and success in the performance of duties assigned by the bureaucracy. There is a strong presumption that a negotiator or representative at a conference should be able to exhibit some 'result', some instrument emerging from the process with appropriate signatures attached. The training of a career person in the foreign service is geared to a permanent stance of ready-and-willing negotiation. This implies a conditioning that blurs, in general, the crucial underlying contours. The mind is immediately channelled into an approach that screens out relevant features of reality beyond manageably isolated packages of technical detail, which offer definite advantages in separating out and converging toward resolvable issues.[27] The 'achievement incentive' that induces negotiators or conference delegations to 'come back' with a signed document of sorts is reinforced by the media. This was made starkly visible in the spring of 1977 on the occasion of Secretary of State Vance's visits to Moscow and the Middle East. It was quite unlikely that these visits would produce any serious results. They should have been understood as a step in the continuous long-run exploration of avenues and positions. Nevertheless, when Secretary Vance repeatedly 'came home' without waving the obligatory piece of paper, the media decided that he had dismally failed in his endeavour. The achievement incentive probably also contributes to the congratulatory optimism of US delegations, described in Senator Moynihan's article included in [*The First World and the Third World*]. Signed-and-sealed documents with implicitly threatening content and language are interpreted as a major success for the United States.

The achievement incentive emerges most particularly in long and drawn-out negotiations. The bureaux and delegations involved, including the appointed top echelons of the respective administration, experience mounting pressure to demonstrate some results to Congress, the media and the public. The pervasive incentives affecting the foreign-service bureaux also produce a subtle confusion between ends and means. The diplomatic political means of 'successful negotiation' replaces the relevant end expressed by a nation's welfare and political position. Events or issues endangering the 'progress of ongoing negotiations' are resented by the bureaux involved even if suspension of negotiations would improve the nation's welfare or allow a deeper reflection on the relation between proper means and relevant ends. The strategy of the Third World under the NIEO manifesto is actually well suited to benefit from this achievement incentive. The confrontation with persistent and wide-ranging lists of demands forces United States delegations, given their conditioning and incentive structure, to reject in 'a process of genuine bargaining' the more extreme demands and to concede the lesser demands. The process blurs their vision and the reports in the press. One obtains an impression of having gained something, when actually concessions are made without any relevant, or with very dubious, returns. This sequence offers, of course, substantial opportunities to both Second and Third World countries to influence the ultimate outcome via manipulation of the demands addressed to western countries.

Another dimension of the incentive structure of a domestic foreign-service bureaucracy requires some attention. This bureaucracy is in regular contact with the bureaucracies of other countries or of international agencies, and there are occasional movements of personnel between national and international bureaux. Foreign-service personnel are involved with the preparation of position papers outlining avenues of exploration and the nature of eventual negotiations or conference participation. They are exposed more substantially and more regularly to foreign and international bureaucracies than to their domestic public or legislative bodies. They are thus exposed to various pressures from their colleagues in foreign and international offices, and these pressures subtly and gradually affect evaluations made and positions suggested by the domestic bureaux. The result is a mutually reinforcing mechanism of narrowly defined achievement incentives with a corresponding exclusion of any broader perspective or socio-political analysis of the issues confronting us.[28] Lastly, the stance of permanent negotiation built into the programme of the NIEO and the operation of international agencies naturally appeals to the conditioned self-interest of the bureaux. It increases opportunities for their specific professional skills. Similarly, an expanding network of international agencies enlarges the range of work for given bureaux or leads to the creation of new bureaux with new career possibilities.[29]

The Marxian theme in the West
The effects of the West's conceptual failure and of the traditional incentives of a bureaucracy are reinforced by a third element. This strand involves the very opposite of a lack of vision. It refers to a socio-political vision that is substantially related to the Marxian theme underlying the New International Economic Order. Unfortunately, American political terminology, with 'liberal–conservative' and 'left–right', has more emotive than cognitive usefulness. The positions so labelled encompass very different views, and the terms blur the issues. The crucial point is that central building blocks of the Marxian theme expressed in the Third World's manifesto and the Second World's ideological imperialism appear as important centrepieces of the socio-political vision governing influential sections of the western intelligentsia. In particular, the 'sociological model of man' has been warmly embraced in some western intellectual circles.[30] Since, according to this model, man is determined by his social conditions, emphasis is put on the need for liberation from his bondage to the one-dimensional, confining and suffocating values of a commercial world. The sociological model necessarily directs attention to 'government' as the instrument of liberation. It thus produces a political view favouring, on balance, the suppression of private property rights or markets and supporting the growth and extension of the government sector with its bureaucratic apparatus. It also fosters a pronounced egalitarian attitude, with implicit advocacy of the coercive institutions required for implementing egalitarianism. One hardly need emphasize that private business, and particularly private corporations, are approached, under the intellectual circumstances

described, with hostility or at least deep reservations. This contrasts sharply with the embrace offered to political institutions and bureaucratic agencies.

My argument will necessarily touch sensitive nerves. But I urge the reader to ponder, beyond an immediate reaction, the essential facts. There should be sufficient observations available to evaluate my thesis. The issue is not whether 'liberal' thinkers, intellectuals or politicians are 'Marxists' or advocates of a New Marxian Manifesto. They need not be. The issue is whether the socio-political vision inherent in some 'liberal positions' is dependent on crucial ideas forming the centrepiece of the ideological war on western societies.

What are the consequences of this situation? It produces feelings of guilt, visible among western intelligentsia and examined in some detail by Peter Bauer in one of his contributions to [*The First World and the Third World*]. A view attuned in basic respects to the ideological theme propagated by the Second and Third Worlds can hardly resist the exploitation strand of that theme. Thus it cannot resist a sense of responsibility for the gap in wealth or 'worldwide hunger and starvation'. Western feelings of guilt provide a useful instrument in the ideological battle surrounding the NIEO. They offer opportunities to the Third World to extend the range of 'institutional weapons' and to enlarge their demands with the reasonable expectation that guilt feelings blur the West's perception. Western advocates of western guilt contribute to the political pressures on western bureaux and representatives. They implicitly accept the principle of 'concessionary transfers' and naturally implore us to cultivate the proper attitude of 'forthcomingness' rightfully expected by the Third World. The implicit Marxian theme in various strands of western thought necessarily weakens western determination. It obstructs, in particular, a proper recognition of the increasing dangers to the survival of free societies. The implicit vision tends to support or actually applaud and reinforce the assault on the United States. While there may be disagreements on the details and technicalities of the NIEO, its central theme and basic political thrust are accepted. Some groups in the West may even be coming to appreciate the political opportunities emerging under the circumstances. US involvement in the diplomatic and bureaucratic tangle of the NIEO promises to yield institutional implementations within the United States that would hasten the trend toward a socialist society desired by these groups. It should be a matter of some concern, therefore, that foreign policy officials who are ideologically sympathetic to the theme behind the NIEO have apparently come to carry more weight in the Carter administration. This development replaces the conceptual vacuum, noted above, with a serious conceptual failure that reinforces the effect of bureaucratic incentives. The likelihood of alternative stances to our foreign policies, encouraging the survival of free societies, hardly seems improved under the circumstances.[31]

Is there an alternative?

The United Nations is frequently presented as man's last hope to prevent the doom of a holocaust. Peace is necessary for the survival of man, and the international organizations are the only means to maintain the chances of peace. We are thus compelled, the argument proceeds, to contribute to the proper functioning of international organizations with a suitable accommodative disposition. A more specific argument with respect to the NIEO bolsters this view. We hear that a refusal by the western nations to 'engage in a process of genuine negotiation' within the framework and premises of the NIEO would unleash disastrous international consequences. An undertone of veiled and dire threats frequently creeps into the discussion.

Both the general and specific arguments badly misconstrue the real situation. The relation between peace and international organizations is substantially more problematic than the standard line assumes. The structure and operation of the international organizations offer opportunities and incentives to search for 'issues' or to play up potential conflicts. The forum provided by an international organization can be used to develop rhetoric and actions encouraging popular support for the ruling oligarchy. In this setting, accommodation by a substantial group of countries neither pacifies opponents nor wins friends. 'Reassurances and accommodation' produce just the opposite, strengthening the opportunities associated with a demanding and aggressive policy by others. Political friends or allies also realize that political friendship yields little benefits under the circumstances. The reality of international organizations and their effect on 'peace' is therefore substantially more complex than the United Nations propaganda line admits. Opportunities for conflict and for avoiding major conflagration in the world depend ultimately on the political perception and will of the United States. Although a less accommodative and reassuring stance may not decrease conflicts, it would change their nature and pattern. It would lower the return on aggressive demands thrown at the West and would induce a more circumspect choice of conflicts to be negotiated. We need to understand that conflicts are not imposed by extraneous social forces, but express to a substantial extent political choices. These choices are, moreover, conditioned by opportunities determined by the mode of operation of the agencies involved and by the behaviour of major countries. A significant modification of these opportunities affects the choices of potential conflicts under consideration and the actual conflicts pursued.

These considerations extend to the specific argument that points to awesome dangers in any refusal to develop a 'concessionary disposition'. But the threatening undertone of the argument requires additional attention. The dire threats of repercussions are not very clear and really make no sense. Suppose the United States explicitly rejects the underlying ideological theme of the NIEO evidenced in the language of resolutions, documents, proposals or even agreements. We may be told that the Third World will form a voting bloc with the Second World. But that has already happened to a large extent. This bloc dominated the meetings of the ILO in the summer of 1977 and the Geneva conference on crime a year earlier. But what else could happen? Do we have visions of African armies marching on Washington, or are we concerned that the African nations may be driven into the Russian orbit, or are we afraid of inviting retaliation by a worldwide raw-materials cartel that would force us to our knees? We may safely disregard the first fear, and the others are extreme versions of a distorted, political perception.

It has been observed by several commentators – among others, by Peter Bauer in [*The First World and the Third World*] – that the Third World does not exhibit monolithic unity or uniformity of interests and situations. It is a highly complex array of societies and countries, with remarkable differences in economic experiences and a substantial variety in levels of real income. The raid on the wealth of western countries is really the only major cohesive force among the countries of the Third World. We should recognize, therefore, the significant fact that the accommodating policies of the major industrialized nations supported and nurtured this cohesiveness by encouraging exploitation of the opportunities discussed above. Less accommodation and reassurance, implicit in a policy based on rational considerations and maximizing the survival opportunities of free societies, lowers the rewards from the single strand of cohesiveness among the large mass of Third World nations.

US policy should thus reject the NIEO and its underlying theme and develop a clear alternative that supports the long-run viability of free societies. Such an alternative requires four general items. First, the United States needs a stable, predictable and reliable line of domestic policies that avoid the worldwide destabilization produced by United States policies in the past years. Second, the United States should lead the western nations in opening their economies by lowering all barriers to international trade. Third, all obstructions to the movement of private investment need to be removed. An increasing number of countries in the Third World might, under the circumstances, re-examine their own economic policies and increasingly shift toward economic development based on innovative explorations and efforts pursued by private investors. Mounting confidence in the reliability and stability of the rules of the game offered by Third World countries would substantially raise the flow of private investments and would thus expand job opportunities and living standards in participating countries. We are led to the fourth and last point: US policy-makers and representatives must recognize the fundamental socio-political issue confronting us and learn to articulate forcefully and without defensive apologies the case for free societies. This should be complemented by relentless attention to Third World domestic policies. This attention includes proposals for institutional reform or alternative economic policies, to be submitted to various Third World countries for their consideration. The Tanzanian and other governments are certainly at liberty to disorganize their economies and lower the quality of life for their citizens, but our articulation should make explicit the consequences of their domestic policies. Our constructive advice may well go unheeded, but an incisive presentation forms an integral part of our coherent articulation.

This alternative programme probably impresses the traditional activist as meagre and 'insensitive'. He need not worry. The political chances for its acceptance as US policy are small. But the apparent insensitivity and modesty of the proposal would assure a rising 'quality of life' for large masses in many countries. In contrast, the 'concerned activism' pursued in accordance with the New Marxian Manifesto entrenches mass poverty, raises the potential of war and conflict as a means of acquiring resources, and intensifies a worldwide system of oppression under the guise of humanitarian concerns.

Notes

1. It includes a set of 'integrated' international cartels to 'regulate the price' of major Third World exports. These cartels are to be operated, with the aid of a common fund financed by the western countries. The free societies of the West are also expected to impose domestic constraints on the development of substitutes for major products supplied by the Third World. Other devices would stabilize Third World revenues from exports. The NIEO also proposes a systematic pattern of preferential tariffs, subsidies and regulations of international trade for the benefit of the Third World. The First World is, moreover, expected to support or encourage 'joint ventures' in the Third World, with the more or less tacit understanding that the First World's contribution establishes no relevant property rights. Any western ventures by private groups with expectations of profit are exhibitions of a 'neocolonialism' endangering the just aspirations of the Third World. Special agencies should be instituted to 'facilitate the flow of technologies' from western countries to the Third World. Similarly, the media and communication systems require apparently substantial changes. This too requires western resources, properly channelled via United Nations agencies in order to satisfy the 'legitimate national interests' of the United Nations' majority voting bloc.
2. Daniel P. Moynihan, 'A diplomat's rhetoric', *Harper's* , January 1976, 44.
3. Charles W. Haynes, 'Can we build on fear?', *New Catholic World*, September–October 1975, 226.
4. The reader is referred to Karl Brunner and William Meckling, 'The perception of man and the conception of government', *Journal of Money, Credit and Banking*, February 1977.
5. It may be objected that the Marxian literature acknowledges the historical progress associated with capitalism. Indeed, one does find appropriate passages in the work of Karl Marx and in Marxian publications describing the human progress from 'feudalism' to 'capitalism'. But one also notes that the attitude described in the text dominates contemporary Marxian views about current socialist and capitalist societies.
6. Peter Bauer offers this quote from Nyerere's speech in 'Ordering the world about: the New International Economic Order', *Policy Review*, Summer 1977.
7. Quoted from 'The New Economic Order', *New Internationalist*, 1975.
8. Jean-François Revel, *The Totalitarian Temptation*, New York: Doubleday, 1977, 107.
9. Further elaborations may be found in Brunner and Meckling, 'Perception of Man'.
10. These aspects were extensively explored by Ernst Topitsch, *Vom Ursprung und Ende der Metaphysik: eine Studie zur Weltanshauungskritik*, Vienna: Springer, 1958.

11. An excellent survey of the issue can be found in William Meckling's 'Values and the choice of the model of man in the social sciences', *Schweizerische Zeitschrift für Volkswirtschaft und Statistik*, 1976.

12. A more detailed examination of the issue beyond this short summary will be presented in a forthcoming paper, 'Substantive Issues in Ideology', prepared for the Fifth Interlaken Seminar on Analysis and Ideology, 1978.

13. The information is based on a report filed by Edwin Dale in the *New York Times*, 25 March 1975. The reader may also note the detailed discussion of this event by Edwin J. Feulner in *Congress and the New International Economic Order*, Washington, D.C.: Heritage Foundation, 1976, 62. After the report containing results quite unpalatable to UNCTAD was leaked to the *New York Times*, it was suppressed and 'eventually released with contradictory conclusions'.

14. Peter Bauer's contributions to *The First World and the Third World*, ed. K. Brunner, Center for Research in Government Policy and Business, 1978, elaborate the theme.

15. Daniel P. Moynihan, 'The politics of human rights', *Commentary*, August 1977, 20, 23. In the last section of the present discussion, some reservations are offered concerning Senator Moynihan's interpretation of 'human rights' as the fundamental sociopolitical issue of our time.

16. Ibid.

17. The facts of the Geneva conference on crime were reported in detail by the correspondent of the *New Zürcher Zeitung*. The reports corroborate in substantial detail the general description advanced by Senator Moynihan in the essay included in [*The First World and the Third World*].

18. It should be noted that President Carter eventually decided against the advice of his foreign-policy bureaux and terminated US membership in the ILO in late 1977. The decision does not excuse the remarkable blindness cultivated in this matter by the State Department.

19. Otto Matzke, a correspondent of the *Neue Zürcher Zeitung*, publishes regular reports on the operation of international agencies. These reports offer some unique and insightful information.

20. A ministerial commission sets a plafond on the Stabex system's five-year budget. The extensive interpretations thus push actual expenditures to the plafond. The bureaucracy's incentives also make it very likely that the operating committee will approach the ministerial commission for additional funds before the first five-year term is ended.

21. Feulner, *Congress and the New International Economic Order*, 13, 14.

22. Ibid., 15.

23. Ibid., 68.

24. Moynihan's 'Politics of Human Rights' brought this speech to my attention. The reader is particularly referred to pp. 24 and 25 of his article.

25. The full statement was: 'Since, moreover, nationalization or, more exactly, state ownership of the economy is the only socialism known to centralized authoritarian regimes, this kind of unofficial or lay Stalinism is, under a pseudo-revolutionary pretext, a throwback to the so to speak prenatal stage of political power, where no distinction was made between control of people and ownership of things' (Revel, *Totalitarian Temptation*, 100).

26. A report published by Marvin Stone on the editorial page of *US News and World Report*, 16 January 1978, is noteworthy in this context. We read: 'Communist boss Gierek told me during an hour-long interview in his Warsaw office: "It seems to me that you Americans make one cardinal mistake in believing that human rights was invented by your side." In his view human rights means the right to food, a job and shelter.' In such terms a prison society satisfies the criteria of human rights most adequately.

27. Some proposals bearing on political prisoners and raised by the United States at the time are instructive in this context. The sour and almost hostile response by western and particularly by English representatives reflects the apprehension of foreign-service career personnel toward procedures and issues violating their traditional conditioning and job perception. Moynihan, 'Politics of human rights'.

28. The pressure mechanism is illustrated by the Federal Republic of Germany's eventual

acceptance of the extensive interpretation of the mandate of the Stabex system. Further examples are provided by the interaction between the more 'progressively accommodating' Scandinavian bureaucracies and other western representatives in preparation for new rounds in the North–South dialogue centred on the common fund and raw-material buffers. Lastly, Switzerland, generally considered by 'opinion makers' as the least-progressive country, produces a remarkable observation. A few years ago the voters rejected, under a 'facultative referendum' and by a large majority, a programme of foreign aid for the Third World. The unease and discomfort of the Swiss government was quite noticeable. It was subjected to criticism, comments, suggestions, demands, etc., at usual and regular contacts with the bureaux of other countries. Within three months of the referendum's outcome, the Federal Council of Switzerland declared that the Swiss government would have to find some means to execute a transfer of wealth in spite of the voters' expressed wishes. Eventually, in October 1977, the Council publicly announced some suitable proposals, which, adjusted for the size of the US economy, would involve about $3.2 billion.

29.   These last remarks explain the State Department's attitude with respect to the ILO. Once negotiations and representation are assigned a value independent of the socio-political context and their consequences for a country's long-run position, one easily concludes that the United States should remain at the ILO and 'maintain contacts'.

30.   This issue was discussed in Brunner and Meckling, 'Perception of man'.

31.   The reader may find of some interest an article by Chalmers Johnson, 'Carter in Asia: McGovernism without McGovern', *Commentary*, January 1978.

10 The New International Economic Order: a chapter in a protracted confrontation*

For a century Marxian literature predicted the collapse of capitalism. It outlined the process ultimately destroying a social system organized by markets and based on 'private property in the means of production'. But most propositions made by Marxian writers that permitted some assessment were falsified by events. They were of course suitably reinterpreted ex *post facto* in order to save the language required for the 'revolutionary purpose'. Among the adjustments appeared a new recognition of the role of the intelligentsia and the instrumental use of mass education facilities. The attention of the 'socialist struggle for human liberation and the termination of pre-history' gradually moved beyond the 'industrial proletariat'. Political conception addressed and incorporated other social institutions or groups.

The crucial function of intellectuals in the erosion of capitalism was fully understood by Joseph Schumpeter. The doctrine of the 'march through the intellectual institutions' emerged in Germany almost two decades after Schumpeter's prophetic analysis. His account of the role played by 'professional articulators' in the evolution destroying capitalism still offers remarkable insights and many stimulating suggestions for contemporary readers. The intelligentsia's role also explains another phenomenon that cannot be subsumed under the standard Marxian scheme. The socialist assault on capitalism, apart from the entrenched and well-observed aggressive hostility of the communist bloc, is spearheaded in recent years by the Third World. We owe some recognition of this circumstance to Daniel P. Moynihan's searching examination in a widely and properly acclaimed article.[1]

The exposure of intellectual elites in the Third World to the influence of Western intellectual traditions expanded the range of the 'Schumpeterian process' over noncommunist regions outside the established industrial nations. The socialist rhetoric cultivated by representatives of many 'new countries' can hardly be missed. Socialist conceptions, moreover, are unmistakably revealed by the trend in economic policy and the prevalent forms of economic organization. This evolution may have affected the position of the United States in some respects. For many years the world's intelligentsia has nurtured an anti-American attitude and expressed political sympathies adverse to our long-run interests. As the leading capitalist country, the United

* Originally published in *Journal of World Affairs*, **20**(1), Spring 1976, 103–21.

States is a major affront, or possibly obstruction, to socialist aspirations. Still, without the vast institutional apparatus offered by the United Nations Organization the evolution sketched above would probably have minor significance for the United States. The infiltration of this apparatus and its exploitation give leverage to the power of the socialist onslaught. The United States thus faces a serious and protracted conflict bearing on the fundamental issues of a society.

The evolution of the United Nations Organization offers a good example of the 'institutional weapon'. Institutions, once created according to some well-meaning intentions, determine incentives guiding their use and development in very different and unanticipated directions. Over the past 15 years the UN has increasingly suggested or approved ideas involving coercive transfers of wealth from the 'developed' to the 'developing' countries. This bias confronts the United States increasingly with a fundamental conflict concerning the future of American society. The institutional facilities of the UN are systematically used to launch persistent and wide-ranging assaults on the 'injustice and oppressiveness' of US capitalism which contrasts so sharply, it appears, with the glowing 'justice and liberation' achieved in 'socialist countries'.

One wonders whether the media and our representatives understand the seriousness of the challenge. The traditional bureaucracies or diplomats in the State Department seem either unwilling or unable to cope with the situation. Any forceful attention to the challenge violates the traditional pattern of diplomatic procedures, and this may explain the blandly uncertain stance cultivated on many occasions by US representatives.[2] Such uncertainty may also be conditioned to some extent by institutional incentives that determine an overlapping range of interests for national and international bureaucracies and operate to weaken the attention devoted by some national bureaucracies to *national* interests. It also explains the reaction of bureaucracies and old-line European diplomats to the major exception in our government. Moynihan apparently understood the nature of the challenge and the prospects of the confrontation. Substantially more than bland acceptance of a socialist rhetoric condemning our society is involved in this failure of US administrations and representatives. The rhetoric accompanies persistent attempts to expand the institutional apparatus of international organizations. Moreover, such expansion would gradually impose, at least in explicit intention, increasing constraints on our domestic arrangement. The 'march through the international institutions' thus becomes one of the means to eventually overcome US capitalism and to transform American society to the levels of 'justice, equality and liberty' to be achieved according to the socialist theories guiding many representatives of the Third World. Even if the rhetoric were just an instrument encouraging the US intelligentsia's supply of guilt feelings designed to foster transfers of wealth, such transfers require institutional arrangements modifying the longer-run nature of our society.

The general pattern governing UN institutions may be exemplified by two resolutions adopted by the General Assembly on 9 and 16 May 1974. On 9 May the Assembly adopted the Declaration on the Establishment of a New International Economic Order designed 'to eliminate the widening gap between developed and developing countries'. The declaration recognizes that 'remaining vestiges of ... colonial domination ... and neocolonialism in all its forms' are among the 'greatest obstacles to the full emancipation and progress of the developing countries'. It also asserts that an 'even and balanced development' was impossible to achieve 'under the existing international economic order', and emphasizes that the inherited economic order 'is in direct conflict with current developments in political relations'. It is thus postulated that developing countries participate actively, fully and equally 'in the formulation and application of all decisions that concern the international community'. And so we read that 'international co-operation for development is the shared goal and common duty of all countries'. The 'broadest co-operation of all States, ... whereby the prevailing disparities in the world may be banished', should be respected; and likewise, 'full permanent sovereignty of every State over its natural resources and all economic activities'.

A week later the General Assembly of the UN launched itself on a supplementary resolution introduced as a Programme of Action on the Establishment of a New International Economic Order. Colonialism and neocolonialism are again properly exorcised and condemned. The actions proposed are subdivided into ranges covering trade and raw materials, transportation, the international monetary system, regulation of multinational corporations, and an array of means strengthening the UN system in the field of international economic co-operation. The provisions under the first item should assure larger real revenues from exports, more aid and financial contributions in one form or another. Transportation costs should be lowered (somehow), at least for the developing countries. In the range of international monetary problems, developing countries wish to be 'fully involved as equal partners' in all decision-making. Return to a system of fixed exchange rates is mentioned with some emphasis. This proposal requires supplementary attention to the provision of international liquidity that would be linked to financial grants offered to developing countries. The 'link' is thus naturally tied to the restoration of a fixed exchange rate system. The last section of the action programme lists an extensive schedule utilizing or expanding UN institutions and in this manner raising the leverage to be exercised by Third World countries.

In case some innocent reader of the UN resolutions misses the meaning of the exercise covered with beautiful phrases about justice, peace, equality, liberty and humanity enunciated by representatives of a large assortment of minor or major tyrants, we may fortunately refer to the useful interpretation supplied by a self-styled moralist. On 17 March 1975 Gunnar Myrdal delivered a Nobel Memorial Lecture on 'The Equality Issue in World Development'. Myrdal's world view opens with the old 'colonial empires' neglecting or possibly exploiting their less-developed regions, which 'stagnated in poverty'. The spreading independence of the postwar period encouraged an awareness of the inequality between developed and other countries. A moral issue emerged which should dominate our attention. Myrdal acknowledges that some aid was given over the years, but he finds such aid thoroughly inadequate and usually given for the wrong motives (except, of course, by Sweden). Both morality and rationality, in his view, demand the establishment of a new world order. This new world order should be designed to remove inequality and introduce an egalitarian justice.

The egalitarian principle immediately reflects the appropriate morality, and rationality is expressed by Myrdal's judgement that substantial reductions in western societies' consumption levels are 'in the best interests individually and collectively', of all members of these societies. Implementation of such moral rationality requires national planning to achieve lower levels of consumption in order to release resources for transfer to the developing countries. He notes in particular that the United States would have to be prepared 'to initiate and co-operate in planned intergovernmental action in a way pointing towards "a new world order" asked for by the underdeveloped countries, which in turn would necessitate the rational restriction of our lavish utilization of resources'. The new world order thus introduces a system of 'integrated national planning' for the sole purpose of effecting a massive transfer of wealth from the industrialized nations to the majority of members of the United Nations Organization. Myrdal understands quite clearly that this 'new order' cannot be realized without vast institutional changes covered by the expression 'national intergovernmental planning'. He observes in passing that an economic organization relying on markets seems not to be conducive to 'rational actions' bearing on consumption demands.

The issue confronting the United States is thus clearly defined. We are addressed by a majority of members of the UN and 'intellectual or moral leaders' to accept in essence and initiate a transition into a socialist world and a socialist society. It may be appropriate at this point to clarify our use of the term 'socialist' as applied in this discussion. Two closely associated characteristics of social organization crucially determine important aspects of human life: the extent to which allocation and use of resources are guided by prices formed on markets, and the range or content of private property rights.

There is no society without markets and some price-guided activities, and similarly, no society without private property rights (or entitlements) to resources or use of resources.[3] It is important in this respect to understand the nature and consequences of an 'entitlement structure'; consequences vary substantially with the range, explicitness, predictability, stability and tradeability of the entitlements.

Socialist programmes essentially lower the various dimensions of private entitlements and also lower the range allotted to market mechanisms. This description implicitly rejects the Lange-Lerner conception of a market-oriented socialist society. Their notion is certainly possible, but it should also be recognized that it possesses little empirical relevance. The erosion of private entitlements to resources and their use is usually accompanied, as a matter of empirical fact, by replacing markets and market-determined prices with a political-administrative allocation mechanism. This attrition of private entitlements, according to socialist literature and rhetoric, forms a necessary condition for the transition from 'prehistory to human history' – a necessary condition to assure human dignity and a 'meaningful level of the quality of life'.

This view has infiltrated the discussion at UN conferences on a wide range of issues, be it population, food, pollution or crime. It is also clearly reflected in the documents emerging from UNCTAD, UNIDO or the General Assembly bearing on the New International Economic Order to be established. The challenge confronting the United States should be fully recognized and accepted. We should also unhesitatingly accept the criteria advanced for judging a social organization, viz., criteria stated in terms of 'human dignity and the quality of life'. Although these terms are vague, somewhat ambivalent and require some further circumscription for adequate analysis, this is hardly the purpose of the current discussion. It is sufficient here to emphasize most decisively that the case for capitalism should not shirk these standards. On the contrary. Usefully formulated in a non-evasive mode, they should be fully embraced as the relevant standards of our judgement.

In this respect there is indeed a moral issue in the choice between social organizations, and it subsumes a cognitive obligation to analyse with reliable means the *comparative* operation of different institutional structures. This analysis extends to the human patterns fostered by different arrangements, the attitudes reinforced and the values permitted. It is in these very terms that the case for capitalism should and can be made. But so far we see little evidence that US representatives at international organizations and conferences understand the nature of the challenge or find it useful to fit the confrontation into their accustomed political game. Their neglect is in my judgement not entirely harmless for our long-run interests. The onslaught on our social system is a persistent and pervasive fact reflected by the verbalism and phrasings incorporated by UN documents.

A dominant and basic theme expressed by many formulations encountered in the rhetoric offered by the Third World centres on the Marxist–Leninist idea of 'exploitation'. The Leninist extension of Marx's original notion to international relations explains the difference in wealth between western industrial nations and the Third World in terms of a colonial history, or more generally, in terms of subtle and pervasive forms of political coercion. Western exploitation impoverished the Third World and enriched the western nations. The story is impressionistically plausible and has influenced public attitudes substantially beyond faithful members of the Leninist branch of the Marxist church. One frequently encounters the assertion that the colonies and politically dependent territories stagnated in poverty, with progress occurring only after independence. Myrdal's Nobel lecture elaborates on this theme, and the rhetoric of the above-mentioned UN resolutions clearly reflects this view.

'Decolonization' is introduced as a necessary and primary condition of economic progress. Such progress seems impossible to achieve under a colonial regime. But it also appears that abolition of colonialism is not sufficient. The socialist doctrine claims that exploitation continues in new forms, covered by the term 'neocolonialism'. Neocolonialism emerges whenever private transactions occur between 'developed' and 'developing' nations. It occurs in particular whenever private corporations do business in developing nations. In a sense the label is attached to every transaction proceeding with the expectation of a *quid pro quo*. Abolition of neocolonialism thus involves by definition the desired transfer of wealth to the Third World – a flow of real resources without a *quid* for the *quo*.

One should easily recognize a sense of rationality in these notions. They offer opportunities to justify an extraction of wealth. They also offer to established elites and bureaucracies in the Third World opportunities for enrichment.[4] These opportunities are partly conditioned by the somewhat bemused responses encountered among members of our intelligentsia. The basic theme likewise justifies the claim to 'reparations' made on developed countries as a compensation for the 'obvious damages' wrought by colonialism and neocolonialism. The flexible definition of 'neocolonialism in all its forms' and the claim for reparations embodied in the UN resolutions define an open-ended invitation with pervasive incentives to use expanding UN facilities for an unending stream of action programmes raising political pressures on western governments. The persistent demands also maintain the attention of western media and professional articulators.

These prospects of a protracted confrontation suggest that the socialist rhetoric with its apparently substantive claims should not be blithely disregarded in the manner cultivated by US representatives at UN happenings. It seems important that the claims and the associated rhetoric be forcefully and explicitly contested. One wonders occasionally whether western representatives are sufficiently aware of the dubious case underlying the standard rhetoric. Some general indications of the weakness inherent in the socialist claim seem appropriate in this context.

We should note first that 'exploitation' occurs according to socialist doctrine *by definition* whenever resources (means of production) are owned privately. The extent of 'exploitation' can be measured by the portion of national income absorbed by ownership of resources. All transactions occurring under capitalist arrangements are thus necessarily 'exploitative'. It is important to recognize that this language has a motivating purpose directing moral-political actions. It is used to assert that abolition of 'private property in means of production' liberates the working mass and generally raises economic welfare and human dignity. But the Marxian story, while plausible as are many other stories, fails precisely in its most vaunted virtues. Marxian writers emphasize the superior insights into crucial social relations summarized by the *Produktionsverhältsusse*, the relation between men determined by men's relation to productive resources. But the Marxian account misses completely the important entitlement structure shaping the political, social and economic process and therefore fails to offer any systematic account of political-economic events or processes under socialism.

It is not a matter of chance that socialist writings and the rhetoric about the socialist state barely penetrate beyond some essentially metaphorical or metaphysical elaboration mixed with a touch of the Nirvana approach. Neither is it a matter of chance that Marxian, and more generally socialist, literature cultivates a 'Karamasov fallacy'. One notes instances of injustice, frustration or unhappiness advanced as evidence against capitalism. One also notes that in a socialist country specific groups of the population enjoy more decent housing than before the 'socialist liberation'. This is suggestively used to convey that the whole pattern is generally improved. Such comments and observations are a useful ploy in a political struggle. However, they provide little information bearing on a systematic assessment of alternative institutional arrangements and economic organizations. Such assessment is not possible under Marxian or socialist conception. The doctrine offers no intellectual handle and no analytic perception about the working of socialist institutions; no understanding of the incentives emerging under these institutions and the resulting nature of the social process. It therefore usually fails to offer any relevant interpretation of the problems typically arising under socialist organizations. The permanent agricultural crisis in the USSR offers a good example of the general situation.

Attempts by Marxian philosophers to struggle seriously and honestly with the institutional workings and mode of behaviour determined under socialist regimes reveal in explicit detail the flaws of Marxian sociology. The sociological model of man used in this literature obscures reality and prevents intellectual access to men's responses to incentives inherent in different institutional arrangements. It is unable to explain the system of side-payments and 'unofficial or private' transactions arising under socialist institutions, the patterns of corruption dictated by these arrangements, the power structure or the nature of political competition, and similar problems.[5]

A semi-religious attitude or commitment, which frequently replaces the necessary analysis and evidence, is scarcely conducive to a useful and rational assessment of alternative social systems. But such an assessment over a broad range determines the essential case for capitalism. It is not a case based on guaranteed and uniform justice, happiness, liberty and the like; rather, it emphasizes the circumstance that a system based on wide-ranging private property rights diffuses arbitrary power more effectively than any alternative social organization. While 'justice, liberty and equality' are not guaranteed, it offers more opportunities, and more persistent opportunities, for justice at a lower cost (i.e. than forfeited or sacrificed human values). It also offers more alternatives at a lower cost than the institutional arrangements typically imposed by a socialist regime. In particular, a broader range of alternatives for work and to express a variety of lifestyles erodes patterns of servility and subjection.

The 'open institutions' of capitalism do not assure 'equality', but they loosen established and inherited inequalities to a larger extent than 'closed institutions' of socialist societies that are justified with an egalitarian rhetoric. Moreover, the private cost of dissent – expressed in terms of opportunities sacrificed by political, intellectual, moral or artistic dissent – is certainly positive in *any* social system ever realized or still to be realized. This circumstance frequently encourages a peculiar blindness revealed by absolutist assertions that freedom or liberty is equally missing in most social systems. But the occurrence, even under the best of circumstances, of positive private costs of social dissent should not blind us to the large differences in these costs. Their magnitude is systematically associated with the prevailing pattern of the entitlement structure, and they tend to vary with the range, content and reliability of private property rights. A persistent erosion of such rights eventually raises the cost of dissent and nonconformist behaviour in politics, morals, literature and the arts.

Lastly, the greater opportunities and wider range of alternatives available at lower cost to the average man under a system of private property rights assures better protection of human dignity than can be expected under an essentially political-administrative apparatus. The manifest preference of established bureaucracies and intellectual elites in the Third World for socialist arrangements should be quite understandable, for the attrition of private property rights and the replacement of markets with political-administrative institutions raises the power of both bureaucracy and elite. An extensive reliance on markets erodes such powers and lowers opportunities for wealth transfers and enrichment via political activities. Some members of the elite and the bureaucracies recognize the potential for large rewards – at the cost of the average citizen – under socialist arrangements.

A suitable and highly articulated rhetoric obfuscates the transfer of internal wealth to established elites and bureaucracies. It is also an important instrument in the intellectual offensive directed at an international wealth transfer. Under the circumstances it is vital to understand precisely the human achievement of the social organization covered by the 'capitalism' label. We will undoubtedly find pockets of oppression and injustice in capitalist economies. The world's intelligentsia has persistently emphasized the evils perpetrated in Chile, in Greece under the military junta, in Rhodesia, South Africa, Spain, and possibly also in Brazil. One can indeed observe oppression in these countries, and the cost of dissent is probably higher than elsewhere in western Europe or the United States. But the hysterical rhetoric of the world's intelligentsia has apparently abandoned a sense of proportion in judging the human situation. The cost of nonconformist behaviour in these countries is substantially below the level prevailing in countries accepting the Marxian faith or in numerous socialist countries claiming membership in the Third World.

This observation justifies no complacency about our own institutions or acceptance of the social patterns in the above countries, but it needs some emphasis. It reminds us that a wider range of private property rights is not sufficient to remove a substantial imposition of political constraints on individual activities. Yet these countries also offer useful elaborations on our theme. For one thing, within them an important area of daily life associated with one's work and economic activities remains free from detailed coercion and harassment. Political discussions within small or private groups are to a substantial extent feasible at little risk and very small cost. There is intermittently even a measure of public discussion of nontrivial social or political aspects. Moreover – and this is a crucial point – the persistence of a diffused range of private and reliable entitlements lowers the survival probability of the confining political system. The pervasive property rights prevent an 'institutionalization' of the political system and thus raise the chance of transition to a political-social organization with greater freedom, i.e. entailing a smaller cost for nonconformist behaviour.

We notice some serious discussions and a hopeful expectation about Spain's emergence from the ossified forms of a Falangist dictatorship. Similar developments in Chile and Brazil are not entirely improbable. Does anyone seriously contend that Yugoslavia will 'open its institutions' after Tito's death, or that the Soviet Union will let 'a thousand flowers bloom' after Brezhnev's death? The answer is obvious, and the difference in opportunities and prospects is anchored in the prevailing entitlement patterns. We are eventually led to realize that a *Gulag Archipelago* typically emerges under a socialist regime and with it develops the systematic use of arbitrary terror to browbeat citizens into well-patterned conformity.[6]

It seems important to stress that patterns of subjection and servility fostered by vast political-administrative machineries lower access to alternatives over a wide range of life. A trend to the emergence of such machineries is implicit in Myrdal's programme. His authoritarian position is clearly revealed by his peculiar conception of 'rationality' – meaning that his judgement and the judgement of a peer group of his friends should prevail. The average consumer 'needs to be told what's good for him'. Myrdal effectively exemplifies the group of professional articulators who fail to appreciate that most people have a definite idea concerning the quality of *their* life. Many prefer life-shortening consumption habits to the chance of experiencing senile uselessness. Many prefer skiing, mountain climbing, car racing or flying to a safe, stodgily 'rational' existence. Myrdal focused on a central issue of our time by pointing up the arrogant claim of 'intellectual and moral leaders' to control the fate of our societies. Proposals to institute a comprehensive administrative control apparatus are a natural consequence of this claim and the supporting view that most people are ignorant and incapable of addressing their own interests.

In this context the 'colonialist theme' so ardently cultivated by the Third World deserves our particular attention. It determines the moral fervour and offers a justification of the claim for a New International Economic Order, but the rhetoric of 'colonial' or 'neocolonial' exploitation by western industrial nations is a legend substantially falsified by historical events. According to the standard exploitation thesis, poverty and economic stagnation should increase in relation to the density of transactions with capitalist economies. Yet we systematically observe the opposite. Over the past hundred years regions with the least commerce, the smallest exposure to capitalism and only marginal transactions with western nations have remained the poorest and most truly stagnating areas (e.g. Ethiopia, Afghanistan). Almost without exception the colonies experienced substantial economic progress under colonial status and benefited from a net flow of real resources from industrial economies. The dramatic expansion of population, the improvement of life expectancy, the appearance of public transportation and modern cities resulted from economic relations with the West. Western investments raised real income beyond the levels that would otherwise have been achieved.

This description holds regardless of the regular repatriation of certain profits earned on these investments. Similarly, the use of exhaustible resources contributes to raise real income, at least over time. And with suitable reinvestments of savings accruing from raised levels of real income, real income could be raised permanently. The issue can be stated most effectively in the words of Peter Bauer, who has studied the problems confronting developing economies for many years. Referring specifically to Africa, he says:

> All the foundations and ingredients of modern social and economic life present there today were brought by Westerners, almost entirely during the colonial era. This is true of such fundamentals as public security and law and order; wheeled traffic (sub-Saharan Africa never invented the wheel); mechanized transport (transport powered by steam or gasoline instead of muscle – almost entirely human muscle in Black Africa); roads, railways, and man-made ports; modern forms of money (instead of barter or commodity money, such as cowrie shells, iron bars, or bottles of gin); the application of science and technology to economic activity; towns with substantial buildings, water, and sewerage; public health and hospitals and the control of endemic and epidemic diseases; and formal education.
>
> In short, over the last hundred years or so, contact with the West has transformed large parts of the Third World for the better. Southeast Asia and West Africa provide well-documented examples. For instance, in the 1890s Malaya was a sparsely populated area of hamlets and fishing villages. By the 1930s it had become a country with populous cities, thriving commerce, and an excellent system of roads, primarily thanks to the rubber industry brought there and developed by the British. Again, before the 1890s there was no cocoa production in what is now Ghana and Nigeria, no exports of peanuts or cotton, and relatively small exports of palm oil and palm kernels. These are by now staples of world commerce, all produced by Africans, but originally made possible by European activities. Imports, both of capital goods and of mass consumer goods designed for African use, also rose from negligible amounts at the end of the 19th century to huge volumes by the 1950s. These far-reaching changes are reflected in statistics of government revenues, literacy rates, school attendance, public health, infant mortality, and many other indicators, such as the ownership of automobiles and other consumer durables.[7]

We conclude that there is little merit in the well-publicized idea that Western countries effected a transfer of wealth from the colonies to their own economies, a transfer impoverishing the colonies and enriching the mother-countries. The remarkable economic progress of capitalist economies over the last 150 years seems to support the exploitation thesis, but only if one fails to recognize the parallel development in the colonies. When real income per capita in Western economies rose persistently, in spite of Marxian predictions to the contrary, this economic progress also benefited the colonies. In any case, all the relevant indicators show an increase in economic welfare for these regions. In contrast to some popular beliefs, trade *is* mutually beneficial. Moreover, decolonization often produced economic stagnation and even economic decline. The sub-Saharan region, Sri Lanka, Burma, Uganda, Bangladesh and Pakistan are outstanding examples of this. Other countries may fare a little better, but even those like Algeria or India show little progress in comparison with previous phases of their economic evolution, whereas a colony like Hong Kong has continued to thrive.

These divergent patterns exemplify the irrelevance of colonial status and decolonization to economic progress. Such progress is crucially conditioned, instead, by the trend in policies and institutions developed. The comparative stagnation following 'decolonization' in numerous cases resulted from a pronounced shift to 'socialist programs and institutions', or from a rapid increase of political instability and uncertainties about the 'social rules of the game'.

A notion evidently cherished in UN resolutions refers to a member country's right, in order to be respected by others, to 'sovereignty over its resources'. One might respond with a shrug of the shoulders and easily assent to an obvious meaning. But the phrase involves a rather specific meaning subtly associated with the exploitation thesis. 'Sovereignty over resources' is realized by 'nationalization' and suitable ownership by 'government'. Moreover, 'determination of one's own economic fate' is exercised by a system of political-administrative controls over the size and allocation of (nonhuman and human) resources. The rhetoric cultivated by the UN resolutions thus refers to a concentration in *de facto* entitlements to the use of resources among a ruling oligarchy, its articulators and bureaucracies. 'Sovereignty' and 'determination' involve the establishment of a socialist economy with eroded private property rights and a political-administrative machinery replacing markets over a wide range of activities. Acquisition of 'sovereignty over resources' and active 'determination of a nation's economic fate' subject the vast majority of inhabitants to the political machinations of a ruling oligarchy using these means to foster its political position and enrich its patronage and clientele.

Still, the notions appeal to wide circles which find it difficult to grasp that a developing economy could hardly advance its welfare better than by letting foreigners buy its natural resources and thus involve their active interests in economic development. Whether this inflow of foreign capital necessarily leads to political influence and domination depends very much on the prevalent institutions. Foreign business firms will invest in political influence and manipulations only to the extent that such investments are expected to bear returns. The 'relative density' of government in society is the crucial factor. In face of a comparatively small government sector and modest regulatory powers, investment in political manipulations brings little return and remains on a small or even vanishing scale. The political problem posed by foreign business firms operating in a developing country results essentially from the established and pervasive influence of bureaucracies and government officials. It increases with a socialist trend in policy and institutions, becoming an 'endemic disease' of such institutions as the operators of the government's administrative machinery find it advantageous to exploit opportunities determined by their position. Yet such (illicit) transactions probably raise general economic welfare above the levels achievable in the context of a rigid 'sovereignty over resources' and a militant 'determination of economic fate'.

The exploitation theme also shapes the issue raised about terms of trade. It is occasionally asserted that western industrialized nations manipulate the terms of trade to their advantage and impoverish the raw-material-producing Third World. But the terms of trade of primary producers were, according to Sir Arthur Lewis, much more favourable in the 1950s than for the previous 80 years, and they improved even further in the late 1960s. The overall picture covers a diversity of experiences for different parts of the developing regions. Moreover, deliberate manipulation of the terms of trade by industrial nations for their benefit would require rising export tariffs on manufactured goods in conjunction with rising import tariffs on raw and primary materials. Yet we find no such pattern. There remains the obnoxious fact that the United States, Australia and Canada are major suppliers of some primary commodities on the world market. Under the circumstances 'manipulation of the terms of trade' should be dismissed as a politically useful fabrication. Bauer's comments are again noteworthy in this connection:

> When changes in the cost of production, the greater improvement in the range and quality of imports, and the huge increase in the volume of trade are taken into account the external purchasing power of the exports of the Third World in the aggregate is now very favorable, probably more so than ever before. This in turn has made it easier for governments to retain a larger proportion of export earnings through major increases in royalty rates, export taxes, and corporation taxes.[8]

The conflict regarding the foundations of social and economic organization cannot be exorcised with pious platitudes. We may prefer tranquillity, serenity, undisturbed quiet with all contentious engagements far removed, but the issues bear on our life and the prospects of our society. What should the position of the United States be on these issues? Certainly it would be desirable for Washington to re-examine the trend emerging in recent years in various UN organizations. We should seriously question the wisdom of blandly following this trend with some muted reservations. But what may be a feasible alternative to a thoughtless accommodation? An alternative action programme expressing the long-run interests of the United States, in my judgement, involves five major strands, as follows.

The US economy forms a vital centre of the world economy, and the consequences of American domestic policies are felt throughout the world. Financial instability in the United States contributed substantially to the emergence of world inflation in the late 1960s and early 1970s. Financial policies pursued in the United States also determined the final breakdown of the system erected at Bretton Woods and eventually produced – reinforced by the massive transfers of wealth engineered by OPEC – the 'stagflation' observed in western economies. Such economic vagaries and uncertainties impose severe adjustment costs on many countries. Restoration and maintenance of financial stability is thus the first obligation US policy-making should accept. This means that Washington must evolve a set of policies and institutions assuring stable monetary growth at a noninflationary level, and a controlled budget with at most a modest deficit. Restoring a reliable pattern of financial stability would require a major political effort and a substantial break with recent and current trends.

The second and third strands of a positive programme would be directed toward a substantial opening of our economy. All trade barriers should be removed or drastically lowered. Import quotas of any kind and obstacles to imports should be systematically abolished – this action including the reduction and removal of tariffs. The elimination of trade barriers would offer other countries opportunities to sell their products and acquire the means to finance an increasing range of imports while substantially helping to expand their real income levels. The same policies would also contribute to a more efficient use of resources in the US economy and would in the longer run benefit US residents. Moreover, the systematic removal of trade barriers should be supplemented by a removal of all barriers to private investments in foreign countries or obstructions to private loans made available to foreign businesses and residents. The flow of capital would depend to a large extent on conditions in foreign countries and particularly on the predictability and stability of the rules of the game applied to foreign business and foreign investors. The policies and institutions of the Third World would thus form a major determinant of the capital flow and the contributions made by industrial economies to the rate of development.

As for the fourth item on the programme, it is imperative that the United States formulate a coherent conception of the conditions relevant to economic growth and rising welfare. Uncertain growth and 'stagnating poverty' are not the result of a colonial history or the consequence of 'neocolonialism in any of its forms'. Over the postwar period most developing countries settled on a course of policies and a pattern of institutions systematically obstructing or retarding their economic development. In a growing number of countries economic reality has been sacrificed to the rising demands of ideology. Representatives of the US government should learn to argue a coherent case for alternative programmes and policies that would release the shackles imposed on developing economies. These programmes and suggestions should be formulated with the full acknowledgment that members of the Third World have the right to proceed according to their own lights. But their insistence on policies and institutions obstructing their development and lowering their welfare sets no moral obligation on the western nations to bail them out with a massive transfusion of resources. The manifest failure of government-offered economic aid revealed it to be wasteful and inefficient.[9] All aid should be replaced by voluntary transactions executed on open capital and credit markets.[10]

Attention to policies emphasized in the previous paragraph introduces the last item in a positive agenda. US representatives (and hopefully even some intellectuals) should forcefully contest socialist claims in the world market for ideas. The case for capitalism as a set of flexible institutions best designed to assure a continuous striving for human dignity and human achievement requires some impassioned articulation. We should not hesitate to offer a vision of our humane potential, though this may involve some radical changes of established procedures and well-entrenched habits, as revealed by the first press conference of Ambassador Moynihan's successor reported in the European press. According to these reports, Ambassador William Scranton emphasized that no fundamental issues of principle leading to a confrontation exist between the United States and major portions of the world. This view may simply represent the standard verbalism of a 'diplomatic bureaucracy', but the fact remains: we *are* confronted with a serious challenge and a severe test of our understanding of fundamental issues of social organization. Why US representatives persistently fail to recognize or to admit the existence of an underlying confrontation, therefore, is a puzzlement. Perhaps, since our own domestic trend has veered sharply in the direction implicitly advocated by the New International Economic Order, many politicians and professional articulators may respond sympathetically to the socialist rhetoric supplied by UN organizations and the Third World. But the longer-run cost measured in human values will be high on this road. We can still learn and delineate a vision of human opportunities to be offered to the world.

Notes

1. See Daniel P. Moynihan, 'The United States in opposition', *Commentary*, March 1975.
2. The report published by the correspondent of the *Neue Zürcher Zeitung* in August 1975 on the occasion of the UN Conference on Crime Prevention held in Geneva is most revealing in this respect. It summarizes the onslaught on western countries and the United States in

particular and notes the silence among Western representatives, stating specifically that they refused to respond to the barrage in order 'to avoid polemics'. This attitude reveals a serious failure to comprehend the new international reality, or a serious misjudgement concerning our strategy to meet these onslaughts.

3. Observers of the German Democratic Republic note that janitors at the Leipzig Trade Fair charge about $80 for 'private use right' to a toilet for the fair's duration. Speedier access to medical doctors requires side-payments; so does more rapid attention by automobile mechanics. Along with the official and formally decreed system, an informal market system has emerged based on *de facto* entitlements of the janitor, the medical doctor, mechanics and others. They all control *some* dimension of resource use which determines opportunities for transactions.

4. The reader may wish to refer to Omotunde Johnson's instructive investigation into 'The economics of corrupt government', *Kyklos*, **28**, 1975, fasc. I.

5. An examination of this sociological model may be found in a paper prepared by William Meckling for the Second International Interlaken Seminar on Analysis and Ideology, held in June 1975. The paper will be published in 1976 by the *Schweizerische Zeitschrift für Volkswirtschaft und Statistik*. A full session of the Third International Interlaken Seminar on Analysis and Ideology will explore the issue still further with papers presented by co-authors Gerard Gäfgen and Hans Georg Monissen and by Willi Meyer. Among the serious writings by Marxian philosophers are some published by the group at the University of Belgrade – with specific reference to Stojanovich.

6. A short comment should be added apropos of Rhodesia-Zimbabwe and South Africa. That apartheid involves a wealth transfer to the white population was clearly recognized by the South African labour unions in the 1920s. At the time, the market operated toward gradual integration, and this occurred most particularly on the 'marriage market'. But recognition of the internal wealth transfer implicit in apartheid should not blind us to the fact that the economic welfare of the blacks in South Africa, on the average, probably exceeds the levels reached (or descended to) in any other African country.

    One should also note the intriguing statement made in Mozambique by one of the black leaders of Rhodesia-Zimbabwe. Making clear that a rigid socialist regime will be instituted in Zimbabwe, he warned particularly that it would have no room for assorted competing black politicians whose socialist ideology is suspect. A comparison of future patterns in Mozambique, Zimbabwe and Angola with the life patterns feasible in 'oppressive white Rhodesia' or apartheid South Africa will certainly be interesting.

7. Peter Bauer, 'Western guilt and Third World poverty', *Commentary*, January 1976.

8. Ibid.

9. See Peter Bauer's 'Politicization of knowledge: development economics', prepared for the First International Interlaken Seminar on Analysis and Ideology in June 1974, and subsequently published in the *Schweizerische Zeitschrift für Volkswirtschaft und Statistik*, 1975.

10. The pervasive concern about a permanent food crisis should stimulate US representatives to present alternatives to the established agricultural and land tenure policies of the Third World. Tanzania recently accepted the Soviet model and collectivized agriculture. The resulting effect on her agricultural output is predictable. Subtler ramifications bearing on agricultural output and population emerge from other land tenure systems. Arthur DeVany demonstrated, for instance, in an interesting study using Mexican data (prepared for the April 1976 Carnegie–Rochester Conference on Public Policy) that the ubiquitous usufruct system creates incentives lowering output and raising the average family size.

11 The socio-political vision of Keynes*

Some background

The moral crisis of our world in this century has been pondered and discussed by many learned and thoughtful men. The old orientations offering meanings, valuations and interpretations of life, the universe and man's relation to this universe, transmitted by the Christian churches, ultimately crumbled and decayed. Nietzsche expressed this evolution in a famous passage describing a man with a lantern searching vainly and announcing that 'God is dead'. The English philosopher G.E. Moore expressed, late in the last century, the resulting state of mind facing an empty world and explored the necessity for a new orientation in life. And so have the churches in recent decades. They increasingly filled the void with a social and political activism. They fulfilled thus the prophecy of the German philosopher Feuerbach, a post-Hegelian contemporary of Karl Marx. He argued that the void would be filled by a new religion – and politics would form the new religion of western man.

Keynes was born into the early period of intellectual and moral fermentation. His 'early beliefs', adhered to during a lifetime according to his own testimony, were decisively shaped by G.E. Moore. This philosophy attempted to cope with fundamental ethical questions posed by the void. Attention was redirected away from eternity and the salvation of the individual soul and concentrated on man's finite life on earth. In the resulting process the social consensus among members of society, particularly among the educated classes, gradually decayed. The nature of a desirable human society became a central focus of political thinking and political activity. This focus actually underlies most of the political issues at this time, whether it is pollution, energy, health care or the environment. These issues are essentially used by influential groups as an instrument to restructure society in some manner.

The moral order, consisting of the prevailing more or less conscious or explicit rules of behaviour and general norms of conduct, together with explicit social and political institutions inherited from the past, was increasingly questioned. The search for a new orientation induced by the experience of the void also produced a questioning and critical attitude with respect to the social patterns constituting the existing society.

* Originally published in *The Legacy of Keynes*, ed. David A. Reese, San Francisco, Cal.: Harper & Row, 1987, 23–56. I wish to acknowledge gratefully many discussions bearing on issues covered in this paper with Allan H. Meltzer (Carnegie-Mellon University). Thomas Lys (Northwestern University) also contributed a useful clarification on Keynes's 'Beauty Contest' interpretation of the stock market.

188

Keynes was deeply involved in this dissolution of a consensus. His 'early beliefs' drove him unavoidably down this particular intellectual road. We should recognize that Keynes's intellectual horizon and driving concerns reach a long way beyond his work as a 'technical economist' understood in our twentieth-century sense. His concern for social and political issues beyond the range of a narrowly conceived economic analysis moves him closer in intent, but not in content and ideas, to the eighteenth-century moral philosophers. He appears, however, very little touched by their most important and durable contributions. His thoughts and ideas seem more attuned to the rationalist eighteenth-century French tradition. His deep concern and pronounced interest in the nature of a viable, humane society was time and again expressed in a wide-ranging series of essays.

The diversity of essays bearing on the socio-political theme are united by a common theme, namely, the need, in his judgement, of a new society with a different structure of government and a different economic organization. The *General Theory*, the central arch of his professional work with a lasting influence in the profession, fits remarkably well into the structure of his social and political thought. It provided an important intellectual underpinning for the social, economic and political proposals advanced over the years.

Keynes, as a social and political-economic thinker, forms the theme of my essay. I wish to explore with you the nature of his ideas and arguments and give a critical assessment of both. But first we prepare for this exploration and assessment with a description of the major socio-political visions of society contending in this century for attention and advocates. This classification may help us to place Keynes into the context of our modern world. The result may reveal a strange and possibly problematic mixture of ideas and positions.

The socio-political spectrum
It is tempting here to follow the simplistic American custom and order the political world and its ideologies into 'liberal' and 'conservative'. But this is really too crude and uninformative. This standard description is almost an exercise in disinformation. The characteristic features of alternative visions of a desirable society are more usefully approached in terms of social and political institutions including, most particularly, the prevailing pattern of property rights. This choice determines the general nature of political and economic organizations. The European tradition offers us a rough but useful classification for our purposes. Four views are typically distinguished: the socialist, the social democrat, the liberal and the conservative position. The American custom combines the first two as a 'liberal' position and joins the last two under a 'conservative' label. The positions joined in this manner exhibit, however, significant differences that should be explicitly recognized.

The socialist vision considers the most radical restructuring. It offers, however, not a monolithic blueprint. One version accepts the Russian model with some variations and approximations revealed among the satellites of the Soviet empire. Its crucial characteristic is the abolition of private property in the means of production. Some more or less restricted property rights in agriculture and some other areas may occasionally survive. A residue of markets and market prices usually remains. But the dominant social co-ordination mechanism of the economy's activities does not rely on markets and market prices. A complex political apparatus attempts to co-ordinate all activities. Another version emerged over the postwar period. The experience with 'real socialism' disillusioned reform socialists. They mostly abandoned the Soviet model and hope for salvation with some variations of the Yugoslav model, that is, a system of worker-owned firms. But the property rights of the workers are severely limited and a dominant political control remains.

The social democrat conception centres essentially on an extended and encompassing welfare state. The political apparatus is designed for the extraction of a massive redistribution. This is supplemented by an extended range of government enterprises or semi-independent but politically controlled corporations. This list includes in particular transportation, public utilities, communication, banks, insurance, health-care business, and so on. A wide range of activities operate thus essentially beyond market influences and are controlled by the working of political institutions. Private property rights, even in means of production, still remain. But these rights are typically restricted in various dimensions. The wave of 'employment protection' legislation observed in several countries over the past 20 years offers a good example in this respect. A range of activities co-ordinated by markets and market prices continues, however. But the social democrat position will always look at this market sector with suspicion and unease,[1] ever ready to implement further institutional restriction with opportunities of political control.

The liberal vision offers an entirely different solution. Many western countries satisfy at this stage much more closely the social democrat model than the liberal vision. The latter offers thus, measured against our political and economic reality, a somewhat radical solution. It differs fundamentally from the other three positions by a severe constitutional limitation on the range of admissible government activities. It also involves a much stricter constitutional anchoring of property rights. The socialist position is obviously firmly opposed to such ideas. The possible occurrence of constitutional provisions in social democrat and conservative thought bearing on both aspects generally means very little. They are qualified and subjected to conditions that would actually allow the political process to modify property rights quite arbitrarily. The constitutional emphasis of the liberal position implies, of course, a dominant reliance on markets and market prices as a social co-ordination mechanism.

The conservative position is more difficult to describe. We already outlined the crucial difference with the liberal vision. It shares the welfare state with the social democrat vision. It also favours an institutional arrangement that relies on government and private corporations within a set of complex political institutions. The corporativist theme traditionally formed an important component of conservative thought. The system of interlocking institutions linking government and private business firms would be controlled mostly by private interests or jointly by political and private representatives.

It may be objected that concentration on the institutional aspects emphasized in the previous passage is insufficient. An important dimension seems omitted. Each vision offers also a rationale that supports the institutional programme. This rationale is indeed important. It offers a promise of a 'good life' in the context of the institutional programme advocated by the vision. It is a crucial element in the marketing of the vision. The rationale centres in each case on a moral conception. These conceptions differ radically among the four positions. The socialist vision expects to change man's moral nature by social engineering, whereas the conservatives plan to constrain his immorality by suitable social constraints administered by the state. But the actual consequences of the visions' attempted realizations depend on the detailed nature of the established institutional arrangements. The ideological rationale offers then a useful scale against which to assess the actual performance of the institutionalized vision. The relation between the ideological justification and the institutional programme is moreover an important subject for a critical analysis.

Our description suggests a systematic ordering of socio-political visions in terms of two conditions: the extent of constitutional limitations on the political sector and the guarantees or protection offered to private property rights together with their admissible range. The latter includes the right to sell and buy on any market with the right to open new firms or close old firms. Measured against this scale, we may note a substantial overlap between the social democrat and the conservative positions. It need also be noted that the classification should not be confused with party labels. The European socialist parties include both advocates of socialism and social democracy. The liberal parties frequently exhibit both social democrat and conservative strands. And similarly, some conservative parties show clear social democrat intrusions. Hayek did not in vain address his book, *The Road to Serfdom*,[2] to the 'socialists of all parties'.

Keynes's socio-political vision

Where do we place Keynes's socio-political vision in this spectrum? We discover easily enough his rejection of the liberal solution. He finds the severe limitation imposed on government unacceptable. The matter requires, in his judgement, a thoroughly fresh approach: 'Perhaps the chief task of Economists is to distinguish afresh the Agenda of Government from the Non-Agenda, and the companion task of Politics is to devise forms of Government within a Democracy which should be capable of accomplishing the Agenda.'[3] Keynes published in 1925 an informative article 'Am I a Liberal?'[4] He surveyed the three political parties in England of his time and pondered whether he could be a member of any one of them. He rejects the labour party:

> It is a class party and the class is not my class ... but the class war would find me on the side of the educated bourgeoisie. ... But, above all, I do not believe that the intellectual elements of the Labour Party will ever exercise adequate control; too much will always be decided by those who do not know at all what they are talking about; and if ... the control of the party is seized by an autocratic inner ring, the control will be exercised in the interests of the extreme Left Wing – the section of the Labour Party which I shall designate the Party of Catastrophe.[5]

The Conservative party also appears quite unattractive:

> It leads nowhere, it satisfies no ideal; it conforms to no intellectual standard; it is not even safe, or calculated to preserve from spoilers that degree of civilization that we have already attained.[6]

There still remains the Liberal party. He finds that it still is 'the best instrument of future progress – if only it had strong leadership and the right programme'.[7] Keynes notes in particular that the Liberal Party is too much tied to the past and its issues. Past issues provide no political momentum to a party. So he addresses the question of what 'the Liberal Party ought to be'. A programme of five points is roughly outlined, composed of the peace question (pacifism), questions of government, sex, drugs and economic affairs. A few crucial points may be selected:

> The government will have to take on many duties which it has avoided in the past. For these purposes Ministries and Parliament will be unserviceable. Our task must be to decentralize and devolve whenever we can, and in particular to establish semi-independent corporations and organs of administration to which duties of government, new and old, will be entrusted – without, however, impairing the democratic principle of the ultimate sovereignty of Parliament.[8]

And the message bearing on the economic question involves a most definite rejection of the liberal vision:

The transition from economic anarchy to a regime which deliberately aims at controlling and directing economic forces in the interests of social justice and social stability, will present enormous difficulties. ... The New Liberalism should seek the solution of these difficulties.[9]

Does Keynes opt for socialism under a new name? Let us consider his own words:

Like other new religions, Leninism derives its power not from the multitude but from a small minority of enthusiastic converts whose zeal and intolerance make each one the equal in strength of a hundred indifferentists. Like other new religions, it is led by those who can combine the new spirit, perhaps sincerely, with seeing a good deal more than their followers, politicians with at least an average dose of political cynicism, who can smile as well as frown, volatile experimentalists, released by religion from truth and mercy but not blind to facts and expediency, and open therefore to the charge ... of hypocrisy. Like other new religions, it seems to take the color and gaiety and freedom of everyday life and to offer a drab substitute in the square wooden faces of its devotees. Like other new religions, it persecutes without justice or pity those actively resisting it. Like other new religions, it is unscrupulous. Like other new religions, it is filled with missionary ardor and ecumenical ambitions. But to say that Leninism is the faith of a persecuting and propagating minority of fanatics led by hypocrites is, after all, to say no more nor less than that it is a new religion and not merely a party, and Lenin Mahomet, not a Bismarck. If we want to frighten ourselves in our capitalist easy chairs, we can picture the communists of Russia as though the early Christians led by Attila were using the equipment of the Holy Inquisition and the Jesuit missions to enforce the literal economics of the New Testament.[10]

This is a harsh indictment of the Soviet model. But the issue of socialism appears somewhat unresolved in the context of Keynes's further comments. He concludes that the communist implementation of socialism contains an old, but important, strand of a true religion of the future: 'It tries to construct a framework of society in which pecuniary motives as influencing actions shall have a changed relative importance, in which social approbations shall be differently distributed, and where behavior which previously was normal and respectable, ceases to be either the one or the other.'[11]

Let us consider also the following passage:

To me it seems clearer every day that the moral problem of our age is concerned with the love of money, with the habitual appeal to the money motive in nine-tenths of the activities of life, with the universal striving after individual economic security as the prime object of endeavor, with the social approbation of money as the measure of constructive success. ... The decaying religions around us, which have less and less interest for most people unless it be as an agreeable form of magical ceremony or of social observances, have lost their moral significance just because ... they do not touch in the least degrees on these essential matters. A revolution in our ways of thinking and feeling about money may become the growing purpose of contemporary embodiment of the ideal. Perhaps, therefore, Russian Communism does represent the first confused stirrings of a great new religion.[12]

We also note his complaint that capitalism offers no moral guide or moral sense within an encompassing orientation. Its members move in a peculiar vacuum. The basic thrust of these comments certainly suggests that Keynes found little attraction in the Soviet Russian implementation of socialism but that he does strongly approve of the central strands of the socialist vision.

But what are his suggestions for institutional implementation of the fundamental directive provided by the moral problem of our time? There is no simple acceptance of a standard socialist programme. We find some clues in his paper. 'The End of Laissez-faire', published in 1926,[13] ten years before the *General Theory*. We find a strange mixture of ideas drawn from the socialist vision and social democrat and conservative programmes. In his own words:

> I suggest that progress lies in the growth and the recognition of semi-autonomous bodies within the state – bodies whose criterion of actions within their own field is solely the public good as they understand it, and from whose deliberations motives of private advantage are excluded, though some place it may still be necessary to leave, until the ambit of man's altruism grows wider, to the separate advantage of particular groups, classes or faculties – bodies which in the ordinary course of affairs are mainly autonomous within their prescribed limitation, but are subject in the last resort to the sovereignty of democracy expressed through Parliament.[14]

Keynes observes that the trend toward a system of autonomous bodies is already under way. He refers to 'the Universities, the Bank of England, the Port of London Authority, even perhaps the Railway Companies' (private corporations at the time). He continues: 'More interesting ... is the trend of Joint Stock institutions, when they have reached a certain age and size, to approximate to the status of public corporations rather than that of individualistic private enterprise.'[15] Big enterprise gradually 'socialized' itself: 'A point arrives in the growth of a big institution ... at which the owners of the capital, i.e., the shareholders, are almost entirely dissociated from the management, with the result that the direct personal interest of the latter in the making of great profit becomes quite secondary.'[16] Keynes admits that this evolution is 'not ... an unmixed gain; [it is associated with] many of the faults ... of State Socialism, [but it is] nevertheless ... a natural line of evolution. The battle of Socialism against unlimited private profit is being won in detail hour by hour.'[17] The following passage also reflects Keynes's ambivalent position concerning socialism:

I criticize doctrinaire State Socialism not because it seeks to engage men's altruistic impulses in the service of Society, or because it departs from *laissez-faire,* or because it takes away from men's natural liberty to make a million, or because it has courage for bold experimentations. All these things I applaud. I criticize it because it misses the significance of what is actually going on.[18]

The seed of its problem seems to be, so we read, its Benthamite origin.

Keynes also addresses the choice of a criterion for the agenda of government: 'The important thing for government is not to do things which individuals are doing already and to do them a little better or a little worse, but to do those things which are not done at all.'[19] Keynes notes here emphatically that 'the greatest economic evils of our time are the fruits of risk, uncertainty and ignorance'.[20] He compares economic life with a lottery, so that 'great inequality of wealth comes about'.[21] The same patterns create, so he thinks, unemployment and impair efficiency and production. Keynes argues that the cure for these evils lies outside the sphere of the individuals and belongs to the agenda of government. It is particularly noteworthy that Keynes expresses, ten years before publication of the *General Theory*, deep doubts about the social function of the investment–saving nexus: 'Some co-ordinated act of intelligent judgment is required as to the scale on which it is desirable that the community as a whole should save, the scale on which these savings should go abroad in the form of foreign investments, and whether the present organization of the investment market distributes savings along the most nationally productive channels.'[22] These matters, concludes Keynes, should not be left 'to the chance of private judgment and profits'.[23]

The general direction of Keynes's socio-political thoughts had thus already emerged many years before he wrote the *General Theory*. Some strands of his thought, in particular the doubts about the investment–savings nexus, anticipated a central point of the *General Theory*. But his argument remained vaguely conjectural and totally undeveloped. It was no more than a passing sentence. There was moreover no adequate rationale offered for his general vision of the institutional structure characterizing a New Liberalism. This vacuum was partly filled with the *General Theory*. It provided the underlying vision of the socioeconomic process in an extensive analytic context. The socio-political programme outlined over the prior decade naturally fitted with the *General Theory* into a coherent story of modern western society. A closer look at the argument developed in the *General Theory* is thus necessary in order to understand and critically assess his socio-political thoughts.

The general theory

We need not, for our purposes, delve into the full detail of Keynes's theory of employment. It is sufficient to trace the broad contours and the dominant patterns introduced by Keynes. It is particularly important to probe 'behind' the usual formal textbook representation into Keynes's underlying rationale.

The prevailing level of output and employment is determined by the interaction between aggregate real demand for output and aggregate real supply. The realization of 'full output' and 'full employment' requires that aggregate real demand reach the level of full output. The central purpose of Keynes's book is to argue that this will not happen in general. Modern economies typically produce an aggregate real demand below full output. The interaction between aggregate demand and aggregate supply settles in modern economics (for deep structural reasons) at a level below full employment and full output. There is moreover not much to be achieved with financial tinkering. Lower money wages or increases in the money stock may induce temporary deviations from the underemployment equilibrium and contribute to movements of the system around the central position. But there operates no feedback mechanism to establish full employment within the basic structure of a modern market economy. A fundamental failure is thus built into these economies. No automatic readjustments raise aggregate real demand to the full employment level. And within the structure of the market system no such feedback can possibly emerge. Basic structural reform of the system offers the only remedy for the evils of widespread unemployment, wasted resources and pronounced inequality. In spite of the book's title, interest rates and money are but an appendage of little relevance to the basic problem. The underemployment level is dominated by real – that is, nonmonetary – conditions. The business cycle – the 'trade cycle' in Keynes's words – is similarly controlled by nonmonetary conditions. The nature of those conditions implies moreover that monetary policy exerts a negligible influence on the real situation expressed by output and employment. This theme differs radically from the 'mainstream' Keynesian position established most particularly in the United States over the past 20 years. Keynes's emphasis on the dominant role of nonmonetary conditions yields another implication conflicting with standard Keynesian views. The latter developed, with the so-called Phillips curve representing labour market patterns, the idea of a permanent tradeoff between unemployment and inflation. Shifting financial policies to induce a higher level of inflation would lower the prevailing rate of unemployment. Keynes's analysis doesn't accommodate such an idea. The dominant role of real conditions prevents such a permanent tradeoff. Monetary expansion thus unavoidably raises the price level even around the underemployment equilibrium. Unemployment cannot be 'inflated away' under the circumstances. This solution was not available to Keynes.

But let us consider now the nonmonetary conditions placed by Keynes on centre stage of the economic drama. We examine for this purpose the composition of aggregate real demand. It is a sum of three components: real consumption expenditures of the household sector, investment expenditure of the business sector, and government expenditures on goods and services. Consumer expenditures are presented as a somewhat passive entity. They are governed, in Keynes's scheme of the world, by a reliable pattern linking these expenditures to income. Consumer expenditures rise with income but at a lesser rate, that is, a given increment in income produces a smaller increment in consumer expenditures. This means that the proportion of consumers' expenditures to income falls as the level of income rises. The mirror image of that fact is thus the rise in the savings ratio with rising income. Savings – that is, the gap between consumers' expenditures and income – expands more than proportionately with income. Investment and government expenditures must fill this gap in order to achieve full output. Their sum must balance the level of savings forthcoming at full output level. Employment and output settle at a lower level, should investments (plus government) expenditures remain below full output saving. Keynes's basic point emphasizes that the investment–savings nexus does not function in a socially useful manner. It provides no adequate mechanisms linking savings with investments. We read that savings and investment decisions are made independently and to a good extent by different groups of individuals. A fundamental market failure in the investment–savings nexus is thus responsible for endemic underemployment suffered by modern economics. Investment expenditures are generally, for deep structural reasons, insufficient to fill the gap between consumers' expenditures and full output. The villain in this economic drama is the operation of the mechanism represented by the stock exchange, which links savings with investments. The *General Theory* elaborates in a lengthy chapter the nature of the short allusion made ten years earlier.

Investment decisions proceed in a more complex and tenuous setting than consumers' expenditures. They are influenced by the expected yield of the investment over its lifetime and the rate of interest adjusted for a risk premium. This risk premium reveals the sense of pervasive uncertainty surrounding all investment projects. Keynes elaborated the importance of this uncertainty with great emphasis. It shapes the premium added to the interest rates in order to obtain the best estimate of the investment projects' present value. Projects with a present cost below the present value will be executed.

The prevailing uncertainty raises the discount rate and lowers investment expenditures forthcoming at any given interest rate. The assessment of future yields and the discount rate are unavoidably quite volatile in the context of a diffuse uncertainty beyond any calculable risk. This volatility was reflected by investment expenditures. Keynes stresses also that investment expenditures, even with unchanged assessment of a murky future, respond only to a small extent to changes in interest rates and thus to manipulation of monetary policy. Two circumstances contribute to this result. One is the fact that a given change in the interest rate produces a much smaller proportionate change in the discount rate. The other reason is the rapid decline in the present value of projects as one delves deeper into their potential list. This is reinforced by a simultaneous increase in the cost of investment projects as the rate of investment expands.

But this is not yet the full story behind endemically insufficient investment and low underemployment. The stock exchange magnifies the prevailing uncertainty and fails to offer a channel for the rational allocation of saving. The behaviour of stock prices, which reflects the market's current evaluation of existing real capital, is determined by the interaction of two groups of operators on the stock market. The 'enterprisers' assess the 'fundamentals' shaping the profile of yields to be expected from investment projects. They invest resources to inform themselves about the best estimate of a project's value in a rational manner. Speculators, on the other hand, proceed very differently. They seem little concerned about 'fundamentals'. They address their effort to guess the stock prices prevailing in the near future. But this is not the end of their game. They wish, after all, to form a guess about market prices resulting from interaction between all operators. The average of all agents' guesses is thus more relevant than their own guess. So each agent makes again his or her own guess about the average of the first-round guesses. The guessing game need not stop, however, at this stage. Agents may guess the average of the second round of guesses about the average of the first round guesses, and so forth and so on. Keynes argues furthermore that 'speculators' dominate 'enterprisers'. This is presented as an inevitable result of an investment market based on the 'principle of liquidity' involving continuous re-evaluation and trading of existing assets in the context of an uncertain future. The result in Keynes's judgement is an essentially irrational price formation. The stock prices formed on such markets bear little relation to the relevant 'fundamentals'. It follows therefore that the stock market is a poor guide, measured in social terms, to a nation's investment activity. The private interests driving the market cannot be expected to perform a socially useful function. The great uncertainty to which they contribute explains in Keynes's scheme both the insufficient average volume and volatility of investment expenditures. It also explains the poor response of investment expenditures to monetary manipulation. Keynes summarized his argument with the famous metaphor about the beauty contest:

> Professional investment may be likened to those newspaper competitions in which the competitors have to pick out the six prettiest faces from a hundred photographs, the prize being awarded to the competitor whose choice most nearly corresponds to the average preferences of the competitors as a whole; so that each competitor has to pick, not those faces which he himself finds prettiest, but those which he thinks likeliest to catch the fancy of the other competitors, all of whom

are looking at the problem from the same point of view. It is not a case of choosing those which, to the best of one's judgment, are really the prettiest, nor even those which average opinion genuinely thinks the prettiest. We have reached the third degree where we devote our intelligences to anticipating what average opinion expects the average opinion to be. And there are some, I believe, who practice the fourth, fifth and higher degrees.[24]

With the fundamental flaw in the machinery of modern economics thus recognized and characterized, what solution to the resulting evils of unemployment and gross inequality does Keynes propose? He toys shortly with the idea of a large transfer tax on trading securities in order to break the beauty contest game. But this is hardly sufficient in his judgement. A more fundamental approach is required.

It is interesting to note that Keynes did not propose the solution of mainstream postwar American Keynesianism. The standard textbook discussion forcefully directs attention to fiscal policy as the government's crucial instrument to hold aggregate real demand around full output. Postwar Keynesianism thus developed the notion of a fiscal steering wheel for the economy expressed in fiscal activism and 'fiscal fine-tuning'. The textbook interpretations, whether in terms of the simple 'Keynesian cross' or the so-called IS/ LM framework, naturally fostered such conceptions. The maintenance of full employment became in this view the chief responsibility of fiscal policy. Monetary policy was simply assigned the role of an accommodating player controlling interest rates at a 'politically acceptable level'.

But this was not Keynes's cure of the problem. Fiscal policy management would not suffice to cope with the social and economic ills his diagnosis revealed. Fiscal policy would not remove the 'inherent irrationality associated with the beauty contest game' played on the stock exchange. Nor would it remove the pervasive and obstructive uncertainty and the volatility of investment decisions imposed on the economy by the interaction of private interests. Lastly, Keynes was very much concerned with the accumulation of real capital in modern economies. He considered it quite feasible to accumulate with a suitable 'institutional policy' sufficient real capital to drive interest rates to zero and to make real capital a nonscarce free good 'within two generations'. It required, however, on the basis of Keynes's own diagnosis of the system's basic flaw, a different approach than that chosen by mainstream Keynesians. Keynes's answer to the problem was the 'socialization of investment'. The economy's investment activities should be removed from the sphere of private interests centred around a 'beauty contest game' with socially irrational consequences. He understood that this socialization of investment need be supplemented by exchange controls. He also understood that such controls would have to be rather far-reaching and also cover domestic transactions related in some manner to international transactions. It was possibly these conceptions that influenced the statement in the preface of the German editions that his theory can be applied more easily to the conditions of a totalitarian state than could the inherited classical theory.

A critical examination

This section examines the relevance of the intellectual heritage conveyed to us. This heritage involves two issues. One refers to Keynes's diagnosis of a market system's inherent flaws. The other addresses a fundamental question of political economy. This second issue, in contrast to the first, was transmitted to the Keynesian postwar tradition. It typically characterizes the policy discussion and the vision of policy institutions associated with mainstream Keynesianism.

On the diagnostic level, I address Keynes's factual assertion and inference associated with the 'beauty contest game'. The inference of 'social irrationality' of the stock exchange as a guide to investment activity seems quite plausible. Some probing examination appears, however, advisable. The problem starts with the first-level estimates of the stock prices in the near future made by speculators. These estimates are either based directly or indirectly (by observing the enterprisers for signals) on 'market fundamentals', or they are simply random guesses. Consider now, in the first case, the sequence of estimates made in ascending levels. Each step in the sequence exploits additional and new (for each speculator) information beyond what was available in the first round of estimation. This process, contrary to Keynes's irrationality claim, reveals speculators' endeavours to improve their substantive assessment. The process thus raises the efficiency of the market. We also should note here that the analogy with a beauty contest fails on a crucial point. The sequence of rounds guessing the average stock price adds relevant new information about the assets traded. The rounds in the beauty contest game add, on the other hand, no new information about the prettiness of faces. It only adds information about other agents' attitudes about prettiness but offers no information about the inherent quality of prettiness.

Two alternative situations need be distinguished in the second case. Suppose the first-level estimates are unbiased random guesses. The sequence of guesses emphasized by Keynes also increases the information available to speculators and consequently contribute to market efficiency. But what happens in case the first-round estimates are biased, contemporaneously correlated across speculators, and also serially correlated? The last property would correspond to the 'waves of optimism and pessimism fuelled by animal spirits' emphasized by Keynes. But the last feature is not compatible with well-established observations. Even critics of the efficient market and random walk hypotheses concede that serial correlations of changes in stock prices, if positive, are so low as to make it very difficult to distinguish from a random walk. And should the speculators' guesses be systematically biased, then we should observe over time a redistribution of wealth between speculators and enterprisers in favour of the latter. Even speculators, preferring profits to losses, would learn over time under the circumstances and attend more to fundamentals or exploit in one way or another information about the enterprisers.

This leads us to a factual issue. Keynes argues that at the New York Stock Exchange speculators dominate enterprisers. This assertion seems most doubtful. A large host of financial analysts, specializing on various branches of the economy or groups of firms, diligently invest valuable resources to probe the 'fundamentals'. The same analysts and their customers may also re-evaluate their estimates exploiting information signalled by others. This seems both privately and socially rational. It appears to me, at this stage, that Keynes's central arch of his structure is poorly and dubiously supported by his argument. The facts are wrong and the inference, so crucial for his socio-political purpose, fails. I submit that his argument in the *General Theory* offers no rationale for his socio-political blueprint. But we should add also a warning. Keynes's emphasis on uncertainty beyond calculable risk is very important and should find more attention in our professional work. He simply confused the 'barometer of uncertainty' with its source. It would seem a useful task for economists to probe the nature of this pervasive uncertainty. Its occurrence bears importantly on policy problems and analysis. Most of the policy discussions and policy analysis proceed with a denial of such uncertainty. The application of the resulting policy analysis to our world is consequently highly questionable. Most importantly, we should respond to Keynes's challenge with a careful examination of institutional arrangements – that is, choice of institutional policies – that contribute to lower uncertainty and its impact on our economic or political affairs.

Such institutional problems are closely associated with our second issue, namely, Keynes's social-political vision. It was already noted that his views on socialism are quite ambivalent. He proposes to 'socialize' the investment goods sector but not the consumer goods sector. The market system raises no problems in this sector of the economy and attends with reasonable efficiency to the consumers' preferences. His diagnosis locates the flaws of the economic machinery in the investment goods sector. But the socialist vision contains major strands of thought of which he approves. This attitude reveals an important aspect of Keynes's thought and character exhibited by many members of the intelligentsia and college-educated classes.

Among the strands so favoured by Keynes is the 'love of money', which the market systems allow to bloom and possibly dominate people's hearts. The expression is somewhat unfortunate and misleading. The moral problem 'of our age' addressed by Keynes is really the 'love of wealth'. He clearly disapproves in principle but apparently not so much for his person. He finds particularly attractive that the socialist vision challenges and engages men's altruism to serve society. Keynes shares with many advocates of the socialist vision two fundamental fallacies, a factual and a moral one.

The factual fallacy involves the inherent self-expression of people associated with their basic historical-biological nature. The socialist vision is usually based on the assumption of a perfectly malleable human nature completely shaped eventually by the social environment. Man is believed to be born an empty slate to be filled in any particular way according to his social experience. Proceeding from this Rousseauesque basis, the socialist vision asserts that man's nature changes once private property is abolished and opportunities for private profit-seeking and wealth accumulation are removed. The institutional arrangements of a socialist state destroy the old temptations. The slate can be rewritten and human nature is radically changed. The social conditions suppressing profit seeking and wealth accumulation unavoidably channel men's energies, so we hear, into altruistic expressions of activity. People will be socially oriented and act in accordance with the public spirit and interest. A new social atmosphere and a new dimension of life opens up as a result.

This dream is a sad fallacy and is the fatal illusion of our time. Indeed, man cannot live on bread alone. But the old dream dissolved for the intelligentsia and this void was unbearable. Feuerbach's prophecy thus came true, and Keynes's socio-political thoughts form a revealing strand of this development. We know at this stage, beyond the romantic-rationalist tradition of the eighteenth century still floating around in contemporary socio-political thinking, that people are not born as an empty slate to be covered with the right kind of writing by social engineering. They are born with a genetic endowment. And this endowment shapes each individual's most fundamental life expression, that is, self-interest and self-realization. It is important not to confuse this with egotism. Man is neither egotistic nor altruistic. He spans the full range of possibilities within his self-interested behaviour. The latter simply means that, given a choice, people prefer not to delegate decisions affecting their own person irrevocably and unconditionally to others. They prefer in general to make their own decisions about their lifestyle. Whatever altruistic gestures may emerge, they are conditioned by each person's own assessments and volitions. This is made clear by the fact that we are discriminatingly altruistic and not anonymously and uniformly.

Proper recognition of man's basic nature substantially shapes our valuation of the socio-political issues raised by Keynes. Institutional arrangements suspending profit seeking and private wealth accumulation do not suspend self-interested behaviour. A prevalent custom to equate the latter with the first is simply naive. A short visit in Washington, DC, or a look at church organ-

izations or many other nonprofit organizations should inform us better. Variations in institutional arrangements only modify the specific form of individual self-realization. It follows that socialism does not engage men's altruism in the service of society. People will adjust to the prevailing institutions.
Profit-seeking and the 'love of money' are replaced by a competitive striving
for power, status and influence. Men still pursue their own interests. And even
their attention to the 'public good' is qualified and conditioned by their own
perception and interests. Keynes plays artfully with an old human dream, a
dream resulting in oppression and systematic cruelty whenever it was
coercively imposed on human societies. Keynes, like many social visionaries,
fails to understand the fundamental socio-political problem. The basic problem is not to change men's nature by a felicitous or 'rational choice' of our
social and political institutions. This is futile and illusionary. The relevant
problem is just the reverse. It was clearly understood by the Scottish moral
philosophers of the eighteenth century. We need to accept man's basic nature
in all its ambivalence and consider what institutions offer the best chance,
never an absolute guarantee, that this self-interested behaviour will be channelled into socially productive directions beneficial to the members of society. A social co-ordination in the context of a market system with private
property offers still the best opportunity in this respect. The market system
provides a feedback, a link, guiding self-interested behaviour to some extent
according to the values and preferences prevailing in society. The power
system developed under socialism provides no such feedback. On the contrary, it suppresses or disregards the values and preferences expressed by
members of society. This property is an inherent feature of socialist systems
not much appreciated by our contemporary social dreamers.

But I can hear an objection to the effect that to accept man's basic nature is
immoral. The moral problem of our age, to paraphrase Keynes, is to change
this nature by suitable social engineering. But we have abundant historical
evidence that social engineering fails miserably in its endeavour. The result is
a coercive imposition of the desired moral posture with the aid of suitably
chosen political institutions. The reality of life in such societies hardly measures up to the moral motivations for their existence.

But let us attend to another fundamental moral issue. Keynes, as many
other social dreamers, was concerned to find institutional arrangements that
remove all, or most, moral problems or dilemmas and protect man against
their occurrence. Society needs to be programmed to protect man from such
exposure. Dostoevsky's Grand Inquisitor would agree. But such a society is
fundamentally immoral. Coerced actions have no moral dimension, for the
moral problem confronts individuals in their free choice between the options
of life. Francis of Assisi faced a deep moral question when he pondered
whether he should accept the life-style of a businessman or become '*il*

poverino'. The confrontation with moral problems and moral dilemmas is an expression of our essential humanity. Ants and bees have no moral problems. But man encounters such problems and moral virtue appears just because he can exercise lifestyle options. An essentially human society can thus only exist where we have the option to make the wrong moral choice. A society deliberately constructed to prevent man from making moral lapses really attempts to convert people into creatures similar to ants and bees. It essentially dehumanizes man. The social dreamers might usefully reflect under what institutional arrangements do moral lapses, life decisions to immorality, affect society more seriously. It seems to me that the potential damage to third parties is significantly smaller under a market system than under socialist institutions. We need simply to understand that fallible man's basic nature is unchanged under variations of institutional arrangements. The pattern of specific actions changes and self-realizing and self-interested behaviour explores different avenues. A market system, however imperfect, diffuses and disciplines power much more than in the context of the concentrated power of a socialist apparatus. This conclusion also applies upon further examination to the Yugoslav model of a socialism based on worker-owned firms and apparent self-management. The elaboration of this point needs, however, to be suspended for another occasion.[25]

The moral issue addressed by Keynes touches fundamental questions of our time bearing on the choice of social orders and political organization. It also touches on the role of religion, understood as comprehensive orientations of life in society and our universe. The relation between social order and religion looms in this context with particular weight. Keynes interpreted the social order created by Lenin as an attempt to implement a 'new religion'. The realization of a specific socio-political order appears as a necessary (and possible sufficient) condition for the 'new man' to express the 'new religion'. The politics of modern man's new religion thus mobilizes emotive energies on behalf of a particular social order to be anchored and maintained by political means. This view of the 'new religion' clearly affects Keynes's judgement of capitalism: 'Modern capitalism is absolutely irreligious, without internal union, without much public spirit, often ... a mere congeries of possessors and pursuers.'[26] Keynes considers that 'irreligious capitalism' can only survive against 'religious communism' in case it is 'immensely' more successful in economic terms.

An incidental point may be addressed first. Since Keynes wrote these passages about 60 years ago, we have learned much about the problems emerging in a socialist society. The tension between its ideology, that is, its religion, and the reality of life under socialist institutions induced major adjustments in attitudes and forced specific behaviour patterns conducive to effective survival in the world. It fostered in particular a singular attention to the game of power characterizing the social scene. The religion became a facade to cover a brutal reality with pleasant words. The religious fervour on behalf of *some* socialist state continues, however. It gradually shifted directions to hopefully alternative implementations of the dream. So we had better attend to the issue posed by Keynes.

The passage quoted above from Keynes's discussion of the Soviet model emphasizes an unpleasant similarity of all new religions. Its well-modulated phrases and imaginative metaphors convey a plausible impression. But Keynes misses a crucial distinction. New religions may all have the unpleasant characteristics (intolerance without mercy to deviants, and so on) attributed by Keynes. But the human and social significance of these characteristics differs radically in accordance with the social status of the religion. A new religion may simply assemble a community competing in an open society with alternative religious options. This is essentially the situation under capitalism. The open institution of a market system severely constrains any possible effect of the characteristics deplored by Keynes on the majority of the society's members. This constraint vanishes, however, in the context of a 'politics as the new religion'. Under the circumstances, the religion controls the political apparatus and the social organization. Its agents possess thus the power lever to affect the members of society. Brutality and cruelty without compassion or mercy on a massive scale usually characterized a religion enthroned in the state's apparatus expressing a dream about the nature of the social organization.

A religion addressed to the 'politics of society' yields a human catastrophe. Our century extended the historical record already available from the Inquisitors, the American Colonial experience (in moderate form), and other examples with a terrifying proportion. The irreligiousness of capitalism, deplored by Keynes, forms thus an important virtue of the system. Of course, it offers for this very reason no attraction to the modern disciples of Feuerbach's prophecy. But the importance of a social organization relying on markets for social co-ordination follows from the protection it offers against the political tyranny of a political religion. But a market system does not survive without some emotively grounded support by the citizens. It encounters on this level in our time a serious difficulty. Some reflection should indicate, however, that religiously involved people, searching for new orientations, should welcome the social framework of capitalism as the best opportunity to pursue their dreams. The social framework allows the formation of any community with some committing religious messages to compete freely for members. Such 'moral communities', attempting to offer satisfying life orientations, need to recognize their dependence on an open society. Such a society can only survive if its 'moral order', expressed by rules of conduct and norms of behaviour, is generally respected. The array of competing moral-religious communities needs thus (at least) to provide an emotive thrust committing members of society to accept this common basis. But our modern clerics are engrossed with the new religion as politics. Contemporary man's attempts to fill the inherited void confront us therefore with a dangerous problem.

The crucial argument developed in the previous passages also bears on two incidental points made by Keynes. He emphasized the opportunity for experimentation under socialism and the (minor) loss in liberty to make a million. The last point disposes of the basic issue concerning liberty under socialist institutions in a remarkably cavalier manner. We find this attitude quite frequently among social dreamers. The institutional arrangements of the socialist state necessarily lower substantially the range of decisions granted to individual members of society. Individual members are moreover confronted by a pervasive uncertainty cultivated by an overpowering and autonomous bureaucracy without accountability to the members of society. There is in a sense no citizenship under the circumstances. It is somewhat strange that Keynes brushed off the issue posed by liberty so easily after his perceptive remarks made on other occasions on Soviet socialism. It would appear that Keynes invested little time to think in detail and in some depth about alternative structures of societies. The intellectual issue was, of course, somewhat different at the time. Political economy (that is, the so-called public-choice analysis) and 'institutional analysis' evolved over the past years into major, fascinating research branches of economics. These instruments and insights were not available to Keynes. Still, this did not prevent Ludwig von Mises from writing a penetrating and challenging analysis of socialism[27] at the time of Keynes's socio-political essays.

The case for more experimentation under socialism is left similarly unclear and underdeveloped. It just occurs as a claim formulated in short clauses of a long sentence. But the problem is worth pondering. One should particularly consider whether the open institution of a competitive market system does not foster substantially more experimentation on a broad front than the centralized bureaucratization of a socialist economy. Much evidence bearing on that problem has accumulated over the past decades. We know, for example, about the severe bureaucratic obstacles in Soviet Russia to implement scientific results and develop concrete applications.

But let us remember now that Keynes, however favourably impressed with socialism, did not propose a socialist organization of society. His diagnosis of modern economies indicated to him that a socialist conversion was not necessary. His analysis found no fault with the consumer goods sector. The 'socialization' of investment was quite sufficient to remove the flaw obstructing the functioning of modern economies. But none of his essays ever elaborates in the slightest the content of this proposal. We do not know in what form the socialization should be implemented. The institutional choices are never examined and there was hardly an opportunity or intellectual challenge to assess the consequences of such socialization. The only clues from some of his earlier essays are contained in his vision of a New Liberalism. The socio-economic organization should be built on the basis of a system of large autonomous bodies, each one encompassing major branches of economic activity. The democratic principle of 'parliamentary sovereignty' should, however, be maintained. The 'autonomous bodies' must be accountable to Parliament. Keynes also invokes here a strand of his socialist dream. He writes that, of course, the management of these autonomous bodies can be expected not to be 'motivated by private advantage'.[28] The 'public good' will dominate the managers' actions. Whatever Keynes wrote in this matter never reaches beyond a level of wishful verbalization of 'beautiful thoughts'. One would hardly guess from the material of the essays that a social scientist, even economist, had written the essays. Any social dreamer of the intelligentsia could have produced them. Crucial questions bearing on such a system are never faced or explored.

The general sense vaguely points to a sort of corporativist system appealing to President Theodore Roosevelt, discussed by French conservatives, instituted by Fascist Italy and continued in the postwar regime by the Christian-Democrat party. But the detailed institutional arrangements, or even the broad contours, remain hidden in a thick fog of wishful good feeling. We receive, for example, no clue as to how property rights would actually (not nominally) be structured – that is, the assignment of admissible action to specified persons with respect to specified objects. But this assignment of relevant rights crucially determines the operation of such a system. The idea that managers of 'autonomous bodies' will not be motivated by consideration of private advantage need not detain us much longer here. We should, of course, reasonably expect that the managers will diligently attend to their private advantages in many dimensions, incidentally touching also on pecuniary gains. We may hear, of course, that parliamentary accountability would control such temptations. But analysis of the implicit agency problem and evidence from the operation of autonomous bodies in the United States and Europe should make us very doubtful about the hopeful invocation of parliamentary sovereignty. Members of Parliament frequently lack the relevant information for a proper supervisory job, in particular as the flow of information is controlled to a good extent by the autonomous bodies. They frequently lack the necessary incentives. They are associated or linked via their interests with the managers in various ways. They may be members of the same party with a tacit agreement between the parties as to their respective range of control over autonomous bodies. Parliamentarians may typically also serve on the board of directors or expect appointments as executive of these bodies. The absence of any relevant accountability is not replaced by a discipline imposed by the market. Whatever discipline the market may still exert can usually be offset through politically manipulated benefits and protective schemes. The result of such institutional structures leads to a concentration of power costly to challenge with a substantial disposition for corruption, waste and inefficiency.

Some final remarks

My essay offers no rounded and full appreciation of Keynes, the economist or the intellectual. Harrod and Skidelsky[29] attended excellently to this difficult task. My critical judgement of Keynes as a socio-political thinker should not obscure the full ambivalence of Keynes as a man, an ambivalence mirrored in his legacy. There was a trace of genius in Keynes and a power recognized by Hayek.[30] Some dimensions of his thoughts and interests attract my sympathy. I should mention here his indefatigable attention to important issues of our reality and his interest in policy problems. His general approach to policy problems is well exemplified by his sensible discussion of German reparations. His general methodological thrust deserves some attention, most particularly today. He expressed early an interesting doubt about the attempt to represent an economy's functioning in an encompassing econometric model. His 'Marshallian analysis', in contrast to a 'Walrasian approach', emphasized the importance of felicitous simplification in the best tradition of economics with the courageous disregard of second- and lower-order aspects. He also cautions us implicitly not to chase the illusory goal to anchor every piece of empirical analysis on 'first principles'. All this we might usefully heed.

And the *General Theory*: I submit that it was a blind alley, but a very useful blind alley. It raised unresolved and important open issues economists should ponder and develop. Keynes's central emphasis on pervasive uncertainty especially requires our attention. Its ramification for policy-making and institutional choice has not been sufficiently recognized by the profession. But Keynes's socio-political thoughts are an entirely different matter and reveal an unexpectedly strange dimension of a complex personality. When shifting to these broader social issues, he became a romantic and utopian dreamer. But this may have been his way, conditioned by his early intellectual experiences and 'Bloomsbury', to cope with the void inherited by modern intellectuals.

Panel discussion I

BUCHANAN: I'd like to ask Professor Brunner a question. I was a little confused at one point in the middle of his discussion where he made the point that Keynes did not reject state socialism for several reasons, but he left out that ultimately he did reject state socialism. He didn't reject it because of the overcoming *laissez-faire*, he didn't reject it because of other reasons, but I gathered that he did ultimately reject it. But why? I think he left that out in his discussion.

BRUNNER: I did, yes. I did not mention it because I saw my watch was getting ahead of me. The point is really this. Given the analysis that he has, the analysis only indicates that what is required is a socialization of investment. He's very explicit about this; there's no need to socialize the consumer goods sector. As a matter of fact, the consumer goods sector does not pose any problem at all; it doesn't create any waves, according to his analysis. And, therefore, the consumer goods sector can be left open to private property and market co-ordination, and he said the market co-ordination will function quite efficiently and adequately. This is why Keynes doesn't want state socialism according to his own analysis.

RAMEL: I would like to ask you a question about how Lord Keynes looked upon the politicians who tried to follow his theories and to follow up in practical policies his ideas – Roosevelt and the New Deal. How did he look upon the New Deal and how Roosevelt and his administration tried to carry out Keynesian policies? How did he look upon what was done in Great Britain and in Scandinavia?

BRUNNER: I suspect that Geoffrey Harcourt has more information about that than I do. I have not sufficiently read whatever he has to say on the Roosevelt situation, on the National Industrial Recovery Act (NIRA). There is one point, however, that interests me. The NIRA was really, in terms of its institutional arrangements, approaching what Keynes proposed. It was a huge cartelization arrangement where there was the development of interlocking bodies, setting prices and wages, and in many ways, it seemed to be sort of a halfway house getting toward a kind of corporate state.

HARCOURT: Though I don't know that much about the details of Keynes's attitudes to Roosevelt, what I have read suggests that they passed in the night. Keynes liked Roosevelt, particularly because he admired his hands. This was a very important thing, for Keynes, in summing up people, looked at their hands. He didn't like your President Wilson because he had a fine body and a fine face, but when he got to his hands, he was disappointed with them, and that was one of those things that he brought out in his portrait in the *Economic Consequences of the Peace*. But when he met Roosevelt, he found that he had very nice hands, and, therefore, he was very favourably disposed to him. Keynes thought after he had his first meeting with Roosevelt that he had made a big impact and that perhaps it would have an effect on his policies. But as I understand it, when he left, Roosevelt turned to his advisers and said, 'I didn't understand a word the man said'. I think that Professor Brunner and Professor Buchanan have raised very important points because Keynes has come down to us in the textbooks as very unlike the very complicated and sophisticated and subtle minds that Keynes and many of his close colleagues had. We tend to forget that when Keynes was trying to tackle the very deep unemployment of the late twenties and the thirties and then thinking about unemployment after the war, the orders of magnitude of unemployment that he thought could be tackled by what we call Keynesian policies now were amazingly high. The orders of magnitude that Keynes had in mind to bringing unemployment down by the sorts of things that he was proposing and that he thought his arguments in the *General Theory* were relevant for were very high orders. He didn't want to stop there, of course, but then he would have been inclined to have joined hands sometimes, I suspect, with Milton Friedman in some of his proposals for information and retraining and relocating and sometimes with Roosevelt with his industrial organization and microproposals. Keynes was very pragmatic and didn't have an absolute commitment to the competitive model with Smithian roots. So, I suspect that the link between Keynes, his policies and Roosevelt was not that strong, at least in the early part of the thirties when the New Deal was on.

RAMEL: I thank Dr Harcourt for this explanation of why Keynes was not in favour of *laissez-faire* liberalism. You said that he liked hands so much, and yet he didn't like the invisible hand.

THUROW: I enjoyed both of the talks, but I'm going to accuse them of a defect, which you're going to think is peculiar. I think they were both too clear, too logical, and too antiseptic. We first had a talk on the intellectual development of Keynes that made it a very clear, logical process. We then had a talk on how Keynes's political and social views in a very clear and logical way led to the *General Theory*. In both of those talks there were two key words that were never mentioned: *Great Depression*. The *General Theory* would not have been written without the Great Depression.

On my last sabbatical, instead of working in a university, I spent 1979 working for the *New York Times*. Since 1979 was the fiftieth anniversary of the great stock market crash, I was assigned by the editors to go back and read the newspaper every day from the first of January 1928, through the end of December 1933, to get a feeling for what it felt like to be there at the time, and then write an article about these events. Now you remember the stock market went down 95 per cent, unemployment rates of 25 per cent (still almost 20 per cent ten years later) existed for a decade. If you read the newspapers over that period of time, what you get is a feeling of confusion, chaos, and a system out of control.

Now we can't do it, but I suspect that if you could go back and put yourself in Lord Keynes's mind, between 1929 and 1933, you would've found a lot of confusion, chaos, and a feeling that the system was out of control. What we've made it sound this morning is all much too reasonable and all much too antiseptic, in the sense of not being affected by real world events. I think that's the academic's disease. If you're an academic, you like to think that ideas affect ideas and ideas affect events; but events have relatively little effect on ideas. I think if you look at the truth, it's more the other way around. Ideas seldom affect events, and events often affect ideas.

If it had not been for the Great Depression, what we now know as Keynesian economics would not have existed. I would venture to bet that Keynes would just be one of many economists of that period and that we would not be here today thinking about Keynesian economics. Keynesian economics became the 'bible' as to how you get out of the Great Depression. Whether it was an accurate bible doesn't make any difference; people regarded it as the bible you had to study to think about that problem. So, one of the things I want you to throw into this calculus is a lot of confusion, chaos, and a system out of control. If you don't put that into Keynesian economics and the development of Keynesian economics, I think you miss both the reason for its development and something that has to be very important to its development.

TOBIN:　I found both of the talks extremely interesting and Professor Brunner's scope breathtaking. I don't believe I've absorbed all that he had to say yet. I agree with Professor Thurow though. I don't see a case for relating Keynes's *General Theory* so closely to things that Keynes wrote in the 1920s. I think he was looking for a diagnosis of the world economic crisis of the Great Depression, as Professor Thurow said, and for a way out of it. Now, I don't put that much stock and serious advocacy of political and social organization in the phrase *socialization of investment*. I think that could mean a lot of different things. It could mean something as loose as the French plan, in which, with a bit of consultation with government authorities, private businessmen try to gain a common, realistic appreciation of where the national economy is going and gear their investment in a co-ordinated but noncompulsory way to that vision of the future of the economy. It's the sort of thing that John Monnet was trying to do in France in the wake of the Second World War. It could have meant that. It could have meant using public investment just as a balance wheel, public investment and infrastructure as a compensatory amount that would make up for inevitable fluctuations in private industry. I don't think it meant the corporate state, at all. I don't think it meant socialization in the sense of eliminating in any important way private property, or even private control of business decisions. I also note that in the *General Theory*, Keynes says that he has no quarrel with the way that a capitalist economy allocates the resources that it employs. His quarrel is with the fact that it doesn't employ all the resources, not with the allocation of the resources that are employed. I think he was too generous to a capitalist economy, perhaps in that phrase, but that's what he said. In many ways, I think you can interpret the *General Theory* as a relatively painless and conservative way of getting capitalism out of the worst crisis of its history, in a time when most of the critics of capitalism believed that it was fundamentally flawed and doomed because its structure was just incapable of sustaining prosperity. Keynes comes along and said that's not true. With a relatively easy set of remedies, largely using the powers that a democratic capitalist country already gives its government, we can save the day.

As for Keynes and Franklin D. Roosevelt – I think the record will show that Keynes didn't much understand Roosevelt any more than Roosevelt understood Keynes. I'm confident that Keynes deplored the National Recovery Association. That was not the kind of recovery programme that he had in mind. He also deplored the increases in taxes and the attempts of the Roosevelt administration to balance the budget in their first years in office. He hoped that Roosevelt would engage in bold spending programmes – larger in compass than they did at first, but of the nature of the Works Progress Administration. He also approved of the Roosevelt administration's monetary policy. The revaluation of gold – essentially depreciation of the dollar – was essential to American recovery, just as the depreciation of the pound sterling had triggered the British recovery two years before. However, one technical matter in what Professor Brunner said is not true. As I understand the *General Theory*, it's not true that Keynes's underemployment equilibrium could not be moved by monetary expansion. It could be. In fact, that is often what Keynes wanted to do. So he was not saying that we were stuck at some real equilibrium that monetary policy and fiscal policy, either one or both together, could not remedy.

HARCOURT: I just want to answer Professor Thurow very quickly. I've been called lots of things, but never antiseptic. Keynes, of course, was a very political figure, as came out from Professor Brunner's lecture, and he was always actively involved in the very pressing problems of his time. And, of course, I agree that the Depression was an extraordinarily important prerequisite for the *General Theory* to be written; otherwise he wouldn't have responded to that problem. But that was not my brief. I see no place for a social scientist who isn't politically active. I have always belonged to either the Australian or British Labour Party or both; I'm a Christian Socialist; and for five and a half years I lived the antiwar movement when Australia was the only respectable ally of America in the Vietnam War. So I know a hell of a lot about political activity, and so did Keynes. So I am not antiseptic.

Notes

1. Arthur M. Okun, *Equality and Efficiency: The Big Tradeoff*, Washington, D.C.: Brookings Institution, 1975.
2. Friedrich A. Hayek, *The Road to Serfdom*, Chicago: University of Chicago Press, 1944.
3. John Maynard Keynes, *Essays in Persuasion*, New York: Harcourt, Brace, 1932, 373.
4. Ibid., 323–38.
5. Ibid., 323–4.
6. Ibid., 324.
7. Ibid., 325.

8. Ibid., 331.
9. Ibid., 335.
10. Ibid., 297–9.
11. Ibid., 302.
12. Ibid., 308–9.
13. John Maynard Keynes, *The End of Laissez-faire*, London: Hogarth Press, 1926.
14. Keynes, *Essays in Persuasion*, 313–14.
15. Ibid., 314.
16. Ibid., 313.
17. Ibid., 315.
18. Ibid., 316.
19. Ibid., 317.
20. Ibid.
21. Ibid., 318.
22. Ibid.
23. Ibid., 319.
24. John Maynard Keynes, *The General Theory of Employment, Interest and Money*, New York: Harcourt, Brace, 1936, 156.
25. The reader may find a more detailed discussion of the issues raised in the previous paragraphs in Karl Brunner and William Meckling, 'The Perception of man and the conception of government', *Journal of Money, Credit, and Banking*, **9**(1), part 1, 1977, 70–85; and Karl Brunner, 'The perception of man and the conception of society', *Journal of Economic Enquiry*, July 1987.
26. Keynes, *Essays in Persuasion*, 306–7.
27. Ludwig von Mises, *Socialism*, Indianapolis: Liberty Classics, 1981.
28. Keynes, *Essays in Persuasion*, 313.
29. R.F. Harrod, *The Life of John Maynard Keynes*, London: Macmillan, 1951; Robert Skidelsky, *John Maynard Keynes: Hopes Betrayed 1883–1920*, London: Macmillan, 1983.
30. Hayek, *Road to Serfdom*.

12 Reflections on the political economy of government: the persistent growth of government*

The issue

A central theme of our time concerns the role and interpretation of 'government'. Two contrasting views influence intellectual attitudes and affect the social evaluation of political institutions. One view emphasizes the importance of a 'limited government' with severe constitutional constraints on the admissible range of political action. Political institutions offer a stable and predictable general framework guiding the detailed voluntary interaction among the members of society. A constitutional consensus establishes and legitimizes the existence and limited scope of 'government'. It is moreover expected under this view that the consensus can be effectively established and even usefully monitored with the aid of suitable social designs.

An alternative view essentially rejects the idea of a limited and controlled government. It denies that human affairs are in general better served under a strictly limited government. The position denies in particular that limited government assures a better chance for evolving human welfare. Political institutions appear in this view as the essential instrument of 'human progress'. 'Government' is the 'objective representation of the principles of justice, equity and human values'. An increasing 'government' and a widening reach of political institutions are presented as necessary conditions of human achievements. Responsible political action thus requires deliberate removal of constitutional limitations. It also requires a conscious effort to expand the range of political action in man's social affairs. Political institutions need be more, according to this view, than a *general* framework for social interaction. They should properly attend to specific and detailed intervention in social transactions over an open-ended range with little inhibition by general and stable rules.[1]

The case for 'limited government' seems a lost historical cause at this stage. We hardly need comment on the state of affairs in the Second and the

* Originally published in *Schweizerische Zeitschrift für Volkswirtschaft und Statistik*, **3**, 1978, 649–79. Many discussions with William Meckling and Allan H. Meltzer over the past years have shaped my thinking on the issues examined in the paper. The contribution made by these discussions is gratefully acknowledged. The paper forms part of a project bearing on socio-political aspects of inflation supported by a grant from the National Science Foundation. The first draft of the paper was prepared as a visitor at the Hoover Institution (Stanford University) during the winter 1977–8.

Third Worlds. The dominant role of political institutions among the mass of member countries in the United Nations is well documented. More important for our immediate purpose is the longer-run evolution in western democracies. The broad facts summarized in the second section of the paper reveal that any constitutional consensus about limited government ever existing in the past substantially vanished over time. But the historical erosion of the thesis advising severe limitations on government does not establish the validity of the second position linking human achievement with 'unlimited government'. The historical evidence effectively dismisses any such claims. More significant in the present context is the simple fact that the second view offers no explanation of the relevant observations. It advances an interpretation of government as the salvation of mankind and justifies an appropriate political activism. But such normative constructions are logically incapable of providing useful accounts of our reality. We also note that the historical evolution, described in the following section, emerged in all western societies irrespective of extent and political organization of the 'ideological commitment' expressed by the second position.

The political events in numerous countries actually revealed in recent years a rising concern about the growing burden imposed by government. President Carter mobilized during his campaign for the Presidency the voters' frustrations fostered by an increasing exposure to an expanding government. Local 'rebellions' of tax payers emerged in the USA with rising frequency and their recent 'rebellion' in California has projected a wide shadow. But the meaning of these political events remains unclear until we possess a coherent explanation of the observed trend. They may be disturbances at the surface without import for the basic thrust of the social process producing an ever-expanding government sector in western democracies. Similarly, promises and attempts to raise efficiency and performance levels of government bureaux may just form an exercise in useless frustrations. The relevance (or irrelevance) of such attempts depends on the nature of the underlying social process. The evaluation of recent events depends thus on our systematic interpretation of the social forces shaping the growth of the government sector. This general and persistent growth attracted increasing attention in the social sciences. A growing number of economists applied over the past 15 or 20 years their analytic tools to explorations of this problem. My paper draws on these contributions and offers a programmatic analysis of the crucial interaction between voters, legislators, bureaux and the judiciary which produces the unrelenting growth of government irrespective of the specific intentions pursued by participants in the process. Some major implications of the analysis bearing on current trends and the future are explored at the end.

The facts

The growth of government has not been invented by the 'New Politics' of the 1960s. It also emerged before the latter-day saviours of mankind relying on political institutions and political processes. Neither was the growth of government produced by the 'Keynesian Revolution'. Admittedly, any measures used to trace our phenomenon contain a variety of more or less serious errors. Measurement procedures are usually faulty and the data obtained rarely correspond adequately to the analytic concept most appropriately used for the specific purpose on hand. Still, the potential errors do not obscure the broad and dominant pattern revealed by diverse measures obtained by a number of authors.

Two distinct measures were presented by Allan H. Meltzer. He examined the relative magnitude of tax collection and the relative absorption of labour by the government sector. The real value of taxes collected by the Federal Government in the United States rose since 1792 at a rate of 5.5 per cent per annum. This growth rate exceeds the rate of growth of private-sector output over the same period. The growth rate was however not uniform. It moved along to 4.75 per cent from 1792 to 1902 and rose to about 7 per cent in the twentieth century. Both figures exceed the growth rate of real gross national product. Total real taxes (accruing to all levels of government) grew over the twentieth century at a rate of 5.4 per cent per annum, whereas real gross national product increased at a lower rate of 3.2 per cent. A similar pattern prevails for government employment. According to this measure, the government of the United States expanded over this century at more than twice the rate of the private sector.[2]

Tables 12.1 and 12.2 present additional information for this century about the United States from another source.[3] The share of public employment (Table 12.1) increased from 1900 to 1970 by a factor of more than 3. Even if the defence establishment is disregarded, the growth in the share over the 70 years is only slightly less than 200 per cent. The expansion in the proportion of national income absorbed by the government sector, exhibited in Table 12.2, confirms the general pattern. This proportion measured 6.8 per cent in 1902. This share rose by 1970 to 34.1 per cent. The relative absorption of national income by the government sector thus expanded over 70 years by approximately 400 per cent.

We should look beyond the United States, however. Warren Nutter published recently an informative summary of the trends prevailing over the postwar period in OECD countries.[4] The patterns exhibited by government expenditures are summarized by Tables 12.3 and 12.4. The sample median (for the fixed sample) of the share of government expenditures in national income rose from 34 per cent in 1953 to 49 per cent in 1973. It rose from 31 per cent in 1950 to 52 per cent in 1974 for the variable sample. The fixed

Table 12.1   Public employment as a percentage of the labour force in the United States

Year	%
1900	6.0
1910	6.4
1920	8.2
1930	9.8
1940	12.2
1950	15.2
1960	17.9
1970	20.1

Source: 'One hundred years of public spending, 1870–1970' in *Budgets and Bureaucrats: The Sources of Government Growth*, ed. Thomas E. Borcherding, Durham, 1977, 26.

Table 12.2   Total government expenditures in constant (1929) dollars as a percentage of gross national product in the United States

Year	%
1902	6.8
1913	8.0
1922	12.6
1932	21.3
1940	20.3
1950	42.7
1960	30.1
1970	34.1

Source: As Table 12.1

sample median increased between 1953 and 1973 by somewhat more than 40 per cent, whereas the variable sample median increased from 1950 to 1974 by slightly less than 70 per cent. The boundaries of both sample ranges rose concurrently with the median. Supplementary information is contained in Table 12.4. It presents the average annual growth rate (over indicated periods) for the share of government expenditures in national income. The data cover 16 countries. The largest growth rate of the *share* of government expenditures (for the period 1960–74) is observed at 1.84 per cent per annum for Sweden. The smallest growth rate is shown at 0.44 per cent for France

Table 12.3   Government expenditures as a percentage of national income:
median and range for samples of OECD countries, selected
years, 1950–74

Year	Fixed sample[a]		Variable sample[b]	
	Median[c]	Range[d]	Median[c]	Range[d]
1950			31	22–39
1953	34	19–44	34	19–44
1955	35	19–42	35	19–42
1960	39	22–43	38	22–43
1965	41	25–49	42	25–48
1970	48	24–57	48	24–57
1973	49	27–62	49	27–62
1974			52	29–64

Notes:
[a]   Covers the same 13 countries in all years, excluding Australia, Luxembourg, and Sweden.
[b]   Covers varying countries: 9 in 1950; 14 in 1953 and 1955; 16 in 1960, 1965 and 1970; 15 in
     1973; and 13 in 1974. For lack of data, the following countries are excluded in the desig-
     nated years: Australia, Belgium, Italy, Japan, Luxembourg, Norway and Sweden in 1950;
     Australia and Sweden in 1953 and 1955; Luxembourg in 1973; and Austria, Italy,
     Luxembourg and the United States in 1974.
[c]   The middle percentage in the sequence of percentages arranged in ascending order for the
     countries covered.
[d]   The lowest and highest percentages recorded for the countries covered.

Source: W. Nutter, *Growth of Government in the West*, Washington, D.C.: American Institution for Policy Research, 1978.

(covering 1950–74). Apart from Sweden, a growth rate of at least 1 per cent
per annum can also be noted for Denmark, Norway, the Netherlands and
Belgium. The median growth rate of the sample is 0.69 per cent per annum.

Several aspects of the broad facts should be noted at this stage. The
information provided by data from the United States reveals that the growth
of government is neither a postwar nor a post-Keynesian experience. It developed over many decades and stretches over the history of the United States. I
conjecture that this pattern extends beyond the United States. This seems
certainly worth exploring in further research covering a variety of European
nations. The postwar data indicate moreover the broad perspective required
in approaching the problem. All western democracies are apparently exposed
to the same social process with some obvious variation in detail. We also note
that a persistent operation of the postwar trends would raise the (variable)
sample median of Table 12.3 by the year 2000 to about 68 per cent. The

Table 12.4   *Estimated average annual increase[a] in government expenditures as a percentage of national income: sixteen OECD countries, varying periods, 1950–74*

Country	Average annual increase %	Period
Sweden	1.84	1960–74
Denmark	1.42	1950–74
Norway	1.38	1951–74
Netherlands	1.13	1950–74
Belgium	1.00	1953–74
Luxembourg	0.92	1952–72
Canada	0.82	1950–74
Italy	0.72	1951–73
Austria	0.66	1950–73
Switzerland	0.62[a]	1950–69
United Kingdom	0.55	1950–74
Federal Republic of Germany	0.54	1950–74
United States	0.51	1950–73
Japan	0.49	1952–74
Australia	0.46	1960–74
France	0.44	1950–74

Notes:
[a] The estimated average annual increase is derived for each country from a linear regression of government expenditures as a percentage of national income on a time trend. In the case of countries with more than one OECD series, the regression coefficient is taken from the composite series.
[b] Taken for the series based on former SNA because the composite series is significantly biased.

Source: As Table 12.3

upper boundary of the range would reach 80 per cent. One naturally wonders whether such developments are feasible or probable. Will government continue to grow until government expenditures coincide with national income? Or should we expect that the share approaches an equilibrium level definitely below 100 per cent? What are in this case the characteristics of the social process which determine such an equilibrium, and what is the nature of this equilibrium? Is it a viable state or an essentially unstable position defining a transition to a nondemocratic political arrangement? Moreover, what is the connection between the expansion of the government sector and the mode of financing government expenditures? And lastly, what is the relation between inflation and this mode of financing? These are the major questions guiding an examination of the political economy of government. We should not expect to obtain definite or reliable answers at this time. Serious work beyond the exercises of normative judgements or religious commitments is comparatively young. We possess at this stage an assembly of promising fragments and also, in my judgment, an array of blind alleys. I propose to explore blind alleys and the fragments with potential promise for useful explanation.

A survey of approaches

A.C. Pigou was probably the first to apply an efficiency criterion in order to establish a norm for the relative size of government. The size and composition of the budget maximizes social welfare provided the marginal satisfaction of every dollar spent 'inside' or 'outside' the government coincides for any taxpayer. Government is too small, whenever the marginal satisfaction of a dollar spent via government exceeds for any taxpayer the marginal satisfaction of 'privately spent dollars'. An expansion of the government budget raises social welfare under the circumstances. 'Government' is too large on the other hand whenever the marginal utility of 'publicly spent money' drops below the marginal utility of 'privately spent money' for any taxpayer.

This general norm yields however little information about the division between private and public activities. The efficiency criterion requires supplementary characteristics in order to achieve more content or useful guidelines. The basic idea governing a rational division of labour suggests that the government should provide a range of services and goods with a comparative advantage derived from its monopoly of coercive power. This argument opened two distinct but related avenues. Both avenues circumscribe the range of appropriate governmental activities with the aid of general characteristics or properties attached to goods or activities. One line explored the implication of externalities resulting from private transactions. The occurrence of externalities lowers the welfare of members in the social group. Activities with negative externalities are too large from a social perspective, even if they maximize individual transactors' welfare. Activities producing positive externalities on the other hand are too small in a social context. Such imbalances reveal opportunities to raise the level of general welfare. But this improvement cannot be expected to emerge from the voluntary interaction of private interests. The government possesses the required coercive power to intervene and suitably regulate with various devices the relative magnitude of externality producing activities. The government functions in this manner as an 'internalizer' of privately produced externalities. This argument justifies apparently the operation of government and defines an admissible range for its activities.

The other line of investigation addresses the properties of various goods and services. Samuelson introduced the notion of a 'public good' in contrast to the 'private goods' usually considered in standard price theory. The goods acquired in ordinary transaction are controlled by the purchaser. Others have no access to the use of such goods without the consent of the owner. Such exclusion and separability seems not to extend however to all goods. A public good can be used or consumed by some group without impairing its use by other groups. Any person paying a full price for the public good will realize under the circumstances that others may have access to the good without paying or at a lower cost. The buyer has no exclusionary rights. It follows apparently that the private production of 'public goods' remains too small from a social perspective. The conclusion seemed unavoidable that 'public goods' should be produced by government.

A closer inspection of these arguments reveals that we obtain no useful explanation of our phenomenon. They exhibit essentially a normative character in the tradition of welfare analysis. It is logically impossible under the circumstances to provide an explanation of our observations. Normative statements can be transformed into positive statements bearing on descriptive material with the aid of suitably selected supplementary hypotheses. The 'goodwill theory' or 'public interest theory' of government provides the necessary addition in this case. The normative ideas bearing on socially optimal size and composition of government are transformed into descriptive statements about the world, whenever we assume that 'government' essentially pursues the public interest and attends to the general welfare of all citizens. But this translation still provides no relevant explanation. The 'goodwill theory' of government hardly offers a serious proposition about the reality of observable governments.[5] Moreover, the pattern of activities covered by the government sector is difficult to reconcile with the story emerging from the translation of normative prescriptions. Lastly, it cannot explain the observed growth in the *relative* size of government without speculative and dubious artifices. One would need to argue that economic growth accelerates privately produced externalities or increases the public's demand for public goods at a faster rate. There is however little evidence, if any, in support of these special assumptions. They would appear with an essentially *ad hoc* character not founded in substantial studies.

Some additional considerations cast further doubt on the special assumption. The rejection of the 'goodwill theory' of government frees our view for the actual behaviour of government, its bureaucratic apparatus and its interaction with the legislature. There is little reason to expect that 'government' itself does not produce substantial externalities lowering the welfare of the citizens. A realistic theory of government behaviour offers no systematic expectation that interventions designed to correct privately produced externalities do not create more serious distortions of another kind. Moreover, an examination of externalities suggests that they involve either a specification problem of property rights or are essentially reducible to a distributional problem. Neither aspect requires, *per se*, a large government or a government continuously expanding in relative size.[6]

Similar problems attach to the argument based on 'public goods'. It was demonstrated in recent literature that the exclusion argument actually poses a problem of property rights. It follows that these aspects do not justify government actions beyond the traditional function of enforcing private agreements. 'Publicness' of goods does not obstruct moreover an efficient private production, or private group arrangement to finance the supply of public goods. The leap from 'publicness of goods' to the necessity of government production is generally fallacious and unwarranted.[7]

A second level of work contributed a variety of propositions bearing on the size of government. Barro explored an interesting model on 'the control of politicians'. Citizens can use their income to acquire private goods or obtain via tax payments 'public goods'. Politicians derive some reward or income beyond their salary as legislators from the provision of public goods. A budget constraint links the citizens' tax payments with the total cost of producing public goods. The analysis implies that the size of the government sector, expressed by the amount of public goods supplied to citizens, exceeds the optimal amount desired by the voters. The excess depends on the re-election probabilities faced by politicians. The excess is larger with legislators not confronted with any re-election problems. The analysis thus establishes the nature of the control over the budget exercised by politicians relative to the optimum determined by voter preferences.[8]

Barro's examination addresses the role of politicians in producing, at any moment in time, an 'excessive' government sector. The model offers, as it stands, no information about the relative *growth* of the government sector. Baumol attempted to cope with our phenomenon in the context of a standard two-sector model. The private sector exhibits a systematic growth of factor productivity, whereas the government sector settles on a stagnant productivity level. The renumeration of factors in both sectors is determined however by the marginal product of the private sector. Economic growth raises consequently the real cost of government per unit of public good. With appropriate assumptions about price and income elasticities of the demand for public goods one derives a persistent increase in the cost of government relative to national income.

A more sophisticated analysis of the growth context was developed by Mackay.[9] The citizens behave according to a utility function containing a private good, a public good and a future private good representing current savings. Accumulation of capital is accompanied by a constant growth rate of the population. The supply of the private and the public good is governed by production functions characterizing the two sectors. This analysis implies that the actual output of the public good expands along the steady-state path at the rate of population growth. Moreover, the division of employment between the two sectors is constant along the steady-state path. Similarly, the value shares of the two sectors remain constant on this path, whereas the output of the public good declines relative to the output of the private sector.

The Baumol and Mackay model does not seem to cope adequately with our phenomenon. The Baumol model requires very special *ad hoc* constraints on price and income elasticities in order to yield a relative growth of the government sector. Mackay's model on the other hand cannot be reconciled with the long-run trend of relative growth exhibited by the government sector expressed in terms of employment or in terms of value shares. Relative growth of government has been observed for almost 200 years in the United States. The OECD data seem also difficult to reconcile with the steady state patterns of the model. Mackay's analysis hardly offers a relevant explanation of the observations summarized in the previous section.

Another group of contributions emphasizes a variety of 'biases' built into social conditions and political institutions which affect the relative size of government. Downs' pioneering approach to the political economy of government centres on the role of parties in the political process. Parties compete in a democratic context for power with tax and expenditure programmes. Information about the costs and benefits of programmes are not easily or uniformly accessible to voters. They approach their political options with incomplete information. Downs argues in particular that information (or awareness) is asymmetrical. Voters are, in his judgement, more aware of the costs than of the benefits of government programmes. The value of the benefits appear thus at a discount relative to the cost. The 'government' is therefore smaller than its optimal size determined by fully informed voters.[10]

Buchanan–Wagner offer an opposite asymmetry under the label of 'fiscal illusion'. They argue that for a variety of reasons voters underestimate the tax price of government services. 'Fiscal illusion' emerges as a result of the institutional arrangements shaping legislative processes and most particularly the procedures involved in budgetary policies. The information bias is reinforced by deficit policies and encourages an excessive size of the government.[11]

The arguments based on asymmetric fiscal awareness remain somewhat inconclusive. Some evidence appears to support the contention that a lower 'tax price' of government services raises the demand for such services. But there is little systematic association between deficits and government debt and the size of the government.[12] Most importantly, however, these arguments offer no explanation of the *relative growth* of the government sector. They are preoccupied with a static efficiency problem, the size of the government relative to an optimum defined in terms of voter preferences and full information.

The short survey encounters many interesting ideas and potentially useful fragments. But the candidates for an explanation of our phenomena, reviewed in previous paragraphs, suffer from a pervasive and common flaw beyond the specific reservations noted above. They describe government more or less implicitly as a producer of public goods uniformly available to all voters. The production is financed by general contributions made by voters in the form of tax payments. These aspects of the approaches surveyed cannot be reconciled with the reality of government. The provision of 'public goods' forms a small and declining portion of total government activities. The dominant portion of governmental operations involves the supply of *private* goods, services and benefits to specific groups of voters.[13] The argument also misses the redistributional thrust implicit in every provision of private or public goods. It omits any reference to the redistributional incentives unavoidably built into every government programme. The analysis thus overlooks the crucial consequences of any constituted government. These flaws of the public goods approach expressed by a factual error and a serious omission account for the failure to provide a coherent story about the social process producing the relative growth of government.

The growth of government

The nature of politics
This section presents a general outline for an explanation which essentially defines a programme of future research. The elements and strands of ideas used for our purposes are not new. They were drawn in various combinations from existing contributions and most particularly, of course, from economic analysis.

The starting point is the fundamental ambivalence of government. This ambivalence is expressed by the mixture of benefits and risks associated with a political structure. Hobbes and others have eloquently described the state of anarchy. We also note that anarchy or unstructured social processes appear at most as transition phases. Nozick and Buchanan offer a lucid and detailed analysis of the transition from anarchy to elementary forms of political structure.[14] Both authors demonstrate that anarchy is not a viable state and spontaneously evolves forms of political structure. This spontaneous evolution requires no mysterious 'social' forces beyond man's interests and resourceful endeavours. The social interaction between self-interested men produces the transition into patterns of political structure.

The benefits to individual members of these associations are very substantial indeed. Their security is enhanced and the political structure encourages an economic organization raising the productivity of labour and thus improving the standards of living. This story is clear enough. But the emergence of political structure shifts opportunities and incentives in a peculiar way. Nozick addresses this aspect when he notes that already the constitution of a 'minimal state' unavoidably involves some measure of coercive redistribution of wealth.

In a state of anarchy each individual has essentially three options: to engage in productive activity or voluntary exchange, to allocate efforts to protect his product and possessions, or to engage in piracy and acquire wealth through violent extraction from others. It should be obvious that only the first option increases social wealth. The occurrence of the other two options determines the brutal uncertainty of anarchy and the vanishing incentive to invest any resources or efforts for returns beyond the immediate horizon. The appearance of political structure replaces this vast uncertainty confronting the individual with some 'rules of the social game' represented by specific political institutions. The crucial fact requiring some emphasis in this context bears on the range of options available to individual members of the political association. These options include of course the application of resources controlled by individuals to produce wealth. The evolution of political structure enhances and safeguards this option. But the very nature of political institutions cannot prevent alternative options. Their existence offers opportunities to invest resources in political activity, guided by implicit (or explicit) rules of the institutions, in order to extract wealth from other members of the political association. The occurrence of this option implies the existence of a last option, i.e. investment in political activities designed to fend off extraction of wealth threatened by the political activities of other groups. Under both anarchy and a state of political structure individual agents can thus acquire wealth by productive effort and voluntary exchange or via extractions from others. The ambivalence of political structure is defined by the persistence of socially nonproductive private wealth extraction. This kind of wealth acquisition does not distinguish anarchy from systems exhibiting political structure. The crucial difference appears in the range of uncertainty and the existence of rules confining the processes of wealth extraction in the context of political structure. Such rules lower the uncertainty confronting individual agents. This difference implies that opportunities for socially productive wealth acquisition via productive efforts and voluntary exchange are enhanced. Such enhancement assures the viability of the political structure. Viability is endangered whenever political institutions develop complex and pervasive incentives for potential wealth extractions. There emerge under the circumstances ever widening organizational efforts to exploit the political process for persistent acquisition of wealth at the expense of others. The change from anarchy to political structure may also be formulated as a shifting mixture of a positive-sum game (productive effort) and a negative-sum game (piracy). The negative-sum game looms so large under anarchy that most political structures offer a better mixture of positive- and negative-sum games. But the crucial fact is that every political structure necessarily contains characteristic incentives yielding its own peculiar range of negative-sum games.[15]

Every political institution thus projects opportunities for redistribution. This follows from a permanent and historically invariant pattern of human behaviour. Many aspects concerning human preference systems are culturally conditioned or historically influenced. Human preferences (and beliefs) are quite similar in this respect to the inheritance of capital accumulation. But the most basic and pervasive patterns are independent of institutional setting and historical circumstances. They are revealed by the fact that man forever searches and resourcefully gropes to improve his position. This searching and groping is guided by evaluations of current and prospective states according to individual agents' vision of the world. This basic pattern or drive built into man's life implies that all circumstances, including political institutions, are resourcefully assessed and used to improve his position. The resulting probing eventually disseminates information bearing on the use of political institutions for purposes of wealth acquisition.[16]

The redistributional character of political institutions and political actions can hardly be missed upon closer examination. A few examples should usefully illustrate my point. Economists may be impressed by the rhetoric of stabilization policies. But the political reality of these programmes is at best randomly related to the issues of macro-stabilization. Interested groups may use the general state of the economy as a cover in order to minimize objections or summon support from the intellectuals. But changes in expenditure and tax programmes unavoidly involve specific items affecting distinct groups very differently. The pattern of relative changes on the expenditure and tax side of the budget implicitly redistributes wealth between the members of society. This implicit redistribution proceeding under cover of a stabilization policy attracts the central attention of the political process. The impact of these redistributions on the position of individual agents or groups usually exceeds in their evaluation the results associated with the ensuing general macro-policy. This differential effect is probably reinforced by the fact that information about the distributional consequences is more direct than information about the consequences of the macro-policies as such. It follows that 'stabilization policies' are in general quite tenuously related to the requirement of economic stabilization. The political reality converts 'stabilization policies' into conflicts about redistribution of wealth. The emerging policies hardly qualify very effectively as 'stabilization policies'.

The implicit wealth redistribution associated with any programme for economic stabilization also explains the adamant refusal of Congress in the United States to cede authority on short-run tax and expenditure adjustments for stabilization purposes to the President. This concession would lower the influence of Congress relative to the Presidency. The position of a legislator depends at least partly on his opportunities to affect redistributions in one way or another. He should not be expected to impair voluntarily his opportunities.

President Carter's proposed 'energy policy' offers another instructive illustration. Similar to programmes of economic stabilization the package proposed under the label of 'energy policy' is poorly designed with respect to the essential purpose. This purpose may be described as a rational development and use of energy resources in the United States. It is hardly a secret among professional economists that the legislative proposals will obstruct the development of energy resources and lower the productivity of our labour. The rhetoric of an 'energy policy' is deliberately used to extend the range of political institutions which engineer a massive redistribution of wealth. This redistribution mobilizes the political forces behind the President's energy bill. Moreover, the President's difficulties with Congress in these matters reflect a conflict about the nature of the wealth redistribution. Substantive concern for the future course of our economy associated with a rational exploitation of our energy resources has been submerged by the distributional conflict implicit in the legislative proposal.

A similar fate befell the proposal to restructure the financial system of the United States. There is hardly a competent economist who would not agree on a broad range of measures well designed to improve the efficiency of our financial system. The substantive case is quite clear and well documented. But the general improvement of our welfare possesses no relevant political constituency. The distributional impact on various groups of financial institutions (or borrowers) of changing arrangements overshadows the rise in general welfare. The appropriate proposals, worthy as they are, become unavoidably lost in a morass of distributional conflicts. The same fate affects also any price–wage body instituted by the government to control or curb inflation. It will be converted into a device to extract wealth via publicly sanctioned *relative* price concessions. Its relation to inflation remains restricted to its name.

We need not extend our examples in further detail. It is sufficient to repeat that the distributional conflicts permeate all public institutions, be they state-owned or state-controlled railroads, banks, airlines, or be they tariffs, export subsidies or more traditional aspects of government activities. *The essence of politics is redistribution and political conflicts centre on matters of distribution.* This central aspect of political processes, the very motor force of politics, has been discarded by the public goods approach to 'collective choice' and government, and similar approaches fail to comprehend therefore, in my judgement, the crucial mechanism producing the relative growth of government. The basic flaw of this literature is revealed by the following quotation:

'there remains the question of government involvement in wealth redistribution. There have been efforts to identify appropriate levels of this activity. ... While each of these considerations remains a plausible point of view, neither captures what appears to us to be the essence of the appeal for, nor the defense against, wealth transfer in society. The overriding issues here are ethical ...' And so we read that 'the redistributional aspects ... will be ignored'.[17] One may indulge in the intellectual challenge of ethical studies pertaining to the distribution of wealth. But these studies offer little understanding or explanation of observed political processes or of the relative growth of government. The recent contributions made by Rawls and Nozick are certainly remarkable and worth pondering. Attempts to explain political conflicts in terms of ethical positions are bound to fail however. We need not invoke any ethical systems or moral considerations to explain the incentives of political institutions and observe the responses of men to these opportunities. The function of the scientist concentrates on the development of valid explanation and a proper understanding. It should be recognized that an adequate execution of this function also involves an ethical commitment or moral obligation. The scientist would therefore argue that moral judgement and ethical valuations of social aspects are useless and basically immoral when pronounced independently and in the absence of validated positive explanations. All this does not mean that ethical valuations and moral judgements are *per se* irrelevant. They occur as pervasive social phenomena and their role in the social process deserves some attention. As such, both ethical valuations and moral judgements are frequently used as intellectual weapons of the political conflict. Such occurrences are *part* of the phenomena to be *explained* and cannot reasonably explain the nature of political conflict. Serious studies, exemplified by Rawls and Nozick, may ultimately affect our evaluation of alternative social arrangements and political institutions. But they cannot explain the central contours of political conflict and its relation to the relative growth of government. The quotation thus misconstrues the nature of the problem and proceeds to discard the central mechanism of a potentially usefull explanation.[18]

The pure wealth transfer model

The basic nature of political structure suggests that the fact of wealth redistribution be placed into a central position of the analysis of government, at least for the context of modern democracies. Allan H. Meltzer and Scott F. Richard recently offered an important contribution systematically linking wealth transfers induced by rational behaviour on the part of voters with the persistent growth of government.[19] The authors base their analysis on three postulates consistent with elementary economic analysis. The postulates are stated as follows:

1. Candidates and officials propose many more programmes than they enact. Their purpose is to find issues which attract attention and votes.
2. A voter chooses a candidate who promises to act in his interest and votes to reelect a candidate who does so.
3. Voters compare the benefits they expect to receive to the costs they expect to pay.

The three postulates yield the major conclusions derived by the pure wealth-transfer hypothesis of political processes. Incumbent and aspiring politicians sample the political market with a variety of proposals and programmes in order to discover a package enhancing their longer-run position. Postulates two and three imply that this competition eventually yields a tax structure which redistributes income from the upper parts to the lower parts of the distribution. Wealth is redistributed in this manner from a minority to a majority.

Voters can be grouped according to income classes. The description offered by the Lorenz curve in Figure 12.1 can be usefully exploited for our purposes. The vertical axis measures along OF proportions of national income. The segment OF is necessarily one. The horizontal axis measures on the other hand proportions of voters. The segment OC is again unity. The solid line Lc describes an association between proportions of total income

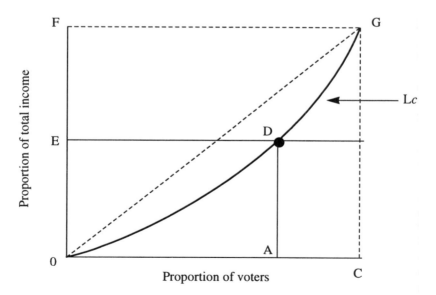

Figure 12.1

and proportions of voters. In particular, a proportion OA of all voters receives just half of total income expressed by OE along the vertical. This means of course that the other half of total income is absorbed by the proportion AC of voters. It is clear upon inspection that the magnitude of the curvature exhibited by the curve Lc indexes the degree of inequality of the income distribution. This curvature also implies that the *median* voters' income level is below the *average* level of income. But this means of course that *more than half the potential voters* experience an income below the *average* level. Voters in the upper tail beyond the median voters' income could possibly form a coalition with the median voter group in order to shift tax burdens to the lower end. Assuming however that differences in coalition costs are small, the interests of the median group are better served by joining and mobilizing the lower portions of the distribution for its purposes. The net gain in wealth to be expected via the political process will be larger. The process can be understood as a continuous sampling of politicians. Competition among politicians implies that the tax schedules preferred by the median group eventually dominates.

The analysis need not assume that all potential voters actually vote or clearly perceive the issues. It is sufficient that a portion of voters recognizes the relative benefits of different tax schedules and vote accordingly. The government's budget thus expands under the persistent incentive for redistribution unleashed by the fundamental properties of an income distribution characterized above.

The story requires at this stage some extension. One needs to explain why the voters under the higher branch of the Lorenz curve, i.e. the voters to the right of the median on the horizontal axis, are not immediately 'taxed down' to an average income. Some additional strands enter the story and these strands account for the gradual and persistent operation of the redistributional process and the essentially incremental growth process of government.

Among the additional strands should be noted that redistribution lowers the incentives for the voters with higher income. Rising taxes lower the relative price of leisure and also the relative price of current consumption. Moreover, redistributional achievements require investment of resources into the political process which are withdrawn from the positive-sum game of productive activities. The redistribution achieved offers income options for voters under the lower branch of the Lorenz curve independent of productive application of their resources. Some substitution from productive application towards leisure should thus be expected also for this group. These social costs of redistribution are eventually revealed by comparatively lower real income or lower growth of real income. An accelerated or cumulative redistribution thus endangers eventually the prospects of the median voter groups. They will suffer increasing uncertainty and hesitate or revise their tax policy conceptions. This hesitation and revision operates in the nature of a brake on the redistributional process. Some forms of democratic processes incorporating strong elements of federalism operate probably also to retard the process.

Another important aspect is the prevailing uncertainty pertaining to the median voter group. Neither politicians nor members of the group are certain about the range of this group. This uncertainty induces a cautious sampling and extensive probing. At any given stage substantial time will be required for the political process to produce further adjustments in tax schedules. The movement may occasionally be interrupted with revisions lowering the progressivity of the tax schedule or lowering the whole schedule, whenever evolving experience reveals that the politicians' sampling misjudged the position of the median voter group.

The gradual extension of the franchise since 1800 contributed in the United States significantly to the process summarized above. The last extensions actually occurred in the postwar period over the 1950s and 1960s with the mobilization of Negro voters. Any broadening of the franchise usually extends the group of potential voters to the left of the established median voters in the Lorenz diagram. The horizontal segment covering the voters and anchored on the right at point C moves on the left closer to 0 with every extension of the franchise. An extension of the franchise thus pushes the median voter group to the left in the diagram and opens new opportunities for redistributional tax policies. It should be noted moreover that the lower income groups among voters in a system of limited franchise have an interest to extend the franchise. Such extensions raise the likelihood of additional restributions benefiting these voter groups. The redistributional adjustments of tax schedules converge eventually over time to an equilibrium state. This equilibrium is however not invariant. It depends on a number of factors including the demographic profile, the preference structure of the voters and the nature of the franchise.

Some aspects of the pure wealth transfer hypothesis of political processes are interestingly supported by observations. Table 12.5 offers remarkable information about the distribution of tax payments among income classes in the United States.[20] We note first that the lower half of the income distribution pays almost no taxes in this country. The upper 50 per cent of income recipients pays 93 per cent of total tax revenues, whereas the lower 50 per cent pays only 7 per cent. The lowest 25 per cent pays less than one-half of 1 per cent of total taxes, whereas the highest 5 per cent of income recipients pays 37 per cent of all the taxes. These facts can be represented with the aid of a diagram. Figure 12.2 describes again a Lorenz curve Lc of gross income.

The curve *tr* describes the distribution of tax payments with an outline reflecting the broad properties exhibited by the table. The third line, *aLc*, introduces an adjusted Lorenz curve based on income net of tax payments.

Table 12.5   *Percentage of total taxes paid by high- and low-income taxpayers, 1970 and 1975*

Adjusted gross income class	Income level ($)		Tax paid (%)	
	1970	1975	1970	1975
Highest 1%	43,249[a]	59,338[a]	17.6	18.7
Highest 5%	20,867[a]	29,272[a]	34.1	36.6
Highest 10%	16,965[a]	23,420[a]	45.0	48.7
Highest 25%	11,467[a]	15,898[a]	68.3	72.0
Highest 50%	6,919[a]	8,931[a]	89.7	92.9
Lowest 50%	6,918[b]	8,930[b]	10.3	7.1
Lowest 25%	3,157[b]	4,044[b]	0.9	0.4
Lowest 10%	1,259[b]	1,527[b]	0.1	0.1

Notes:
[a]   Or more.
[b]   Or less.

Source: *Congressional Record, Proceedings and Debates of the 95th Congress, Second Session*, Washington, 9 March 1978, no. 33.

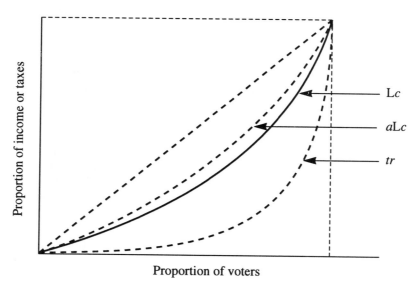

Figure 12.2

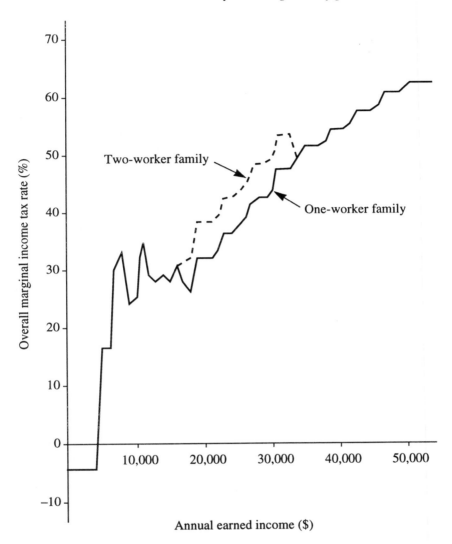

Source: 'The roller-coaster income tax' by Martin Anderson in *The Public Interest*, No. 50, Winter 1978.

Figure 12.3   Marginal income tax rates for a typical family of four in the United States, 1976

The adjusted Lorenz curve is moved substantially closer to the diagonal line. Another interesting item in Table 12.5 is the change in the tax distribution between 1970 and 1975. The tax proportion of the upper 50 per cent of income recipients rose by 3.2 percentage points from 89.7 per cent to 92.9 per cent. The tax proportion of the lower 50 per cent of income recipients fell correspondingly from 10.3 per cent to 7.1 per cent. This tax proportion of the lower branch income distribution thus fell over five years by about 30 per cent.

A previous paragraph emphasized the uncertainty pertaining to the location of the median voter group. It should be emphasized that this problem is reinforced by shifting and uncertain voter participation. The tax schedules governing the redistribution of income which emerge from the political process reflect this information pattern. It implies in particular that the tax schedules exhibit a middle range holding the marginal effective tax rate along an approximately constant level. Figure 12.3 summarizes the pattern for the year 1976 in the United States. An inspection of the diagram reveals immediately that the marginal effective tax rate for typical families of four moves around a horizontal trend for annual incomes between $8,000 and $22,000. The marginal effective tax rate rises rapidly at incomes below $8,000 and continues to increase steadily for incomes beyond $22,000.

An extension beyond the pure wealth transfer model: the entrepreneurial behaviour of politicians and bureaux
The pure wealth-redistribution hypothesis deserves our close attention. It addresses the crucial aspect of political conflict and political processes. It recognizes and fully reflects that politics is essentially concerned with the negative-sum game of human endeavours, proceeding however in a somewhat regulated manner according to an implicitly accepted set of rules. We seem to be offered a useful hypothesis with substantial content. Some reflection indicates however that the pure wealth-redistribution hypothesis is incomplete and only describes one strand of the full story. This can be recognized by the circumstance that the pure wealth-transfer model explains the growth of government by equating the size of government with the magnitude of the budget. But the two phenomena, the budget and the government apparatus, raise separate issues. The pure wealth-transfer model is consistent with a minimal apparatus which essentially operates a fund transfer business. In other words, the pure wealth-transfer hypothesis explains only one facet of the observed trend. It explains the relative growth of the budget, whether measured in expenditures or tax revenues. But the pure transfer model cannot explain, by itself alone, the relative growth of employment in the public sector or the increasing ramifications of the governmental apparatus. Neither can it explain the observable fact that wealth transfers do not occur in the

form of a single, uniform and huge system shifting money from the richer to the poorer. Few programmes actually affect the lower income groups across the whole range of income classes. The mass of programmes are directed towards *specific* and *limited* groups. The programmes are moreover usually organized and implemented in more complicated forms than the basic wealth transfer, *per se*, would require. All these aspects may not be germane for a useful proximate explanation of the relative growth of the *budget*. They are however relevant, in my judgement, for attempts to explain the relative growth of 'government'.[21]

The problem may be approached from a different side. The Lorenz curve L*c* in Figure 12.2 was modified by the tax schedule into the adjusted net income curve *aLc*. This cannot be the final story however. We need to incorporate the effect of government expenditures on the final distribution of real income. The pure transfer model may assume that tax revenues are redistributed in inverse proportion to the size of income. But the nature of the expenditure programmes, noted above, crucially affects the growth of 'government' in contrast to the growth of the budget. Many of these programmes involve provisions of (private) services and goods to specific income classes or particular social groups of society. The resulting distribution of net income including the full array of real services and goods obtained via governmental operations requires thus an independent and separate examination. Important recent work established for the United States that the relevant distribution of net real income is actually substantially closer to the diagonal line in the Lorenz diagram than the original distribution of gross income.[22] It also seems that this net real income distribution moved closer to the diagonal over the past decades. These observations confirm the basic theme introduced in the early paragraphs of this section, a theme interpreting political processes in modern democracies in terms of the negative-sum game of wealth redistribution. But the 'other side of the budget' covering the expenditure pattern forms a crucial link in the social mechanism generating the observed growth in the governmental apparatus. A second strand must be added to the analysis. This second strand involves the entrepreneurial behaviour of bureaux and politicians. Meltzer–Richard properly criticize an approach concentrating on the monopoly power of bureaux or politicians, a monopoly power essentially disregarding voter preferences. Such disregard implies that citizens appear forever doomed to ignorance about the state of affairs. But the recognition of the role of bureaux and politicians is not confined to this objectionable interpretation. A parallel with standard price-theory may clarify the issue. Market phenomena emerge from the interaction between demanders' preferences (subject to constraints) and suppliers optimizing adjustments to these preferences. These preferences are not revealed by a supernatural information channel. They are sampled and explored by the searching behaviour of entrepreneurial suppliers. This entrepreneurial behaviour proceeds with imaginative exploration of potential preferences and the development of production programmes expected to be validated by actual preferences. Entrepreneurial actions are thus a crucial link in the adjustment of services and goods produced in accordance with evolving consumer preferences.

A similar process prevails on the political scene. Bureaux (more appropriately bureaucrats) and politicians (incumbent and aspiring legislators, persons holding or seeking appointments, functionaries of political organizations) correspond to producers in the market place sampling the consumer preferences and adjusting competitively their supplies. Both politicians and bureaux thus respond to the preferences of the citizen. But this response proceeds in the context of information patterns and organizational arrangements which open opportunities for the self-interested behaviour of politicians and bureaux. They operate under the circumstances not just as mere vehicles executing the median voter groups' preferred transfer of funds. Their operation implies that a portion of the total funds collected are absorbed by the 'governmental apparatus'. This absorption corresponds to the normal profit in the competitive market place. The voter benefiting from redistribution cedes this portion of the tax revenues to the political and administrative entrepreneurs organizing the benefits. The nature of the political institutions determines extent and form of the competition between politicians and bureaux, or seen from the 'other side', the extent and form of monopoly achievable by politicians and bureaux and their potential of collusive behaviour. It seems useful for our purposes in order to focus attention on the major strands of the argument to introduce seven 'postulates'.

1. Politicians are entrepreneurs competing in a market for votes and influence. They compete with proposals, programmes and the systematic exploitation of non-cognitive aspects of language. The politicians prefer more votes and influence to less votes and influence. They also share with other men a preference for higher permanent real income
2. 'Bureaux' sample the political market with proposals, reinterpretations of their mandate, and the detailed manner of administering the tasks developed. This entrepreneurial behaviour is designed to maintain or increase the budget.
3. Costs and benefits associated with *general* programmes are more evenly distributed than the costs and benefits of *specific* programmes.
4. Information costs about costs and benefits of *general* programmes are *large* relative to benefits.
5. Information costs about costs and benefits of *specific* programmes are relatively *small* to the 'positively affected group' and comparatively *large* to the 'negatively affected group'.

6. The marginal cost of political operation (for example, lobbying in various forms) is much smaller for *established* than for *potential* organizations.

7. Potential voters weigh expected costs and benefits associated with the bureaux potential offers and with the alternative packages represented by different politicians.

The crucial information patterns are formuled under assumptions 3 to 5. These assumptions differ substantially from the information assumption made by Buchanan or Downs. The latter postulate an 'awareness discrepancy' operating uniformly across all voters and expenditure and tax programmes. The distribution of information costs, recognized here, emphasizes on the other hand a highly uneven incidence depending on the relation between voter groups and types of programmes. This distribution of information costs reflects important aspects of our reality. Rational adjustment by voters to such costs should not be interpreted to express some 'flaws in awareness' or 'ineradicable illusions'. There is no illusion in staying less than fully informed. It is an illusion on the other hand to expect voters to invest in information at a cost substantially beyond the expected return from such investments.

The major consequences of the patterns summarized by the 'postulates' can be summarized according to a previous description:[23]

> entrepreneurial competition thrives on a continued search for *new* proposals, *new* programs, *new* twists, modifications, or *extensions* of existing programs. It encourages a continuous search for suitable means to focus public attention. This is a necessary strategy for politicians to establish themselves in the competitive political market. Continuous market research and sampling of the public market with the aid of an expanding staff is therefore a competitive necessity for the politician.
>
> There are no rewards in attempts to abolish existing laws or programs. This strategy has no competitive market value. According to proposition 5 above, the beneficiaries of a program know the significance with respect to their wealth or political power of a curtailed program. 'Outside groups' will barely appreciate their own welfare gain resulting from the cut in a program. Insiders' opposition to a proposed reduction tends to override consequently the feeble support of 'outsiders' for the change. The basic postulates also imply that 'outside groups' can reasonably expect larger returns for any given costs by investing efforts in lobbying for *new specific* programs adjusted to their special benefits. The returns from political investment in organizing opposition to the other groups' specific programs are comparatively small relative to the cost of investment. It follows that proposals to cut programs are neither frequently offered by politicians (with a few exceptions immediately ridiculed by the media) nor frequently advanced by 'investors in the political marketplace'. A political entrepreneur finds thus in general that offering 'new programs' or 'variations on existing themes' assures a higher survival value in the political market. A recent article in *The Banker* noted with

interest that in the budget debates proceeding in the British Parliament over ten years not a single MP ever proposed a single time to cut expenditures.

The politicians' appraisal is reinforced by the media. An examination of commentators in the press and on television demonstrates a preference for 'fresh ideas', a *new* rhetoric or a *new* fad. The media rhetoric prefers a *new* word to almost any thoughtful proposal to abolish or reduce an obsolete or dangerous program. The media themselves find a higher market value with new words in the mass college education market. Attention to old programs, inherited legislation or institutions may infrequently have some market value. But such occurrences form usually the initial preparations for 'more, better, new and larger programs'. Political entrepreneurs find it more advantageous to propose new legislation favoring this or that other group as a way of 'offsetting' the negative effect of previous legislation. But the global welfare effects are not offset. Total welfare is further reduced, government programs increase, the budget balloons and the range of influence open to a bureaucracy expands.

The asymmetry in the distribution of costs and benefits and also the asymmetry in the distribution of information costs summarized above establishes that the emergence of new programs dominates the removal of old programs. They also determine that *specific* programs dominate *general* programs. The capital value expected by organizers proposing *general* and *undifferentiated* tax reductions or expenditure increases is quite small compared to the returns achievable for the same efforts invested to effect *specific* and *highly differentiated* programs. Complex and differentiated programs concentrate benefits on a smaller (interested) group with comparatively low information costs and impose diffuse costs on the 'outsiders' who suffer high costs of information and organization. It will in general not be worth much effort for members of an outside group to organize opposition to a specific and specialized program before or after its imposition. The capital value of investing political activity in specific new programs, differentiated for specific purposes with suitable complexity, tends to be much higher. This pattern of asymmetry in the distribution of costs and benefits explains the entrepreneurial choices of the prevalent types of programs and proposals offered by politicians. This analysis also reveals the unavoidable emergence and increasing range of complexity in tax law or regulatory arrangements. 'Tax loopholes' should be understood as a necessary result of the process. The indignant rhetoric attacking and condemning 'loopholes' reflects on the other hand the entrepreneurial opportunities politicians acquire from their own previous endeavors. This analysis suggests furthermore the fundamental irrelevance of most chapters in the theory of economic macro-policy and implies that systematic and deliberate macro-policies are somewhat improbable.

The bias for new programmes and extensions of existing programmes inherent in the political process and the associated redistributional mechanism contributes a major strand to the incremental growth of government. We also note that the concentration on specific and relatively complex programmes emerges directly from the entrepreneurial behaviour of bureaux. A particular bureau explores the political market with programmes addressed to well-defined groups in order to exploit the information pattern summarized previously. The relative success of the bureaux sampling determines simultaneously magnitude of budget and government, and also the allocation of the apparatus.

Some attention should be directed at this stage to postulate 6 in this context. The cumulative effect of the incremental growth of the government apparatus gradually raises the expected returns from potential organization by various voter groups. The significant aspect in this context is not the prevailing relative growth of government, but its cumulative effect over time. This rise in expected returns fosters the emergence of new organizations. The resulting wider array of organizations extends the range of political conflict. It extends in particular the range of relative price or income changes, or the range of 'desirable objectives' which induce political activities geared to specific redistributions.

It is important in this context that the organizational evolutions and the redistributional process not be arbitrarily narrowed to pecuniary considera- tion. Voter groups may organize in order to extract directly services and goods from the political process highly valued according to their preferences. The environmentalist movement offers an excellent illustration in this re- spect. The spread of 'single-cause movements' in the United States should also be noted in this context. In all these cases substantial organizational efforts are invested in order to achieve via the political process a guaranteed supply of valued services. A redistribution producing direct utilities for the interested voter group offers an incidental advantage over monetary redistri- bution; it is not subject to taxation. This aspect may not be quite irrelevant in a phase of increasing marginal effective tax rates due to permanent inflation.

The entrepreneurial role of bureaux and politicians may be exemplified with a few selected illustrations. The Department of Health, Education and Welfare of the US Government sampled 'client groups' all over the nation and mailed 100,000 letters in order to survey attitudes pertaining to the programme for a national health insurance. This exercise is a fine example of suggestive exploration or entrepreneurial sampling. It also reveals the inter- action between voter groups, organizations and bureaux. It reveals in particu- lar the entrepreneurial probing of voters' preferences by bureaux and the responses of political organizations.[24] A similar case emerged in the Depart- ment of Housing and Urban Development. The Federal National Mortgage Association (the 'Fannie Mae') developed over the postwar periods an impor- tant position in the national mortgage market. It essentially contributed to the efficient functioning of this market. It acquired in this context over the years large resources invested according to expected returns and risks. But the Secretary of the Department of Housing and Urban Development recognized here a potential opportunity and proposed that a substantial share of the available resources be offered at advantageous conditions to selected groups. An existing institution should thus be converted into a vehicle of redistribution benefiting a clientele to be mobilized for the benefit of the bureaux or their chief officers.[25] We may also mention in this context political proposals in Massachusetts addressing insurance companies located in the state to invest a good part of their resources in politically designated 'assets'. Behind the usual rhetoric justifying the proposal threatens a redistribution of wealth from owners, policyholders and employees to particular voter groups. It is also noteworthy that the agencies responsible for the administration of anti-trust legislation gradually reinterpret apparently their mandate and provide it with a redistributional thrust.[26] We note moreover in passing the battle about 'red-lining'. Financial institutions supplying mortgage funds in major cities are increasingly accused of discriminating systematically against loan applications made from the 'inner city' or more generally from 'disadvantaged areas'. The political rhetoric evolved with little concern or interest about the nature and the validity of the issue.[27] But cognitive truth is hardly the motive force of politicians and bureaux. The motor force behind the rhetoric are systematic attempts to exploit the political process for redistribution at a new front. Politicians and bureaux recognize opportunities to control assets of financial institutions for, as yet, unattended wealth redistribution.

The Equal Employment Opportunity Commission of the Department of Labor changed its procedures recently. The new procedures open avenues of substantially more aggressive behaviour for the bureaux. 'The Equal Employment Opportunity Commission outlined plans to sue companies that it says discriminate' against whole classes of employees. 'Formerly, the government had just tried to make sure that companies had set affirmative action goals for the future and hadn't discriminated against specific individuals.' The new approach of the Commission created a major uncertainty among the business firms affected. Representatives of business objected that the Commission violated established and well understood rules of procedures. A representative of the Labor Department found this objection 'ludicrous'. We learn in particular 'that these rules merely set minimum standards of procedure and specify that the Federal Contract Compliance Director can modify them and request any additional data reasonable for conducting a review'. This response of a 'bureau' to objections reveals with remarkable clarity the bureaux' basic interest to erode constraints and to probe freely for new opportunities of implicit transfers.[28]

The educational bureaucracy and the judiciary also offer useful illustrations for the central thesis advanced in this paper. The educational bureaucracy initiated, over the postwar decade, large changes in the political arrangements bearing on the school system. The number of school districts was radically lowered in the United States. This consolidation was accompanied by a substantial expansion of the bureaucratic apparatus and large increases of the budgets. These changes were probably made feasible by an implicit wealth transfer between former districts consolidated into a larger unit. A similar pattern of entrepreneurial legislatures and bureaux modified in New Jersey the rights of local school boards. The legislature granted the State Education Commission authority to overrule budget decision of local communities. A commission instituted by the state legislature proposes now (spring 1977) that local voters be disenfranchised in matters concerning their local school system. Less-affluent communities can reasonably expect to benefit from this proposal, and more-affluent communities lose the right to determine the quality of their own schools. The initiative of legislature and bureau does not proceed in a vacuum of voter preferences as an expression of 'political monopolies'. They reflect an assessment of politically dominant voter preferences exploitable however in a context of relative monopoly powers determined by the nature of the inherited political structure.

The judiciary also developed in the United States a role which can hardly be overlooked. Litigation increasingly evolved into a major avenue of wealth acquisition. The expansion of the legal profession and the entrepreneurial behaviour of lawyers widened over the decades the range of potentially profitable litigation. But these probing ventures at reinterpretations of existing legislation and the modification of prevailing juridical practices initiated by lawyers are essentially conditioned by expectations of appropriate behaviour on the part of the courts and judges. The courts engage in corresponding entrepreneurial behaviour of their own and open new avenues for legal action involving implicit wealth transfers. They innovate reinterpretations, evidential procedures and standards of punishment, offering new opportunities for private investments in the 'negative-sum game' of wealth acquisition. The sums awarded by courts for torts, damages and liabilities exceed in the United States at this stage any reasonable assessment of the values involved by a multiple. This excess is a measure of the implicit wealth transfer operated via the judiciary and the legal system.[29]

These illustrations are not offered as substantial evidence bearing on a completed and developed piece of analysis. They are designed to elaborate in a suggestive vein the important role of bureaux and politicians in the political process to be determined eventually in the context of a coherent and completed analysis. It is not claimed that bureaux and politicians impose their proposals and procedures on the citizen. They contribute to the incremental expansion of government by probing and searching for ranges of voter preferences to be satisfied. Successful sampling of selected and limited ranges of voter preferences producing appropriate wealth or utility transfers also benefits the bureaux and legislators involved. Successful probing of voter preferences determines the longer-run return to be expected by these political entities.

Concluding remarks

The central theme of the paper addresses the fundamental ambivalence of political structure. Such structures raise the expected returns from productive effort and voluntary exchange. But they do not remove all aspects of negative-sum games. Man's resourceful coping with his natural and social environment unavoidably induces the systematic exploitation of any political institutions for purposes of wealth acquisition via investments in the political process. Political institutions offer opportunities to acquire control over resources via privately productive and socially nonproductive methods. The crucial difference between anarchy and political structure is not the occurrence or nonoccurrence of negative-sum games, but their relative magnitude and the absence or prevalence of more or less explicit rules of this game. This fundamental property of political structure explains, in my judgement, the persistent relative growth of government and the erosion of both concept and practice of limited constitutional government. The interaction between voters, bureaux and legislatures produces a persistent process of wealth (or utility) transfers accompanied by an incremental growth of the government apparatus.

Advocates of a contractarian approach to an examination of 'government' and political structure argue the need or necessity for a 'new constitution' in order to prevent the final emergence of Leviathan. The analysis outlined in the third section reveals however a basic flaw in the contractarian view. The contractarian thesis suggests that an established constitution representing the voluntary transaction of individual agents will in general be maintained in the absence of groups insisting on *total* renegotiation. The contractarian position thus misses the crucial consequence of any political structure and the essence of politics. Every constitutional design defines incentives and offers opportunities to exploit the political structure for socially nonproductive wealth acquisition by specific groups or individual agents. No 'reconstructing' can avoid this consequence. This does not mean that different political structures, even within the broad range of democratic arrangements, do not yield substantially different incentives and opportunities with corresponding differences in the growth of both budget and government.[30] But the crucial fact following from the analysis sketched in the third section should be fully appreciated: the opportunities created by any constitutional design originally contracted by the social partners produce responses by participants in the social game which gradually modify meaning, operation and range of political institutions. No political structure can ever be fixed by a constitutional contract.[31]

But where does the process evolving in democratic nations eventually lead? I venture some tentative and somewhat speculative thoughts in concluding the paper. The speculative element reflects the unfinished and incomplete state of analysis. It also defines lines of future research bearing on various aspects of the 'political economy of government'.

The pure wealth-transfer model explains the relative growth of the budget and its eventual convergence to an equilibrium. This equilibrium is determined by the condition that the median voter group discerns no advantage derivable from additional changes in tax schedules producing a larger wealth transfer. But the extension of the analysis incorporating the role of politicians, bureaux and organizations of voter groups introduces additional considerations. The cumulative effect of persistent relative growth of government encourages the formation of political organizations. The larger and wider-ranging the government apparatus, the larger is the expected private productivity of political organization. The relative growth of government is thus accompanied by a growth in number and importance of political organizations. Investments in these organizations occur whenever the accumulated stock of political institutions reveals opportunities for wealth or utility transfers. At this stage we observe that changes in relative prices or relative incomes affecting particular social groups yield incentives for new political formations. These formations raise the cost to politicians and bureaux of disregarding or neglecting these social groups. The longer-run effects of relative growth of government are thus reflected by an increasing range of political conflict. The frontiers of political conflict cover a widening space of issues. This implies furthermore that the range of negative-sum games in society expands relative to the range of positive-sum games. The cumulative long-run consequences of relative growth in government are thus gradually made visible by a declining rate of real growth and eventual stagnation. The social structure will be moulded more and more in rigid political organizations involved in permanent political conflicts. These conflicts become under the circumstances increasingly irresolvable. The laments deploring the 'ungovernability' of the political structure mount in frequency and intensity.[32] Whatever 'political capital' elected executives or appointed officials may have originally acquired rapidly decays when confronted in all directions with rigid lines of political conflict. This weakens the central administration and exposes the government to aggressions of the larger or weightier political organizations. There emerges thus a danger of increasing instability of the political process. The political evolution leads under the circumstances with rising probability to various forms of nondemocratic societies. This process may evolve gradually over many years. It will also be interrupted by intermittent countermovements. And most particularly, it need not and quite likely will not involve dramatic (or romantic) events of any 'deep significance'.[33]

I have drawn admittedly a sombre scenario. Fortunately, it may be wrong. There is no guarantee that my analysis is correct. Moreover, even accepting the general analysis laid out in the third section, the concluding scenario represents only my *most probable* assessment. Political processes and history are beyond any deterministic schemata, at least in the context of serious cognitive endeavours. Systematic knowledge about political processes and the political economy of government is still in its infancy. We still grope for major answers in a world of pervasive uncertainties. The outline offered and the scenario presented are submitted as an intellectual challenge to cope with this uncertainty.[34]

Notes

1. These two positions can be explained in terms of two alternative perceptions (or theories) about man. The connection between the view of man and the interpretation of government was explored in the paper 'The perception of man and the conception of government', jointly authored by Karl Brunner and William Meckling, *Journal of Money, Credit and Banking*, February 1977.
2. A more detailed discussion can be found in the paper 'Why government grows (and grows) in a democracy', by Allan H. Meltzer and Scott Richard, *Public Interest*, 1978.
3. *Budgets and Bureaucrats: The Sources of Government Growth*, ed. Thomas E. Borcherding, Durham, 1977. Tables 12.3 and 12.4 are drawn from this book.
4. Warren Nutter, *Growth of Government in the West*, Washington, D.C.: American Enterprise Institute for Public Policy Research, 1978.
5. The reader is referred once more to the argument presented in the paper listed under note 1.
6. The reader may consult in this context Cotton M. Lindsay and Dan Norman, 'Reopening the question of government spending', in *Budgets and Bureaucrats*, ed. Thomas E. Borcherding, Durham, 1977.
7. A summary of the issues and of the relevant literature is presented in ibid.
8. Robert J. Barro, 'The control of politicians: an economic model', *Public Choice*, Spring 1973.
9. Robert J. Mackay, 'Private versus public sector growth: a collective choice approach', in *Budgets and Bureaucrats*, ed. Thomas E. Borcherding, Durham, 1977.
10. Anthony Downs, 'An economic theory of democracy', New York, 1957.
11. James Buchanan and Richard Wagner, 'Democracy in deficit'. We should note that James Buchanan and Gordon Tullock offered a different explanation for the emergence of an excessively large government (relative to an optimum determined by voter preferences) in their *The Calculus of Consent*, Ann Arbor, 1962. Buchanan and Tullock argued that benefits of government programmes are mostly addressed to specific coalitions, whereas costs of programmes are borne by the general taxpayer. Coalitions are induced to push for a programme size at which their marginal cost (equal to the general taxpayers' marginal cost) coincides with their marginal benefit.
12. The reader may find an interesting discussion of these issues in the Symposium on 'Democracy in Deficit', *Journal of Monetary Economics*, July 1978.
13. Peter A. Aranson and Peter C. Ordeshook present an excellent argument on this score: 'Incrementalism, fiscal illusion and the growth of government in representative democracies'. The paper was presented at the Fourth Interlaken Seminar on Analysis and Ideology, June 1977.
14. James Buchanan, 'The limits of liberty: between anarchy and Leviathan', Chicago, 1975. Robert Nozick, 'Anarchy, state and Utopia', New York, 1974.
15. Nonproductive wealth extraction is usually labelled as a zero-sum game. But this is false. First, occurrence of such extractions includes defensive political investments. Secondly, and probably more important, it lowers expected returns from productive application of resources. The level of productive application will be lowered.
16. The basic these has been elaborated by William Meckling, 'Values and the choice of the model of the individual in the social sciences', *Schweizerische Zeitschrift für Volkswirtschaft und Statistik*, 1976. The REMM (resourceful, evaluation, maximizing man) model has been developed in the context of economic analysis and contrasts with the VARM (vacu-

ous, aimless, reactive man) model widely appearing in the sociological literature. The REMM model is advanced here as a basic framework of analysis applicable to any human pattern.

17. Cotton M. Lindsay and Don Norman. 'Reopening the question of public spending', in *Budgets and Bureaucrats*, ed. Thomas E. Borcherding, Durham, 1977.

18. Some comments on a frequently encountered description of 'politics' and 'economics' may be appropriate here. One reads on occasion that 'politics is concerned with equity, whereas economics is concerned with efficiency'. This is a remarkable obfuscation of the problem posed by the shifting mixtures of the positive-sum and the negative-sum social games. It is well designed to distract attention from the crucial properties of political institution and the essential characteristic of political conflict.

19. The reader is referred to the paper listed in note 2. The authors also prepared their argument in a rigorous analytic form presented originally at the Fourth Interlaken Seminar on Analysis and Ideology, June 1977.

20. The table was published originally by Paul Craig Robers in an article 'Disguising the tax burden', *Harper's*, March 1978.

21. The nature of the issue should be clearly recognized. It does not concern our ability to predict specific programmes. It concerns the *general* fact that they exhibit pervasive properties of the kind described in the text.

22. Morton Paglin, 'Transfers in kind, their impact on poverty, 1959–1975', Hoover Institution Conference on Income Redistribution, October 1977.

23. Karl Brunner, 'Comments', *Journal of Law and Economics*, December 1975.

24. 'Outreach', *Wall Street Journal*, 17 April 1978, 16.

25. 'The Fannie Mae Raid', *Wall Street Journal*, 24 April 1978, 18.

26. Fred Weston, 'Anti-trust: the coming battlefield', *Wall Street Journal*, 14 April 1978, 14.

27. George Benston (University of Rochester) found in his preliminary results of a systematic examination no support for the political claims.

28. Liz Roman Gallese, 'Battle over bias', *Wall Street Journal*, 17 February 1978, 1.

29. The nature of the institutional incentives responsible for this development in the United States in contrast to other countries deserves some careful research. The reader is also referred to two illuminating articles in the *Wall Street Journal* bearing on the entrepreneurial behaviour of the judiciary. On 31 March 1978 (p. 16: 'Coming attractions, 1984') an editorial addressed a decision made by a National Labor Relations administrative law judge. The issue involved the right to union representation at a specific plant. A secret ballot arranged according to existing regulations revealed that a large majority of workers expressed opposition to unionization. The judge dismissed this result and imposed unionization on the workers involved according to an arbitrarily selected criterion. The history of the Seabrook Nuclear Power Station (*Wall Street Journal*, 24 February 1978, 16: 'Berserk proceduralism') offers some further illustration. It is almost a classic example of the adjustments made by bureaux to limited ranges or organized voter preferences and arbitrary juridical decisions and procedures. The example reveals with particular force the reason for the *negative* sum game built into this specific redistributional process.

30. A comparison of Sweden with the United States and of Switzerland with the United States may offer some useful insights in this respect.

31. The general interpretation of political structure offered in this paper can be usefully extended to nondemocratic regimes. The viability of an oligarchy or dictatorial group depends on suitable redistributional arrangements via the operation of political institutions. Inadequate attention or misjudgement of the appropriate redistribution endangers the viability of the ruling group. A variety of events in Eastern European countries, in Russia or African and/or Latin-American dictatorships offer observations deserving detailed examination from the vantage point elaborated. These investigations would show, according to my conjecture, that even a totalitarian regime *cannot* disregard *completely* the preferences of disenfranchized citizens. Some concessions to these preferences seem a necessary condition for the viability of the regime. A totalitarian regime with all its heavy ideological apparatus cannot escape *some* subtle and indirect influence exerted by the preferences of the citizens. An authoritarian regime with little ideological commitment

and a smaller range of political institutionalization suffers even greater exposure to citizen preferences.

32. The general model corresponds to the patterns observed in Italy and New York City.
33. The importance of May 1968 in France pales somewhat from a ten-year perspective. It formed a residual disturbance in the longer-run process.
34. The analytic programme outlined in the paper needs also to examine the role of socio-political beliefs in the political process. Their pervasive occurrence is hardly disputable and deserves systematic integration into the analysis.

13 The limits of economic policy*

Alternative approaches to economic policy

Academic analysis of economic policy and associated normative conclusions exhibits two distinct traditions. The historical evolution of policy and policy conceptions reflects over the past 200 years shifting influences from both traditions. One addresses an open-ended field of specific actions potentially available to government and explores the consequences of these measures. More importantly, this tradition justifies an action-oriented approach aimed at a wide range of specific results over a loosely limited or practically unlimited range. This policy conception envisions government as an active agent at least approximately concerned with the optimization of some social welfare function. This concern would require a wide array of policy instruments in order to allow the policy-makers unobstructed play in the policy game. The analysis of economic policy examines under the circumstances the relation between instruments and goals expressed by a social welfare function and the useful range of possible instruments. It investigates in particular the dependence of the choice of instruments and their setting on the prevailing state of affairs in view of the desired goals of policy-makers. A substantial literature followed this line exemplified by Tinbergen's *Theory of Economic Policy* (1952) and the work on optimal control (Chow, 1975). Most of the discussions directed by academicians to the public arena address the policy problem in a similar vein. They concentrate on specific actions, choices of instruments or their setting in the past, at the present or in the future. Notes are assigned to policy-makers for the adequacy of their choices or alternative specific suggestions are submitted for urgent attention.

The second tradition is more attuned to classical political philosophy and classical economics. It rejects the action-oriented approach with its characteristic desire to mould the world in some detail and its emphasis on choices of specific instruments or their level of application. The classical tradition emphasizes by contrast the proper choice of rules governing the socio-political or socio-economic game. The difference between the two approaches may be usefully explained with the metaphor of a football game. The policy-makers would be represented by the commissioner of the football league and the players represent agents in the socio-economic game. The classical tradition with its constitutionalist thrust limits policy-makers to formulate, monitor

* Originally published in *Schweizerische Zeitschrift für Volkswirtschaft und Statistik*, **3**, 1985, 213–235.

and enforce the general rules controlling the detailed plays of the game. The choice of strategies, tactical procedures and all the varied details of play are left to the players. The other tradition empowers the commissioner to shape both the general rules and much detail of play in a shifting pattern in accordance with the state of play. The classic approach to policy analysis thus understands policy not as a choice of specific actions but as a choice of general rules usually embedded in a set of institutions. We may juxtapose it under the circumstances as an 'institutional policy' to 'specific action policies'. Analysis of economic policy means in this case an examination of alternative sets of rules. Variations in the rules yield in general different patterns in the socio-economic game. Any normative concern requires thus some careful analysis of the consequences associated with different sets of rules. Opportunities and incentives are in general affected by the choice of rules. The resulting modification of behaviour influences unavoidably the broad pattern of the outcome produced by the social process. An evaluation of this outcome guides the analysts' choice of rules.

Theorists, pragmatists and understanding policy
The discussion of policy is ultimately guided by a desire to provide an understanding of its role and consequences. It should contribute in particular to a reliable assessment of the alternative traditions. Academic contributions, whether made in academia or offered to the public arena, do not exhaust however the public discussions. We also encounter the comments, views and proposals made by the media, suggested by officials or politicians and advanced by policy-makers. Some components in this second strand of the discussion interact quite closely with the academic discussion. But major components evolve according o their own 'logic' and with their own momentum. The discussion surrounding the US budget deficit demonstrates this aspect with remarkable force. The media and other participants in the political process recognize this state and typically reflect it by juxtaposing the pragmatist or practical men of affairs to the academic 'theoreticians'. This juxtaposition involves more than a simple description of facts. It occurs with a peculiar epistemological thrust. It conveys a subtle sense about a difference in the state of knowledge. Practical men of affairs directly immersed in the reality of the policy problem experience somehow an immediate absorption of the relevant knowledge. The academic by contrast approaches reality indirectly via the construction of theories. The underlying message suggests moreover that the epistemological quality of such theories hardly compares with the acquisition of knowledge based on 'direct exposure to reality'. This more or less implicit theme embedded in the cliché represented by the juxtaposition suffers however under a fatal illusion. It thoroughly misconceives the nature of human knowledge. All potential knowledge appears in the form

of theories or hypotheses about various aspects of our physical or social environment. This holds for academics and equally for 'practical men of affairs'. The latter are full of theories about matters concerning them. They are however rarely aware of the essentially theoretical nature of their perceptions of reality. They fail consequently to appreciate that perceptions about reality occurring in the form of some general conceptions (i.e. theories) are not automatically true simply because they were motivated somehow by 'exposure to reality'. They still need to be critically assessed against observations. Most of these ideas would hardly survive this process. An analysis of the remainder reveals moreover that they yield almost no information about the range of important consequences to be expected under different sets of policy actions or under various policy institutions. We encounter here the crucial focus of a minimal understanding of economic policy. A rational evaluation and choice of policy actions or institutions requires some more reliable knowledge of the probable consequences. This knowledge defines in an important sense the relevant limits of economic policy. But such knowledge can only be supplied in the form of theories which survived some first rounds of critical assessment. The 'practical men of affairs', geared for other and quite important functions in life, frequently demanding high levels of intelligence, are in general, with remarkable exceptions however, not equipped for this task. They are by contrast often well equipped to provide us with detailed and useful descriptions of the political decision process with suggestively insightful *theoretical fragments* bearing on the general nature of this process. This state of affairs probably contributes to the prevalent belief in the public arena that practical men of affairs possess superior knowledge about economic policy. This belief confounds descriptive knowledge about the decision process with knowledge about the consequences and meaning of policies. My comment neither implies nor suggests that academic economists can be relied upon to possess such knowledge. An academic position is neither a necessary nor a sufficient condition for this state to occur. The verbal supplies of any economist are not our concern. The crucial point which needs to be made on occasion is the existence of a professional core expressed by economic analysis and represented by the best accumulated work of the profession. This core guides our exploration of 'the limits of economic policy'.

Limits of economic policy

General remarks
This exploration does not represent the basic purpose of this paper. It is motivated by our ultimate interest in the alternative traditions of economic policy. The notion of limits associated with economic policy requires,

however, some careful attention. Any metaphor or usual analogy suggesting a limit would in general blur the real issues posed by policy choices. A sense of the relevant limitation on policy-making emerges once we examine the consequences of policies and the nature of the policy-making process. The implications of the constraints imposed by the social opportunity set and the prevalence of perennially incomplete information about the detailed working of the private and public sector determine the range of issues to be examined in this context. One more comment needs to be made here. The term 'economic policy' is used here in a very inclusive way. It subsumes social policy, regional policy, housing policies, labour market policies, etc. It subsumes in a sense all governmental actions conditioning the use and development of (human and non-human) resources.

Implications of constraints characterizing the social opportunity set

The notion of a social opportunity set   The range of possible states of affairs is not unlimited. Physical nature and the patterns of social interaction constrain the feasible set of states potentially realizable. This limitation has been recognized and analysed for a long time by economic analysis under the label of a set of social production possibilities or a social opportunity set. The general properties of this opportunity set have been examined and belong to the standard material of textbooks. The general idea is simple and straightforward (see Figure 13.1). Suppose for convenience that an economy consists of two activities each one with a specific product (x and y). On the basis of a given endowment of resources existing at a time, the social opportunity set can be represented by a simple graph. The two axes express the output of y and x, the two goods in the economy. The concave line describes the production possibility frontier. The set of points defined by this frontier and the two axes constitutes the social opportunity set. Any combination (y, x) within this set is achievable. Interior combinations of the set are however inefficient. This means that one output could be raised without sacrificing any amount of

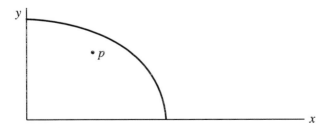

Figure 13.1

the other. The point p reveals this fact. It also reveals that both outputs could be raised simultaneously. It should be noted for our subsequent discussion that the concept of the social opportunity set is not confined to standard goods and services. It can usefully include any dimension of our environment valued positively or negatively.

The social opportunities, whatever the dimensions subsumed, remain limited and the frontier imposes trade-offs with unavoidable choices or associates social costs with all actions. Policy-makers can only move the economy (in the longer run) along the frontier trading off one good for another good. The opportunity set is moreover not just the reflection of a physical environment. It is crucially determined by socio-economic and socio-political institutions. Changes in admissible forms of organizing activities or changes in the admissible range of contractual arrangements modify in general the social opportunity set. We also learned over the past 15 years that variations in policy regime also influence this set. This means that some social costs imposed by policies appear as a contraction of the social opportunity set. This contraction occurs however relative to the expansion produced by economic growths and possible social benefits of policy. Other welfare losses occur as so-called distortions in the use of resources expressed by deviations between marginal social and private costs or deviations between marginal social costs and private relative evaluations (marginal rates of substitutions) expressing the agent's preference system.

The recognition or acknowledgement of such limitations is frequently difficult for 'political entrepreneurs', policy-makers or a politically committed intelligentsia. They will resent an analysis emphasizing inherent limitations and the reality of trade-offs or of social costs. The pursuit of policies which disregard inherent limitations produces unavoidably new problems not expected by the policy-maker and wrongly attributed to a variety of irrelevant conditions. A further round of policies is then introduced to cope with the new problems. They will be quite ineffectual however. They do not, in general, address the crucial conditions and further problems result.

The reality of trade-offs   The general characterization needs some illustrative exemplifications. Two sets of policies based on recent experience and discussions will be adduced. The first set refers to monetary problems. Central Bank officials and politicians attempt (or profess to attempt) on occasion to pursue simultaneously a policy of exchange rate control and a monetary control policy. But this combination is not within the feasible set of possible combinations. An exchange rate policy implies that monetary growth reflects all the random shocks operating on exchange markets. 'Sterilization' or 'desterilization' operations may for a short period appear to reconcile the two goals. This reconciliation cannot persist over the longer run. A monetary control policy on the other hand is consistent with interventions in exchange markets. It is however inconsistent with interventions guided by longer-run exchange rate targeting. The experiences of the past 15 years and most particularly the experience of the Swiss National Bank confirm this point. Monetary authorities and politicians need to recognize the basic facts. They are confronted with a trade-off and they must choose between controlling exchange rates or controlling monetary growth. It is noteworthy that this issue determined Dr Schiller's resignation as Minister of Economic Affairs from the German Government in 1972. The German Government chose to disregard Dr Schiller's warning about a trade-off and was subsequently confronted with the hard facts. We note in passing that the same limitation extends to any attempt to combine a monetary control policy with a policy of controlling some real variables (say, e.g., interest rates). This means also that the constraints imposed by reality exclude the simultaneous realization of a policy avoiding persistent inflationary or deflationary episodes and a monetary policy addressed to control some real variables.

The policy debates of the European Parliament in Strasbourg erupted on occasion with demands for a persistently expansionary monetary policy (*'eine monetäre Vorwärtspolitik'*) substantially raising monetary growth. It seems that advocates of this policy expect with its aid to lower permanently unemployment and to revive permanently the growth or level of output. The reality of the social opportunity set precludes however this option. Its pursuit beyond a deep depression actually reflecting a contraction in aggregate nominal demand involves a serious illusion. Such a policy would under the present circumstances yield at best a very temporary effect on output and ultimately produce a pattern of rising inflation. The same impossibility obstructs the wishful dreams of many politicians who propose to lower interest rates by an accelerated monetary growth.

The US administration's budget forecasts made in past years suffered from politically appealing illusions about feasible achievements on a related issue. The forecasts were based on assumptions bearing on future inflation and interest rates. These assumptions were required to determine the course of revenues and expenditures. But the assumptions were quite inconsistent. No feasible state in the opportunity set could produce the comparatively high inflation jointly with the relatively low interest rates assumed as a basis for the forecasts.

Other examples drawn from agricultural policy, housing policy, tenancy protection, risk regulation, etc., abound. A survey of the range addressed by policy in any country offers a rich menu of possible cases.

Labour market policies pursued in Europe over the past decades yield some particularly important examples. The goal of job security or economic security in a more general sense found increasing favour over the past 20 years in the political arena. The goal was pursued with little recognition of, or concern for, inherent limitations. Such limitations do exist, however, and we can easily appreciate that committed advocates of more (and more) economic security resent being confronted with the reality of such limitations. The limitations impose trade-offs involving economic security, employment, real wages and real fringe benefits. They also impose a trade-off between economic security and economic growth with rising standards of living. The policies addressed to job security or to economic security in general varied between countries. Their gradually expanding implementation within each country proceeded, moreover, with a variety of measures. All these measures, whatever their detail, directly or indirectly raised the real cost of employment. This implies that either employment, real wages or real fringe benefits fall. The inherent nature of the social process thus imposes a trade-off. Its reality exists irrespective of ideological commitments or theological dreams and this reality ultimately confronts us with a choice. Employment will fall or stagnate with an insistent maintenance of real wages. Employment levels can be maintained, on the other hand, with trading-off of real wages. It might appear that these unpleasant choices can be avoided with subsidies to business firms offsetting the increase in the real cost of employment. But such subsidies must be financed, either with taxes or money creation. In the first case, net real wages or net real income from investment will be lowered. And the latter effect discourages investment and lowers growth. The recourse to money creation generates inflation. The political reality of inflation determines moreover a highly erratic inflation with pervasive uncertainty lowering investment and growth. Similarly, an increasingly rigid or demanding policy of economic security impedes economic growth. It obstructs adjustments in the pattern of resource use and lowers incentives to explore new possibilities or opportunities. It contributes to a state of ossification or petrification of society. Most European nations moved along a course trading off employment and stagnation for economic security. But this implicit choice is not recognized in the political arena. The loss in employment imposed by the political choice is insistently attributed by the media and most politicians to the evolution of modern technologies. Any politician who dares to recognize the crucial issue is usually ridiculed and vilified in the public arena. But the professional core of economics informs us that 'technology' is an opportunity for rising general welfare and not the problem asserted. It does become a problem within the institutional arrangements characterizing an ossified or petrified society.

The reality of social costs   The reality of the social opportunity set with the economy's inherent drive to settle in the neighbourhood of the production frontier confronts policy-making with another important dimension. This dimension involves a significant limitation almost systematically neglected in the politics of economic policy. This neglect substantially distorts the balance of social benefits and social costs associated with policy decisions. It encourages economic policies with social benefits less than their social costs. These costs may involve a decline in welfare expressed by a relative compression of the social opportunity set whenever resources are allocated to socially non-productive investments in the political process encouraged by distributional gains associated with the policy-making process. The costs may also reflect larger inputs ('rent-seeking') in the production process required per output unit. But welfare losses also occur whenever policies distort the pattern of resource uses relative to the prevailing preference system within a given opportunity set. In either case, social costs reflect a sacrifice in some dimensions of the social process positively valued by some members of society. Social costs are not an abstract entity beyond human concerns. They ultimately represent underlying human valuations by the only source of human values, i.e. the individual persons in a society.

The regulation of pharmaceutical products initiated in the USA in the early 1960s offers a remarkable example of the consequences associated with the neglect of this particular limitation. The traumatic impact on public impressions made by the tragically crippled and deformed babies resulting from the use of thalidomide by pregnant women influenced new legislation and tougher regulatory policies. Public attention became fixed on a single goal: to lower the risk to zero of admitting new pharmaceutical products with potentially dangerous side-effects. The measures implemented for this purpose substantially raised the costs of development for new products by a large factor. Other measures shortened at the same time the expected pay-off period of new drugs and thus lowered the potential return. Regulatory policies quite generally obstructed the flow of inventions and innovations. Innovation consequently declined by a wide margin and the appearance of new drugs sharply contracted. It would be difficult to dispute that new legislation and regulatory policy provided no benefits. They most probably offered some useful effects. But they also imposed some heavy burdens on the members of society. They obstructed the creation and use of new and effective drugs for a wide array of health problems. Avoidable illness and death due to unavailable but potentially producible drugs increased. Illness and death unrecognized by legislators and regulators forms the social cost of a well-meant endeavour. A detailed research of this problem concluded that the social cost of the new policy vastly exceeded the social benefits it provided to the public. The single-minded obsession with the minimization of risk attached to new drugs failed to recognize the unavoidable alternative risk associated with a lower innovation of useful and health- or life-preserving drugs. A policy addressed to minimize the probability of bad pharma products maximized at the same time the probability of *not* having useful drugs.

The 'obsessive approach' increasingly dominated regulatory policy during the 1970s. This trend was most particularly visible in environmental, health and safety politics. This approach recognized only a single dimension, the desired benefits. The occurrence of social costs were simply neglected. The result was a seriously unbalanced policy process ultimately lowering welfare. Absolutist standards of environmental purity were envisioned. But any serious attempts to realize such standards lower the dimension of the opportunity set and push the production frontier nearer to the origin. The same consequences follow from an obsessive health policy seriously pursuing an absolutist standard. Commitment to such a standard always involves a neglect of social cost in the decision process. Alternatively, a concern for the social cost imposed on the public prohibits an absolutist standard. It forces policymakers to ponder a more balanced approach. Recognition of social costs would not prevent social benefits from environmental and health policies. But the policies would be constrained by the recognition of social costs. The incentives in the political process to recognize social costs remain however weak and uncertain. The emergence of an approximately balanced approach is, under the circumstances, not the result of a recognition of social costs. It emerges usually from a decentralized implementation involving all major interests. A single and central regulatory agency is much more likely to follow an absolutist standard.

Protectionism, cartel legislation and regional policies exhibit a similar pattern. The Swiss Federal Council's report on regional policy presenting arguments for a proposed legislation is quite indicative. It diligently lists the benefits, and here especially the number of jobs saved or created in some regions as a result of the policy. The reader finds however no allusions to any potential social cost. Legislators are not warned that regional policy also means ossification of inherited inefficient structures. It also means that more efficient jobs in other regions are destroyed or thwarted. And it means, lastly, that some non-human resources will be used less efficiently in a social sense. All this implies that the social opportunity set is contracted for the benefit of some 'regional balance or restoration'.

The same argument extends to protectionism and cartel legislation. Benefits and beneficiaries are easily recognized. But these benefits are hardly ever *social* benefits. They usually involve redistributions of income and are matched by corresponding losses elsewhere. These losses, as the gains, are however private. Occurrence of private gain or even of social benefits establishes no social case for such policies. The professional literature determined a long time ago the 'deadweight welfare losses' produced by protectionism and monopolies. These losses are produced by the distortions in the use of resources resulting from such policies. The welfare losses are actually substantially raised by the 'rent-seeking behaviour' of potential beneficiaries. The evolution of public choice theory in the past 20 years directed our attention to this important aspect. The establishment of a privileged position by means of protectionist measures, cartel legislation and its implementation, or on the basis of other monopolizing actions requires substantial investment of resources in the political process. These investments also contract the social opportunity set. 'Rent-seeking behaviour' thus absorbs socially valuable resources and imposes a welfare cost on society. The *social* cost of these policies is usually overlooked in the political process whereas some *private* benefits are much touted as *social* gains. The net effect of these policies involves, however, essentially a redistribution of income and jobs accompanied by a welfare loss due to the dead-weight burden and the rent-seeking behaviour. Dubious benefits are often claimed most particularly for cartel legislation. But these claims need be understood as an ideological fog covering the reality of this economic policy.

The variety of illustrative cases could be multiplied in many directions. Transfer policies (i.e. 'social policies') create incentives in the political process and disincentives for socially productive activities which yield the same general consequences as the measures discussed in the previous paragraph. We note however a crucial difference. In the prior case the redistributional consequences are hidden. On this issue, by contrast, they are the explicit purpose of the policy. Some measure of redistribution expresses probably the political consensus of western democracies. But we also need to recognize that they impose a social cost on society and those costs rise with the extent and complexity of the policies.

The central proposition of this section emphasizes the comparative blindness of the political process to social costs typically associated with economic policy. Political debate centres on the private gains and losses, i.e. on redistributional aspects, and rarely considers the significant limitation expressed by relevant social costs. It is noteworthy that academia suffers under a similar blindness. The standard discussion of market failure resolves the associated welfare problem with suitable interventions by the government. These interventions are moreover supposed to involve no social costs. This is particularly remarkable as many cases of alleged 'market failure' are attributable to the operation of neglected social costs also affecting governmental interventions. It follows that this analysis offers little guidance for rational policy-making.

The problem of information
Legislation and regulatory rules and ordinances encounter a compliance problem. There is no automatic compliance. The norms established by policy-

making must be monitored and enforced. The investment in the apparatus required for this purpose imposes also a social cost on society. Compliance is however linked with another problem involving limitations on economic policy. We need to recognize that the mode of operation of both private and public sector produces a substantial uncertainty about the *detailed* pattern of outcomes. The nature of this problem will be explored in the following two sub-sections.

Uncertainty in the private sector Government interventions confront members of society with a challenge. These measures modify private opportunity sets and thus induce various responses. Many of these responses address an imaginative search to lower the impact of government intervention. This search by many smart operators eventually produces an array of devices, arrangements and procedures which more or less legally at least partly circumvent the government's intervention. The extent of these activities depends on private costs imposed by intervention and search relative to expected private gains. The very nature of these activities implies moreover that many detailed adjustments made in response to an intervention are quite unpredictable. Important longer-run consequences to complex policies remain thus essentially unknown at the time the policies are under consideration. Even the most rational legislator or policy-maker fully devoted to the mythical entity called the 'public interest' suffers under very incomplete information about the *detailed* ramification of policies. Every intervention tends to produce unintended and unexpected consequences which eventually affect the evaluation and usefulness of the intervention. This uncertainty confronts economic policy with another dimension of possible limitations which need to be considered in rational policy-making.

It may be useful to develop the argument in a more general context. The social process governed by spontaneous interaction between agents in market economies operates as a vast system continuously creating and disseminating new information. Acquisition and interpretation of these flows of new information modifies private opportunity sets and expectations of future market conditions. These revisions induce pervasive adjustments in behaviour. The detailed nature of outcome patterns produced by the social process continuously changes as a result. By the very nature of the process conditioned by the dissemination of *new* information (i.e. essentially *unanticipated*), the evolving outcome patterns are unpredictable in their *full detail*. Economic analysis thus explains quite successfully the nature and characterization of the social process. But this understanding of the spontaneous order created by the social process also implies that no analysis can predict beyond the broad contours the *detailed* outcome of the uncertainty. This uncertainty confronts policy-makers with a serious problem. The correlation between actions or policies and intended outcome or desired results is burdened with shadows of doubt. Some components of the total outcome may be quite predictable but many other evolving effects remain unpredictable. The *full* consequences of policies are thus hidden behind the veils of an uncertain future.

Some examples may elaborate the nature of the issue involved. The public's response to radar traffic control in the USA offers a small but intriguing example. The explosive use of radar detection devices and CB radios to circumvent the measure was hardly predicted. The adjustments produced by tax legislation are both more pervasive and important. These adjustments abound with unexpected and unintended consequences, affecting the use and development of resources. These consequences lower the correlation between motivating intention and actual outcome. This modified correlation confronts any ambitious and complex policy programme with a subtle but effective limitation. We may single out at this stage in particular the corporate income tax. We possess no reliable information about who really pays the tax. The public's vision that the 'corporations' pay the taxes is simply an impressionistic illusion. Taxes are ultimately always borne by persons, in this case the recipients of salaries, wages, income on capital invested or consumers via the real price charged on the corporation's product. The corporation forms just the organizational vehicle for the collection of taxes from the persons associated with it. We can specify a variety of conditions which affect the distribution of the corporate tax among ultimate tax payers. But we lack the detailed empirical knowledge necessary for any reliable information in this respect. This uncertainty explains both the political appeal of the tax and its basic problem. When legislators impose a tax on corporations or change their tax rates they do not know who they really tax. Employees may bear the burden in the form of lower real wages and lower fringe benefits or owners suffer the burden as a result of lower returns on their investments. In either case there would be further repercussions on non-human and human capital formation. Equity and efficiency thus suggest the abolition of the corporate tax and its replacement by a personal income tax. This clashes however with the political appeal of corporation taxes. This appeal is crucially conditioned by the uncertainty described. This uncertainty obscures the true limitations of the tax determined by its social costs. The neglect of the social cost by the political process occurs here in the context of a choice favouring a measure with an inherent information problem.

This theme emerges in the range of stabilization policies with particular force. A wide gulf separates the reality of stabilization policy from the official claims and academic rhetoric. The latter proceed as if we possessed detailed and reliable information about the economy's response structure. Once again this information is not available and the information problem confronts any ambitious stabilization policy with a severe and fundamental limitation. Incomplete information about the economy's detailed response structure lowers the correlation between desired or intended and actual performance level produced by 'stabilization policies'. The unknown detail of the response structure conditions ultimately the outcome of the best-meant policy. Attempts at 'stabilization' proceed under the circumstances in contrast to a general belief without any guarantee of stabilization.

The operation of the public sector   Policies emerge from a political process which contributes to a last dimension of the limitations encountered by economic policy. The inherent nature of the process conditions policy-making into patterns poorly correlated with well-meant and sensible proposals measured in terms of general welfare. Politics is not dominated by consideration of public interest or vague feelings of good-will. Self-interested political entrepreneurship affects the resulting pattern of legislation and executive actions. An examination of environmental or regional policy in Switzerland reveals, for instance, that proposals for efficient (i.e. welfare-raising) solutions to underlying problems do not survive successfully in the political process. The outcome is usually controlled by a redistributional conflict associated with any measure to cope with the problem.

The crucial aspect to be emphasized in this context addresses the pervasive uncertainty about the detailed pattern of legislation, executive actions and court decisions unleashed by some intentions or proposals. The previous section considered the uncertainty produced by the searching and coping responses of agents to policy measures. A similar phenomenon occurs within the political process. Legislation passed influences but does not determine the outcome. The implementation of the legislation by the state's apparatus with the aid of rules, ordinances or regulatory actions frequently enjoys a wide field for the crucial detail of policies. The US experience with a pattern of legislation appearing more and more in the form of general mandates offers some important examples. The independent power of implementing agencies tends to rise with the complexity of the material addressed by the legislators' intentions and the generality of the mandate legislated. Implementing agencies acquire thus some range of operative opportunities. They will exploit this range according to their own political interests and perceptions, searching and coping with their own opportunities. It follows under the circumstances that the translation of legislation into specific actions conditioning socio-economic evolution is a highly uncertain process. This uncertainty is heightened by the fact that implementing agencies often change their interpretations and rules guiding their actions. Various sections of the same agency often proceed moreover according to different interpretations of the same rules. The result is a pervasive uncertainty built into the policy-making process. The ramifications and consequences of policy at the original plane of intention, planning and proposals remain somewhat obscure. This is quite consistent with the fact that immediate beneficiaries suffer little doubt, and correctly so, about their *private* advantage in the matter. Not the least among the beneficiaries are the implementing agencies themselves.

Alternative policy conceptions, once more

The reality of the political process
My lecture opened with the juxtaposition of two basically different policy conceptions. An institutional policy was distinguished from an open-ended action-oriented policy. We may also characterize the alternatives as the choice of a set of general rules monitored and enforced by the government on the one side and an activist intervention over an open-ended range on the other side. The two traditions involve thus an essentially limited, or constitutionalist policy conception and an unlimited, open-ended policy. The issues associated with these two policies still need to be clarified. The discussion of the limits confronting economic policy provides the basis for my assessment. The reality of the social opportunity set imposes trade-offs and social costs associated with policy actions frequently disregarded in the political process. An analysis of this process explains some reasons for this neglect and the role of incomplete information in this context. I refer at this stage to my lecture on 'Reflections on the Political Economy of Government' [Chapter 12 in this volume] presented to this Society in 1978 at the annual meeting in Basel. My account exploited important contributions appearing in the evolution of public choice theory. I suggested in particular that the political arena may be understood in analogy to markets in the private sector as a 'political market'.

> Bureaux (more appropriately bureaucrats) and politicians (incumbent and aspiring legislators, persons holding or seeking appointments, functionaries of political organizations) correspond to producers on the market place sampling the consumer preferences and adjusting competitively their supplies. Both politicians and bureaux thus respond to the preferences of the citizen. But this response proceeds in the context of information patterns and organizational arrangements which open opportunities for the self-interested behaviour of politicians and bureaux. They operate under the circumstances not just as mere or passive vehicles executing the median voter groups' preferred transfer of funds. Their operation implies that a portion of the total funds collected are absorbed by the 'governmental apparatus'. This absorption corresponds to the normal profit in the competitive market place. The voter benefiting from redistribution cedes this portion of the tax revenues to the political and administrative entrepreneurs organizing the benefits. The nature of the political institutions determines extent and form of the competition between politicians and bureaux, or, seen from the 'other side', the extent and form of monopoly achievable by politicians or bureaux and their potential for

collusive behaviour. It seems useful for our purposes in order to focus attention on the major strands of the argument to introduce seven 'postulates':

1. Politicians are entrepreneurs competing in a market for votes and influence. They compete with proposals, programmes and the systematic exploitation of non-cognitive aspects of language. The politicians prefer more votes and influence to less votes and influence. They also share with other men a preference for higher permanent real income.
2. Bureaux sample the political market with proposals, reinterpretations of their mandate, and the detailed manner of administering the tasks developed. This entrepreneurial behaviour is designed to maintain or increase the budget.
3. Costs and benefits associated with *general* programmes are more evenly distributed than the costs and benefits of *specific* programmes.
4. Information costs about costs and benefits of *general* programmes are *large* relative to benefits.
5. Information costs about costs and benefits of *specific* programmes are relatively *small* to the 'positively affected group' and comparatively *large* to the 'negatively affected group'.
6. The marginal cost of political operation (for example, lobbying in various forms) is much smaller for *established* than for *potential* organizations.
7. Potential voters weigh expected costs and benefits associated with the bureaux potential offers and with the alternative packages represented by different politicians.

The crucial information patterns are formulated under assumptions 3 to 5. The distribution of information costs, recognized here, emphasizes a highly uneven incidence depending on the relation between voter groups and types of programmes. This distribution of information costs reflects important aspects of our reality. Rational adjustment by voters to such costs should not be interpreted to express some 'flaws in awareness' or 'ineradicable illusions'. There is no illusion in staying less than fully informed. It is an illusion on the other hand to expect voters to invest in information at a cost substantially beyond the expected return from such investment.

The major consequences of the patterns summarized by the 'postulates' may be developed as follows: 'Entrepreneurial competition thrives on a continued search for *new* proposals, *new* programs, *new* twists, modifications, or *extensions* of existing programs. It encourages a continuous search for suitable means to focus public attention. This is a necessary strategy for politicians to establish themselves in the competitive political market. Continuous market research and sampling of the public market with the aid of an expanding staff is therefore a competitive necessity for the politician.

'There are no rewards in attempts to abolish existing laws or programs. This strategy has no competitive market value. According to proposition 5 above, the beneficiaries of a program know the significance of its curtailment with respect to their wealth or political power. "Outside groups" bearing the cost of an existing program will barely appreciate their own welfare gain resulting from the cut in a program. Insiders' opposition to a proposed reduction tends to override consequently the feeble support of "outsiders" for the change. The basic postulates also imply that "outside groups" can reasonably expect larger returns for any given costs by investing efforts in lobbying for *new specific* programs adjusted to their special benefits. The returns from political investment in organizing opposition to the other groups' specific programs are comparatively small relative to the cost of investment. It follows that proposals to cut programs are neither frequently offered by politicians (with a few exceptions immediately ridiculed by the media) nor frequently advanced by "investors in the political market place". A political entrepreneur finds thus in general that offering "new programs" or "variations on existing themes" assures a higher survival value in the political market. A recent article in *The Banker* noted with interest that in the budget debates proceeding in the British Parliament over ten years not a single MP ever proposed a single time to cut expenditures.

'The politicians' appraisal is reinforced by the media. An examination of commentators in the press and on television demonstrates a preference for "fresh ideas", a *new* rhetoric or a *new* fad. The media rhetoric prefers a *new* word to almost any thoughtful proposal to abolish or reduce an obsolete or dangerous program. The media themselves find a higher market value with new words in the mass college education market. Attention to old programs, inherited legislation or institutions may infrequently have some market value. But such occurrences form usually the initial preparations for "more, better, new and larger programs". Political entrepreneurs find it more advantageous to propose new legislation favoring this or that other group as a way of "offsetting" the negative effect of previous legislation. But the global welfare effects are not offset. Total welfare is further reduced, government programs increase, the budget balloons and the range of influence open to a bureaucracy expands.

'The asymmetry in the distribution of costs and benefits and also the asymmetry in the distribution of information costs summarized above establishes that the emergence of new programs dominates the removal of old programs. They also determine that *specific* programs dominate *general* programs. The capital value expected by organizers proposing *general* and *undifferentiated* tax reductions or expenditure increases is quite small compared to the return achievable for the same efforts invested to effect *specific* and *highly differential* programs. Complex and differentiated programs concentrate benefits on a smaller (interested) group with comparatively low information costs and impose diffuse costs on the "outsiders" who suffer high costs of information and organization. It will in general not be worth much effort for members of an outside group to organize opposition to a specific and specialized program before or after its imposition. The capital value of investing political activity in specific new programs, differentiated for specific purposes with suitable complexity, tends to be much higher. This pattern of asymmetry in the distribution of costs and benefits explains the entrepreneurial choices of the prevalent types of programs and proposals offered by politicians. This analysis also reveals the unavoidable emergence and increasing range of complexity in tax laws or regulatory arrangements. "Tax loopholes" should be understood as a necessary result of the process. The indignant rhetoric attacking and condemning "loopholes" reflects on the other hand the entrepreneurial opportunities politicians acquire from their own previous endeavors. This analysis suggests furthermore the fundamental irrelevance of most chapters in the theory of economic macropolicy and implies that systematic and deliberate macro-policies are somewhat improbable' [Brunner, 1975].

The bias for the new programs and extensions of existing programs inherent in the political process and the associated redistributional mechanism contributes a major strand to the incremental growth of government. We also note that the concentration on specific and relatively complex programs emerges directly from the entrepreneurial behavior of bureaux. The relative success of the bureaux' sampling by the political market determines simultaneously magnitude of budget and government, and also the allocation of the apparatus.

The classic policy conception as a co-operative solution to a prisoner's dilemma problem

The reality of the political process explains the systematic neglect of objectively existing 'limitations of economic policy'. The bias is inherent in any loosely limited or essentially unlimited policy process. The incentives embedded in a more or less open-ended policy process unavoidably produce a pattern with a low feedback from social costs of policy programmes. The political process provides no incentives and no mechanisms for a realistic representation and assessment of the *social* trade-offs and *social* costs associated with economic policy-making. No incentives operate, moreover, to foster a recognition bearing on the consequences occurring over a *longer* horizon. The immanent characteristics of the political process produce an externality problem usually overlooked in 'market failure' and welfare discussions. The parties involved assess their strategies in terms of their *perceived private* gains and costs related to the redistributional consequences of the policy game. These perceived private gains and costs are quite generally poorly correlated with the relevant social benefits and social costs. The latter involve aspects beyond the direct redistributional consequences perceived as the relevant costs and gains by agents in the social process. Social costs are thus not sufficiently 'internalized' by political operators. We encounter here a sort of prisoners' dilemma problem. The activist and open-ended policy game contracts the social opportunity set and lowers general welfare. The members of society as a group are worse off as a result of their prevalent behaviour. The game promises, however, to individuals and subgroups separately substantial advantages. These advantages are acquired of course at the expense of other members of society. Our previous discussion indicates, moreover, that this game is not a zero-sum game with little effect on *general* welfare. The crucial problem goes beyond the redistribution of wealth produced by the game. The reality of social costs associated with the game reminds us that we encounter here a *negative*-sum game compressing the social opportunity set. The costs imposed by active rent-seeking behaviour form in this context a major portion of the relevant social burden of the game.

This analysis of the policy process provides the basis for the classic policy programme. It should be understood as an attempt to break out of the prisoners' dilemma. It offers essentially a *co-operative* solution to this dilemma. A constitutionalist approach expressed by a set of general rules severely constraining the government's admissible range of actions would moderate the game by a large margin. But such a set of rules is not unique and its choice would have to be carefully examined. The accumulated discussion in various fields of economics indicates quite clearly the nature and thrust of rules extending the social opportunity set. The choice of rules proceeds however not beyond the political process. It would appear that the conflict bearing on the choice of general rules is less intense and protracted than the conflict surrounding the redistributional schemes proceeding under any label (cartel legislation, agricultural policy, trade policy, housing policies, export risk guarantees, etc.) The detailed implications of general rules with respect to the specific position of individual members or sub-groups are somewhat obscure and uncertain. The consequences of specific actions and proposals with respect to the specific position of interested parties are much more visible and reliably assessable. The discussion of general rules is moreover more likely to direct attention to their effect on the social opportunity set than the conflict-loaded dispute generated by specific schemes of wealth redistribution.

Objections to the classic programme
The classic programme is often characterized by academic critique as a 'retreat from potential opportunities to raise welfare'. Tinbergen's *Theory of Economic Policy* developed formal arguments representing this vision. The traditional argument on behalf of an activist stabilization policy may illustrate the prevalent attitude. This argument emphasizes that a pattern of discretionary interventions offers opportunities to offset a range of exogenous shocks and produce consequently a much better performance of the economy. Such a policy pattern, not confined by general rules, can sensitively adjust to all contingencies. Such adjustments are bound to raise the economy's overall performance level. But this means that the social opportunity set is actually expanded under the circumstances.

The fallacy of this argument has been demonstrated at another occasion (Brunner, 1981). It is based on two conditions which deny the two dimensions of the information problem confronting any adequate analysis of the policy problem. This problem seems rarely recognized by advocates and is implicitly discarded with the assumptions built into their analytic demonstration of the activist case. The first condition invokes full and reliable information by the policy-maker about the economy's dynamic response structure. The possession of such knowledge would certainly guarantee the possibility for an effective application of activist policy sensitively adjusted to evolving contingencies. But a survey of our state of knowledge denies the existence of this condition. The detail required for the rational guidance of an activist policy is not available. It is moreover inherently impossible ever to acquire this information level. We noted before that market processes also function as mechanisms perennially producing new information to agents. This implies a persistent evolution in a random pattern of an economy's detailed response structure. It follows that this detailed response structure is not constant over time to be approximated even more closely by clever econometric estimation. The information problem destroys the case for an activist and contingent policy pattern. The execution of such policies in spite of inadequate and unreliable information contributes with substantial probability to the opposite of the desired stabilization.

The other condition of the activist case pertains to the political economy of policy-making. The activist argument implicitly assumes a public-interest or goodwill theory of government. Government is supposed to pursue policies only guided by a general interest summarized by some social welfare function. But this (romantic) vision hardly describes the reality of policymaking. This reality was described above and is closely associated with the operation of the political sector under a severe information problem. Politicians, policy-makers and bureaucracies interact with constituencies in a context of incomplete and non-uniform information. They are moreover motivated in the light of an essentially self-interested appraisal of their opportunities. The characterization of policy-makers as optimizers of a social welfare function expressing a social consensus is thus remarkably irrelevant. The policy process actually produces, under the circumstances described above, a pattern of uncertain drift reinforcing the pervasive information problem. The reader is reminded in particular that under the incentives controlling the political process 'stabilization policies' usually appear as a camouflage for redistributional activities with minor, if any, real concern for aggregate stabilization. Examples supporting this point may be observed in any country.

The irrelevance of academic objections and the actual driving forces of the political process

Neomercantilist interests   The academic argument supporting an open-ended and activist policy, however seductive it may appear, does not explain the prevalent reality of these policy patterns. The political process may at most exploit these arguments as a rationale to support and cover the really motivating forces at work. The crucial driving forces are found beyond these arguments in neo-mercantilist interests and ideological beliefs. Neo-mercantilist interests systematically exploit opportunities to create and expand some privileged or protected position under any label. Imaginative inventiveness is the only limit to the forms of policies which evolve over time. They may each from import quotes, the subtleties of the 'new protectionism', to housing subsidies, tenant protection, cartel laws, privileged access to banks, etc.

Once the barrier of the classic conception, for reasons not further examined here, has effectively broken down, neo-mercantilist interests experience an open field for their activities. They permeate under the circumstances the reality of the political process summarized above. The essentially unlimited range for potential economic policy offers entrepreneurship on the political market, pursued by politicians, bureaucracies and neo-mercantilist interest groups, a wide and open-ended field. This pattern raises the expected private return from investments in political organization or economic policy organization. There emerge under the circumstances expanding opportunities to use the state and its policy institutions for purposes of wealth redistribution, executed via one or the other of the thousand forms given to 'economic policy'. The range and level of political conflict unavoidably rises over time under the circumstances and 'trade policies' are more bitterly contested between nations. The rising burden of social costs imposed by this evolution lowers the growth of real income and the expansion of opportunities. The search for private wealth derives in this case increasing returns from opportunities associated with investments in the political process at the expense of investments raising the social opportunity set via accumulation of human and non-human resources.

Ideological beliefs   But the complex of neo-mercantilist interests engaged in the exploitation of the political process cannot provide a full explanation of the driving forces at work in contemporary western democracies. We need to recognize more fully the role of ideology and ideological beliefs in this context. My earlier account is thus quite incomplete. We encounter first an extensive use of ideology in the neo-mercantilist struggle for wealth advantages. The ideological component operates here as a camouflage of the underlying relevant interests. The 'Helvetian ideology' surrounding the ongoing efforts for a cartel legislation in Switzerland offers in this respect a particularly interesting example. But ideological beliefs enter the policy process also in a radically different manner. They may still be associated with schemes involving some wealth redistribution. But their crucial aspect for our purposes reaches beyond the political acquisition of wealth fully characterizing the neo-mercantilist interests. Their motivation contains a component which is separate and independent from wealth. This motivation involves basic and radical restructuring of society. The ideological beliefs express a commitment to 'a new socio-economic order' requiring foremost a complete political control over the socio-economic process. The realization of the 'new order' does not rely on revolutionary strategies. It is approached via an 'incrementalist tactic'. Active participation in the policy process is the essential instrument in this game. An unlimited economic policy-making offers thus the necessary field of operation for ideological beliefs. Any potential issue and any measure can be exploited for the purpose of an expanded political control. This 'incrementalist tactic' yields moreover some important benefits. The measures adopted by the political process or executed by policy agencies under the combined influence of neo-mercantilist interests and ideological beliefs frequently create a new pattern of social conditions which can be problematized. The evolution of labour market institutions in Europe exemplifies the point. The various measures of 'job security' raised the real cost of employment. Unyielding real wages impose adjustments on employment and unemployment. Thus emerges a new opportunity for further tactical exploitation. Work-sharing forms the next claim to 'solve the problem'. But once again it will impose a new problem. It will lower the social opportunity set and thus strengthen the incentives for politically engineered wealth redistribution. The more problems the policy process generates along a road influenced by the interaction of neo-mercantilist interests and ideological beliefs the more attractive become the opportunities for 'the incrementalist tactics'.

The experiences with environmental and health policies in the USA offer a wide range of illustrative material for this theme. Environmental and health problems assuredly deserve our careful attention. But they can be approached in very different ways. This field of concern suffers most particularly from the illusion that no deviation from some imagined ideal can be tolerated. Any consideration of social costs imposed by the realization of the absolutist goal is scorned. This implicit refusal to recognize social costs reflects ignorance of either an elitist or an authoritarian attitude. The social costs associated with a given course shaping the use of resources mirror the values attached by members of society to goods and services sacrificed by using resources in this particular manner. A deliberate unwillingness to consider such costs reveals thus a refusal to recognize other people's values. This pattern is unavoidably associated with the role of ideological beliefs in the policy process. The deliberate disregard of social costs in the ideological approach to economic policy is typically supplemented by another pattern. The proposals emanating and issues raised are hardly addressed to the *substance* of a genuine problem requiring serious attention. The proposals and issues formulated are dominated by the ideological motivation directed to an encompassing socio-political vision.

The behaviour of the Ralph Nader group in matters of environmental policy is quite instructive in this context. It seems clearly motivated by a deep hostility towards a society relying on a social co-ordination based on markets and private property. Health policy in the USA, shaped by influential science groups, shows a similar development. A remarkable intellectual establishment effectively suggested that technology and modern industry is responsible for an incipient cancer epidemic. This suggestion crucially shaped important legislation in the USA. A careful examination of the state of scientific knowledge reveals, however, a remarkable absence of supporting evidence for the asserted link between technology and 'cancer epidemic' (Efron, 1984). A further examination shows moreover that these intellectual and scientist groups distorted the scientific evidence in order to serve an essentially ideological socio-political purpose. An absolutist legislation setting almost impossible standards frequently emerges from such operations in the policy process. Such legislation provides a basis for potentially arbitrary and unlimited actions by regulatory bodies 'in the public interest' naturally interpreted by interested groups.

The operation of the so-called 'Hunger Lobby' in the USA offers another interesting example. A remarkable coalition of political agencies, private political organizations and activist groups of scientists justifies a large allocation of government funds to alleviate an allegedly massive hunger syndrome in the USA. The (massive) interests of the various groups in the potential redistribution of income is easily discernible. A deeper examination reveals also the ideological motivation of some important participating groups. Most revealing in this context is the absence of substantial evidence and relevant analysis supporting the strong assertions peddled in the public arena. Independent scholars demonstrated that the reports offered by the 'Hunger Lobby' are unreliable and offer little relevant information bearing on the issue. Ideological camouflage and commitment merge in this case to protect both interests and socio-political goals.

Concluding remarks

Economic policy does not occur in a socio-political vacuum. It forms an essential component of an ongoing fundamental conflict about the future social order of western democracies. Questions bearing on the possible 'limits of economic policy' thus ultimately involve decisions about alternative policy conceptions with substantially different institutional approaches. These differences imply over the longer run divergent social, economic and political evolutions. But the implicit denial of any 'limits of economic policy' expressed by one of the alternative policy conceptions does not suspend their reality. Their neglected operations will increasingly burden societies and moderate our opportunities.

References
Brunner, Karl (1975) 'Comments', *Journal of Law and Economics*, December 1975.
Brunner, Karl (1981) *The Control of Monetary Aggregates: Patrolling Monetary Aggregates III*, Boston, Mass.: Federal Reserve Bank of Boston.
Chow, Gregory C. (1975) *Analysis and Control of Dynamic Economic Systems*, New York: John Wiley.
Efron, Edith (1984) *The Apocalyptics: Cancer and the Big Lie*, New York: Simon & Schuster.
Tinbergen, Jan (1952) *On the Theory of Economic Policy*, Amsterdam: North-Holland.

14 Mephistopheles and inflation*

> Wir wollen alle Tage sparen
> und brauchen alle Tage mehr.
>
> So stempelten wir gleich die ganze Reihe,
> Zehn, Dreissig, Fünfzig, Hundert sind parat.
> Ihr denkt Euch nicht, wie wohl's dem Volke tat.
> Ein solch Papier, an Gold und Perlen Statt,
> ist so bequem, man weiss doch, was man hat.
>
> (Wolfgang Goethe, *Faust*, ii)**

Human history has entered a new phase over the past 15 years. We have moved into an era of permanent and worldwide inflation. This *worldwide* nature of *persistent* inflation confronts us with a remarkable and historically unique event. Inflation itself is, of course, not a new experience. The Roman Empire occasionally suffered from it and so did various regions of medieval Europe. Many countries have experienced inflationary episodes over the past 500 years. The most dramatic cases, of course, are the hyperinflations observed by a small group of nations in Europe after the last two world wars. The United States of America shared this common experience. It has appeared four times over its short history. This pattern contrasts, however, with our most recent historical environment. Permanent inflation has remained confined to limited regions of the world. Other occurrences were usually associated with wars and their aftermath. They emerged as temporary financial emergencies lasting at most for a few years. Hyperinflations in particular could not persist. The nature of their internal process leads to their own destruction.

A rough survey demonstrates the radical change in our fate. Switzerland was the only country which managed for a *few* years during the last decade to avoid the general fate. There remain, of course, massive differences between the many nations. Some countries, exemplified by West Germany and Switzerland, manage to hold inflation on average substantially below 10 per cent per annum. Other countries, like the United Kingdom and Italy, produce

---

* This chapter is a draft of a lecture presented in Caracas, Venezuela, on 8 February 1982.
** A new translation by Philip Wayne (Penguin Books, 1959) reads: We daily try to save and store, / When everyday our needs are more. / We stamped the total series then and there. / Tens, Thirties, Fifties, Hundreds, all to date / You cannot think how people jubilate. / Such paper – wealth replacing pearls or gold, / Is practical: you know just what you hold.

inflation rates averaging 20 per cent per annum, while other nations, such as Brazil and Israel, reach above 100 per cent per annum, and Chile under the Allende regime about 1,000 per cent per annum.

The differences between nations at any given time are matched by remarkable differences over time within the various countries. Swiss inflation moved during the past decade between 0 and 12 per cent per annum. The Brazilian experience shifted between more than 100 per cent and 15 per cent per annum, and of course Chile produced extremes of 1,000 per cent and 10–15 per cent per annum. Lastly, the worldwide experience does not respect the tight controls of totalitarian regimes.

The radical change in the pattern of inflation observed in our most recent history poses a serious political threat to our society. It also confronts us with an intellectual problem. We need to understand the forces at work before we can rationally expect to influence their operation. And perhaps, once we understand the process underlying the new phenomenon, we may wonder whether a change in policy required to control the drift is acceptable in our environment. Still, blindness, incomprehension and misunderstanding offer no intellectually satisfactory position. They produce, moreover, on the political arena – as we shall see – continued opportunities for the operation of underlying inflationary conditions.

What are the conditions responsible for our age of permanent inflation? Can we hope for an adequate explanation? Indeed we can. The scholarly work of many economists contributed over many years to the gradual evolution of a coherent story. Some strands of this story remain quite tentative at this time, whereas others are well established and strongly confirmed by the work of many independent scholars. But let us approach our answer somewhat indirectly with a detour through classically romantic German literature.

Wolfgang Goethe, the Grand Seigneur of German literature, died 150 years ago, after spending a good part of his old age finishing the second part of *Faust*. This drama is in many ways a strange story and has encouraged many different interpretations. It offered marvellous opportunities for an *homme de lettres* to explore the complex fabric of Goethe's metaphysical and mythological imaginations. I have no wish to discuss this activity nor have I any desire to add to it. Within the intricate patterns of the drama occurs, however, the outline of a basic theme with remarkable relevance to our time. This theme contains a clue to several important strands of our answer. You are invited to follow my modest detour and join me for an unsentimental look at this man Faust, his failures, his aspirations and his environment.

The drama opens on a total human failure. Faust ponders his condition after years of learning and teaching. His heart is joyless, his soul empty and his mind blank. Life confronts him as a barren wasteland. He invokes the tellurian forces of darkness for help in his escape from an existential hell.

Thus enters Mephistopheles, offering Faust a deal: the use of magic in exchange for his soul. With the exercise of Mephisto's magic he now follows his aspirations, filling the void of an empty life. These aspirations consist of sexual pleasures and power, the latter increasingly important as the story evolves. We need not linger on the Gretchen episode for our purposes, the witches' Walpurgis night, or the assorted mythological adnumerations apparently required for a German intelligentsia market. Two episodes offer, however, suggestive material for our central purpose. This is Faust at 'the Emperor's' court and Faust the 'visionary builder' in the second part of the drama.

Faust and his companion Mephisto appear at the Emperor's court in the middle of a 'budget debate'. Army commander, chancellor, court marshall and treasurer, all complain to the Emperor about insufficient funding of their manifold activities. Mephisto offers a simple solution and suggests that the Emperor create his own paper money, backed up of course by all the unknown and buried treasure of the earth within the empire (or somewhere). So army commander, court marshall, chancellor and treasurer happily spend the night creating money of increasing denominations. They assuage the Emperor's doubts and seem to convince themselves that the diligent financing of their multiple pursuits with newly created money is truly in the interest of the people's welfare. *'Des Volkes Heil'* and *'Des Volkes Wohl'* are incantations that flow easily from the officials' lips. Mephisto's deceitful argument to overcome the initial doubts of the officials is also noteworthy for our subsequent exploration of the political economy of inflation.

The episode of Faust as a 'visionary builder' towards the end of the drama is in crucial ways more sinister. It also alludes to subtle but pervasive strands shaping political processes in our century. Faust was given some piece of land beside the sea for services rendered to the Emperor. This land becomes his base for an ambitious project to build a huge dam. Faust envisions a vast new land wrested from the sea to offer life and freedom to a vast populace. His dream of a paradisal state is pursued, however, with the ruthlessness of a murderous tyrant. There is no compassion and no concern for those who stand in the way. The 'impossible dream' mobilizes the darkest forces and imposes untold human sacrifices. What Faust considers – under Mephisto's guidance as a masterpiece of human achievement – finally becomes a terrible exercise in inhumanity.

What possible illumination can we derive from Faust's story? It contains several strands which offer clues to the new and worldwide inflation problem. The scene at the imperial court addresses immediately the proximate cause of inflation. Other strands of this scene combined with the pervasive theme of a wasted intellect grasping at power for meaning in life suggestively point to crucial socio-political conditions shaping our drift into permanent inflation.

The immediate and much easier part is the proximate cause of inflation. There is little mystery about this and the explanation need not be complicated. Many influences can indeed shape the movement of the general level. It typically moves quite erratically from one month to the other, or from one quarter to the other. There is no useful purpose, however, in attempting to understand these passing erratic motions. They do not confront us with any serious problem. Any attempt, on the other hand, to tamper with them would create problems for the economy. Large and persistent changes in the price level over many quarters or years are an entirely different matter. They are produced by a systematic driving force. We understand this force and can potentially cope with it. This driving force is a nation's money stock.

In *every* country at *any* time there is some quantity of money in existence. This quantity consists of all assets held by the public used with dominant frequency and regularity for making payments. A persistent rise in their quantity induces a corresponding rise in the price level. Larger masses of money mean that more money will be supplied in exchange for goods and services. As the latter magnitude expands less, less goods are available per unit of money. The markets express this fact by a rise of prices expressed in money. This rise reveals to us that too much money has been created in relation to the goods and services produced in the economy.

We may look all over the world and find the same basic pattern. There exists for every nation a critical benchmark level of monetary growth (i.e. growth in the nation's money stock) determined by its maintained growth of production and some other factors. Wherever we observe the inflationary patterns summarized at the beginning of my lecture, we will also observe an excessive growth of the nation's money stock. And whenever you observe an excessive expansion of the money stock, maintained over a substantial period, then you will also find the persistent inflation characterizing our worldwide scene.

Much more can be observed however. You will note that the broad difference between the nations' inflation rates at any time correspond approximately to the differences in the rate of monetary expansion. Similarly, the large differences in the observed inflation rate *within* a nation *over time* follow the pattern of evolving monetary growth. You will never observe an acceleration of monetary expansion from 0 to 10 per cent per annum or from 10 to 30 per cent per annum or from 30 to 100 per cent per annum without a corresponding rise in the rate of inflation. Our past and recent history demonstrates that it is by far easier and less costly in resources to create money than to create goods. The large variability of the money stock or its growth rate and the ease with which it is pushed beyond the critical benchmark demonstrates this difference.

But where is all that money coming from? Once upon a time most money consisted of metallic coins of one kind or another, minted and issued by kings, princes and cities. The metallic content of money seemed to prohibit arbitrary variations in the total amount. The manipulators of political power understood quite well, however, that issues of money could be used to extract resources from the general public for their political purposes. The new money created could be applied to finance the court, an army or other enterprises a prince wished to consider. This way of financing avoided moreover the political trouble associated with the usual and explicit taxes. King Jean Valois II of France understood quite well the advantage of money creation over standard methods of taxation. So he tinkered with his currency over 70 times during his reign. He created the money for his purposes by lowering the metallic content in the coins. More and more coins could thus be produced out of the available metal.

Mephisto's proposal was certainly more efficient than the French king's technique. It enlarged the princes' power to exploit the monetary institution for their political purposes. Once the financial markets spontaneously developed paper money as a convenient representative and claim against more cumbersome metal, the political powers recognized an improved opportunity to use money creation as a means to finance their expenditures. Banks emerged with special charters that granted the monopoly of issuing bank notes. The privilege of this monopoly charter was usually granted for favours received, and the favour received money created by the bank under the monopoly for the government. These chartered banks with a monopoly of note issues evolved over the past 2,000 years into modern Central Banks.

Our modern Central Banks form the basis of our monetary system. They possess under prevailing regulation a monopoly for issuing 'base money', i.e. currency and reserves held by the banks against their liabilities. Many of these liabilities, consisting of so-called transaction accounts, are also money. Transfers between these transaction accounts are, in modern economics, the major form of executing payments. Modern bank money, consisting of these transaction accounts (e.g. checking deposits) together with the currency issued by the Central Banks, constitutes today a nation's money stock. This magnitude, in spite of its dominant composition by bank money, is closely controlled over time by the 'monetary base', i.e. the total amount of money *directly* issued by the Central Bank. We find that over all periods and all nations large and persistent changes in the nation's money stock are produced by corresponding changes in the monetary base. And this is the crucial point: this monetary base is *immediately* and *fully* determined by the Central Banks' behaviour.

I have belaboured all these somewhat technical points in order to emphasize the technological progress made since Mephisto and the court officials spent the night stamping out paper money. I most particularly want to convey to you that the monetary expansion, necessary and sufficient, to unleash and maintain inflation in modern societies can be traced to the behaviour of our Central Banks. Their behaviour determines, not within days, weeks or a few months, but certainly over quarters and years, the magnitude of our monetary expansion. If you find Central Banks raising their volume of base money by 10 to 20 per cent per annum or more, you will not find the nation's money stock limping along at a growth of a few percentage points. It follows that excessive monetary expansion, the *proximate* cause of inflation, cannot emerge without the Central Banks' specific behaviour. Their behaviour corresponds to the actions of Faust's imperial court so enthusiastically printing out the money the court officials required to attend to 'the people's welfare'. So this is where, ultimately, all the money comes from.

But why do Central Banks behave that way? Well, at this point we approach the harder part of our problem, but the officials at the imperial court and Faust's search for meaning in the context of political power may yet yield a clue. Our answer is buried in the nature of the political process and the peculiar ambivalence of political structures and institutions. The basic theme was already revealed by the imperial court's chancellor when he lamented that though officials try to save every day, they need ever larger revenues to finance their projects. We also observe this basic theme in the exploitation of the monetary institution by potentates, kings and princes. Their perennial search for revenues led them again and again to use their power over money to create money as a means to finance their budgets. But the time of kings and princes is passed and we live under very different political processes. But indeed, it appears in *some* respects not *that* different.

Political structure protects the members of a given society against the 'zero-sum game' of anarchy. Hobbes's description of this state of nature is well known. Men find it to their own advantage under the circumstances to overcome this state. Anarchy hardly ever persists in man's affairs. Their spontaneous interaction, guided by their diverse and personal interests, will evolve some political structure. Such order creates incentives to produce, invest and trade, i.e. activities obstructed by the endemic threat of loss by robbery and piracy through violence under anarchy. The tremendous social productivity of political structure should be quite obvious.

There is another dimension to the story, however. Man's disposition to improve himself and acquire wealth proceeds under any environment. Political structure channels and regulates this disposition in specific ways. But the institutions constituting the political order are not neutral. While they impose the rules of the socio-political game they also offer new opportunities to the participants in the game. All political institutions offer especially opportunities of wealth redistribution.

Participants of the socio-political game can acquire income or wealth by investing resources in socially productive activities, in production and trade.

Their private endeavours at wealth acquisition contribute in this context to raising social wealth, the general level of welfare. But they can also direct their efforts to using political institutions and the political process in order to extract income and wealth from others in the society. This private effort yields, however, no social benefits. It actually diverts valuable resources from socially productive use. But depending on the nature of the political structure, the private gain obtainable from 'political investments' can be very large indeed, even if its social productivity is negative. The ambivalence of political structure is thus determined by its social productivity relative to anarchy, combined with the inherent opportunities offered for wealth redistribution under the more or less implicit rules of the game constituted by the political order. We recognize thus in redistribution the central nature and driving force of the political process. But we need also to recognize that the stability of a political order depends on its incentives and opportunities fostering redistributive efforts and investments. Some basic measure of redistribution is most probably a necessary condition for a stable order. James Buchanan has elaborated this aspect and Robert Nozick recognized this element in the constitution of a minimal state. But an expanding wave of increasingly persistent redistributive activities gradually induces a crisis of the political order. This crisis will be reflected by a more or less tacit but increasing disavowal of the rules of the game. There evolves a spontaneous search for new rules expressed in many countries by the evolution of an 'underground economy'.

Our political theme requires at this stage some further elaboration in order to find a major link between the political process and the monetary expansion directly responsible for permanent inflation. A democracy is characterized by an explicitly regulated competitive game for power. The required regulation is determined by a constitution, the corresponding legislation or simply a well-understood tradition. We also encounter a political apparatus expressed by the bureaux of the government. Politicians and bureaux may be usefully viewed as entrepreneurs operating in a political market. These entrepreneurs pursue their interests addressed to achievable positions and the associated influence over the use of resources. They compete for influence and positions with programmes and ideas offered on the political market. All these programmes or ideas bear, in one way or another, on the government's budget or involve regulatory activities modifying the distribution of wealth between various social groups. Both politicians and bureaux compete thus for support by voter groups with programmes and promises involving benefits for these groups. Some specific properties of the political market determine ultimately the peculiar bias built into the structure of the political process, a bias already noted by Faust's imperial court. This bias follows from the pervasive information problem confronting the members of the political order.

Information about a programme benefiting a particular group is more easily accessible and at much lower cost to the beneficiaries under the programme than to most of the rest. This asymmetry in information costs is reinforced by an asymmetry in benefits and costs associated with the programme. The benefits usually accruing to a well-defined group are comparatively large per person, whereas the costs to be borne by all taxpayers are small per person. This pervasive fact implies that the benefits from investments made in the political market in order to obtain a specific programme are large, whereas benefits on investments made by taxpayers to oppose a programme are quite small and most of the time remain well below the respective cost of investments.

This asymmetry of information and in the distribution of benefits and costs under specific programmes crucially affects the nature of the political process. It implies in particular that the political process typically produces programmes addressed to *specific and well-defined* groups. We rarely find programmes involving a redistributive scheme uniformly across income groups. We also typically find that old programmes hardly ever disappear. The competitive survival of politicians and bureaux thrives on '*new* programmes' or specific *extensions* of old ones. Proposals to abolish or contain old programmes promise no winning strategy for a politician and offer no attraction to a bureau. Promising to offset the burden of old programmes imposed on particular groups by *new* programmes with benefits specially tailored for these groups is a much more effective strategy.

This sketch of crucial aspects of the political process in modern democracies extends with some modifications to various oligarchic structures, including military regimes. These political arrangements are not immune to the basic forces described. They are, moreover, not a monolithic organization. They are usually subject to pervasive internal conflicts for power and influence. The process driven by these conflicts also involves a competitive use of programmes containing a variety of redistributive strands. No oligarchy, military or otherwise, can persist without auxiliary groups beyond the immediate power centres. The more or less active support of these groups is 'bought' by appropriate programmes. The history of military regimes and oligarchies exemplifies this process.

One more step leads us to our goal. The competitive drive on the political market with the built-in bias for ever-new programmes and extended programmes unavoidably expands the budget. This process, revealed by the remarkable increase of the budget relative to national income, has dominated all western democracies. But the same properties of the political process favouring the expansion of expenditure programmes has retarded a corresponding increase in tax revenues. Increasing tax rates induce, moreover, a widening search for effective avoidance of tax payments. The evolution surveyed produces under the circumstances a persistent deficit in the government's budget. The basic nature of the process will also create a pervasive impression of 'uncontrollable forces' producing an 'uncontrollable budget with an intractable deficit'.

Deficits need to be financed. If the political process refuses to adjust taxes, i.e. politicians quaver and citizens' groups benefiting from expenditure programmes march on the legislature, the government may borrow or accept Mephisto's advice. As it happens, financing a deficit, at least to some extent, with new money created by the Central Bank offers great advantages to governments and politicians. They obtain revenues to finance their expenditure programmes without the political difficulties associated with the legislation of explicit taxes. It also avoids the political problem that emerges in response to massive and persistent borrowing on domestic or foreign capital markets. Lastly, countries with capital markets underdeveloped or emasculated as a result of past policies find recourse to the Central Bank easier and politically most feasible. The evolution of events in Italy and the United Kingdom over the past 15 years illustrates our general description with remarkable clarity. So does the history of many Latin American countries. And, as we know, the United States has hardly been immune to Mephisto's problem. One minor qualification: the monetary expansion induced by the political process may on occasion be associated with policies independent of the budget. They may result from implicitly redistributive arrangements involving more or less direct credits from Central Banks to portions of the private sector. The pursuit of some exchange rate policies offers one example.

Some remarkable passages in Faust's drama alert us to an important aspect of the political process. We noted above how the veil that screens the crucial facts from the full perception by the citizens contributes to the evolution of an 'overgoverned society with a built-in inflationary bias'. This incomplete information shaping the nature of the political process is pervasively reinforced by the pattern of systematic *disinformation* created by the competition between politicians and bureaux for position and influence. Mephisto lies and misleads the Emperor. He sneers at the initial hesitation of the court officials to misdirect their attention, in a passage which, incidentally, was frequently quoted by the intelligentsia with great approval. Note also Mephisto's impressive flow of words to produce some Orwellian inversions of impressions and meanings. Lastly, once the court officials have understood the advantages to them accruing under Mephisto's proposal they smoothly convince the Emperor that everything proceeds for the people's welfare and benefit.

The disinformative use of language forms an essential by-product of the political process. Frank Knight, one of the great economists of this century, once remarked at a Presidential address to the American Economic Association, that 'truth has no political function'. His statement refers to the phenomenon observed at the Emperor's court. Political programmes and ideas seem more easily sellable on the political market if their benefits are exaggerated, particularly to those who barely benefit, and their costs underestimated. According to some account, most Congressmen in the USA hardly appreciate the consequences of most of the legislation they vote on. Nor do they know even in roughest outline the cost their actions impose on citizens. But then, there is really very little incentive to obtain this information. Such effort requires some costly investment (at least some valuable time) and adds little to their survival in the political market.

Most important for our problem is the disinformation spread over the political market in matters bearing on inflation. A coalition of politicians, bureaux and Central Banks can be expected to supply the citizens with pronouncements attributing inflation to a shifting variety of conditions. This disinformation makes it more difficult for citizens to perceive the nature of the issues and in particular to perceive the nature of the inflation problem. The resulting misconception or confusion protects politicians and Central Banks from any effective public accountability for their responsibility. Politicians and members of bureaux who know better and fully understand the issues will find it difficult and occasionally quite painful to articulate their views. Truth, as Knight reminded us, has an uncertain political appeal and an ambiguous function in the political market. Words become under the circumstances increasingly an instrument of manipulated impressions.

The role of the media and the intelligentsia needs also to be considered in this context. The media share with the political market a muted attention to relevant information. Their purpose is dominated by entertainment in one form or another or by a more or less explicit devotion to a political creed. A perceptive articulation of budgetary, regulatory or monetary problems finds few buyers in the media market. There are, as in the political market, always some exceptions. But they do not represent the broad pattern dominating the media or the political market. The interaction between the two markets reinforces the disinformation process which lowers the pressure for a relevant accountability of policy-makers and legislatures. And lower accountability entrenches the inflationary bias even more into the political process. It also entrenches even more the spreading tentacles of a growing Leviathan.

The intelligentsia, as Schumpeter noted in his classic study *Capitalism, Socialism and Democracy*, moves with an ambivalent role in this process. It provides the themes on the media market and supplies the emotion-controlling buzz-words and word pictures. The intelligentsia appears with the claim to grope for a critical examination and search for an assessable truth. This claim represents indeed an ever-present potential. But an important strand in Faust's story conveys to us basically the ancient theme of a *trahison des clercs*, the betrayal by the intelligentsia of their claims for access to power and influence on the political market. The intelligentsia has wilfully offered over the centuries its services for the disinformation so usefully marketed by the political apparatus. The most sinister part of the story refers, however, to the intelligentsia's not-infrequent ability, less frequent among professional politicians, to justify its committed disinformation in terms of a parochial state, beyond the socio-political ruins of the present society, with their advice and operation in the media and political market.

The lines of my argument were unavoidably tightly drawn without the necessary qualification and the important nuances still to be observed in our societies. I deliberately drew the lines with some harsh definition beyond my sense of assurance in this matter. It is my hope that my presentation may stir some thoughts about our road. My theme was essentially simple. Permanent inflation appears as the syndrome of a pervasive political crisis of our societies. It reveals a socio-political process moving us ever closer to Leviathan, i.e. the monster behind Faust's vision and Mephisto's artful help.

Are we condemned to march along this road? The prevailing shades and nuances do fortunately offer us opportunities and hope. We may also be told that Mephisto ultimately failed. Faust was redeemed: a redemption I never could understand, however. But this may be the crux of any redemption. Still, redemption applies to an individual person and his soul. We cannot rely on the hope that the socio-political process will somehow encounter a redeeming redeemer. Such redeemers without fail are servants of Leviathan. Whatever needs to be done, *we* will have to accomplish it. We also accomplished, with our past policies and actions, our present state and current trend. The institutional changes required to break the ongoing process and reverse the grasp of the political apparatus on our lives have been discussed by many scholars deeply concerned with the survival of a free and open society. The crucial conditions in all these endeavours involve some structuring of the political order which effectively limits the range of political action again. Man's resourcefulness may yet find a path, perhaps in a later future only. But man, after all, with all his dubious dimensions, is more remarkable and potentially more meaningful than the miserable and empty creature Faust really was.

15 Economic development, Cancun and the western democracies*

Conferences rarely settle the fate of nations.[1] Social and political developments are shaped by more pervasive currents. But conferences are frequently indications of underlying social trends. They provide significant links in the political process. They offer tactical opportunities to influence future approaches to issues. Processes of negotiation and 'political exchanges of views' are neither neutral nor irrelevant events. They often help to focus a political trend more clearly and to condition a legacy of political and social problems that, sooner or later, have to be faced in the future.

The North–South conference of heads of government that took place in Cancun, in Mexico, last October has to be appraised in such a context. It confronted the United States and other western democracies generally with a set of social and political issues inherited from past decades. This inheritance is the product of a trend substantially influenced by the policies that have been pursued by the United States, and by other western countries, over recent years. This legacy, partly shaped by the conceptions and actions of policy makers in key capitals, calls for careful examination. The issues may appear, at first glance, to involve little of substance beyond a few financial and diplomatic technicalities. But such a view would seriously misconceive the fundamental importance of the issues that were posed at the Cancun summit. Such a view would fail to recognize the nature of the problem confronting the western democracies. The President of the United States, along with his counterparts from other western countries, was faced at Cancun with questions bearing on the nature of the international economic order, those questions having serious implications for the future of what are termed open societies.

It might be said, and indeed it has been said, that little was achieved at the Cancun summit. The fact is, though, that since it took place a renewed effort has been made, and is continuing to be made, to initiate 'global negotiations' on economic development. What would be the substance of those negotiations is not clear. But the governments of western countries are divided over what approach to them should be adopted, and in the United States, if not in other countries, there are apparently serious differences between the department responsible for the conduct of foreign policy in general and the depart-

* Originally published in *World Economy*, 5(1), 1982, 61–84.

ments, and other agencies, concerned more directly with economic policy. But the questions at Cancun remain.

These questions are closely associated with a basic issue to do with the social organization of the United States or, more generally, that of the western democracies. The nature of the issue may be more clearly perceived against the background of the Reagan administration's determined effort to reverse the course of socio-political developments in the United States. President Reagan faced in Cancun the legacy of a socio-political trend radically opposed to his conception of the social and political organization of an open or free society. This trend is represented in effect by the proposals for a 'new international economic order' (NIEO), some elements of which go back to the early sessions of the United Nations Conference on Trade and Development (UNCTAD), the first having taken place in Geneva in 1964. Indeed, the political forces advocating a 'new order' have increasingly exploited, over the past two decades, the institutional opportunities offered by the United Nations. The strategic conception of a *Marsch durch die Institutien*, articulated by Marxist groups in West Germany during the 1960s, has been successfully pursued by NIEO proponents in United Nations fora.

A series of conferences within the United Nations system, including the Conference on the Law of the Sea, as well as meetings of the General Assembly, have provided the political focus for the promotion of the NIEO proposals. The report of the Brandt Commission,[2] informally initiated by the World Bank, gave a fresh impetus to the NIEO proposals in the world's political market. Thus an understanding of the problem facing policy-makers in the western democracies requires an examination of the nature of the ideas advanced by NIEO proponents and by groups supporting the Brandt Report's recommendations. A clarification of the issues inherent in this set of ideas should ultimately influence the direction and content of American policy – and, too, it might be hoped, the policies of other countries.

The next section of the article outlines the general thrust of the NIEO proposals and those of the Brandt Report. The following section explores the conception inherent in these initiatives and critically evaluates the ideas advanced. Then, having examined the issues posed by the NIEO proposals in the context of the Conference on the Law of the Sea, the article puts forward an alternative course that is consistent with the Reagan administration's fundamental socio-political position, which is concerned with the survival of free societies, and is also consistent – in my view – with improving the welfare of the peoples of developing countries. The issues raised in this article are weighty matters and it is difficult to avoid being, and it may even help to be, somewhat provocative in presenting a different perspective in necessarily succinct terms.

Proposals for a New International Economic Order

A snap review of events at the United Nations highlights the nature of the political endeavours and the issues facing President Reagan and other western leaders.[3] Two important resolutions were adopted in 1974 at the sixth special session of the General Assembly.

First, the General Assembly adopted the *Declaration on the Establishment of a New International Economic Order* designed 'to eliminate the widening gap between developed and developing countries'. The Declaration recognizes that 'remaining vestiges of ... colonial domination ... and neo-colonialism in all its forms' are among the 'greatest obstacles to the full emancipation and progress of the developing countries'. It also asserts that an 'even and balanced development' is impossible to achieve 'under the existing international economic order' and emphasises that the inherited economic order 'is in direct conflict with current developments in political relations'. It is then proposed that developing countries should participate actively, fully and equally 'in the formulation and application of all decisions that concern the international community'. And so it is stated that 'international co-operation for development is the shared goal and common duty of all countries'. The 'broadest co-operation of all States ... whereby the prevailing disparities in the world may be banished' should be forthcoming and the 'full permanent sovereignty of every State over its natural resources and all economic activities' should be respected.

Secondly, the General Assembly launched itself on a supplementary resolution introduced as a *Programme of Action on the Establishment of a New International Economic Order*. Colonialism and neo-colonialism are again properly exorcised and condemned. The actions proposed are subdivided into categories covering trade and raw materials, transport, the international monetary system, regulation of multinational enterprises and an array of means for strengthening the United Nations system in the field of international economic co-operation. The provisions under the first item are intended to assure developing countries of larger real revenues from exports and more aid and financial contributions in one form or another. Transport costs are to be lowered (somehow) – at least for the developing countries. As for international monetary problems, developing countries are to be 'fully involved, as equal partners', in all decision-making. Return to a system of fixed rates of exchange is mentioned with some emphasis. This proposal requires supplementary attention to the provision of international liquidity linked to financial grants for developing countries. Thus the 'link' is naturally tied to the restoration of fixed rates of exchange. The last section of the action programme lists an extensive schedule for utilising or expanding United Nations institutions and in this way increasing the leverage of Third World countries.

A long line of conferences sponsored by the United Nations that are somewhat separated from the centres of NIEO rhetoric also deserve attention.

The Conference on the Law of the Sea was aimed at various levels of territorial jurisdictions bearing on the control over the surfaces and bottoms of the seas. The increasing value of fishing resources and of resources embedded in continental shelves induced unilateral actions imposing differential and extended jurisdictions with respect to fishing rights, the extraction of mineral resources and political sovereignty. New technologies promise future access to the mineral deposits in the oceans through vast investments with corresponding returns. The wealth of the seas that is rendered accessible by the evolution of technology and business organization inevitably stirs many interests. These temptations became visible in the proposals discussed at various sessions of the Conference on the Law of the Sea over many years.

The crucial proposal, supported by Henry Kissinger, as Secretary of State in the United States, would have instituted an international authority controlled by member countries of the United Nations. This authority could have licensed private operators for a limited period. Most importantly, however, the proposed Deep Sea-bed Authority would have had its own organization (the Enterprise) extracting deep-sea minerals. The international agency would have enjoyed remarkable powers of implicit taxation over the citizens of the First World. It would have been authorized to impose changes and fees on private operators. Most particularly, it would have enjoyed the power to force private operators to provide their technology to the Deep Sea-bed Authority's Enterprise. The voting arrangement and the institutional structuring of the proposed agency, designed to exploit the 'common heritage of mankind in the interest of mankind', clearly implied that the developing countries would dominate policies, procedures and the wealth of the agency at a severe social cost to the developed countries. Thus this aspect of the Conference on the Law of the Sea corresponded fully to the ideas launched by NIEO proponents. And it forms an integral part of the institutional restructuring urged by the Brandt Commission.

The Brandt Report revived the basic theme of the NIEO proposals, with appropriate diplomatic vagueness on important details, supported by a rather dramatic vision. The Brandt Commission views the restructuring of the international economic order as a crucial condition for assuring peace and fostering the economic development of the Third World with prosperity for all. Peace, development and prosperity are to be achieved, moreover, by means satisfying the requirements of justice. The economic development of the Third World forms, in fact, the key to everything else in the Brandt Commission's vision of the world. War seems to be dominantly caused by poverty and the political frustrations that ensue. Thus economic development produces prosperity and lowers the level of, and scope for, potential conflict. The North–South dialogue offers the decisive political instrument for affecting man's chances of survival. Moreover, the suitable institutionalization of this dialogue, in accordance with the NIEO programme, satisfies the 'mutual interests' of both the 'North' and the 'South', it is said.

The NIEO proposals would substantially modify, if put into effect, the two basic conditions allegedly maintaining the poverty of the Third World, it is argued. Persistent poverty is attributed, by the vision which guided the Brandt Report, to insufficient natural resources and to the imbalance of political power between the countries of the First World and those of the Third World. The NIEO proposals would remove the first obstacle by a massive transfer of wealth from the 'North' to the 'South' channelled by a wide array of old and new international agencies. The second obstruction to rapid economic development would be corrected with the aid of a new set of socio-political arrangements. These arrangements are designed to provide the countries of the Third World with some political control over the planned redistribution of wealth. The Brandt Report visualizes the enlargement of the range and power of international institutions and agencies.[4]

Social analysis and global approach inherent in the NIEO proposals and the Brandt Report

The vision and the social message influencing the NIEO proposals and, more particularly, those of the Brandt Report conform to a powerful trend in western thinking. They fit naturally into a pervasive socialist conception of the world with the corresponding socio-political and normative aspirations. The usual appraisals of this influential intellectual tradition suffer unfortunately from a disposition to ignore their implicit cognitive basis. The intelligentsia seems to be dominated by a sense that these issues essentially express 'ideological commitments' which have to be judged in terms of their normative appeal. This is regrettable and hardly serves a rational approach to the assessment of alternative social organizations. 'Ideology' may enter discourse and intellectual endeavours in many ways, but beyond the operation of ideological attitudes there remains a substantive core among the problems envisaged; and that core challenges cognitive aspirations and also challenges a commitment to rational and effective action. The moral or normative appeal of the message advanced with NIEO proposals, or with those of the Brandt Report, provides no rational basis for the policies advocated. In particular, it offers no assurance that the global approach to restructuring the world economy will ever produce consequences approximating to the promises of peace, development and general prosperity. It is necessary to penetrate beneath the layers of moral feelings to the substantive core of the 'vision' which has produced the Brandt Report and, before it, the NIEO demands.

A vision of the world

The vision of the world – that is, the underlying theory about the world – guiding these policy prescriptives is ultimately controlled by two basic strands of thought. One strand advances a specific view of man living in a social context. The other strand involves a notion of justice probably influenced by ancient biological conditioning from the earliest phases of human evolution.[5] The two strands jointly determine an approach to political issues and social organization outlined by the views summarized above.

The first strand, bearing on our intellectual perception of man, is well represented among the social sciences by a sociological model of man. This model envisages man as an essentially passive agent controlled by social norms and forces beyond his interacting reach and imposed on him as alien events. Man's *general* disposition to behave, beyond specific actions and responses, is seen to emerge from cultural conditioning determined in the context of prevailing social environments. Profit-seeking usually identified with self-interested behaviour, is interpreted as resulting from a social context organized by markets based on private property. Self-interested behaviour is expected to wane in the context of non-market institutions with little, if any, relation to private property.

The second strand supplements the perception of man in society with an end-state conception of justice. This conception defines justice in terms of a specific outcome pattern of the social process. The inequity of a society is measured, according to the circumstances, by the deviation of its characteristic operation from the outcome pattern deemed to represent the standards of justice. The argument associated with this notion of justice advances the claim that a political organization of society must be designed to assure outcomes closely approximating to the standards of justice.

The two strands of thought, while logically separate, jointly imply that non-market institutions (that is, a political structure) should control the economic and social co-ordination of society. Moreover, the perception of man assures us that the institutional requirement imposed by an end-state notion of justice poses no real problem. This model determines the essential malleability of man necessary for this purpose. The same perception also implies that replacing co-ordination by markets with political mechanisms lessens the attraction of 'commercial values' and raises the quality of *human* attention. This implication of the sociological model reinforces a commitment to an end-state view of justice.[6]

An alternative view of the world

The two basic strands of thought influencing a great deal of contemporary social thinking were challenged by the development of the social sciences. They need to be juxtaposed to two alternative views which shaped professional thinking in these matters for a substantial period. Economic analysis, influenced by the remarkable insights of the Scottish philosophers of the eighteenth century, emphasized the resourceful, evaluating and maximizing behaviour of man. A searching behaviour copes with the environment and gropes for improvements in accordance with the agents' interest and own understanding. This model of man yields radically different implications about the operation of market processes and political mechanisms than the sociological model. It acknowledges that *general* dispositions to behave essentially form an evolutionary heritage independent of the social environment. Self-interested behaviour is recognized, according to the circumstances, to express a pervasive disposition built into man's nature. It follows that profit-seeking is only one *particular* form of self-interested behaviour. Other forms will dominate in the context of non-market institutions. Thus the variability of specific actions and behaviour patterns emerges in the context of *general* dispositions in response to the peculiarities of the social environment.

The alternative vision implies in particular that the consequences of complex political institutions and agencies usually differ substantially from their motivating intentions. It also implies that all attempts to institutionalized end-state views of justice are doomed to dismal failure. Ultimately, they produce economic stagnation, with a serious loss of freedom. Most importantly, the end-state pattern of justice will never be realized and remains, forever, a futile hope. Accordingly, the alternative perception of man is typically linked with a process conception of justice which defines justice in terms of the characteristics of the process, or the rules of the social game, irrespective of its detailed outcome.

The choice between the two perceptions of man essentially involves a selection between two alternative empirical hypotheses. The evidence ranges from crime to marriage, divorce and many other events and patterns beyond the usual market place. This evidence, covering many different cultures, political organizations and historical periods, substantially confirms the intellectual position of the Scottish philosophers. But the non-cognitive and normative appeal of the sociological model with its prospects of social salvation maintains its political thrust in the public arena. This thrust is well sustained by the linkage with the end-state notion of justice which is threatened by the alternative view of man.

Brandt Report: central message and diagnosis
The alternative views of man and concepts of justice provide a framework for a critique of the social 'messages' and political proposals advanced in the Brandt Report. Major strands of thought in the Report are conditioned by the underlying model of man and conception of justice.

Several commentators have noted, for example, the pronounced attention given in the Brandt Report to the distribution of wealth (or redistribution), with little or no attention given to the production of wealth. This emphasis is accentuated by a systematic preference for political 'solutions' over a social co-ordination based on market processes. This pattern favouring an increasing use of political regulation and controls is reinforced by a remarkable disregard for their unintended and often overwhelming consequences. The redistributionist message naturally conforms to the 'common interest of mankind'. We are told in a similar vein that the mineral deposits at the bottom of the seas form the 'common heritage of mankind'. We can note, also, the pervasive disposition to define categories of 'needs', requiring specific political actions directed to each 'need'. The explanation of poverty in terms of inadequate natural resources and 'political imbalance' and the explanation of wars or political conflicts in terms of poverty are further examples. Thus there is a wide range of arguments and detailed judgements which are ultimately determined by the basic vision guiding the Brandt Report and justifying the NIEO demands. An examination of the argument developed by the Brandt Commission demonstrated, however, the crucial role assigned to the explanation of poverty in this whole structure of thought. This specific explanation, harnessed to the overall vision, determines a host of detailed views and proposals. My critique therefore addresses this central arch of the intellectual building presented by the Brandt Commission.

Brandt Report: its explanation of poverty
The more or less deliberate or conscious commitment to an end-state principle of justice gives rise, immediately, to the emphasis on redistribution. The sociological model of man justifies, in this context, the required shift from market processes to political institutions and non-market arrangements. It also assures us that we need not worry about any negative effects on production and resource allocation produced by the operation of the institutions transferring wealth from the 'North' to the 'South'. This result follows from the model's neglect of the role of specific incentive structures associated with various institutional arrangements. It disregards, therefore, the most crucial conditions fostering economic growth and raising the welfare of broadly defined social groups. The 'vacuous, aimless, reactive man' visualized by the sociological model cannot rise by resourceful groping and coping in the context of prevailing opportunities. Changes in opportunities due to lessened political constraints and regulations produce no systematic change in behaviour. Wealth acquisition seems predetermined, according to the circumstances, by the bounty of nature or the relative power of the nation. This theme, permeating the views developed in the United Nations over the last decade, dominates the Brandt Report's vision.

The role assigned to political relations and the 'imbalance of political power' determines the emphasis attributed to 'colonialism and neo-colonialism'. A colonial relationship produced, in this view, a redistribution of wealth from the colony to the 'controlling country'. The colonial powers enriched themselves at the expense of their colonies. The thesis of neo-colonialism asserts that the formal independence of the former colonies does not change, by itself, the basic reality of 'exploitation'. With the persistence of political imbalance favouring the western countries, the pattern of wealth redistribution from the 'South' to the 'North' persists in many subtle ways. Thus there emerges the contention that the massive transfer of wealth from the 'North' to the 'South', proposed in the NIEO programme, should be understood as compensation required by the standards of justice for inequities imposed by colonial and neo-colonial patterns.

This explanation of poverty, with its further ramifications, essentially rejects the insights attributed to Adam Smith. These insights became the core of modern economic analysis and have been successfully applied ever since to the social organization of western societies. The pervasive influence of entrenched ideas, however, is revealed with a remarkable force by the Brandt Commission. The statements are advanced by a group of intelligent and sincerely concerned people. Moreover, the statements are made in spite of the falsehood, almost plain to the naked eye, of the claims advanced. An array of countries with bountiful or meagre resources visibly demonstrates that possession of natural resources is poorly related to economic development and relative affluence. Similarly, there is an absence of any significant correlation between political status and affluence. The facts, as they speak for themselves, thoroughly reject the Brandt Commission's central allegations. Relative poverty or the wealth of nations cannot be reduced to the comparative state of natural resources and political power.

The alternative hypothesis combined with the rejection of an end-state principle of justice directs attention to a very different set of policies that are more effectively designed to combat poverty and hunger. Little virtue is attributed to massive redistribution. It has no moral claim and only obstructs processes of economic improvement in both the 'North' and the 'South'. The political arrangements that are required for persistent and large redistribution lower the incentives to use current resources efficiently or to develop future resources. They increase, on the other hand, the incentives to invest resources in the political process. Moreover, the large flow of resources made available to countries of the Third World will be used in accordance with the political interests of the ruling oligarchies. The whole structure of thought, guided by the underlying perceptions, fails to understand that ultimately poverty can only be alleviated by raising the productivity of man's effort and by encouraging man's incentives and opportunities to *apply* such efforts.

Apart from vague references, the vision associated with the NIEO proposals and the Brandt Report denies the relevance, or the importance, of domestic institutions and policies. The sociological model of man hardly alerts us, as the alternative view does, to the entrenched obstacles to economic improvement that are built into the institutional structures and are fostered by the economic policies of many countries in the Third World. A massive transfer of wealth would not remove these impediments and therefore it would contribute little to economic development. Indeed, it would impoverish the First World, lower its rate of growth and retard the increase in welfare of the mass of its citizens.

Thus the Brandt Commission and the 'official line' of the United Nations misdirects our attention. There is a need to recognize, beyond political power and the rich possessions of non-human resources within specific national locations, the role of institutions and their consequences bearing on man's opportunities. A social co-ordination, organized by political mechanisms and agencies, stifles opportunities and obstructs imaginative and probing initiatives. By contrast, an open society, co-ordinated by market processes, unleashes the energies of *human* resources. A pattern of political control hardly ever produced the lofty promise of improving welfare for widely dispersed segments of the population. The political control structure yields in general a kind of police state, economic stagnation, permanent poverty and a highly unequal distribution of affluence. The experience of the period since World War II demonstrates the remarkable differences within the Third World between market-oriented and state socialist economies. The operation of markets assures, in general, a substantially closer association between costs and returns of individual projects and activities. Individuals can also expect to capture the potential rewards from activities within the range of their opportunities.

The empirical irrelevance of the political explanation of poverty effectively destroys two central pillars supporting the NIEO proposals. The contention of systematic exploitation by the 'North' of the 'South' can no longer be maintained. Nor does there exist any empirical support for a more explicit Marxist reinterpretation of the 'colonial relationship'. An economic analysis of colonial history tentatively suggests that 'colonialism' was characterized by a redistribution of wealth within the 'mother country' benefiting the groups associated with the colonial venture at the expense of all other groups. This internal redistribution was accompanied by an external redistribution favouring the colonies quite directly. We can assert with more certainty that colonialism raised in general the economic welfare of the people in the colonies.[7] The moral claim for compensation vanishes along with the contention of past (colonialist) and current (neo-colonialist) exploitation. The support for redistribution must rely solely on the end-state principle of justice. Such reliance cannot be reconciled with any relevant empirical analysis of social and political institutions without forfeiting all hope for a society offering some chances for human achievement.

The Brandt Commission's explanation of war and conflict is closely associated with its theory of poverty. Given the underlying vision, it argues that levels of conflict rise with large differences in wealth; and it also argues that a complex set of institutional arrangements transferring wealth to the poorer countries lowers the level of conflict. But this position cannot be justified by economic analysis. Nor is it compatible with the facts. The patterns of political conflict are not dominated by relative wealth positions. We do not possess at this point a positive theory of conflict yielding a full range of adequate explanations. We have sufficient knowledge, however, to establish the inadequacy of *some* explanations. We also know enough about the operation of political institutions to conclude that the arrangements proposed in the NIEO programme, and incorporated in the Brandt Report, would actually *raise* the level of political conflict. The existence of political institutions controlling the redistribution of wealth offers strong incentives to those who want to appropriate wealth and those who want to generate wealth. Those who want to appropriate wealth invest in political institutions to achieve their purpose and those who want to generate wealth do so to defend themselves. This behaviour inevitably raises the level of conflict.

The approach to deep-sea resources as an example of the NIEO approach
The above critique of the NIEO proposals advocated by international organizations and the Brandt Commission need not be confined to its general characteristics and consequences. We have been offered a specific and important example of the political thrust inherent in the NIEO proposals. An examination of this representative case provided by advocates of a globally negotiated international economic order reveals the fundamental problem confronting the United States administration and other western governments.

The existence of vast resources at the bottom of the seas has been well known for many decades. Improving technologies and the expectations of rising real prices of major resources changed the economic significance of deep-sea mineral deposits. The world became aware of the potential wealth in the seas beyond the resources embedded in continental shelves and the potential for fishing. Access to these resources attracted political attention at various levels bearing on different dimensions of potential control. The resulting re-examination led to some differentiation in jurisdictional claims. The range covering fishing rights and access to continental shelves was substantially extended in relation to the limits of territorial sovereignty. The geographically more extensive rights are weaker in the sense that they are limited to specific resources without constraints on 'innocent' use of the surface. These changes were set in motion over the past decades and seem to converge to form an international consensus without having the benefit of an international treaty.

The negotiations for such a treaty, however, proceeded over many years. They attempted to impose, beyond the settlement of jurisdictional changes, a pattern of international control and regulation – under the auspices of the United Nations – on the economic exploitation of deep-sea mineral resources. These negotiations were suspended by the Reagan administration just before the American delegation prepared for a final agreement. At the end of January the administration announced that is was ready to resume discussions, having formulated some changes in the draft treaty that it wanted to advance, but nobody has forecast plain sailing in the negotiations ahead.

I have already stressed the close connection between the treaty proposal under negotiation over the past decade and the conceptions governing the NIEO proposals. Execution of the draft treaty as it stands would have been a great victory for NIEO advocates. The arrangements specified in the draft would have imposed substantial transfers of wealth on western countries. An impressive political slogan seemed to obscure the prospects that presented themselves. It was claimed that the resources of the sea bed are the 'common heritage of mankind'. This formulation appeared to justify without further argument the institutional arrangement addressed by the global negotiations. Moreover, the delegation of the United States seemed to be in the hands of a coalition formed by the departments of State and Defense that was unable, or unwilling, to assess the consequences of the treaty in terms of relevant socio-political criteria. American representatives hardly contested the political phraseology enshrined in many documents. They seemed either unaware of the political significance of the phraseology or found it irrelevant in terms of their own tactical purposes. But this meant that the new United States administration under President Reagan simply had to articulate a new course of policy.

What course? The lesson thus far was clear. There is really neither use nor need for any further global negotiations. The United States, it could be said, should effectively cancel what had been agreed. In the event, President Reagan has not gone that far, but I would like to quote at this point from an interesting study dealing with the issues:

> The sea-bed provisions would indeed be massively inefficient from the perspective of the world as a whole and quite hostile to the economic interests of the United States. Unfortunately, these defects are not cancelled out by so-called advantages elsewhere in the treaty, as the conventional wisdom appears to hold. Almost every other group of treaty articles at best conveys advantages for the United States that we cannot realistically expect the treaty or the parties to it to

enforce and at worst conveys real disadvantages for the United States relative to the state of the world without the treaty. The navigational protections for which we have traded away so much of our economic interests are either unnecessary or redundant; the coastal articles are inferior for us to the coastal-state resource rights that would exist without a treaty; and the sea-bed provisions are beyond reason.

The treaty would be so unsatisfactory to the United States that the Senate would probably reject it. In view of this the wiser course of action would be for the Reagan Administration to reject it straightforwardly at the conclusion of its own inter-agency review. Setting aside this huge but flawed experiment in multilateral negotiations will make the world as a whole wealthier, have more fish and less pollution and have greater supplies of increasingly scarce minerals. But these objectives can be realized only if the United States reverses the course of its present ocean policy and thereby ends a decade-long bipartisan mistake.[8]

What else could the United States administration do? Congress has already passed legislation enabling business firms to operate in the deep seas. Such operations would proceed in the tradition of enclosures applied to unowned resources. A detailed assessment of this state of affairs indicates that the absence of formalized and internationally codified property rights would not seriously affect incentives to invest. The cost of general search and then detailed explorations of the sea beds, even for locations close to already operating enclosures, prevents the occurrence of a 'free-rider' problem with its resulting under-investment. Nor will there occur a common-pool problem, typically appearing in oil extraction, leading to over-investment. The enclosure procedure would seem to approximate to an efficient use of resources ultimately beneficial to everybody in the context of an open competitive system. Lastly, the United States administration should invite other countries to pass similar legislation. The mutual recognition of such legislation involves the corresponding mutual recognition of the respective enclosures. Thus there would emerge some international arrangement better geared to raise general welfare than the redistributional scheme with the delegation of implicit taxing powers of the original treaty proposal. Whatever risks may still face private operators would remain small compared with the uncertainty produced by the regulatory miasma that could be expected under the treaty provisions administered by a body essentially hostile to the United States.

A rational policy for the United States
A critique of past trends and associated proposals is not sufficient. What is needed is a positive programme for an international economic order offering a better promise for human aspirations and welfare. This programme follows immediately from the underlying analysis guiding the critique of the Brandt Commission's report.

General aspects of the programme and the need for articulation
A reversal similar to the redirection of American domestic policies needs to be initiated over a broad front. It would involve a shift from an essentially political conception of social co-ordination controlled by public agencies and institutions to a market-oriented approach. The international trend depicted in earlier sections, while not fully accepted in detail by the United States administration, was neither opposed nor really understood by the country's foreign-policy establishment. More or less subtle concessions by representatives of the United States on important issues were frequently characterized as tactical behaviour by the administration. This behaviour reflected little strategic sense about the nature of the problem confronting the United States and its implications for the country's future welfare. The signs of strategic failure in the making of American international economic policy can be noted over a wide range of activities. We observe them in pretentious reports to the Department of State about the results and achievements of conferences. Such reports managed to turn strategic failure and incomprehension of basic issues into positive achievements of American policy.[9] The long series of meetings on the negotiations bearing on the exploitation of sea-bed resources were hardly ever systematically analysed. For instance, there is no evidence that Dr Kissinger, or other important officials of the Department of State, understood the serious consequences associated with their proposals supporting an international authority controlling the extraction of mineral deposits. We have also observed meetings and conferences covering a wide range of issues where the position and view of the western countries, and most particularly that of the United States, was not articulated. Immediate tactical concerns addressed to the state of the conference in question overshadowed strategic considerations pertaining to the longer-term course of international economic policy.

We also need to consider whether past decades confronted American policy-makers, within the range of American interests, with radically new situations and problems. The application of an 'institutional weapon' and the extensive use of 'ideological warfare' are comparatively new developments for which the foreign-policy establishment of the United States is not really prepared. Traditional training and reflexes offer no guidance on how to develop a rational strategy to meet this new type of assault on the position of the United States.

The 'institutional weapon' involves a systematic infiltration of existing institutions and agencies. This infiltration is designed to exploit the available apparatus for specific interests and purposes in a long-range strategy of political control. The 'ideological warfare' supplements this 'institutional' infiltration. It uses an integrated and global set of ideas which are systematically exploited to advance a particular political interest. This set of ideas offers a comprehensive and alluring interpretation of the world. This interpretation is designed to 'explain' all actions pursued by one side to the protracted conflict as expressions of a desire for peace and justice and to reveal all actions of the other side as expressions of evil designs that are hostile to peace and justice. Some major patterns of such 'ideological warfare' with a corresponding erosion of the western position in the political arena may be recognized in the effective propagation of key words and their meaning in the public vocabulary. We are frequently inclined to dismiss questions of language and the use of specific words as matters of minor significance. But words and formulations often develop a momentum in the political market. They impose constraints on future negotiations, affect the questions to be examined and how they will be considered. They subtly influence the nature of agendas and the expectations or meaning associated with a programme. Words and formulations are not neutral; their implications condition future behaviour. A party to the conflict can be effectively weakened by subtly imposing on it a defensive attitude via an implicit acceptance of linguistic regulations determined by the opponent.

This pattern emerges with a remarkable clarity in the series of meetings in the United Nations on the NIEO proposals, at conferences on other issues such as crime, at conferences of the United National Educational, Scientific and Cultural Organisation (UNESCO) or at meetings on the law of the sea. I have already noted in this last case the effective use made by interested parties of the slogan that deep-sea minerals are 'the common heritage of mankind'. This characterization was hardly neutral. It was advanced to justify a specific political programme (but a programme which would have yielded little benefit for mankind).

The American representatives at the Conference on the Law of the Sea, or at the General Assembly of the United Nations, have seemed in general not inclined to counter this political slogan with an alternative articulation. It appeared that they considered it a minor exercise in semantics with little substantive import. The Brandt Commission's use of 'mutual interests' between the 'North' and the 'South' works in a similar vein. One might be easily inclined to accept the existence of 'mutual interests' in some sense. But the Brandt Report identifies such interests with a specific interpretation and a particular programme. Thus an alluring term is used with a very definite meaning determined by an interpretation and a proposal hardly consistent with the relevant facts and mankind's long-term interests. We may also note the use of the terms 'global negotiations' or 'internationalism' in order to prod the United States administration into a specific pattern determined by the NIEO programme. The word 'peace' has been similarly exploited by Soviet propaganda in Western Europe to produce an increasingly prevailing attitude equating 'peace' with the Soviet Union's foreign policy.

Several factors may explain the observed failures in American international economic policy. One factor involves the incentives built into the foreign-policy establishment and the stock of inherited views pertaining to its performance characteristics. The tradition fostered by the establishment's institutional incentives conditions the bureaucracy to concentrate its attention on tactical issues and procedures. The prevailing incentives encourage a pattern-evaluating performance essentially in terms of immediate tactical moves. The interaction of the foreign-policy establishment with the media and legislature seems to reinforce such incentives. The immediate task of negotiation dominates the attention of foreign-policy officials. Negotiations often evolve in the context of a weak strategic conception their own momentum. This became visible in the United States' administration's approach to the NIEO proposals and at the Conference on the Law of the Sea. Even western diplomats, fully aware of the serious inadequacy of the treaty proposal emerging from the latter, were offended by the Reagan administration's suspension of the matter after many years of persistent labours.

Another factor involves the interaction between different branches of the government. The course ultimately emerging typically appears to be a compromise between conceptions, strategies and tactical considerations governing different departments or different groups within departments. Shifting coalitions between and within departments produce correspondingly shifting 'policies' with no sense of a coherent overall strategy. This situation results in negotiators concentrating on tactics without regard for strategic considerations.

The patterns mentioned in the above paragraphs may not exhaust the reason for the failure of western governments to cope more effectively with the assault on western positions institutionalized via international agencies. The failure seems to have been reinforced by a subtle influence within the policy establishments of western governments of some ideas underlying the Brandt Report and the NIEO proposals. The absence of a clear conception about the role and importance of western social organization and its contribution to human welfare weakened the ability of the United States to cope with the ideological warfare launched against it. The confusion within the United States about the meaning of 'human rights' and associated political conceptions offers a good example in this respect.[10]

The new scenario in the field of international economic policy suggests some changes in the attitude and procedure of the United States. First, it is necessary to develop a strategic conception compatible with American long-term interests and consistent, too, with a social organization appropriate for a free society. Secondly, it is necessary to articulate explicitly, and in detail, the position and views of the United States. The foreign-policy establishment has usually avoided such articulation for tactical reasons or in order 'to prevent a confrontation'. I submit, however, that this articulation acquired some major importance in the world with new forms of conflict and political tension. It is important that representatives of the United States should learn to cope with this world and learn most particularly to explain the American case. What is involved is much more than a matter of disdainful ideology. It involves matters bearing on the core of American society, on the way of life of a free society, on the institutional arrangements fostering economic welfare and freedom in human society. The foreign-policy establishment of the United States needs to understand that a rational and eloquent case can be made beyond shallow ideological attitudes.

Major strands of a strategy

President Reagan has repeatedly formulated the basic thrust of his domestic economic policy. He explicitly presented, in some detail, the reasons for the reversal in policy, a reversal characterized by greater reliance on markets and less political controls and regulations. The same basic thrust should be extended to international economic policy. There is hardly any doubt that the President and at least some appointees in the Department of the Treasury understand the problem. There still remains some doubt whether other branches of the administration understand the situation. An outline of major components in the strategy may therefore be useful.

A stable financial framework   The international monetary system established after World War II was constructed by a process of international negotiations. The agreement concluded at Bretton Woods provided for an international agency operating under a set of general rules. The arrangements, however, were inherently inadequate for their purposes. The necessary condition for a fixed exchange-rate system remained submerged under a complex set of provisions. The agreement and its institutional execution could not assure a pattern of domestic monetary policies geared to maintain a system of fixed rates of exchange. The necessity to have the balance of payments dominate the movements of the monetary base appeared to be politically difficult for the participating countries to accept. This fault in the system was reinforced by the failure of American policy-makers to recognize the importance of a central economy within a fixed exchange-rate system. The world gradually moved under the Bretton Woods arrangement to a 'dollar standard'. The United States, as the centrepiece of the system, was faced with a special obligation. Maintenance of a functioning system required that the United States should reliably pursue a non-inflationary financial policy with a stable policy-making framework. The United States refused to acknowledge that obligation and this settled eventually the fate of the 'Bretton Woods' international monetary system.

An international system based on fixed rates of exchange offers substantial advantages for trade and investment. A well-functioning international monetary system should thus be considered to be a major goal of American policy. This goal should not be approached with the aid of international negotiations, agreements, treaties and new or renewed international agencies. Such an approach, appealing as it is to professional negotiators, will not yield any useful results. An alternative strategy fully under the control of the United States promises more relevant results. The United States should develop a stable and predictable framework for its monetary and fiscal policy involving a definite pre-commitment to a specific course over the longer term. Implementation of constant monetary growth at a non-inflationary level, or a similar institutional pre-commitment (lowering the uncertainty about future monetary evolution), forms one component of the required strategy. A corresponding framework for fiscal policy also needs to be developed. This framework would yield some assurance of a controlled budget growing at a comparatively slow rate and with small variations in the deficit averaging at a low level. This framework for a stable and reliable financial policy would foster the attractiveness of the dollar as an international means of payment. It would also offer a strong inducement to other countries to peg their currency to the American dollar. Thus an area with fixed rates of exchange would emerge quite spontaneously without a complex of negotiations and treaties. All countries interested in non-inflationary policies could participate voluntarily and spontaneously. Other countries would only endanger any negotiated system and render it essentially inoperative. But the United States could organize in this way a central core of countries forming a system of stable financial relations. This system, moreover, would determine an implicit but clearly determined division of responsibilities. The United States is responsible for a non-inflationary policy and the remaining participants are responsible for setting their respective rates of exchange relative to the dollar.

Capital markets, trade and aid   The United States administration should encourage open and well-functioning capital markets all round the world. It needs to eliminate existing institutions or prevent the emergence of new policy arrangements which impair or distort the operation of capital markets. In the context of over-controlled and over-regulated West European domestic capital markets, the United States should view all attempts to control the Eurocurrency markets with some critical hesitation. It should be recognized that an open Eurocurrency market satisfies an important function for the social co-ordination of resources worldwide. Well-functioning capital markets are particularly important as a constructive and ultimately more useful alternative to the Brandt Commission's obsession with redistribution. Countries of the Third World have access to resources for investment in accordance with their prospects which are determined by their own domestic policies.

An open international trading system forms another important strand in the American conception for an international economic order. An international accord, the General Agreement on Tariffs and Trade (GATT), providing a framework of rules and procedures, has operated for many years in this field. We cannot expect this accord to offer, by itself, the focus of a political force pushing for open international markets. This political force needs to be mobilized by the government of a 'core' country. The United States must assume political leadership in this field. It will have to control with some determination its own protectionist impulses and exert a corresponding influence on other countries. The GATT offers a potentially useful institutional framework for this purpose. It needs to be added, however, that the opening of trade should be extended beyond a traditional range of goods appearing in a 'trade balance' to all potentially tradeable services.

A thorough and credible commitment to free trade forms a crucial component in American strategy. The suspension of *economic* aid from government to government, directly or via international agencies, would be more difficult to maintain without a determined approach towards free trade, particularly in the conduct of American trade policy. The record of economic aid extended between governments, as an instrument of raising welfare, does not justify its continuation. The United States administration should terminate such programmes. It would not obstruct, however, the organization of aid by private organizations. Nor should an end be put to aid – in one form or another – as one of our instruments of foreign policy.

Range of international agencies   Whatever the initial intentions associated with many international agencies and institutions may have been, they frequently evolve into political conduits for the redistribution of resources. The resulting pattern of redistribution usually benefits some groups, but these seem typically concentrated around the ruling oligarchies. The distortions in the use of resources consequently lowers the level of achievable economic development around the world. The Reagan administration, if not other governments, needs to re-examine systematically the role of various international agencies. Selected aspects of the central institutions of the international economic order are touched on below, although I have touched on the GATT already, my concern below mainly being with the financial institutions.

The breakdown of the Bretton Woods system substantially eroded the function of the International Monetary Fund (IMF). In order to maintain a political role, the agency moved, over time, to expand its range of 'soft loans'. It also advocated an extension of Special Drawing Rights (SDRs) along the lines proposed by the Brandt Commission. A variety of new facilities are supposed to transform the IMF into a major transfer agency on behalf of Third World countries.

The position of the United States should be quite straightforward in this matter. The IMF should return to its relevant function of short-term advances intended to cover transitory balance-of-payments deficits. All traces of redistributional transfers, in whatever form and however indirect, need to be terminated. It would also mean no further expansion in the volume of SDRs issued by the IMF. There is really no monetary role for such issues in the context of the international monetary system described above. International liquidity requires no regulation by an international agency. It can more satisfactorily be determined via the exchange-rate policies of countries participating in the fixed exchange-rate system. An increased demand for international liquidity would appear in the context of the approach described above as an increased international demand for dollars. This trend could also be incorporated into the benchmark level of non-inflationary monetary growth in the United States. Such adjustment of monetary growth would lower the frequency of resetting exchange rates.

There still remain some useful functions for the IMF. It integrates a world-wide financial information system. This information bears on the interaction between balance-of-payments, fiscal and monetary policies of all countries. It offers a meeting ground beyond the Bank for International Settlements (BIS) for Central Bank or finance ministry officials and government functionaries in general. This meeting ground provides opportunities to exchange views and to explain policies. The IMF offers, furthermore, an appraisal and monitoring service for the international capital market. This service has suffered somewhat in recent years and the IMF could usefully provide this service again. The IMF enjoys a singular advantage which allows it to couple lending activities with appropriate monitoring and appraisal in a mode that is not achievable by private commercial institutions. The successful development of this monitoring and appraisal service in the nature of an international Moody's would contribute to the operation of capital markets in the field of international private lending. Lastly, the IMF can provide the expertise required to develop commercial and central banking, and to organize credit markets, in developing countries.

The World Bank should eliminate all redistributionist schemes and political loans. It should operate in the manner of a private commercial bank. It would specialize in international investments around the world. Its effectiveness and business should depend on the comparative advantages that are most probably present in its specialization in information and procedures bearing on a wide complex of international situations. It probably also enjoys a comparative advantage in packaging major projects with the complex expertise required. Its operations offer also an opportunity to dissociate long-term investments from occasionally difficult bilateral arrangements between directly involved governments. In the absence of such comparative advantage the World Bank should be driven out of business by the competition from private lenders. By contrast to the IMF, the World Bank should concentrate, moreover, on longer-term loans to private firms around the world. It should not be used as a conduit for American funds to foreign governments or nationalized industries

The roles of other international institutions, such as the Organization for Economic Co-operation and Development (OECD) and the different parts of the United Nations system, such as the Food and Agriculture Organization (FAO), also need to be reappraised in the light of the essentials of the kind of international economic order that has been discussed in this article. What is required is a much more critical approach to international organizations with a view to ensuring that they devote their resources to the development of policies attuned to the welfare of broad population groups.

Domestic policies of Third World countries
The Brandt Report did include a short paragraph referring to domestic economic policies of 'developing nations'. But this recognition remains somewhat incidental; the emphasis on it is marginal. It hardly fits the basic vision and the resulting diagnosis of the problem. But there is ample evidence bearing on the crucial role of domestic economic policies. This is revealed by major differences in economic development among the countries of the Third World. A variety of policies and institutions in many developing countries obstruct the development of agriculture, the most important component of many developing economies, while the usufruct system of landholding in many of them discourages investment and soil improvements. With the political base of ruling oligarchies usually centred in the cities, the resulting policies typically impose low prices on agricultural products, which means that transfer of wealth from rural to urban parts of the population discourages productive effort and lowers agricultural output. Potentially productive land remains unused.

The American position should be very clear in this respect. It is indeed necessary to be concerned about the fate and welfare of developing countries. This concern rationally determines the interest of the United States, and other developed countries, in effective long-range measures that can be expected to raise general standards of living in the countries of the Third World. The problems posed for economic development by the domestic policies of diverse countries should thus be understood and recognized by developing-country governments. This recognition needs to be articulated and argued in the international fora. It needs to be argued at summits and, especially, at meetings of the kind held in Cancun.[11] The domestic policies to be considered among the developing countries need to include a range of legal and contractual aspects. Direct investments raising a country's productive capacity will be encouraged with the reliability of contractual arrangements. Uncertain property rights and unreliable contractual conditions curtail direct investments and concentrate their occurrence to short pay-off periods.

A final statement

'Peace and prosperity' are welcomed by most people. The incantation of the words does not assure the conditions they represent. A 'global programme' for 'peace and prosperity' still requires critical examination, even when it is launched by a prestigious commission, or by an international peace organization. The United States should, indeed, raise its voice in a 'global context', advocating peace and rising welfare for broad groups. It should also express its concern about the fate and welfare of Third World countries. Peace, however, is better achieved by avoiding arrangements which increase the prospect of domestic and international conflict. Moreover, rising welfare is fostered by suspending policies, and removing institutions, which emasculate opportunities of millions of workers and farmers. The United States administration needs to recognize, as President Reagan has, that the inheritance of the 'global approach' defined by an international bureaucracy advances neither peace nor prosperity. Fortunately the United States administration can develop an alternative programme. There is really no reason to continue an international negative-sum game.

Notes

1. This article is the revised text of a lecture in commercial diplomacy, the sixth in a series, sponsored by the Trade Policy Research Centre and given at the Royal Commonwealth Society in London on 28 September 1981. I gratefully acknowledge useful discussions, bearing on the matters covered in the article, with Michele Fratianni, Jerry Jordan, William Meckling and Allan H. Meltzer.
2. Independent Commission on International Development Issues, *North–South: A Programme for Survival*, London and Sydney: Pan Books, 1980.
3. This section draws extensively on my essay, 'The New International Economic Order: a chapter in protracted confrontation', in Karl Brunner (ed.), *The First World and the Third World*, Rochester: University of Rochester Policy Center Publications, 1978.
4. It might be noted in passing that the emphasis on the redistribution of wealth that is developed by the Brandt Report finds strong support in a report on a programme for worldwide full employment which has been prepared by a Dutch group that included Jan Tinbergen, a Nobel Laureate, and Joop den Uyl. The report is being distributed by the Federation of Socialist Parties in the European Community.
5. An interesting analysis of this issue is offered in F.A. Hayek, *New Studies in Philosophy, Politics, Economics and the History of Ideas*, Chicago: University of Chicago Press, 1978.
6. A more detailed discussion of these strands of thought may be found in Karl Brunner and William Meckling, 'The perception of man and the conception of justice', *Journal of Money, Credit and Banking*, February 1977; and Brunner, 'The perception of man and justice and the conception of political institutions', in Fritz Machlup, Gerhard Fels and Hubertus Müller-Groeling (eds), *Reflections on a Troubled World Economy: Essays in*

Honour of Herbert Giersch, London: Macmillan, for the Trade Policy Research Centre, 1983.
7. P.T. Bauer, 'Western guilt and Third World poverty', in Brunner (ed.), *The First World and the Third World*.
8. Ross D. Eckert, *United States Interests and the Law of the Sea Treaty: Myths versus Realities*, Discussion Paper, Department of Economics, Claremont College, Claremont, 1981.
9. Daniel Patrick Moynihan, 'The United States in Opposition', in Brunner (ed.), *The First World and the Third World*.
10. The reader may find some material bearing on this issue in my contribution to ibid. Also see Deepak Lal, *Resurrection of the Pauper-labour Argument*, Thames Essay no. 28, London: Trade Policy Research Centre, 1981, where a specific example of confusion over 'human rights' is discussed in the chapter on 'Fair Labour Standards as a Matter of Human Rights'.
11. In my view, President Reagan's address at the annual meetings of the IMF and the World Bank in October 1981 was an excellent example, one that should be emulated by the foreign-policy establishment.

16 A fascination with economics*

The study of economics in the context of an institutionalized vacuum of knowledge is a peculiar experience. You reach in all directions with no sense of discrimination. Good fortune may intervene on occasion and guide you to the inheritance left us by great thinkers. But such exposure is disturbing. It stirred an awareness that my doctoral dissertation, marking the ritual exercise assuring entry into the academic confrerie with the blessing of the University of Zürich, be immediately committed to oblivion. Still, I was more than ever fascinated by the spectacle of man and his problems in society. I also judged, with better intuition than reason, that economics could offer me the best avenue to satisfy my curiosity. But the intellectual wasteland characterizing the social sciences at Swiss universities compelled a crucial decision between adaptation or departure. The offer of a grant by the Rockefeller Foundation determined the outcome. Four months at Harvard University and one and a half years as a visitor at the (then) Cowles Commission for Research in Economics (University of Chicago) introduced me to the American scene.

This experience produced utter confusion and urgent questions. The environment enjoyed at the Commission was in many ways admirable, valued in human terms and measured by the skilled intelligence and technical expertise. But all this impressive exhibition of human ingenuity remained blurred and out of focus. What did all these layers of adroit analytics involve, what was their point and what did really matter? Was it the superior skill in using a mathematical theorem within a context of 'economic' vocabulary? Was it the 'technical complexity' and 'sophistication' of an argument, or was it the felicitous re-articulation of views bearing on economic policy within the dominant postwar consensus, or an 'innovative variation' of a well-defined game fixed by some paradigmatic formulation? A master of the German postwar university scene advised me at the time to be guided by 'astounding and new ideas'.

My encounter with Milton Friedman indeed opened new and astounding vistas. He violated the prevalent pattern of suggestively vague criteria addressed to the selection and evaluation of professional work. Most distressing was moreover the encounter with a group of economists systematically

* Originally published in *Banca Nazionale del Lavoro Quarterly Review*, no. 135, December 1980, 403–26. It was a contribution to a series of recollections and reflections on professional experiences of distinguished economists. This series opened with the September 1979 issue of the *Review*.

applying economic analysis (i.e. price theory) to social problems of our world. The resulting confusions yielded fertile ground for the right environment, and UCLA at the beginning of the 1950s was for me the right place. The permanent discussion with a subtle mind (Armen A. Alchian), the impact of a lucid philosopher of science (Reichenbach), and the good fortune of questioning and determined students (Allan H. Meltzer, Tibor Fabian, later on Jerry Jordan and others) dispersed the intellectual fog and gradually structured my thinking about economics and its role in our endeavour to understand the world.

This background influencing the evolution of my thoughts addressed to the role and use of economics, guided my attention to three distinct major groups of problems. One covers the range of monetary analysis and policy and a second involves the nature of our cognitive endeavours expressed by our pursuits. The last strand of my persistent interests developed over time from my occupation with the previous two problems. There evolved a gradual understanding that economic analysis offers a systematic approach to the whole range of socio-political reality. These three distinct strands, however separated they may be on purely logical grounds, emerged in the actual practice of my thinking with a connected pattern. I wish to invite the reader to trace with me some of these aspects and interrelations.

Issues in monetary analysis and monetary policy

The development of a 'money supply' analysis

Monetary problems already attracted my interest as a student. But I became, as many others, absorbed with the 'Keynesian Revolution' and the study of Keynes's work. My old interest re-emerged however during the early years at UCLA and the detachment from the Keynesian orthodoxy was under way. This detachment was guided by many uneasy questions bearing on the profession's dismissal of the classical programme for monetary analysis. It was also encouraged by many discussions with Allan H. Meltzer during his doctoral work bearing on the money supply process. So began a long and productive association which crucially influenced my work and ideas over many years.

My interest focused during the 1950s most particularly on the total separation between 'policy' and monetary analysis. This separation was best revealed by the occurrence of two unrelated and independent languages used for the discussion of policy and the formulation of analysis. This analysis offered little help for a systematic approach to important aspects covered by policy discussions. And the latter frequently proceeded with arguments and formulation unrelated to any economic analysis. This feature still lingers at many Central Banks. Our professional literature contained around the middle of the 1950s suggestive approaches attempting to trace the behaviour of money stock or earning assets of banks in response to actions undertaken by the monetary authorities. These approaches were indeed rather 'mechanical' in the sense that the behaviour patterns used in the arguments showed no exposure to economic analysis. But this failure was not an inherent property of what became known as the 'multiplier approach' to the analysis of the money stock. It occurred to me that a suitable exploitation of inherited attempts could articulate the problem within the context of an economic analysis recognizing the operation of relative costs and yields on the crucial behaviour patterns. The result was an analysis of the money supply process describing the joint behaviour of money stock, earning assets and interest rates resulting from the interaction between banks, the public and the monetary authorities. The behaviour of the money stock was made understandable by this approach as an outcome determined by interacting asset markets operating in response to Central Bank behaviour.

The formulation was deliberately chosen in order to navigate the analysis between the empty exercises represented by (what I called once) a 'Forest of Jacobians' and the standard econometric approach relying on large models. The multiplier approach lacks the neat elegance much appreciated by our profession but does offer a procedure with useful advantages for anybody concerned with the real problems confronting us. I suggested a natural way to impose order constraints assuring a range of definite propositions about the results of the asset market interaction. It offered moreover a framework effectively geared to subsume important institutional aspects of the monetary system. The role of a shifting interbank deposit structure, or the consequences of changing reserve arrangement or of waning membership in the Federal Reserve System could be systematically evaluated in the context of this analytic framework. It offered also an opportunity to examine the dominant patterns shaping the behaviour of the money stock and to appraise the many assertions usually encountered in this respect. Thus emerged an assessment of the relative importance of the public's, the banks' and the authorities' behaviour in the evolution of the money stock over shorter and longer horizons. It yielded in particular a clarification of the conditions generating a 'reverse causation' in the relation between money and income. The occurrence of this phenomenon depends on very specific institutional arrangements. It requires either a massive interest elasticity of the banks reserve and borrowing behaviour or a pronounced interest sensitivity in the supply of the monetary base. The latter condition is probably more important. But such patterns are not a natural property of monetary processes. They are the product of a Central Bank's institutional policy. Variations of these arrangements over time modify the relative contribution of reverse causation to the observed association between money and income.

The analysis clarified moreover the meaning of loan ceilings occasionally imposed by important countries. It showed that this instrument hardly affected money stock and total earning assets. It created a captive market for government securities and lowered the relative cost of public borrowing and raised the cost of private borrowing. It presented a typical example of wealth redistribution proceeding under the rhetorical cover of an anti-inflationary device. And lastly, the monetary control procedure developed by the Swiss National Bank or experimentally applied by Professor Robert Rasche on behalf of the Shadow Open Market Committee emerged basically from this equilibrium analysis couched in terms of a multiplier approach.[1]

The study of Federal Reserve policy-making
This research on the money supply process prepared the ground for a detailed examination of Federal Reserve policy-making jointly undertaken with Allan H. Meltzer. This work initiated a growing attention to the political economy of political institutions. We examined in particular the nature of the ruling conception guiding policies over the past decades. We also investigated the strategy associated with the ruling conception and the interpretations of events and actions made in this context. It became very clear that the Federal Reserve's policy-makers shared with all other men the characteristic of a 'theorizing animal'. Their view of the world was controlled by a theory associated in the 1920s with their major figures. Federal Reserve actions and interpretations during the Great Depression were rationally conceived in terms of this theory. The problem centred on the adequacy of this theory developed without any connections with or exposure to systematic economic analysis. This theory, centred on the notion that banks are inherently reluctant to borrow (irrespective of costs and yields), gradually changed into the free-reserve doctrine of the early postwar period. This tradition eventually faded away in the late 1960s and was replaced with the idea that the money stock is determined by a volatile money demand in the context of a more or less explicit IS-LM framework.

Several major results of our investigation were impressed on my mind. The history of monetary policy-making in the USA revealed to me, confirmed by many observations over the subsequent years, that only very special circumstances will produce a substantial change in conception and procedure well entrenched in the bureaucracy manipulating a political institution. It also revealed that policy-making is indeed rational. It involves however a rationality relative to the long-run interests and survival of a political institution not necessarily linked with systematic attention to the social welfare of the nation. A careful study of the minutes summarizing the meetings of the relevant policy committee indicated moreover the tragic and persistent misinterpretation of monetary actions and monetary events all through the Great Depression. This judgement does not depend on hindsight. It can be justified by the knowledge available at the time. Lastly, the persistent misinterpretation of monetary evolutions, also visible in the public record, was ultimately expressed by the *negative* association between the Federal Reserve's actions and rhetoric description. This Orwellian inversion (i.e. expansionary becomes contractionary and vice versa) of language affects the media's reporting and permeates the financial world to this day.[2]

The major issues in the 'monetarist' controversy
The discussion gradually evolving over the 1950s proceeded however with a broader focus beyond the issues considered so far. The monetarist 'counter-revolution' addressed some central tenets of the Keynesian position. The array of issues governing the discussions can be organized under four major groups. These problems refer to the nature of the transmission mechanism, the impulse patterns driving the economic process, the internal stability of the system and the relation between allocative processes and aggregative behaviour. The controversies proceeding under the various headings involved substantially more than erudite scholarly games. They reflected ultimately important aspects of the world bearing on the rationale of specific policies or of general approaches to policy-making.

The transmission mechanism   The Keynesian tradition subsumed two interpretations of the transmission mechanism associated with two alternative interpretations of the famous IS/LM apparatus. One version guides the econometric approach to macro-analysis and most of the textbook discussion. It emphasizes the substitution between money and financial assets represented by bonds and excludes substitution between money and real assets. Monetary impulses are conveyed under the circumstances by the play of interest rates on financial assets. The interest sensitivity of money demand and of major expenditure categories in the national income accounts determines therefore the impact of monetary policy. This interpretation explains investigations bearing on the efficacy of restrictive monetary policy organized by the US Department of Commerce in 1967 which concentrated on the response of business firms' capital budgeting to the observed increase in interest rates. It also explains the rationale developed by the Council of Economic Advisors for an activist use of fiscal policy supplemented with an accommodative stance of monetary policy. This particular version of the Keynesian transmission mechanism directed attention to the operation of borrowing costs associated with specific expenditure categories. The framework guiding policymakers' interpretation produced the conclusion that monetary impulses reach the economy via a narrow segment of total national expenditures most exposed to the impact of borrowing costs. This sector became identified with construction activity. The burden of monetary policy would be imposed under the circumstances on an industry with high 'social and political priorities'. This 'social cost' of monetary policy could be avoided by confining monetary policy to an accommodation of prevailing trends guided by an interest rate set in accordance with the 'needs of the housing sector'. Activist management of aggregate demand was assigned on the other hand to fiscal policy.

Other policy issues reinforced attention to the nature of the transmission mechanism. This range of questions, motivated by policy problems, encouraged the systematic re-examination of this particular Keynesian strand. This re-examination was guided by an analysis of the social function of money as an asset emerging from the interaction between individuals in a social group. The self-interested search of interrelated individuals yields a pattern of asset uses minimizing information and transaction costs in a world where information and transactions require the investment of valuable resources. But money as a transaction-dominating asset substitutes in all directions, and most particularly over the whole array of assets. The textbook version of the Keynesian story centred on interest rates and borrowing costs could not subsume the monetary evolutions of countries without an organized capital market. Observations from a wide array of countries suggest that money substitutes beyond financial assets with real assets. This broad sweep of substitution relations radically changes the nature of the mechanism transmitting monetary impulses to the economy. This change lowers the significance of Keynesian 'interest rates' as conveyors of monetary impulses and dismisses the role of relative borrowing costs. Some of the empirical studies designed to explore the efficacy of restrictive (or expansionary) policy appear thus to be misconceived or irrelevant. The monetary policy of accommodation loses moreover its justification.

A broader view was already contained in an alternative version of the IS/LM apparatus developed by Lloyd Metzler. In order to subsume an analysis acknowledging the full substitutability of money over all assets into a framework admitting only two assets all non-money items were lumped into a single asset juxtaposed to money. The interest rate refers in this case beyond rates on financial assets also to returns on real assets. But the procedure severely constrains the relevant range of application available for the analysis. It could only be used for episodes exhibiting comparatively negligible variation in relative yields between financial and real assets. This limitation excludes most of the cyclic fluctuations unfolding in contexts of modest inflation. These fluctuations usually produce shifts in relative yields affecting the interaction between asset markets and the real sector. A useful analysis would thus explicitly represent the important strands of the money substitution process. This motivated the analysis of a three-asset model of interacting asset and output market jointly developed with Allan H. Meltzer by the late 1960s.

This revision of the transmission process affected most particularly the crucial conditions ensuring the occurrence of monetary effects in the real economy. Keynesian analysis typically yielded statements emphasizing the role of the interest elasticity of money demand. Samuelson and others actually characterized the difference between a Keynesian and a non-Keynesian view in terms of the relative magnitude of this interest elasticity. This characterization reflected a persistent misconception maintained over the years by the Keynesian establishment. This misconception assumed that everybody shared the basic assumptions yielding the specific economic content of the IS/LM approach. It reflected thus a pervasive failure to recognize the nature of the issue. Our analysis implies in contrast to the accustomed Keynesian view the comparative irrelevance of the absolute value of the interest elasticity of money demand. The essential (i.e. necessary and sufficient) condition assuring the transmission of monetary impulses involves an order relation, irrespective of absolute magnitudes, between interest elasticities on the credit market and on the money market. The extension of the transmission mechanism affected furthermore standard interpretations offered by our Central Bank bearing on the observed variability of monetary growth. This variability was usually interpreted to express corresponding disturbances in money demand. The extended analysis determines however that *all* disturbances from *all* over the economic system are converted into corresponding gyrations of monetary growth whenever policy is geared to accommodate interest rates. This difference in interpretation affects again the evaluation of monetary policy.[3]

The internal stability of the economic system   The internal stability of the system opposed a dominant Keynesian position that the private sector is inherently unstable. This issue was again associated with important policy problems and determines very different views of policy-making. It modifies in particular the role assigned to the public sector. The Keynesian tradition views the government as the stabilizer of a flawed system. Under the alternative view the government's actions contribute, in conjunction with other shocks affecting supply and demand conditions, to maintain the system in motion. The system's internal stability operates to absorb these shocks and assures that the system converges forever to its normal position. Persistent deviations from this position, as in the 1930s, do not result from an inherent instability. They are produced by a long and massive series of negative shocks lowering aggregate demand beyond the system's shorter-run absorption capacity impaired by the information load imposed by the long series of shocks. Such a series is moreover (and usually) the creation of government.

This conclusion contributed to the proposal that government policy would best serve the economy with a stable framework of reliably predictable actions.

The view of an unstable or meta-stable process contrasting with the classical notion of a system absorbing all shocks in a perpetual convergence around its normal position seems difficult to reconcile with pervasive patterns of monetary experience. These aspects attracted my attention in the late 1950s when I pondered in many discussion with Allan H. Meltzer and Armen Alchian the large differences in the level of monetary growth observed at peaks or troughs of cyclic fluctuations over time within a country or across time between countries. It dawned on us that neither the level of monetary growth nor of the money stock could be expected to affect significantly the real variables. The inherent stability of the system projects the persistent patterns bearing on these magnitudes into the price level or the inflation rate. We settled at the time, as Milton Friedman did, on the idea that real effects are produced by monetary accelerations not yet absorbed into the prevailing price structure. It followed that a general recognition of persistent accelerations would shift the real effects to higher-level time derivatives of the time path followed by the money stock. The role assigned to a non-passive and economically relevant aggregate supply interacting with aggregate demand determines ultimately the stabilizing property of the private sector process. This interaction assures that monetary impulses cannot raise output permanently beyond its normal level. The property of an internally stable process precludes this result by eventually translating such impulses into price effects. The evolution of these ideas was spread over many years and became eventually fixed in our analysis by the end of the 1960s.[4]

The impulse problem   The impulse problem dominated initially to some extent the public debate. Keynesians usually advance a thoroughly eclectic position with respect to cyclic fluctuations in real variables. This eclectic position has recently been extended to explanations of inflation. The vision bearing on this issue is closely connected with the alleged flaws of the price mechanism associated with the denial of the system's internal stability.

The monetary analysis emerging during the 1950s attributed to monetary impulses a dominant role in the process generating business cycles and most particularly in the inflation process. The second strand bearing on inflation fully acknowledges the operation of real shocks modifying an economy's underlying condition. These shocks may significantly affect the price level and over time our economic welfare. Their contribution to the persistent inflation remains however at the most quite modest. The first strand involving the fluctuations around the normal level is much less robust and more sensitively influenced by specific historical conditions. The contribution of monetary accelerations (and decelerations) to economic fluctuations changes over time with the comparative mixture of monetary and real shocks. This mixture explains, at least in part, the variability of the lags acknowledged in the literature. This operation of monetary impulse in a context of shifting and unpredictable mixtures of shocks re-enforced the notion of a non-activist approach to monetary policy-making.[5]

The relation between allocation processes and aggregative behaviour The last issue, centred on the relation between allocative processes and aggregative evolutions of the economy, may appear to be somewhat remote from policy issues. The rationale of large-scale model construction, pursued by the translation of a Keynesian tradition into an econometric language, was based on the idea that allocative processes determine the economy's aggregative behaviour. The monetary analysis evolving since the 1950s does not deny all possible spillovers from allocative processes into aggregative patterns. It contends however that this spillover is comparatively small and remains confined to the shorter-run noises in the aggregate data. This position reflects an assumption that aggregative evolutions and the detail of allocative processes are approximately separated to an extent increasing with the lapse of time.

The alternative conjectures about the processes governing an economy's aggregative evolution may be formulated in terms of a probability distribution covering the relevant dimensions of an economy. Monetary analysis asserts that the force shaping the *position* of this distribution are approximately independent from the forces controlling the location of individual elements *under* the distribution. The Keynesian tradition motivating an approach to large (and larger) econometric models asserts in contrast that the forces shaping the location under a distribution also determine its position. This difference affects in particular alternative proposals to control inflation. The first conjecture requires suitable monetary policy actions whereas the second usually leads to sequential proposals of incomes policy. The second conjecture influences furthermore the views bearing on the impulse patterns. It tends to encourage a diffuse eclecticism in this matter. Economic fluctuations are dominantly attributed to shifting combinations of allocative disturbances widely ranging over the private sector. The government possesses under the circumstances the only opportunity to smooth the aggregative fluctuations generated by the array of allocative processes.[6]

Government deficits and 'crowding out' The structure of this analysis evolving over the 1960s and early 1970s influences our approach to a systematic evaluation of permanent deficits in the government's budget. This issue moved in the middle of last decade beyond the pages of learned journals and was submitted to the public attention by the Shadow Open Market Committee.

The analysis anchored on the interaction between a credit market and a money market implies that persistent and large increases in government debt induce portfolio adjustments. The resulting pressures on relative yields eventually lower the stock of real capital in the private sector. Government thus crowds out real capital and lowers normal output. This conclusion is strongly contested on two grounds however. One strand invokes the public's rational expectations of tax increases matching the increased obligation to pay interest on new debt. The other strand emphasizes that new tax liabilities change the agents' risk pattern. They restore with suitable hedging their preferred risk position revealed in a prior state. They purchase under the circumstances the new debt issued in accordance with their expected tax liability. The first strand removes the wealth effect and the second strand exorcises any substitution effect of deficits financed by issues of debt. With both effects removed the financial choice between taxes and debt is immaterial. Crowding out does not result from a *financial* decision but from a *real* phenomenon expressed by the relative size of the government's absorption of real resources and the characteristics of the government sector's production process. Further reflection about this matter suggests that the difference between the alternative conjectures developed within monetary analysis do not bear significantly on the longer-run outcome under appropriate assumptions about the public sector's production process. They influence mostly the views about the shorter-run impact on the economy. But the relative magnitudes of the effect on aggregate demand involved in this controversy seem to be of second-order significance.

The contribution of 'rational expectations analysis'
Rational expectations entered our scene during the last decade and substantially affected the nature of our discussions. Originally introduced by Jack Muth 20 years ago it lay dormant for many years until Robert Lucas effectively resurrected this idea. Its central theme advances a systematic extension of economic analysis to information problems. People are not passive engineering particles. They grope and cope with their natural and social environment. They will thus exploit whatever information they may acquire. This theme was moreover developed in the context of new analytic formulation which extended the opportunities for useful explications of intuitive ideas. Such explication is hardly ever a trivial endeavour and the history of science demonstrates its creative dimension. This dimension became again visible with the appearance of rational expectations analysis. It opened aspects to our attention beyond the direct explication of initially available ideas. This point may be exemplified for our purposes with the analytic explication obtained for the idea mentioned above that money stock and monetary growth exert no real effects. Rational expectations analysis provides an explicit form for the

intuitive notion that we need to consider monetary acceleration for this purpose. It generalized the idea and directed our attention to unpredictable or surprising movements in the money stock not discounted into the current prices or prevailing price movements. It also provides a more powerful formulation addressed to an examination of the conditions controlling the absorption of monetary (or fiscal) impulses by price movements with little deviation of output from its normal level. Prior analysis could produce similar results in a somewhat mechanical fashion by suitable adjustments in the elasticity of price expectations with respect to the current level.

Rational expectations analysis sharpened our awareness of the information problem. An intuitive sense of this awareness was brought to our work from many discussions with Armen Alchian during the early 1960s. These discussions led us to the nature of the information problem explaining the emergence of a wide range of social institutions, including money, middlemen, specialists of various kinds, etc. We understood also that rationally behaving agents' exposure to incomplete information could explain the conjunction of 'long-run' neutrality of nominal impulses and their 'short-run' non-neutrality. The emergence of rational expectations analysis made us aware however that monetary analysis needed to attend more explicitly to the specification of the relevant information structure confronting agents. Two distinct patterns of incomplete information have been used in recent years. The pioneering work initiated by Lucas, Sargent and Barro relied on Phelps' 'island story'. It argues basically that local information is cheaply available whereas global information is costly. Global information beyond an agent's location accrues thus with a lag. Agents face under the circumstances an inference problem defined by insufficient information to separate local and global effects in observed local price movements. They do not know whether changes in specific prices represent relative or aggregative price changes. Their behaviour would moreover substantially differ with the interpretations of the observations. The structure of incomplete information determines ultimately the optimal inference made. Even thus best inference deviates however from the true but unknown state. This wedge, produced by the specific form of incomplete information, assures the (transitory) real effect of monetary impulses. An alternative structuring of the problem emphasizes incomplete information about the composition of contemporaneously known allocative and aggregative shocks. Agents face continuous changes in relevant conditions, but they do not know to what extent these conditions are 'permanent' or 'transitory'. Their behaviour over a wide range of activities depends on the other hand sensitively on their inferences made in this respect. Their best inferences will generally deviate from the true composition of the shocks. This deviation defines in this case the potential leverage of monetary impulses on real variables.

The second approach to the structuring of incomplete information offers in my judgement substantial advantages. The second type of inference problem affects the behaviour of agents much more pervasively than the first one. This would be confirmed by observations showing vastly larger investments to cope with a more reliable interpretation of contemporaneously known shocks than with the problem of lagging global information. Beyond these immediate factual issues loom important empirical problems exemplified by the credibility of Central Bank policy or the lamented unresponsiveness of prices to current conditions. These issues can be usefully subsumed under the second but cannot be explicated with the first inference problem. The range of relevant empirical problems requiring our attention thus suggests that the pattern of incomplete information be advantageously explicated according to the second version really initiated many years ago by Milton Friedman.[8]

The monetarist policy rule
One subject, usually dominating the attention of wider circles, has been omitted so far. The 'monetarist rule' of a constant monetary growth is frequently assigned centre place in many of our disputes. It addresses indeed an important problem. This should not obscure however the central cognitive issues surveyed above. The monetarist rule derives from two distinct justifications. One strand is based on the internal stability of the system supplemented with the dominance of monetary impulses. These conditions would indeed be sufficient to justify a monetarist rule. But this argument lacks substantial force and depends too much on seriously contested conditions. There is an alternative and in my judgement much more pervasively relevant argument in support of a constant monetary growth. The argument evolves from an examination of the case made on behalf of activist regimes or 'discretionary policies'. A close scrutiny of these arguments reveals without exception two crucial conditions invoked to establish the efficiency of activist policy-making expressed in one form or another. The first condition assures the policy-makers' perfect information about the detailed structure of the economic process. The second condition rests on a particular implication of the sociological model of man expressed by the goodwill theory or the public-interest theory of government. Both conditions are blatantly falsified by massive evidence. Our vision of the structure governing the economic process suffers under a diffuse uncertainty, whatever the policy-makers', their staff's and academic advisers' subjective feeling may be. This diffuse uncertainty is exemplified by the array of econometric models producing very different answers to the quest for an optimal policy. An activist regime may thus 'luck in' and actually stabilize the economy, or 'luck out' and substantially destabilize the economy. An analysis of this problem shows moreover that the risks are asymmetrically tilted towards potential

destabilization. It follows that in the context of diffuse uncertainty a neutral strategy of constant monetary growth is optimal.

This conclusion is reinforced by the rejection of the second strand more or less implicitly adduced in support of an activist regime. A political economy analysis of political institutions determines the basic ambiguity of such institutions. The information problem confronting citizens imposes very high costs on effective monitoring of a political agency. Such monitoring costs create opportunities for trade-offs enjoyed by the personnel operating political agencies. Private and self-interested behaviour replaces to some extent attention to the public interest. These trade-offs are moreover reinforced by the diffuse uncertainty about the economy's basic structure and the resulting vagueness of the public interest. This environment fosters discretionary policies exhibiting shifting patterns of unpredictable activism imposing serious information problems on economic agents. The subtle temptations of office shaped by inadequate monitoring opportunities resulting from the pervasive information problem need to be removed by a constitutional or legislated constraint. Thus emerges the case for a neutral strategy operated as a policy of constant monetary growth. Diffuse uncertainty about the economy's structure and the political economy of political institutions constitute the crucial conditions of the justification. This argument needs however to be supplemented by an analysis addressed to the choice of benchmark level of monetary growth, and also to the important institutional and implementation aspects of such a policy.[9]

Beyond monetary problems

The search for a sense in our intellectual activities sharpened an awareness beyond the range of monetary phenomena. The struggle about purpose and content compelled my efforts to acquire a better comprehension of the logical aspects of our endeavours. It increasingly occurred to me that our behaviour and procedures expressed most particularly by prevailing language patterns frequently obstruct whatever degree of provisional and partial resolution could possibly be achieved. The nature of this obstruction observed in my judgement some exploration.

The cognitive enquiry beyond 'money' involved also the vision about the content and range of economics. The inherited division of the social sciences appeared increasingly without logical or empirical justification. The broad sweep of Adam Smith's vision had been narrowed and confined to 'economic issues'. But economic analysis offers in my judgement the only usable analytic core in the social sciences. Political science and sociology define an important range of problems but provide no developed analytic framework to cope with these issues. The fashionable appeal to sociology over an expanding range of problems cultivated by many professionals seemed to sacrifice a potentially useful framework with a substantial empirical foundation for essentially *ad hoc* verbalisms and programmatic classifications or promises.

The rules of the game and the idea market

The market for ideas and intellectual products may be examined as any other market. We may investigate the patterns shaping the supply of intellectual products or affecting the demand. We may question the conditions controlling the survival of ideas in this market. We may particularly probe the dominant rules of the game which contribute to determine the supply and survival of ideas competing for our attention. A close examination of many argument patterns widely used in textbooks or in papers published in leading professional journals influenced eventually my conjecture that our prevailing rules of the game contain important strands obfuscating the nature, significance or irrelevance of our intellectual activities and their products.

We hear on occasion that the social sciences address a subject matter inherently more difficult than the natural sciences. It would appear that the gods controlling social processes play an essentially hostile and non-cooperative game with the economics profession, whereas the gods controlling 'natural' processes play a co-operative game with the scientists. There is however an alternative conjecture emphasizing the rules of the game dominating our activities. It is argued in particular that the rules of the game actually influencing our intellectual conduct contribute somewhat hesitantly to the relevant sorting between competing ideas. We should note however that the truth of this conjecture would not remove the other conjecture bearing on an inherent difference between natural and social processes. The truth of the second conjecture could simply aggravate the problem already recognized by the first conjecture. The immanent difficulties posed for the comprehension of social processes could thus reinforce the obstructive effect of questionable rules of the game. A selection of some of our patterns cultivated in our learned endeavours drawn from a large sample may exemplify my concern.

The pervasive occurrence in many variations of the 'modality fallacy' offers some instructive information. We may encounter for instance a long series of possibility statements bearing on monetary policy. Somehow, by the end of the series of statements rather miraculously a categorical statement denying (or asserting) any relevant impact of monetary policy emerges. Alternatively, we find that monetary policy 'does not necessarily' modify the money stock (or anything) and is therefore potentially impotent. Both types of statements are inherently ambiguous and require careful scrutiny. A strictly logical interpretation of possibility statements simply conveys the information that the sentence subjected to the possibility modifier involves an empirical (i.e. non-logical) assertion. Similarly, the denial of necessity on a strictly logical interpretation means that the connections asserted are empirical and not of a logical nature. This meaning of the argument pattern is however quite innocuous and offers no grounds for the conclusions asserted.

The context of these argument patterns suggests however an alternative interpretation. The modality 'it is possible that something' is meant to convey that the 'something' should be considered to occur with a probability exceeding one-half. The denial of necessity appears furthermore to reflect on many occasions the existence of an alternative conjecture asserting the operation of different patterns. Statements are categorically judged in this manner simply on the grounds that an unsupported (stochastic) hypothesis can be invented or formulated. The argument pattern so widely encountered offers either no adequate grounds for the categorical statement advanced or no reason for the rejection of a particular conjecture addressed. The reader is lulled by the impressionistic effect of the linguistic evolution into a judgement lacking any relevant logical justification. This procedure is particularly rampant in critical objections addressed to a hypothesis (or theory) on the grounds that another hypothesis can be conceived (is possible). The substitution of impressionistic responses to a logical analysis of propositions subsumed by an analysis can be recognized moreover in many comparative judgements bearing on competing structures. The criteria seem occasionally affected by purely formal aspects with little attention to the empirical content obtained.

The role attributed to 'assumptions of a hypothesis' (or theory) offered for many years the most pervasive example of the ambiguous operation of the prevailing rules governing the idea market. A standard argument regulated the cognitive status of a hypothesis on the basis of the 'realism of its assumptions'. Milton Friedman's intuition understood very early the logical fallacy in this argument. In the absence of an explicit logical analysis of this issue the discussion initiated by Friedman's famous essay concentrated on intuitive and basically analogistic examples used by Friedman. The profession, represented by the published responses, refused to examine the logical merits of the problem and interpreted the needed clarification essentially as an ideological exercise. But an explicit logical analysis of the structure of hypotheses and their confirmation procedures establishes unambiguously that Friedman's intuition was right, whatever the relevance and effect of his argument may be. The standard argument pattern is logically untenable. Other patterns of our linguistic habits could be adduced to buttress my case but I wish to introduce just one additional example of great importance which has troubled me for many years. Econometrics emerged with a promise of ultimately assuring the victory of the cognitive adventure constituted by science. But this promise, still potentially inherent in the instrument shaped by econometric theory, has been converted into a travesty by the effort directed at large-scale model construction. The cognitive effort has been replaced by a numerological exercise on a level with astrology. Most of the models violate the essential requirements imposed on an empirical hypothesis, i.e. their empirical content remains on many occasions a mystery. Their actual use is a rigmarole of technical *ad hoc*ery frequently conflicting with some of the explicitly advanced stochastic hypotheses used to infer a quantitative structure from the data. They are moreover logically impossible to test in their present form. They also contributed to an unfortunate confusion between forecasting exercises on the one hand and logically acceptable test procedures on the other hand. At this stage large-scale model construction should be understood not so much as a relevant cognitive effort but as rational wealth-maximizing behaviour. The use of such models among political institutions directs moreover our attention to the peculiar socio-political incentive structures of political agencies. But this leads us to the last major strand of my intellectual experience.[10]

The renaissance of Adam Smith's vision
Our examination of Federal Reserve policy-making in 1963–4 alerted me to the importance of institutional problems. It occurred to me at the time that our profession had unnecessarily and without adequate grounds sacrificed Adam Smith's broad vision of economics. Any cognitive efforts coping with monetary policy or inflation increasingly directs our attention moreover to consideration of socio-political aspects. But political science or sociology offered no analytic help in these matters. Many problems listed under these headings seemed on the contrary well designed for a systematic exploration with the aid of 'economic' analysis. I gradually accepted as a working hypothesis that economic analysis constitutes the basic apparatus potentially unifying the social sciences. The traditional partitions would at best survive, if at all, as specializations of interest over sub-classes of social phenomena.

The social sciences offer, however, beyond economic analysis a highly influential but also very undeveloped and ultimately very questionable alternative approach to social processes. The nature of this issue is best recognized by an examination of the intellectual background motivating radically different approaches to society. This background produces most particularly divergent evaluations of political institutions or of the operation of political agencies. It seems customary to reduce differences in views about socio-political arrangements to a purely 'ideological' dimension. The media and many professionals argue as if all views bearing on political institutions are condemned to a range beyond assessable cognition. This pervasive attitude is in my judgement fundamentally wrong and intellectually pernicious. The different evaluations of the operation of political structures reflect ultimately, so I began to recognize, two radically distinct perceptions of man. One perception was introduced to the social sciences by the Scottish moral philosophers of the eighteenth century. Man occurs in this view as a resourcefully coping, groping and evaluating agent persistently bent on improving his lot according to his own best lights. This basic pattern of behaviour proceeds irrespective of any specific institutions. Such arrangements only modify the particular forms of man's self-interested expressions. An influential socio-logical tradition produced on the other side an entirely different perception. In this view man is totally shaped by exogenous social forces or entities. He is, in the words of my colleague Michael Jensen, a vacuous, aimless and passively reactive man. He plays a role determined by his position in society. He reveals no basic patterns invariantly operating over the whole spectrum of institutions. According to this perception man's self-interested pursuits are limited to the range of private property or the market place but wane in the context of political institutions.

The alternative perceptions present essentially two very different empirical assertions about man's conduct in society. They determine the different views and evaluations pertaining to social arrangement and most particularly to the role of political institutions. These differences can thus be recognized as the product of underlying perceptions which are in principle analysable and assessable. The easy reduction of all disputes about socio-political aspects to an 'ideological' dimension thus fails to recognize a cognitive problem of fundamental importance.[11]

The perception of man formalized by economic analysis appears to be substantially confirmed by a vast array of historical evidence. An application of suitably adjusted economic analysis to the operation of political institu-tions thus promises useful insights and answers to important socio-political issues. We obtain in this way, for instance, a better appreciation of the ambivalence of 'stabilization policies'. We begin to understand why 'stabilization policies' are at best randomly stabilizing and mostly designed for purposes of wealth redistribution. We also recognize more clearly the dangers associated with any kind of policy-activism. The problem addressed in the context of monetary policy actually characterizes the full range of government activities. Activist policy-making pursued by agencies imposing massive monitoring costs on the citizens usually produces the swamp of 'discretionary policies' with unreliable shifts, or stop and go. This erratic performance reinforces however the adjustment burden imposed by natural shocks and destabilizes the economy over time and on the average.

Lastly, the failure to recognize the alternative perception of man contrib-utes to a widening influence of more or less indirect or subtle forms of essentially sociological explanations of inflation. Interpretations of price move-ments as 'self-generated, self-propelled and self-sustained autonomous pro-cesses' rely basically on a sociological role-playing pattern and cannot be reconciled with a 'resourcefully evaluating maximizing man'. The funda-mental issue influences at this stage our approach to the inflation problem. It affects in particular our judgement on how to cope with it most effectively. Whatever the detail of the sociological approach may be, it will always favour, for reasons inherent in its basic perception, a complex set of political institutions controlling prices or wages. Once we recognize more fully the underlying nature of these differences we may discard easy ideological accusations and seriously consider the cognitive issues at stake. The rising importance of socio-political problems and institutional issues raises in my judgement the significance of economic analysis. The range of problems posed by our social evolution may encourage a new appreciation of Adam Smith's broad vision guiding our intellectual discipline. My own appreciation slowly evolving along the intellectual road was shaped by many discussions with many colleagues in the profession. It was decisively influenced however by my colleagues and friends in Rochester (foremost William Meckling) and by my long-time friend Allan H. Meltzer. A younger and international group of friends has contributed its share in recent years. And I naturally hope that fate grants me future opportunities to continue to learn from them.

Notes

1. The reader will find a list of the major papers bearing on the issues discussed in the paper jointly authored with Allan H. Meltzer, 'Time deposits in the Brunner–Meltzer model of asset markets', *Journal of Monetary Economics*, January, 1981. My paper on 'A diagrammatic exposition of the money supply process' published in the *Schweizerische Zeitschrift für Volkswirtschaft und Statistik*, 1973, summarizes the essential features of the accumulated analysis.
2. A detailed argument bearing on these issues may be found in 'Some general features of the Federal Reserves approach to policy', February 1964, 'The discrepancy between Federal Reserve policy and Federal Reserve statements', February 1964, 'The Federal Reserve's attachment to the free reserve concept: a staff analysis', May 1964, 'An alternative approach to the monetary mechanism', August 1964, *Subcommittee on Domestic Finance. Committee on Banking and Currency. House of Representatives*, 88th Congress, Second Session, 1964, (with Allan H. Meltzer).
3. Some material pertaining to this section may be found in my paper on 'The monetarist revolution in monetary theory', in *Weltwirtschaftliches Archiv*, 1970. My 'Survey of selected issues in monetary theory', *Schweizerische Zeitschrift für Volkswirtschaft und Statistik*, 1971, also contains some relevant material. Lastly, the paper and comments jointly authored with Allan H. Meltzer and published in *Monetarism*, ed. Jerome Stein, Amsterdam, 1976, may also be usefully consulted.
4. Relevant material on this point is contained in my paper on 'The monetarist revolution in monetary theory' and 'Inflation, money and the role of fiscal arrangements', in *The New Inflation and Monetary Policy*, London: Macmillan, 1976.
5. Note here also my paper on 'The Monetarist revolution in monetary theory', op. cit.
6. Note here also my paper 'The monetarist revolution in monetary theory', op. cit.
7. Aspects of crowding out appear in the paper published in *Monetarism*, op. cit., and also in the second paper mentioned in 4.
8. This section refers to current work jointly undertaken with Alex Cukierman and Allan H. Meltzer. A first piece has been published in the *Journal of Monetary Economics*, October 1980. Several other pieces bearing on the issues discussed in the text are in progress.
9. The reader will find an extensive argument in my paper 'Controlling monetary aggregates' to be published in 1981 by the Federal Reserve Bank of Boston. A summary statement appeared in the *Lloyd's Bank Monthly Review* in the winter 1980–81.

10. The following papers provide additional information on these issues: 'Assumption and the cognitive quality of theories', *Synthese*, 1969; 'The importance of rules in the competitive market for ideas', *Schweizerische Zeitschrift für Volkswirtschaft und Statistik*, 1962; 'Econometric practice between numerology and empirical science', *Journal of Economic Literature*, 1973; 'Some reflections on the state of econometric practice', *Vielfalt der Wirtschaftspolitik*, Zurich, 1969.

11. The crucial ideas were developed in a paper jointly authored with William Meckling on 'The perception of man and the conception of government', *Journal of Money, Credit and Banking*, 9(1), Part 1, Feb. 1977 [reprinted as Chapter 5 in this volume].

Index

administrative systems 3–4
  corruption in 77, 80, 140–1, 151, 153,
    157, 177, 179, 184, 189, 208
  cost of dissent under 179–81
  costs under 7, 12–13
  exploitation under 8, 178–9
  and externalities 12–13
  'human rights' imposed by 162–3
  inadequate analysis of 8, 14–16, 70–
    1, 120–2, 178–9
  and individual choice 181, 187, 195,
    206
  power incentives under 14–16, 103,
    110, 116–19, 120, 121–2, 140–1,
    149, 153, 180, 183–4, 203, 207–
    8
  religion and 110–11, 116, 119, 120–3,
    140–1
Adorno, Theodor 66
Affluent Society (Galbraith) 8–9, 17
Africa
  apartheid in 187
  colonialism in 182
agency problem 74, 207
agriculture, organization of 38–9, 113,
    136, 149, 150, 178, 187, 190, 300
Albert, Hans 60
Alchian, Armen A. 5, 22, 26, 83, 95,
    304, 310, 313
alienation 6, 73, 132
Allen, W.R. 5
American Economic Association 44, 60,
    61
anarchy 34, 95, 117, 224, 225, 274, 275
Anderson, Martin 233
anthropology, subject matter of 64
apartheid 187
Aquinas, St Thomas 129
Aranson, Peter A. 244
Argentina, natural resources of 32, 112
assets, substitutability of 25–6, 307–9
assumptions 26, 43–5, 59
  as constituent sentences of theories

with theory as class of universal
  sentences describing body of
  general laws and 49–51
with theory as deductive system
  and assumptions as non-
  logical postulates of system
  48–9, 61
Friedman's argument 26, 43–4, 60,
  62, 317
psychologism and logical analysis
  57–9
'realism' defined 44, 60
as semantic rules 56–7, 62
as sentences not constituting theories
  with assumptions as antecedent of
    general implication 54–6, 62
  with assumptions as antecedent of
    material implication 53–4, 62
  with assumptions as selected types
    of observation statements 52–
    4
  with assumptions of a theory
    constituting a higher level
    theory 51–2, 62
attention, mutual, differences in 100
Australia, government expenditure in
  219
Austria, government expenditure in
  219
Axelrod, Robert A. 94

Banker, The 237, 262
Bank for International Settlements (BIS)
  299
Barrash, David 86
Barro, Robert J. 222, 313
Bartley, William Warren III 80
base money 273–4
Bauer, Peter 152, 166, 168, 170, 182,
  184, 302
Baumol, W.J. 222, 223
'beauty contest game' 198–9, 200
Becker, Gary 79, 83, 124

importance of 16
and inadequate analysis of administrative systems 8, 14–16, 70–1,
120–2, 178–9
and inadequate analysis of capitalism
7–8, 10–13
incorporated into economics 104,
133–4
separation of cognition from 1–2, 3,
9–10, 16
and social order 82–3
see also man, perceptions of;
religion
traditional orientations and 1–2, 9, 17
universities and 3
Vanberg, Viktor 79
Vance, Cyrus 164
VARM (Vacuous, Aimless, Reactive
Man) model *see* man, perceptions of
Vatican 120, 121
'veil of ignorance' 118

wages and unemployment 11–12, 196
Wagner, Richard 223
Wall Street Journal 76, 245
war, explanation of 290
wealth creation
colonialism and 181–2
equality and 107–8, 112–15, 138–9
human capital and 33–4, 139
impediments to 34, 35–6, 37–41, 113,
117–18, 122, 225–6, 242
market systems and 7, 14, 15, 35, 36–
7, 114–15, 137–8, 287, 289
natural resources and 32, 112, 113,
137, 284, 287, 288
political power and 32–3, 112, 113–
14, 141, 284, 287, 288

political structure and *see* political
structure
wealth redistribution
economic policies and consequences
for 226–7, 255–6, 267, 268
loan ceilings and 306
political power and 32–3, 113–14,
288, 289
political structure and 34, 35–6, 40–1,
114, 117–19, 121, 122, 225–8,
242, 244, 275, 315
'redistributive state' 36, 37–9
pure wealth transfer model 228–34,
243
with entrepreneurial behaviour of
politicians and bureaux 235–
41, 243, 245, 260–3, 266,
275–6
limitations of 234–5
to Third World 37, 148, 149, 152–3,
156–9, 166, 171, 175, 177, 180,
284, 287–90, 291, 298, 301
international financial agencies and
298–300
see also equality conception of
justice
welfare state 13, 39, 73, 115, 190, 191
Weston, Fred 245
White, Lynn 97
worker-owned firms 190, 204
work ethic 91
work-sharing 267
Works Progress Administration 212
World Bank 108, 281, 299–300, 302
World Council of Churches 112, 120,
121, 131, 138

Yugoslav model 190, 204

Economists of the Twentieth Century

Monetarism and Macroeconomic
Policy
Thomas Mayer

Studies in Fiscal Federalism
Wallace E. Oates

The World Economy in Perspective
Essays in International Trade and European
Integration
Herbert Giersch

Towards a New Economics
Critical Essays on Ecology, Distribution and
Other Themes
Kenneth E. Boulding

Studies in Positive and Normative
Economics
Martin J. Bailey

The Collected Essays of Richard E.
Quandt (2 volumes)
Richard E. Quandt

International Trade Theory and Policy
Selected Essays of W. Max Corden
W. Max Corden

Organization and Technology in Capitalist
Development
William Lazonick

Studies in Human Capital
Collected Essays of Jacob Mincer, Volume 1
Jacob Mincer

Studies in Labor Supply
Collected Essays of Jacob Mincer, Volume 2
Jacob Mincer

Macroeconomics and Economic Policy
The Selected Essays of Assar Lindbeck,
Volume I
Assar Lindbeck

The Welfare State
The Selected Essays of Assar Lindbeck,
Volume II
Assar Lindbeck

Classical Economics, Public Expenditure
and Growth
Walter Eltis

Money, Interest Rates and Inflation
Frederic S. Mishkin

The Public Choice Approach to Politics
Dennis C. Mueller

The Liberal Economic Order
Volume I Essays on International Economics
Volume II Money, Cycles and Related Themes
Gottfried Haberler
Edited by Anthony Y.C. Koo

Economic Growth and Business Cycles
Prices and the Process of Cyclical Development
Paolo Sylos Labini

International Adjustment, Money and
Trade
Theory and Measurement for Economic Policy,
Volume I
Herbert G. Grubel

International Capital and Service Flows
Theory and Measurement for Economic Policy,
Volume II
Herbert G. Grubel

Unintended Effects of Government
Policies
Theory and Measurement for Economic Policy,
Volume III
Herbert G. Grubel

The Economics of Competitive Enterprise
Selected Essays of P.W.S. Andrews
*Edited by Frederic S. Lee
and Peter E. Earl*

The Repressed Economy
Causes, Consequences, Reform
Deepak Lal

Economic Theory and Market Socialism
Selected Essays of Oskar Lange
Edited by Tadeusz Kowalik

Trade, Development and Political
Economy
Selected Essays of Ronald Findlay
Ronald Findlay

General Equilibrium Theory
The Collected Essays of Takashi Negishi,
Volume I
Takashi Negishi

The History of Economics
The Collected Essays of Takashi Negishi,
Volume II
Takashi Negishi

Studies in Econometric Theory
The Collected Essays of Takeshi Amemiya
Takeshi Amemiya

Exchange Rates and the Monetary System
Selected Essays of Peter B. Kenen
Peter B. Kenen

Foundations of Modern Econometrics
The Selected Essays of Ragnar Frisch
(2 volumes)
Edited by Olav Bjerkholt

Growth, the Environment and the
Distribution of Incomes
Essays by a Sceptical Optimist
Wilfred Beckerman

The Economics of Environmental
Regulation
Wallace E. Oates

Econometrics, Macroeconomics and
Economic Policy
Selected Papers of Carl F. Christ
Carl F. Christ

Strategic Approaches to the International
Economy
Selected Essays of Koichi Hamada
Koichi Hamada

Economic Analysis and Political Ideology
The Selected Essays of Karl Brunner,
Volume One
Edited by Thomas Lys

Growth Theory and Technical Change
The Selected Essays of Ryuzo Sato
Volume One
Ryuzo Sato

Employment, Labor Unions and Wages
The Collected Essays of Orley Ashenfelter
Volume One
Edited by Kevin F. Hallock

Education, Training and Discrimination
The Collected Essays of Orley Ashenfelter
Volume Two
Edited by Kevin F. Hallock

Economic Institutions and the Demand and
Supply of Labor
The Collected Essays of Orley Ashenfelter
Volume Three
Edited by Kevin F. Hallock